T0301443

Fraud Data Analytics Methodology

The Wiley Corporate F&A series provides information, tools, and insights to corporate professionals responsible for issues affecting the profitability of their company, from accounting and finance to internal controls and performance management.

Founded in 1807, John Wiley & Sons is the oldest independent publishing company in the United States. With offices in North America, Europe, Asia, and Australia, Wiley is globally committed to developing and marketing print and electronic products and services for our customers' professional and personal knowledge and understanding.

Fraud Data Analytics Methodology

The Fraud Scenario Approach to Uncovering Fraud in Core Business Systems

LEONARD W. VONA

WILEY

For general information on our other products and services or for technical support, please contact our Customer Care Department within the United States at (800) 762-2974, outside the United States at (317) 572-3993 or fax (317) 572-4002.

Wiley publishes in a variety of print and electronic formats and by print-on-demand. Some material included with standard print versions of this book may not be included in e-books or in print-on-demand. If this book refers to media such as a CD or DVD that is not included in the version you purchased, you may download this material at http://booksupport.wiley.com. For more information about Wiley products, visit www.wiley.com.

Library of Congress Cataloging-in-Publication Data:
Names: Vona, Leonard W., 1955- author.
Title: Fraud data analytics methodology : the fraud scenario approach to uncovering fraud in core business systems / Leonard W. Vona.
Description: Hoboken, New Jersey : John Wiley & Sons, [2017] | Includes index.
Identifiers: LCCN 2016036161 | ISBN 9781119186793 (cloth) | ISBN 9781119270348 (ePDF) | ISBN 9781119270355 (epub)
Subjects: LCSH: Auditing. | Forensic accounting. | Fraud—Prevention. | Auditing, Internal.
Classification: LCC HF5667 .V659 2017 | DDC 658.4/73—dc23
LC record available at https://lccn.loc.gov/2016036161

Cover design: Wiley
Cover image: © kentoh/Shutterstock

10 9 8 7 6 5 4 3 2 1

This book is dedicated to my family, Patricia, Amy, David, and Jeffrey, for supporting me in my quest to explain fraud auditing. In the memory of my dad, who told me to go to college, and the memory of the women who shaped my life.

Contents

Preface   ix

Acknowledgments   xi

Chapter 1: Introduction to Fraud Data Analytics   1

Chapter 2: Fraud Scenario Identification   17

Chapter 3: Data Analytics Strategies for Fraud Detection   41

Chapter 4: How to Build a Fraud Data Analytics Plan   81

Chapter 5: Data Analytics in the Fraud Audit   109

Chapter 6: Fraud Data Analytics for Shell Companies   127

Chapter 7: Fraud Data Analytics for Fraudulent
Disbursements   149

Chapter 8: Fraud Data Analytics for Payroll Fraud   183

Chapter 9: Fraud Data Analytics for Company
Credit Cards   205

Chapter 10: Fraud Data Analytics for Theft of Revenue
and Cash Receipts   227

Chapter 11: Fraud Data Analytics for Corruption
Occurring in the Procurement Process   247

Chapter 12: Corruption Committed by the Company 269

Chapter 13: Fraud Data Analytics for Financial Statements 285

Chapter 14: Fraud Data Analytics for Revenue and
Accounts Receivable Misstatement 311

Chapter 15: Fraud Data Analytics for Journal Entries 333

Appendix A: Data Mining Audit Program for Shell
Companies 349

About the Author 363

Index 365

Preface

Even the world's best auditor using the world's best audit program cannot detect fraud unless their sample includes a fraudulent transaction. That is why fraud data analytics is so essential to the auditing profession.

Fraud auditing is a methodology tool used to respond to the risk of fraud in core business systems. The methodology must start with the fraud risk identification. Fraud data analytics is about searching for a fraud scenario versus a data anomaly. I have often referred to fraud data analytics as code breaking. The fraud auditor is studying millions of transactions in the attempt to find the needle in the haystack, called the *fraud scenario*. It is my hope that my years of professional experience in using fraud data analytics will move the auditing profession to become the number-one reason for fraud detection.

This book is about the science of fraud data analytics. It is a systematic study of fraud scenarios and their relationship to data. Like all scientific principles, the continual study of the science and the practical application of the science are both necessary for success in the discovery of fraud scenarios that are hiding in all core business systems.

The methodology described in the book is intended to provide a step-by-step process for building the fraud data analytics plan for your company. The first five chapters explain each phase of the process. Later chapters illustrate how to implement the methodology in asset misappropriation schemes, corruption schemes, and financial reporting schemes.

The practitioner will learn that fraud data analytics is both a science and an art. In baseball, there is a science to hitting a baseball. The mechanics of swinging a bat is taught to players of all ages. However, you can read all the books in the world about swinging a bat, but unless you actually stand in the batting box and swing the bat, you will never truly learn the art of hitting a baseball. Likewise, the fraud auditor needs to learn to analyze data and to employ the tools to do so in order to be able to find fraud scenarios hiding in your data systems.

Acknowledgments

To my friends at Audimation Services: Carolyn Newman, Jill Davies, and Carol Ursell. It is because of working with you that I developed the art of fraud data analytics.

To Sheck Cho (Executive Editor), who encouraged me to write my books, and to the editors at Wiley, without you I could not have written this book.

To Nicki Hindes, who keeps my office going while I travel the world.

To all those people who have inspired me. Thank you!

CHAPTER ONE

Introduction to Fraud Data Analytics

The world's best auditor using the world's best audit program cannot detect fraud unless their sample includes a fraudulent transaction. This is why fraud data analytics (FDA) is so critical to the auditing profession.

How we use fraud data analytics largely depends on the purpose of the audit project. If the fraud data analytics is used in a whistle blower allegation, then the fraud data analytics plan is designed to refute or corroborate the allegation. If the fraud data analytics plan is used in a control audit, then the fraud data analytics would search for internal control compliance or internal control avoidance. If the fraud data analytics is used for fraud testing, then the fraud data analytics is used to search for a specific fraud scenario that is hidden in your database. This book is written for fraud auditors who want to integrate fraud testing into their audit program. The concepts are the same for fraud investigation and internal control avoidance—what changes is the scope and context of the audit project.

Interestingly, two of the most common questions heard in the profession are, "Which fraud data analytic routines should I use in my audit?" and, "What are the three fraud data analytics tests I should use in payroll or disbursements?" In one sense, there really is no way to answer these questions because they assume the fraud auditor knows what fraud scenario someone might be committing. In reality, we search for patterns commonly associated with a fraud scenario or we search for all the logical fraud scenario permutations associated with the applicable business system. In truth, real fraud data analytics is exhausting work.

I have always referred to fraud data analytics as code breaking. It is the auditor's job to search the database using a comprehensive approach consistent with the audit scope. So, the common question of which fraud data analytics routines should I use can only be answered when you have defined your audit objective and audit scope. A key element of the book is the concept that while the fraud auditor might not know what fraud scenario a perpetrator is committing, the fraud auditor can identify and search for all the fraud scenario permutations. Therefore, the perpetrator will not escape the long arm of the fraud data analytics plan.

Once again, the question arises as to which fraud data analytic routines I should use in my next audit. Using the fraud risk assessment approach, the fraud data analytics plan could focus on those fraud risks with a high residual rating. The auditor could select those fraud risks that are often associated with the particular industry or with fraud scenarios previously uncovered within the organization—or the auditor might simply limit the scope to three fraud scenarios. Within this text, we plan to explain the methodology for building your fraud data analytics plan; readers will need to determine how comprehensive to make their plan.

WHAT IS FRAUD DATA ANALYTICS?

Fraud data analytics is the process of using data mining to analyze data for red flags that correlate to a specific fraud scenario. The process starts with a fraud data analytics plan and concludes with the audit examination of documents, internal controls, and interviews to determine if the transaction has red flags of a specific fraud scenario or if the transaction simply contains data errors.

Fraud data analytics is not about identifying fraud but rather, identifying red flags in transactions that require an auditor to examine and formulate a decision. The distinction between identifying transactions and examining the transaction is important to understand. Fraud data analytics is about creating a sample; the audit program is about gathering evidence to support a conclusion regarding the transaction. The final questions in the fraud audit process:

Is there credible evidence that a fraud scenario is occurring? Should we perform an investigation?

It is critical to understand that fraud data analytics is driven by the fraud scenario versus the mining of data errors. Based on the scenario, it might be one red flag or a combination of red flags. Yes, some red flags are so overpowering that the likelihood of fraud is higher. Yes, some red flags simply correlate to errors. The process still needs the auditor to examine the documents and formulate a conclusion regarding the need for a fraud investigation. It is important to understand the end product of data analytics is a sample of transactions that have a higher probability of containing one fraudulent transaction versus a random sample of transactions used to test control effectiveness. One could argue that fraud data analytics has an element of Las Vegas. Gamblers try to improve their odds of winning. Auditors try to improve their odds of detecting fraud. Figure 1.1 illustrates the concept of improving your odds by reducing the size of the population for sample selection.

Within most literature, a vendor with no street address is a red flag fraud. But a red flag of what? Is a blank street address field indicative of a shell company? How many vendors have no address in the accounts payable file because all payments are EFT? If a vendor receives payment through the EFT process, then is the absence of a street address in your database a red flag? Should a street address be considered a red flag of a shell company? Is the street address linked to a mailbox service company? What are the indicators of a mailbox service company? Do real companies use mailbox service companies? Fraud examiners understand that locating and identifying fraudulent transactions is a matter of sorting out all these questions. A properly developed fraud data-mining plan is the tool for sorting out the locating question.

To start your journey of building your fraud data analytics plan, we will need to explain a few concepts that will be used through the book.

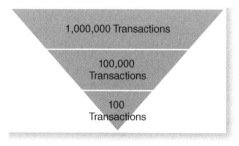

FIGURE 1.1 Improving Your Odds of Selecting One Fraudulent Transaction

What Is Fraud Auditing?

Fraud auditing is a methodology to respond to the risk of fraud in core business systems. It is a combination of risk assessment, data mining, and audit procedures designed to locate and identify fraud scenarios. It is based on the theory of fraud that recognizes that fraud is committed with intent to conceal the truth. It incorporates into the audit process the concept of red flags linked to the fraud scenario concealment strategy associated with data, documents, internal controls, and behavior.

It may be integrated into audit of internal controls or the entire audit may focus on detecting fraud. It may also be performed because of an allegation or the desire to detect fraudulent activity in core business systems. For our discussion purposes, this book will focus on the detection of fraud when there is no specific allegation of fraud.

Fraud auditing is the application of audit procedures designed to increase the chances of detecting fraud in core business systems. The four steps of the fraud audit process are:

1. *Fraud risk identification.* The process starts with identifying the inherent fraud schemes and customizing the inherent fraud scheme into a fraud scenario. Fraud scenarios in this context will be discussed in Chapter 2.
2. *Fraud risk assessment.* In the traditional audit methodology the fraud risk assessment is the process of linking of internal controls to the fraud scenario to determine the extent of residual risk. In this book, fraud data analytics is used as an assessment tool through the use of data-mining search routines to determine if transactions exist that are consistent with the fraud scenario data profile.
3. *Fraud audit procedure.* The audit procedure focuses on gathering audit evidence that is outside the point of the fraud opportunity (person committing the fraud scenario). The general standard is to gather evidence that is externally created and externally stored from the fraud opportunity point.
4. *Fraud conclusion.* The conclusion is an either/or outcome, either requiring the transaction to be referred to investigation or leading to the determination that no relevant red flags exist. Chapters 6 through 15 contain relevant discussion of fraud data analytics in the core business systems.

What Is a Fraud Scenario?

A fraud scenario is a statement as to how an inherent scheme will occur in a business system. The concept of an inherent fraud scheme and the fraud risk structure is discussed in Chapter 2. A properly written fraud scenario becomes the basis for developing the fraud data analytics plan for each fraud scenario within the audit scope. Each fraud scenario needs to identify the person committing the scenario, type of entity, and the fraudulent action to develop a fraud data analytics plan. The auditing standards also suggest identifying the impact the fraud scenario has on the company.

While all fraud scenarios have the same components, we can group the fraud scenarios into five categories. The groupings are important to help develop our audit scope. The groupings also create context for the fraud scenario. Is the fraud scenario common to all businesses or is the fraud scenario unique to our industry or our company? There are five categories of fraud scenarios:

1. *The common fraud scenario.* Every business system has the same listing of common fraud scenarios. I do not need to understand your business process, conduct interviews of management, or prepare a flow chart to identify the common fraud scenarios.
2. *The company-specific fraud scenario.* The company-specific fraud scenario in a business cycle because of business practices, design of a business system, and control environment issues. I do need to understand your business process, conduct interviews of management, or prepare a flow chart to identify the common fraud scenarios.
3. *The industry-specific fraud scenario.* The industry specific fraud scenarios are similar to the common fraud scenario, except the fraud scenario only relates to an industry. To illustrate the concept, mortgage fraud is an issue for the banking industry. This category of fraud scenarios requires the fraud auditor to be knowledgeable regarding their industry. However, using the methodology in Chapter 2, a nonindustry person could create a credible list of fraud scenarios.
4. *The unauthorized fraud scenario.* The unauthorized fraud scenario occurs when an individual, either internal or external to the company, commits an act by overriding company access procedures.
5. *The internal control inhibitor fraud scenario.* The concept of internal control inhibitor is to identify those acts or practices that inhibit the internal control procedures from operating as designed by management. The common internal control inhibitors are collusion and management override.

Chapter 2 will explain the concept of the fraud risk structure and how to write a fraud scenario that drives the entire fraud audit program. Chapter 2 will also cover the concept of fraud nomenclature. In the professional literature, we use various fraud words interchangeably, which I believe creates confusion within the profession. Words like *fraud risk statement, fraud risk,* and *inherent fraud schemes, fraud scenario, fraud schemes,* and *inherent fraud risk* are used to describe how fraud occurs for the purpose of building a fraud risk assessment or fraud audit program. Within this book, I will use the phrase *fraud scenario* as the words that drive our fraud data analytic plan.

What Is Fraud Concealment?

Fraud concealment is the general or specific conditions that hide the true nature of a fraudulent transaction. A general condition is the sheer size of database, whereas a specific condition is something that the perpetrator does knowingly or unknowingly to cause the business transaction to be processed in the business system and hide the true nature of the business transaction.

To illustrate the concept, all vendors need an address or a bank account to receive payment. On a simple basis, the perpetrator uses his or her home address in the master file. On a more sophisticated level, the perpetrator uses an address for which the linkage to the perpetrator is not visible within the data—for example, a post office box in a city, state, or country that is different from where the perpetrator resides. The fraud data analytics plan must be calibrated to the level of fraud sophistication that correlates to the specific condition of the person committing the fraud scenario. In Chapter 3, the sophistication model will describe the concepts of low, medium, and high fraud concealment strategies. The calibration concept of low, medium, and high defines whether the fraud scenario can be detected through the master file or the transaction file. It also is a key concept of defining the audit scope.

It is important to distinguish between a fraud scenario and the associated concealment strategies. Simply stated, the fraud scenario is the fraudulent act and concealment is how the fraudulent act is hidden. From an investigation process, concealment is referred to as the intent factor. From a fraud audit process, the concealment is referred to as the fraud concealment sophistication factor.

What Is a Red Flag?

A red flag is an observable condition within the audit process that links to the concealment strategy that is associated with a specific fraud scenario. A red flag exists in data, documents, internal controls, behavior, and public records.

Fraud data analytics is the search for red flags that exist in data that links to documents, public records, persons, and eventually to a fraud scenario.

The red flag is the inverse of the concealment strategy. The concealment strategy is associated with the person committing the fraud scenario and the red flag is how the fraud auditor observes the fraud scenario.

The red flag theory becomes the basis of developing the fraud data profile, which is the starting point of developing the fraud data analytics plan. The red flags directly link to the fraud concealment strategy. The guidelines for using the red flag theory are discussed in Chapter 3.

What Is a False Positive?

A false positive is a transaction that matches the red flags identified in the fraud data profile but the transaction is not a fraudulent transaction. It is neither bad nor good. It simply is what it is. What is important is that the fraud data analytics plan has identified a strategy for addressing false positives. Fundamentally, the plan has two strategies: Attempt to reduce the number of false positives through the fraud data analytics plan or allow the fraud auditor to resolve the false positive through audit procedure. There may be no correct answer to the question; however, ignoring the question is a major mistake in building your plan.

What Is a False Negative?

A false negative is a transaction that does not match the red flags in the fraud data profile but the transaction is a fraudulent transaction. From a fraud data analytics perspective, false negatives occur due to not understanding the sophistication of concealment as it related to building your fraud data analytics plan. Other common reasons for a false negative are: data integrity issues, poorly designed data interrogation procedures, the lack of data, and the list goes on.

While false positives create unnecessary audit work for the fraud auditor, false negatives are the real critical issue facing the audit profession because the fraud scenario was not detected.

The false positive conundrum: Refine the fraud data analytics or resolve the false positive through audit work.

There is no real correct answer to the question. The fraud data analytics should attempt to provide the fraud auditor with transactions that have a higher probability of a person committing a fraud scenario. The fraud data interrogation routines should be designed to find a specific fraud scenario. That is the purpose of fraud data analytics. However, by the nature of data and fraud, false positives will occur. Deal with it. The real question is how to minimize the number of false positives consistent with the fraud data analytics strategy selected for the fraud audit.

Remember, fraud data analytics is designed to identify transactions that are consistent with a fraud data profile that links to a specific fraud scenario. There needs to be a methodology in designing the data interrogation routines. The methodology needs to be based on a set of rules and an understanding of the impact the strategy will have on the number of false positives and the success of fraud scenario identification.

The reality of fraud data analytics is the process will have false positives; said another way, there are transactions that will have all the attributes of a fraud scenario, but turn out to be valid business transactions. That is the reality of the red flag theory. Unfortunately, the reality of fraud data analytics is that there will also be false negatives based on the strategy selected. This is why before the data interrogation process starts, there must be a defined plan that documents the auditor judgment. Senior audit management must understand what the plan is designed to accomplish and why the plan is designed to fail. Yes, based on the correlation of audit strategy and sophistication of fraud concealment, you can design a plan to fail to detect a fraud scenario. At this point in the book, do not read this as a bad or good; Chapter 3 will explain how to calibrate your data interrogation routines consistent with the sophistication of concealment.

To provide a real-life example, in one project involving a large vendor database, our fraud data analytics identified 200 vendors meeting the profile of a shell company. At the conclusion, we referred five vendors for fraud investigation. In one sense, the project was a success; in another sense, we had 195 false positives.

If I could provide one suggestion based on my personal experience, the person using the software and the fraud auditor need to be in the same room at the same time. As reports are created, someone needs to look at the report and refine the report based on the reality of the data in your database. Fraud data analytics is a defined process and with a set of rules. However, the process is not like the equation $1 + 1 = 2$. It is an evolving process of inclusion and exclusion based on a methodology and fraud audit experience. So, do not worry about the false positive, which simply creates unnecessary audit work. Worry about the false negative.

FRAUD DATA ANALYTICS METHODOLOGY

I commonly hear auditors talk about the need to play with the data. This is one approach to fraud detection. The problem with the approach is that it relies on the experience of the auditor rather than on a defined methodology. I am not discounting audit experience, I would suggest that auditor experience is enhanced with a methodology designed to search for fraud scenarios. In fact, the data interpretation strategy explained in Chapter 3 is a combination of professional experience and methodology.

The fraud data analytics methodology is a circular approach to analyzing data to select transactions for audit examination (Figure 1.2).

- *Fraud scenario.* The starting point for building a fraud data analytics plan is to understand how the fraud risk structure links to the audit scope. The process of identifying the fraud scenarios within the fraud risk structure and how to write the fraud scenario is discussed in Chapter 2.
- *Strategy.* The strategy used to write data interrogation routines needs to be linked to the level of sophistication of concealment. For purposes of this book there are four general strategies, which are explained in Chapter 3.

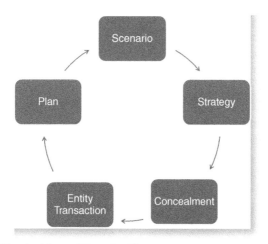

FIGURE 1.2 Circular View of Data Profile

- *Sophistication of concealment impacts the success of locating fraudulent transactions.* A common data interrogation strategy for searching for shell companies is to match the addresses of employees to the address of vendors. While a great data analytics step, the procedure is not effective when the perpetrator is smart enough to use an address other than a home address. So, at this level of concealment, we need to change our strategy. A complete discussion of fraud concealment impact on fraud data analytics is in Chapter 3.
- *Building the fraud data profile is the process of identifying the red flags that correlates to entity and transaction.* All fraud scenarios have a data profile that links to the entity structure (i.e., name, address, etc.) and the transaction file (i.e., vendor invoice). The specific red flags will be discussed in Chapters 6 through 15.
- *The plan starts with linking the fraud scenario to the fraud data profile.* Then it uses the software to build the data interrogation routines to identify the red flags and overcome the concealment strategies.
- *In reality, the search process is seldom one-dimensional.* It is a circular process of analyzing data and continually refining the search process as we learn more about the data and the existence of a fraud scenario in the core business system.

Assumptions in Fraud Data Analytics

1. *The certainty principle.* The degree of certainty concerning the finding of fraud will depend on the level of concealment sophistication and the on/off access to books and records. When the fraud is an on-the-book scheme and has a low level of sophistication, the auditor will be able to obtain a high degree of certainty that a fraud scenario has occurred. Consequently, with an off-the-book fraud scenario and high level of sophistication, the auditor will not achieve the same degree of certainty that a fraud scenario has occurred. Therefore, the auditor must recognize the degree of certainty differences when developing the fraud audit program.

   The difficulty in ascertaining the degree of certainty directly influences the quality and quantity of evidence needed. If an auditor assumes a low level of certainty with regard to a fraud scenario occurring, then the auditor may not incorporate the gathering of credible evidence at all. However, if an auditor is well versed in fraud scenario theory and, therefore, establishes some degree of certainty that a scenario has occurred, the audit plan needs to incorporate the obtaining of the appropriate amount and quality of evidence to justify that degree of certainty.

Specifically, as part of the fraud audit plan, it should first be determined what elements of proof will be necessary to recommend an investigation. Then a decision is needed to determine if the chosen elements are attainable in the context of a fraud audit based on the specific scenario, concealment sophistication, and access to books and records.

2. *The linkage factor.* The term *link* is used extensively throughout the entire book as it aptly highlights the relationship between the various fraud audit program components and objectives. For example, the fraud audit program is built by linking the data mining, audit testing procedures, and audit evidence considerations to a given fraud scenario found in the risk assessment. At its core, the concept of linkage is a simple one; however, with the traditional audit program as a frame of reference, many auditors have difficulty grasping the idea that fraud audit procedures should be designed, and therefore, linked to a specific fraud scenario. The entire book is based on the linkage factor. All fraud data analytic routines must be linked to a fraud scenario or all fraud scenarios must be linked to a fraud data analytics routine.

3. *Cumulative principle.* Seldom is one red flag sufficient to identify a fraud scenario within a database. It is the totality of the red flags that are indicative of a fraud scenario. The process should incorporate a summary report of the tests to score each entity or transaction. When we search for fictitious employee, commonly referred to as a ghost employee, a duplicate bank test will identify false positives because two or more employees are family members. However, when one of the employees is a budget owner and the second employee has a different last name, address, no voluntary deductions, postal box address, and no contact telephone number, it is the totality of the red flags versus anyone red flag. This is an important concept to incorporate into the fraud data analytics plan.

4. *Basis for selection for testing.* Fraud data analytics is all about selecting transactions for fraud audit testing. The basis for selection must be defined and understood by the entire team.

THE FRAUD SCENARIO APPROACH

The approach is simple. In essence, you develop an audit program for each fraud scenario. The starting point is to identify all the fraud scenarios within your audit scope. Within the audit project this is the process of developing your fraud risk assessment. The final step in the fraud risk assessment is the concept of residual risk. The dilemma facing the profession is how the concept of residual risk should impact the decision of when to search for fraud in core business systems. The question cannot be ignored, but there is no perfect answer to the question. It is what I call the likelihood conundrum.

The Likelihood Conundrum: Internal Control Assessment or Fraud Data Analytics

Does the auditor rely on internal controls or does the auditor perform fraud data analytics? There is no simple answer to the question; I suspect one answer could be derived from the professional standards that the auditor follows in the conduct of an audit. In my years of teaching audit professionals the concept of fraud auditing, I have seen the struggle on the auditors' faces. The reason for the struggle is that we have been told that a proper set of internal controls should provide reasonable assurance in preventing fraud scenarios from occurring. There are many reasons why an internal control will fail to prevent a fraud scenario from occurring. The easiest fraud concept to understand why internal controls fail to prevent fraud is the concept of internal control inhibitors. We cannot ignore collusion and management override in regard to fraud.

We need to understand that fraud can occur and comply with our internal controls. I suspect this is an area of great disagreement in the profession between the internal control auditors and the fraud auditors. Even if you believe that internal controls and separation of duties will prevent fraud, what is the harm in looking for fraud? So, we give management a confirmation that fraud scenarios are not occurring in the business system. We do the same confirmation with internal controls: Because we see the evidence of an internal control we assume that the control is working. If the auditor is serious about finding fraud in an audit, then the auditor must start looking for fraud. For me, the likelihood conundrum is much ado about nothing. Management, stockholders, and boards of directors all think we are performing tests to uncover fraud.

How the Fraud Scenario Links to the Fraud Data Analytics Plan

With each scenario, the auditor will need to determine which scenarios are applicable to fraud data analytics and which fraud scenarios are not applicable to fraud data analytics. For example: A product substitution scheme can occur when the receiver accepts an inferior product but indicates the product conforms to the product requirements. This fraud scenario does not lend itself to fraud data analytics because the clue is not in the data. However, a vendor that consistently submits invoices exceeding the purchase order within the payment tolerances can be identified. Once the list of scenarios relevant to the plan are identified the next step is to understand how the three critical elements of the scenario impact the plan.

The elements of scenarios that are relevant to creating an effective fraud data analytics plan are: the person who commits the scenario, the type of entity, and the type of action we are looking for.

To illustrate the concept, as a starting point we will consider the "who" as either the budget owner, accounts payable function, or a senior manager. A common test is to search for vendors created in the master file at off-periods. If the scenario is focusing solely on the budget owner, is the off-period test relevant to the scope of the project? Now let's change the person committing the scenario to someone in the accounts payable function. Now the off-period test is relevant to the audit scope.

The second aspect of a scenario is the type of entity. Are we searching for a false vendor or a real vendor? If the vendor is real, then searching for vendors with P.O. boxes is not relevant because real vendors tend to use P.O. boxes, whereas if we are searching for real vendors operating under multiple names, then a duplicate test on the address field is relevant.

The third aspect of a scenario is the fraudulent action. If the vendor is real and the fraud scenario is overbilling based on unit price inflation, then searching for a sequential pattern of invoices is not relevant. The test should focus on changes in unit price or comparisons of unit prices for similar items among common vendors.

The fourth element of a fraud scenario is the impact statement. While critical to the fraud scenario statement, the impact statement is not typically associated with the data analytics plan but is critical to the investigation process. The following two scenarios illustrate the concept:

1. Senior manager acting alone or in collusion with a direct report/causes a shell company to be set up on the vendor master file/causes the issuance of a purchase order and approves a false invoice for services not received/ **causing the diversion of company funds.**
2. Senior manager acting alone or in collusion with a direct report/causes a shell company to be set up on the vendor master file/causes the issuance of a purchase order and approves a false invoice for services not received/**depositing the funds in an off-the-book bank account for the purpose of paying bribes.**

A close examination of the two fraud scenarios reveals that the fraud data analytics plan is exactly the same for both scenarios. In both scenarios, the fraud data analytics is searching for a shell company and a pattern of false invoices.

From a fraud investigation plan, the first scenario is an asset misappropriation scenario while the second scenario is associated with a corruption scheme mostly connected to an FCPA violation.

SKILLS NECESSARY FOR FRAUD DATA ANALYTICS

Building a fraud data analytics plan requires a defined skill set. The absence of one skill set will diminish the effectiveness of the plan. The audit team needs to ensure all the right skills are contained within the team:

- *Knowledge of fraud.* Since fraud data analytics is the process of searching for fraudulent transactions, the auditor must have a full understanding of the fraud concepts.
- *Fraud scenarios.* This skill relates to how to write a fraud statement that correlates to developing a fraud data analytics statement. For an analogy, the scenario approach should be considered the system design aspect of the project and creating the routines is the program aspect of the project, or the scenario creates the questions and the fraud data analytical plan creates the answers.
- *Information technology knowledge.* Data reside in large, complex database systems. The ability to communicate with the IT function to locate and extract the data is the starting point of the data interrogation phase of the plan.
- *Audit software knowledge.* Coding software, whether writing scripts or using software functions, is necessary to write the data interrogation routines. The ability of the auditor to clean data, reformat data, combine data, and create reports is an absolutely necessary skill.
- *Audit knowledge.* Fraud data analytics is just one aspect of conducting an audit. Understanding fraud risk assessment, building audit scopes, designing audit steps, and formulating conclusions based on audit evidence rules is what fraud data analytics is all about. Second, designing fraud test procedures for the selected items is just as important as the fraud data analytics.
- *Understand data from a real-world perspective.* In each data column there is information. We need to understand how to use that information.

To illustrate the concept, using something as easy as an address field in a vendor database, the information in the field may correlate to a payment address, a physical address, a public mailbox service address, a nonpublic mailbox service address, mail forwarding services, or a bookkeeping service company. Yes, you must understand the data in a data field from a business perspective to develop a data interrogation routine. A vendor invoice number may have several patterns, depending on the industry and size of the business. The patterns are: no invoice number, date format, sequential ascending project number with a progress billing number, numeric or alpha format, and a sequential number linked to a customer number. So, how does the pattern link to the fraud scenario or the fraud concealment?

SUMMARY

As a conclusion to Chapter 1 and throughout the remainder of the book, I would like to offer some of the lessons learned throughout my fraud audit career. First, note the important points to understand about fraud data analytics, and then note some of the common mistakes one can make in fraud data analytics. I hope you find the points useful as you conduct your next fraud data analytics project.

Axioms of Fraud Data Analytics

- The world's best audit program and the world's best auditor cannot detect fraud unless their sample includes a fraudulent transaction.
- I do not know what a perpetrator will do, but I do know everything the perpetrator can do.
- While we do not know how a perpetrator will commit a fraud or how he will conceal the fraud, we can determine the logical permutations.
- The better you can describe the fraud scenario, the more likely you will be able to find it.
- False positives will occur. You try to resolve false positives either through your fraud data analytics or through an auditor performing audit procedures.
- In fraud data analytics, fraud likelihood is based on data versus the effectiveness of internal controls.
- We search for transactions that mirror the red flag theory of the fraud scenario.

- The better we understand data, the better we can use data to search for a fraudulent transaction.
- Errors and fraud have a lot in common.
- Red flags correlate to both errors and fraud.
- Data are not perfect.
- Databases contain data errors, caused either by mistake or with intent.
- We can only search data when the data reside in our databases.
- Fraud data analytics is both a science and an art.

Common Mistakes in Fraud Data Analytics

- No plan. Please do not jump in without a plan.
- Starting the fraud data analytics process without a clearly defined fraud scope.
- Creating reports that do not link to a specific fraud scenario.
- Searching for data exceptions versus the red flags of a fraud scenario.
- Assuming that a data integrity issue is an indicator of fraud.
- Failure to understand the integrity of the data being examined.
- Failure to understand the type of data that reside in a data field.
- No effective plan for false positives.
- Not worrying about false negatives.
- The fraud data analytics strategy is not calibrated for the level of fraud concealment sophistication.
- No planned audit procedure for the fraud data analytics report.

Chapters 2 to 5 are intended to provide a methodology for building your fraud data analytics plan. The remaining chapters are intended to describe the common fraud scenarios in a core business system and how to build your fraud data analytics plan to locate the fraud scenario in core business systems.

2

Fraud Scenario Identification

To start with an old saying, the house is only as strong as the foundation. In this chapter, the fraud data analytics plan is the house and the fraud scenario is the foundation. The purpose of this chapter is to explain the fraud risk structure and how to write a fraud scenario. In one sense, it sounds like an easy task. In another sense, it is a daunting task. If you have read my other books, you will hear a similar reading, but hopefully the methodology is refined based on more years of practical experience.

The purpose of the fraud risk structure is to define the scope of the fraud audit project. The purpose of the fraud scenario is to act as the design plan for the programmer. Using the fraud scenario the programmer creates the search routines of databases for transactions that meet the data profile for each fraud scenario. The red flags associated with each fraud scenario provide the basis of the selection of transactions for audit examination. The programming can only be as good as the fraud scenario statement. The red flags can only be as good as the integrity of the data in the database.

Fraud risk identification requires a methodology and standards to be followed in identifying and writing a fraud scenario. This chapter will focus on the methodology as it is related to fraud data analytics plan. As such, not all aspects of the fraud risk structure will be covered in this book. Only those aspects that are relevant to fraud data analytics are covered in the book.

At the risk of repeating a concept throughout the book, the fraud data analytics is about searching for transactions that are consistent with the fraud data profile associated with a specific fraud scenario. This is my point; the word *fraud* is too broad to be useful as a search concept. Therefore, we need a way to determine what type of fraud we are searching for within our data analytics project and which fraud scenarios.

FRAUD RISK STRUCTURE

The fraud risk structure shown in Figure 2.1 is a tool used to establish the scope of the fraud data analytics project. In a sequential manner, it entails the primary classification of fraud, the secondary classification or subclass of the primary category of fraud, the inherent fraud schemes, and lastly, the fraud scenarios.

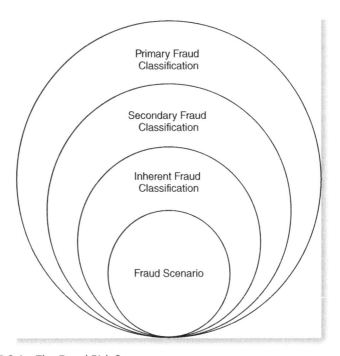

FIGURE 2.1   The Fraud Risk Structure

HOW TO DEFINE THE FRAUD SCOPE: PRIMARY AND SECONDARY CATEGORIES OF FRAUD

In its simplest of definitions, the *fraud risk structure* is a comprehensive classification system to identify all the possible fraud scenarios facing an organization. Fraud is complicated, and we want to make its identification as effortless as possible. However, its complexity tends to be caused by layering and overlapping; therefore, we have broken down the schemes into two levels, denoted herein as primary and secondary. Within each secondary category there are inherent schemes that are composed of an entity structure and a fraud action statement. From the inherent scheme structure, the fraud auditor creates the fraud scenarios that become the basis of the fraud data analytics plan.

The primary and secondary classification system defines the overall scope of the project. Are we searching for financial reporting, asset misappropriation, or corruption schemes? The secondary classification of each primary classification category further defines the scope question. Within the secondary classification, not all categories are applicable to fraud data analytics. An easy example, in financial reporting, is the misuse of generally accepted accounting procedures (GAAP). We can search for transactions that violate GAAP, but not the misuse of GAAP to achieve a desired financial result. The distinction is important from a fraud data analytics perspective.

Each primary classification category is the starting point of the fraud data analytics plan. Financial reporting is designed to search for an error that would cause the financial statements to be misstated on a material basis. Asset misappropriation is searching for theft of assets caused by either internal or external parties. Primary corruption has two focal points:

1. Has the internal selection process (i.e., the purchasing, hiring, or customer process) been corrupted within a company?
2. Is there evidence that our organization is involved in a corrupt act—in essence, an FCPA violation or price fixing?

Now we move from the primary category of the scope question to the secondary category of the scope question:

Financial reporting secondary level defines errors caused through recording fictitious transactions or improper recognition of transactions. It also considers whether the transaction is recorded through a source journal or through a manual journal entry. Transactions that are not recorded can be identified through an inference test.

Asset misappropriation secondary category has three levels of consideration:

1. *The asset that is misappropriated.* The primary categories are theft of monetary funds or theft of tangible assets. Other asset misappropriation schemes are: misuse of an asset; theft for resale; personal expenditures; selling assets below fair market value; and expenditures that do not benefit the organization or project.
2. *Who perpetrates the scheme?* It could be an internal source, external source, or both parties operating in collusion.
3. *The nature of the account.* This categorizes the misappropriation in terms of revenue or expenses.

The corruption secondary category is more difficult to define than the secondary category of asset misappropriation. To properly define the secondary category of corruption, the following questions must be answered:

1. In which core business system is the corrupt act occurring: revenue, procurement, or human resources?
2. Who is initiating the corrupt act? Are we corrupting someone, or is someone corrupting our organization?
3. Within the core business system, which decision is being corrupted?

A common point of confusion occurs through the difference between corruption schemes and asset misappropriation schemes. Vendor overbilling schemes (discussed in Chapter 7) involving both an internal person and a vendor may be either an asset misappropriation or corruption scheme. In one sense, the category is not critical. However, from defining the scope of the project, the difference is absolutely critical. Vendor overbilling is an asset misappropriation scheme because the scheme involves the loss of assets. The overbilling scheme is a corruption scheme because it involves collusion, a necessary element for corruption. The approval process is corrupted because the internal person approves the vendor invoice with knowledge that the invoice is inflated. Most likely, only a fraud geek would delve into the debate of the proper category. So, to make it easy from a scope perspective, each cycle should be divided in half. In the expenditure cycle, the first half is procurement, the land of corruption schemes, and payments to vendors is the land of asset misappropriation schemes. The idea of splitting each cycle can be applied to each business cycle. Remember, it is all about an easy way of defining the scope.

To use an analogy, fraud is like running a marathon. The race is defined by mile markers. Runners understand the need to pace the race by mile markers. Is the runner going to fast or too slow in order to meet the goal, referred to as his or her personal record (PR)? The search for fraud is similar. The primary category is the race: Boston or NYC marathon. The secondary categories are the challenges in the race: flats and hills. The inherent schemes and fraud scenarios are the mile markers. While fraud data analytics is not about personal records, the process is about identifying transactions that are consistent with the course.

The fraud auditor starts the process by having a clearly defined project scope, which occurs by understanding what fraud scenarios are included in the scope of the project and what fraud scenarios are not included in the scope. The second aspect of defining the fraud scope is to identify the inherent schemes that link to the primary and secondary categories. Remember, scope and fraud likelihood are two different questions. Once the scope is defined, the internal control likelihood analysis drives the scenarios in the "marathon" the fraud auditor will search for in the fraud data analytics plan.

UNDERSTANDING THE INHERENT SCHEME STRUCTURE

An inherent fraud scheme will correspond to a secondary fraud classification whereby each secondary fraud classification will have one or more inherent fraud schemes. In turn, each inherent fraud scheme typically has two components. One component involves the direct linking of each business transaction to an entity, such as an employee, vendor, or customer. The entity structure used by the perpetrator of the fraud scenario is either a real or fictitious entity. In the case of a real entity, it is either knowingly complicit or unknowingly involved. In the case of a fictitious entity, the entity is either a created or assumed entity structure. The other component of the inherent fraud scheme is the fraud action statement that occurs, such as billing for services never provided. The action statement will depend on the core business system.

In terms of building a fraud risk register for the business system, the inherent fraud scheme provides the auditor with a starting point to identify and describe the fraud scenarios facing a business system. Therefore, the key principles of an inherent fraud scheme are:

- Each business system has a finite and predictable list of inherent fraud schemes.
- Each inherent scheme has two parts: the entity structure and action component.

- Each inherent fraud scheme has a finite and predictable list of fraud permutations.
- Each fraud scheme permutation creates a finite and predictable list of fraud scenarios.
- How the inherent scheme occurs will be influenced by the business processes and internal controls.

The key points to remember are that fraud is predictable with regard to the schemes that occur, and there is a finite number of schemes that can occur in a given business system. Through a permutation process, the potential number of scenarios facing an organization can be identified and computed with mathematical precision. Now that the fraud risk structure is defined for the project, the next step is to start building your fraud data analytics plan.

THE FRAUD CIRCLE

The fraud circle (Figure 2.2) illustrates the relationship between the inherent scheme and the development of the fraud scenario and the fraud data analytics plan. Appendix 1 provides a fraud scenario matrix which corresponds to

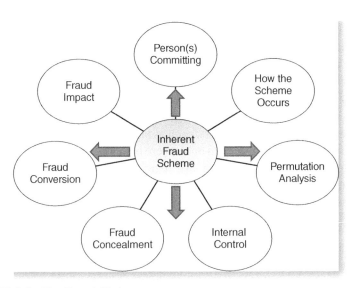

FIGURE 2.2   The Fraud Circle

the fraud circle. The auditor should use the fraud scenario matrix in the brainstorming session to develop the fraud audit program. Appendix 2 in this chapter illustrates a completed fraud scenario matrix.

The ability to describe how an inherent scheme occurs within your business system is a critical skill for the fraud auditor. The skill is a combination of professional experience and a defined methodology. The science of naming fraud risks is an important aspect of building a fraud data analytics plan. Every science has its own nomenclature. The fraud circle provides a systematic way of naming fraud scenarios. The circle also demonstrates how the critical questions of fraud auditing link to the inherent scheme. Now that the fraud auditor sees the relationships of the inherent scheme to the fraud audit, the next step is using the fraud scenario matrix.

In a sports team, every team member has the playbook. By understanding the inherent scheme approach, the fraud auditor in essence has the perpetrator's playbook. You can identify all the fraud scenarios—understand how the fraud is concealed, recognize the financial impact on the organization, and build a complete fraud data analytics plan. Understanding the perpetrator's playbook evens the playing field between the perpetrator and the fraud auditor. The reader should refer to both the fraud circle and fraud scenario matrix located in Appendix 1 of this chapter while reading the next section:

1. *Person committing.* Every fraud scenario is committed by a person or a group of people. The person committing generally needs to have access to the system. For purpose of fraud scenario identification, the fraud auditor will need to understand the concept of direct and indirect access. Direct access occurs when the person's job duties or computer access provides the opportunity to execute a transaction. Indirect access occurs when a direct access person executes a transaction based on an indirect person who has the authority to initiate or approve a transaction. Said another way, indirect access occurs when the authorized actions of a manager cause the direct access person to initiate or record the transaction consistent with the authorization of the indirect person.
2. *Permutation analysis.* There are three required elements of consideration:
   a) Person committing the fraud scenario.
   b) Entity type is derived from the inherent scheme structure. The first answer is based on the business system: employee, vendor, or customer.
   c) Fraud action statement is derived from the inherent scheme structure.
      i. The fraud action may have several levels. The type of levels will differ by financial reporting, asset misappropriation, and corruption.

The first level is called the primary level. The primary level tends to be a high-level description of the fraud action. The goal of the fraud auditor is to describe the fraud scenario at the lowest possible level. To illustrate the drill-down process of determining the lowest possible level for the fraud action statement the following example uses vendor overbilling:

1. Vendor overbilling in the expenditure cycle is the primary level.
    a. Vendor overbilling through product substitution is the secondary level followed by the third and fourth level.
        i. Fitness issue scheme.
        ii. Knock-off scheme.
        iii. Manufacturer false label scheme.
            1. False description of the chemical composition of the product.
            2. False statement as to where the product was manufactured: country of origin.
    ii. Transaction type. This concept is little more nebulous. Transaction types occur from system codes, how internal controls are applied to a transaction, or company's business culture. This knowledge is critical to developing the fraud data analytics plan. To illustrate the concept of transaction type using a process example and then a code example:
        1. The payment process has two methods of approving an invoice for payment. Vendor invoice is matched to a purchase order as part of the payment internal controls, or vendor invoice is paid with no purchase order but based on the budget owner's approval.
        2. Vendor code is either active or inactive.
    iii. The generic fraud action will need to be converted to a fraud scenario specific statement for the business system.
3. *Fraud impact.* This describes the monetary or nonmonetary impact the fraud scenario will have on the organization. The fraud impact statement describes how the fraud scenario impacts the organization from either the monetary impact or nonmonetary impact. As a matter of style, instead of an impact statement, the fraud auditor could substitute the fraud conversion statement, which is how the perpetrator financially benefits from the committing the fraud scenario.
4. *How the scheme occurs.* The fraud scenario statement describes the fraud risk using the inherent scheme nomenclature. In this stage, the auditor

describes how the fraud scenario would occur in the business system. In other words, how and what would need to happen for the fraud scenario to occur in your company? In the fraud scenario matrix, refer to the vulnerability section of the matrix.

5. *Internal controls.* These are intended to mitigate the fraud scenario; the linkage of the internal control to the fraud scenario is the purpose of developing a fraud risk statement. The linkage is also the core of a fraud risk assessment.

6. *Fraud concealment.* Fraud concealment strategies associated with the fraud scenario are a critical step in developing a fraud data analytics plan. We will discuss in Chapter 3 how to apply this concept in the fraud data analytics plan. All perpetrators understand the need to make a fraudulent transaction look like a real transaction. However, by identifying the concealment strategies, the fraud auditor can distinguish between a legitimate transaction and the fraudulent transaction.

   Red flags associated with the concealment strategy become the basis for the data interrogation routine. A red flag is an observable event that links to a concealment strategy. The red flag becomes the essence of the fraud data profile.

7. *Fraud conversion.* This explains how the perpetrator of the fraud scenario obtains the financial benefit from committing the fraud scenario. How the perpetrator obtains the financial gain helps the auditor or management understand how the perpetrator benefits from committing the fraud scenario. I have called this the *believability factor* for management. The financial conversion is either recorded on the company books, such as with internal credit card frauds, or off the books, such as a kickback. On-the-book conversion can be incorporated into the fraud data analytics: person committing the scenario. Off-the-book conversions generally cannot be incorporated into the books.

Vulnerabilities in the Fraud Scenario Matrix

Every business system has inherent vulnerabilities to fraud. These vulnerabilities include both where and how a fraud scenario is committed. This is the essence of the fraud data analytics plan. The description or understanding of *where* fraud most likely occurs is the basis of the fraud data analytics plan. Through the understanding of the *how*—the natural weaknesses in the internal control system—the fraud auditor is better able to design fraud audit procedures and better able to design the fraud preventative and fraud detective controls.

Internal control failure is the result of understanding the *how* and *where* vulnerabilities that can occur in your business systems. Remember, internal controls provide reasonable assurance versus absolute assurance. Internal control failures occur for many reasons, which are beyond the scope of this book. However, understanding the vulnerability questions is an integral part of building your fraud data analytics plan.

Inherent Schemes to Fraud Scenario

The following illustrates how an inherent fraud scheme becomes a fraud scenario. Starting with the inherent scheme and then using the elements of the fraud scenario matrix the fraud auditor creates a fraud scenario.

The inherent scheme elements are:

1. Entity is a created shell corporation.
2. Fraud action is a sales representative pass-through scheme.

One fraud scenario derived from the inherent scheme is:

Sales representative at a real supplier (person committing is an external person) sets up a shell company (entity structure) and convinces the budget owner or senior member of management to purchase from the shell company (how or why) versus the real supplier. The budget places orders for goods through the shell company. The shell company places an order with a real supplier, the real supplier ships directly to the budget owner company, the real company invoices the shell company, and the shell company invoices the budget owner (fraud action statement for a pass-through scheme) at an inflated price, causing the diversion of company funds (impact statement), or budget owner receives a kickback from the sales representative for directing the contract to the shell company (fraud conversion statement).

 THE FIVE CATEGORIES OF FRAUD SCENARIOS

The fraud risk structure is the starting point of the fraud nomenclature. The fraud scenario structure has five categories of fraud scenarios. The purpose of the categories is twofold. First is how our profession defines scope of an audit. The second is to better understand the *how, when,* and *where* questions to identify fraud scenarios.

Many consultants or auditors state that to identify the fraud risk, it is necessary to conduct interviews with management and document the business system. However, if the "common fraud scenarios" are common to all business systems and common to all companies, is there a need to conduct the interviews to start the fraud risk identification process? By recognizing the *common to all business systems* concept, it provides a starting point for the fraud risk assessment.

The "company-specific fraud scenario" occurs through the inherent weaknesses or limitations in the internal control process. So, these fraud scenarios can only be identified with an understanding of the business process and the internal controls.

The unauthorized and internal control inhibitors focus on the vulnerabilities associated with the internal controls. The industry-specific scenarios correlate to a specific industry.

The five categories of fraud scenarios are:

1. *Common to all business systems.* This is the category of all scenarios that face every core business system. To use an analogy, being hit by an automobile is a common physical security risk every time you cross a road. Yes, the likelihood of being hit by a car crossing the Arc de Triomphe in Paris might be greater than being hit by a car in my hometown of Valatie. But likelihood and inherent to a business process are two different questions. The common attribute is the risk of crossing the road. The common fraud scenarios are a natural part of all business systems.

2. *Company-specific.* This addresses a fraud scenario that could occur due to how your business systems are designed, business structures, business philosophies, etc. Company-specific fraud scenarios are identified as part of documenting the business system and internal control phase of the audit. *To illustrate the concept of company-specific:*

   In one fraud data analytics project we discovered, a company downloaded to Excel from its database the payment file, and the Excel file was immediately encrypted and uploaded to the bank to initiate the payment process. The company-specific fraud occurred at the point the payment file was downloaded to Excel because someone could have changed the payment file. The fraud data analytics was to match the downloaded file to the bank payment file.

3. *Unauthorized access.* This is a broad category. It is not my intent to address technical computer security issues in this book. In this category, I generally focus on avoidance of the authorization levels or password administration issues, allowing someone to approve transactions in your name, poor

approval procedures, and so on—in essence, anything that diminishes the approval control. *To illustrate the concept of authorization avoidance*:

Purchase orders were intentionally created below the threshold to avoid the second approval. In one fraud data analytics project we discovered the internal control avoidance was rampant. Interestingly, in this company, I believe the purchase order was split for perceived operational efficiency versus control avoidance. While this might be the motive for the exception, the control avoidance still provides fraud opportunity. Unfortunately, the practice of splitting purchase orders in that company diluted the value of the red flag analysis of internal control avoidance.

4. *Internal control inhibitor*. This is the action that causes an internal control not to operate as management planned. The three most typical internal control inhibitors are collusion, management override, and nonperformance of an internal control procedure. *To illustrate the concept of an internal control procedure inhibitor*:

The quantity on a receipt or usage transactions were intentionally changed after the fact to cause the spare part inventory to match the physical inventory balance. As a result, theft of spare parts could be easily hidden.

5. *Industry-specific*. Here, those fraud scenarios are unique to an industry. *To illustrate the concept of industry specific*:

In the travel industry, fraud scenarios involving the theft of points would be an example of an industry-wide fraud scenario. In banking, mortgage fraud would be an example.

At this time, we have asked all the fraud scope questions and have all the fraud scope answers to start building our fraud data analytics plan. The next step is to start writing the fraud scenarios that can occur within your fraud scope.

 ## WHAT A FRAUD SCENARIO IS NOT

I have introduced the idea of a standard nomenclature to writing a fraud scenario. Just like being able to speak the local language is critical to an international business traveler in order to communicate in that country. Therefore, a fraud scenario is not how the fraud is concealed or how a perpetrator benefits from committing a fraud scenario. The fraud scenario is intended to provide fraud auditors with the necessary elements to build their fraud audit program.

Within the context of this book, the following statements are not fraud risks (how some people refer to a fraud scenario):

- *Bribery fraud risk.* A bribe is how the person benefits from committing a fraud scenario, the fraud conversion statement.
- *False document scheme.* A false document is how a perpetrator creates the illusion that the transaction is real, the fraud concealment statement.
- *The fraud concealment statement.* Also, from a legal perspective, creating false business documents may be a violation of law.

It is not my intent to take exception to someone else's nomenclature but rather to create a common language throughout this book so the reader and I speak the same language. The statement *bribery fraud risk statement* does not provide the auditor with the necessary description to design a fraud data analytics routine. Remember, the intent of the fraud scenario is to provide the programmer with the necessary specifications to design the fraud data analytics plan.

 ## HOW TO WRITE A FRAUD SCENARIO

A fraud scenario describes how the inherent fraud scheme occurs within your core business systems. The fraud scenario is an extension of the inherent fraud scheme. The fraud scenario has three components that impact the fraud data analytics plan:

1. *The person committing the fraud scenario.* The starting point is to identify the internal and external parties associated with a business function. From an internal perspective we start with three groups of individuals who commit a fraud scenario. The first person has direct access to create or change the database. The second person is the budget owner, which is the location where the transaction is recorded—in essence, the home of the fraudulent transaction. The third person is senior management, which can override the direct access point or the budget owner. From an external perspective, the parties are determined by the nature of the transaction. From the starting point, the person committing the fraud scenario can be expanded based on the complexity of the system and who performs the internal control procedures.

   In the process of identifying the person committing the scenario, the fraud auditor must understand the concept of direct access and indirect access. *Direct access* is any person who can add or change an entity or a transaction through their normal job duties. *Indirect access* to data occurs when manager-authorized duties cause a person with direct access to add or change an entity or transaction. Indirect access is an abstract concept but is critical to understanding fraud opportunity. As an example, if an operating manager submits an invoice to accounts payable within their approval level for a vendor not on the vendor master file, then most likely accounts payable will add the vendor to the master file. Even though the operating manager did not add the vendor with a keystroke, the manager effectively did add the vendor to the master file. Indirect access is one aspect that makes fraud risk different from traditional control risk.

2. *The entity structure.* The term *entity* is intended to denote what the transaction is attached to in the business system. In payroll, the entity is an employee; in procurement cards, the entity is a card number; in financial reporting, it is a combination of the general ledger account and the entity associated with the business system (employee for payroll accounts). The next section in this chapter will discuss the permutations of the entity from a fraud perspective.

3. *Fraudulent action statement.* The first step is to identify the fraudulent action. The second step is to understand how to link the fraudulent action links to the database. The fraudulent action will be determined by the fraud risk structure of the primary and secondary fraud risk category. The second aspect will be determined by the nature of the business system. Later chapters will discuss the fraudulent action statements for each core business system.

   Transaction type or transaction codes define a subtransaction with the core business system. The transaction types generally occur because of a system process or a code within your database. The transaction type is a subset of the fraud action. It is also linked to the company-specific type of scenario. *To illustrate the concept of transaction type*:

   ▪ For subtransaction: Payment of a vendor invoice with no purchase order versus paying an invoice matched to a purchase order.
   ▪ For business code: In revenue, there is a credit code that controls the highest balance for a customer's accounts receivable.

UNDERSTANDING ENTITY PERMUTATIONS ASSOCIATED WITH THE ENTITY STRUCTURE

All business transactions have an entity structure. Revenue has a customer; human resources have an employee; and the expenditure cycle has vendors.

The entity structure may also correspond to an intangible identifier such as an inventory number, or in a call center, the entity might be a complaint number. Most entity structures have a unique number identifier and a unique name. Associated with entity structure is information that links to the entity: address, telephone number, government identification number, and bank account number, to name a few. There is also information that describes the date and time the entity was created, who created the entity, and who changed the entity.

The starting point of the process is to recognize that the entity is either false or real. There are two types of false entities: a created entity or an assumed entity. There are two types of real entities: complicit and not complicit. Each entity structure can reside in your databases on either a permanent or temporary basis.

False Entity

The created false entity is an entity created by the perpetrator, and the perpetrator causes the entity to be added to the master file. The vendor, customer, or employee is added to the master file. It occurs directly through a direct input function's, authorized duties or indirectly through a budget owner's authorized request.

The assumed identity, for purposes of data analytics, is an entity that is on the master file and the perpetrator takes over the identity of the entity. Typically this involves changing the address or the bank account information. Another consideration is whether the takeover of the entity is permanent or temporary. This concept may have many meanings. *To illustrate the concept of taking over the identity*:

- Permanent takeover indicates that the entity is used multiple times over an extended period of time to process fraudulent transactions.
- Temporary takeover indicates a limited use of the entity over a short duration. I am avoiding assigning a frequency because the number of transactions depends on the perpetrator.

The concept of permanent or temporary can be applied to both a created entity and real entities in terms of frequency of occurrence; however, the concept is generally intended to be used in the takeover identity scheme.

For purposes of data analytics, the created entity focuses on new entities whereas the assumed identity focuses on changes to entities.

Real Entity That Is Complicit in the Fraud Scenario

The real entity that is complicit in the fraud scenario has three permutations: entity alone; entity in collusion with an internal source; and entity in collusion with another entity. With complicit entities, the second part of the question is linking the person committing the scenario to the entity. From a pure logic perspective, the permutations are as follows:

- Real entity alone takes advantage of internal control weaknesses or poor oversight by internal management.
- Real entity in collusion with an internal source circumvents internal controls.
- Real entity in collusion with another real entity (external source).
- Real entity that fits the definition of a conflict-of-interest entity.

Real Entity That Is Not Complicit in the Fraud Scenario

The concept of a real entity that is not complicit means that the transaction was processed using the name of the real entity but the transaction was not recorded in the books and records of the real entity. The following illustrates the concept: An employee uses his company credit card (a real entity) to purchase personal items at a retail store accessible to anyone. Yes, the transaction occurred at the retail store, but the store was not knowingly involved in the fraud scenario.

Strictly from a fraud data analysis perspective, whether the entity is complicit or not complicit is generally not relevant. From an investigation perspective, complicit or not complicit is very relevant.

Practical Example of Permanent versus Temporary Takeover

Here is a practical example. A customer service supervisor takes over the identity of a customer to commit a false refund scheme. The change field would be either an address field for a paper check or a bank account for an electronic transfer of funds. For simplicity, we will assume an electronic transfer in the two examples.

In the temporary takeover, the customer services supervisor changes the bank account for a short duration and processes one fraudulent refund under the customer number. The pattern recognition is two changes to the bank account number in a short duration. The first change is to a bank account under the control of the perpetrator; the second change is converting the bank account back to the customer's original number. We will assume only one false refund during the change period. The data analysis has two possibilities: first a duplicate bank account number test associated with the change file or second a high frequency of temporary changes attached to one user ID.

In the permanent takeover, the customer supervisor permanently changes the bank account number and processes multiple fraudulent refunds to the same bank account. The pattern recognition is the same, a change to a bank account. The frequency analysis would identify a high number of refunds to one customer.

The point is simple: The data analyses for a temporary takeover and a permanent takeover are different. If both permutations are not considered, the fraud data analysis plan will be incomplete.

PRACTICAL EXAMPLES OF A PROPERLY WRITTEN FRAUD SCENARIO

I am sure that an English teacher reading this statement might cringe when I say a "properly written fraud scenario." I do not mean from a grammar perspective but rather the fraud scenario has the necessary information to write a fraud data analytics interrogation routine. That is the goal.

To illustrate the concept, I have provided two fraud scenarios. One fraud scenario is for accounts payable and the second fraud scenario is for payroll. In one sense, the two scenarios are very different. In another sense the two fraud scenarios are exactly the same. The two scenarios are different from the perspective of accounts payable and payroll, which means the data will be different. The two scenarios are the same from the perspective of the inherent scheme structure and the fraud data analytics.

First Illustration: Accounts Payable

Accounts payable function acting alone or in collusion with a direct report/causes a shell company to be set up on the vendor master file/processes a contract and approves a fake invoice for goods or services not received/causing the diversion of company funds.

1. "The accounts payable function" is the person committing the fraud scenario. The accounts payable function has direct access to the system.
2. "Causes a shell company to be set up on the vendor master file" is the entity statement. The entity is a false entity created by the perpetrator.
3. "Processes a contract and approves a fake invoice for goods or services not received" is the fraudulent action. The fraud action statement is a false billing scheme because no goods or services were received.

Second Illustration: Payroll

Payroll function or a budget owner/causes a fictitious person to be set up on the employee master file/the budget owner or payroll submits false time and attendance records for the fictitious person/causing the diversion of funds.

1. "The payroll function or a budget owner" is the person committing the fraud scenario.
2. "Causes a fictitious person to be set up on the employee master file" is the entity statement.
3. "Submits false time and attendance records" is the fraudulent action statement.

Let's look at the similarities between the accounts payable and the payroll fraud scenario:

1. The person committing the scenario in both examples has direct access to the data files.
2. The entity in both scenarios is a false created entity.
3. The fraudulent action is for something that is false or did not occur.

The point is that the fraud data analytics plan for the two scenarios is very similar; it is the data or the red flags that differ for the two fraud scenarios.

 ## STYLE VERSUS CONTENT OF A FRAUD SCENARIO

The content of a fraud scenario has four elements: person committing; entity; fraud action statement; and impact. How the fraud auditor articulates the content is a matter of writing style. The style used by the fraud auditor needs to be consistent with the operating style of the organization and consistent with the extent of detail desired by the chief auditor. From a fraud data analytics perspective, the style needs to provide the fraud auditor with the necessary elements to write the data interrogation routine.

To illustrate the style concept, we will use the inherent scheme of vendor overbilling using the product substitution involving both an internal party and the vendor.

Impact Statement:
The impact statement could be written in a generic method: resulting in the loss of company funds.
The impact statement could be written from a nonmonetary method: resulting in adverse publicity caused by product failure.
The impact statement could insert the conversion statement: resulting in an internal employee receiving a kickback.

Person Committing the Scenario Statement:
The person committing statement could reference a department: the Accounts Payable Department.
The person committing statement could reference a title in the department: Accounts Payable Manager.
The person committing statement could reference a specific name (most likely only in an investigation).

How-and-Where Statement or Internal Control Vulnerability Statement:
Another common style differential is describing how and where the scenario occurs versus the fraud scenario statement used for fraud risk identification.

So, what is the difference between a fraud scenario and a statement on how the fraud scenario occurred? The difference is an important question. In the fraud circle, the concept of vulnerabilities was introduced. The purpose of the vulnerability question is to answer the "*how* question." How did the fraud scenario occur in your core business system? The *how* question is also relevant to the internal control questions. The vulnerability question helps in identifying which fraud scenarios to include in the fraud data analytics plan. While similar to the concept of residual risk, the vulnerability recognizes the inherent weaknesses in all business systems. The "*where* question" is relevant to the fraud data analytics plan.

As a general style rule, the concealment concept is not included in the fraud scenario statement unless the concept is necessary to understand the scenario. In the accounts payable example, the phrase "a false invoice" was used in the fraud action statement. While the scenario could have used *the invoice* versus *false invoice*, the term *false invoice* suggests that the invoice was created by the person committing the scheme.

It is suggested that the audit function determine the writing style at the beginning of the fraud risk identification phase versus at the end of the process to avoid the proverbial review note. Style is a matter of the person writing the fraud scenario; content is a matter of developing a complete fraud data analytics plan.

HOW THE FRAUD SCENARIO LINKS TO THE FRAUD DATA ANALYTICS

The use of fraud data analytics to search for fraud in core business systems is important to our profession. The ability to prepare a comprehensive fraud assessment is important to our profession. Understanding how the fraud scenario links to the components of the fraud audit is important to our profession. The fraud scenario circle illustrates the relationship (Figure 2.3).

I started the book with the following quote:

The world's best auditor using the world's best audit program cannot detect fraud unless their sample includes a fraudulent transaction.

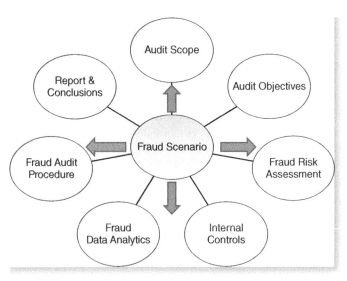

FIGURE 2.3 The Fraud Scenario

The fraud scenario approach provides the fraud auditor with the methodology to build a fraud data analytics plan and ability to locate fraud in core business systems. The fraud scenario establishes the specifications for designing the search routine to locate the fraud scenario. Without specifications the fraud auditor is hoping to come across the fraud based on their experience versus a methodology. There are many software tools available to the fraud auditor but the software is nothing more than a tool in the hands of the craftsman. The fraud auditor is the person using the tool to search databases for indictors of a fraud scenario. In summary, let's be sure we understand how the fraud risk structure relates to the building of a fraud scenario:

The fraud risk structure is necessary to establish the scope of the fraud data analytics project. The reality in our profession and all professions is that projects have limited resources in terms of time, people, and money. Establishing your scope, knowing what is included and what is not included, is important to maintain project quality and efficiency. We start with the primary and secondary fraud categories.

Once the fraud audit scope is established, the inherent scheme structure is the linkage to the data tables within your database. The inherent fraud scheme structure directly links to our database structures. Each inherent fraud scheme has an entity structure referred to a master file. Each inherent scheme has a fraud statement, which is referred to as the transaction file of the database.

The fraud scenario becomes the basis for developing the fraud data profile, which is discussed in the Chapter 3. The fraud scenario has all the necessary elements to write the fraud data interrogation routine to locate a specific fraud scenario. It tells the programmer exactly what you are looking for. The programmer, the craftsman of the software tool, will know how to use the features of the software to examine the data.

The sophistication of the fraud concealment strategies associated with the fraud scenario is how we calibrate the data interrogation routine to search for the fraud scenario. The red flags linked to the level of sophistication of the concealment serve as the selection criteria in the data interrogation routines. Without considering the sophistication of the fraud concealment, the fraud auditor will have false negatives. These concepts are discussed in Chapter 3.

The fraud risk structure, the inherent scheme, the fraud scenario, and the fraud concealment are all necessary to understand and define as part of your sample selection process. Fraud data analytics is about creating a sample of transactions consistent with the fraud data profile of the fraud scenario. The fraud audit procedure is the process of examining the transactions.

Illustration of the Sample Selection Process

The primary category of fraud is asset misappropriation, the secondary category is theft of monetary funds, and the inherent scheme is a false entity with an assumed identity and fraud action is paying for services not performed. The fraud scenario is:

Budget owner/causes an employee who terminates employment without notifying human resources to remain on the payroll on a temporary basis (i.e., four pay periods)/and the budget owner submits time and attendance records for the terminated employee/causing the diversion of company funds or causing the payroll payment to be deposited in a bank account the budget owner controls.

The Fraud Data Analytics Plan

Master file has two key data fields. First data field is the code changing the employee from active to inactive. Second data field is the bank account, assuming all employees have direct deposit; then there has to be a change to the bank account.

Transaction file is the time report. In one sense, there is nothing in the electronic database that would provide a clue, unless the supervisor increased the employee's hours worked during the fraud period or the supervisor's ID code links to the time report record.

The sample selection is a list of all employees who have a termination code and a change to the bank account. The fraud auditor's job is to examine the underlying records for evidence of whether the fraud scenario is occurring.

 **SUMMARY**

One more time: Your fraud data analytics plan is only as good as your ability to identify all the fraud scenarios within your audit scope. Without a methodology, your data analytics plan will be like a buffet. The plan will include a little of this type of fraud and a little of that type of fraud.

APPENDIX 1

Fraud Scenario Matrix

Primary & Secondary	Person Committing	Person Committing	Entity	Action	Impact
Asset misappropriation Corruption Financial reporting Identify secondary type	Always think about: First, What a person can do by himself Second, What a person can do with collusion	Use for collusion	Supplier, employee, or customer False: Created or assumed Real: Complicit or not complicit Permanent or temporary	Identify the fraudulent action	Loss of company funds Or Specific monetary or nonmonetary impact
Conversion	**Concealment**	**Red Flag**	**Vulnerabilities How?**	**Vulnerabilities Where?**	**Internal Control Failure**
How the person receives the financial gain	Listen for the document Listen for the representation that causes the action	Remember red flags link to the concealment strategy Each concealment strategy must have one or more red flags	You will learn this from: Procedure manuals Interview of process, listening for lack of a procedure or weakness in procedure	You will learn this from: Class of transactions, physical location, department, etc.	Identify the internal control, which is either missing or does not operate as intended by management

APPENDIX 2

Fraud Scenario Matrix

Primary & Secondary	Person Committing	Person Committing	Entity	Action	Impact
Primary: Asset misappropriation Secondary: Theft of monetary funds	Budget owner	Blank	Entity is a supplier shell company Permanent	Payment for services not provided	Loss of company funds
Conversion	**Concealment**	**Red Flag**	**Vulnerabilities How?**	**Vulnerabilities Where?**	**Internal Control Failure**
Payment to a bank account in the name of the shell company	Create shell company Create false invoice False approval	New company Small business software Forged signature	New vendor procedures are not risk based	Professional service categories are most prone to this scenario	New vendor procedures did not detect that the company existed in name only

CHAPTER THREE

Data Analytics Strategies for Fraud Detection

N ow that the fraud scope is established and the fraud scenario register is created, the next step is to select a strategy for each fraud scenario and understand how the strategy is impacted by the sophistication of the concealment. Your initial use of this process will seem overly bureaucratic. However, eventually the process will become just a way of thinking. The thought process is important to understand what your data analytics plan is designed to detect and what the data analytics plan will not detect.

This chapter is intended for the fraud auditor who wants to understand fraud data analytics in the later chapters. In the real world, you will need to adapt the suggestions contained in the book to your data files. You will be eventually requested to perform data analytics in business systems for which you have no practical business experience or you will use fraud data analytics to perform an investigation. You will need to develop a fraud data analytics plan where no auditor has gone. I believe the guidelines will serve you well. For the auditor who simply wants a software vendor to provide you with a list of tests, you should pass over this chapter and proceed directly to Chapter 7. For that auditor, I will provide my top three reports that you should create for the business system as part of the chapter summary.

In Chapter 2, I referenced the building of a house. I said the fraud scenarios provided the foundation to the house and the fraud data analytics plan was the blueprint for building the house. Furthering that example, the strategies outlined in this chapter are the building code requirements used by the building inspector to ensure the house is sound.

The strategies provide the basis for developing the search routines to identify the red flags based on the sophistication of the concealment strategies. The two key terms for red flag identification are *patterns* and *frequency*. Understanding the data patterns that link to the fraud scenario versus common data errors is critical to the efficiency of the project. The frequency analysis helps identify if the occurrence of the pattern is consistent with the fundamental fraud theories. Therefore, the first step is to identify the patterns and frequency of red flags that correlate to the fraud scenario data profile.

The last section of the chapter is intended to provide practical guidance on developing the actual search routines in using the data commonly found in all business transactions. The methodology for developing fraud data analytics search routines is covered in Chapter 4.

Before we discuss the data analytics strategies, the fraud auditor needs to understand how the sophistication of concealment will affect the selected fraud data analytics strategy and the eventual sample selection. In reality, the sophistication factor and the right data analytics strategy is a lot like the phrase: Which comes first, the chicken or the egg? Both concepts need to be considered; in what order is based on the fraud auditor's style. However, ignoring either concept will result in building a fraud audit program that is designed to fail.

UNDERSTANDING HOW FRAUD CONCEALMENT AFFECTS YOUR DATA ANALYTICS PLAN

We have developed a simple system of ranking fraud concealment sophistication based on low, medium, and high. There are two sides of the definition. From the perpetrator's perspective, it is the ability or intent to conceal its fraudulent actions from detection. From the auditor's perspective, it is the ability of fraud data analytics to identify the fraudulent action for audit examination.

Concealment is either a general condition of the database or a specific action committed by the perpetrator. However, do not think of this as cloak-and-dagger. In some ways, the general conditions are what allow the fraud scenario to go undetected. However, the specific concealment actions become the basis of our fraud data profile.

General Concealment Actions:

- Number of records processed in a year.
- Number of records that an employee approves in a year.
- Real or perceived time pressure to process a transaction.
- Changes in how society conducts business; mailbox service companies have become very popular.
- Societal changes; area code does not link to a physical address due to the telephone portability act.
- New technology changes the way we look at an address or bank account. The cloud can serve this function in disguising the ultimate receiver.
- Natural vulnerabilities within internal control systems.

Specific Concealment Actions:

- Keeping all fraudulent transactions within the perpetrator's control level.
- Ensuring the dollar value of the fraud does not exceed internal budgets.
- Understanding how controls operate in other areas of the business system.
- Realizing that smaller-dollar-value transactions tend to get less scrutiny than large-dollar transactions.
- Management override can occur without a paper trail or data trail.
- Documents or transactions that look real tend to get less scrutiny.
- Creating the illusion of compliance with internal controls.
- Creating a legal entity that provides the illusion of a real company.

So, how do we define the concealment concepts and how do we integrate the concepts into our fraud data analytics plan? That is the million-dollar question.

 ## LOW SOPHISTICATION

The perpetrator's footprint is visible in the entity data or the pattern recognition in the transactional data is visible to the naked eye through the use of data interrogation routines. Footprint in the entity data is typically identified through missing data analysis, matching routines, duplicate routines, or specific anomaly testing. The duplicate routine is searching for duplicate data in the same database. The matching routine is searching for a match of two or more databases where the entity could logically exist. A high degree of missing entity data indicates that someone is manually controlling the process versus the automated system. In transactional data the pattern recognition tends to allow for specification identification. In low sophistication, the pattern recognition tends to be an exact match. The three types of matches are discussed later in the chapter.

To illustrate low sophistication:

- If a vendor has neither a street address nor a bank account, how is the payment being delivered to the vendor?
- Regarding low sophistication of concealment within the entity data: Searching for a vendor operating under two different names or a duplicate telephone or email address would provide the linkage.
- Regarding low sophistication of concealment within transactional data: Vendor invoice numbers follow a sequential pattern (pattern recognition). The number of occurrences and the date range of the sequential pattern would be the basis for sample selection.

MEDIUM SOPHISTICATION

The perpetrator's personal identity and the fictitious entity's identity have a limited or vague connection. There is no exact match on the complete address, but there is a match on the postal code. The match or duplicate test is not sufficient by itself to cause the entity to be selected. The transactional data may show an avoidance of internal controls or an anomaly to general business practices or business expectations.

To illustrate medium sophistication:

- In the entity data, vendor postal code matches the postal code of the head of purchasing.
- In the transactional data, there is a regular frequency of invoices being structured to avoid dual-signature controls. The invoice dates are not an exact match but a close match.

HIGH SOPHISTICATION

The perpetrator's personal identity and the fictitious entity have no overt connection within the entity data. The transactional data generally conforms to the internal controls. For real entities committing the scenario alone, the success of the pattern recognition is the auditor's ability to benchmark the internal data to business expectations or through the use of outlier or frequency analysis. For external real entities in collusion with an internal source the key is the internal source needs to control the volume of the fraudulent data. For external sources complicit with the internal perpetrator, either the perpetrator is the only internal source to use the real non-complicit entity or the volume of transactions, either quantity or dollar value, exceeds business needs. There could be a change in the use of the external entity in conjunction with a change in the internal management team.

To illustrate high sophistication:

▪ In the entity data, there is no match on address, bank account, or government registration number.
▪ In the transactional data, the number of journal entries below a control threshold is illogical for the company.

In building the fraud data analytics plan, the fraud auditor needs to consider the scenario, the fraud data mining strategy, and the sophistication of the concealment strategy. Without calibrating the plan for the sophistication of concealment, the fraud auditor will not know what the plan is intended to find and what the plan cannot find by the way the interrogation plan was designed.

As a guideline, fraud auditors should start building their fraud data analytics plan to locate fraud based on low or medium sophistication, whereas investigations based on sufficient predication should consider high sophistication. Figures 3.1 through 3.3 are intended to reflect our experiences with fraud data analytics.

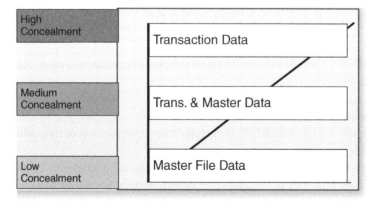

FIGURE 3.1 Fraud Concealment Tendencies

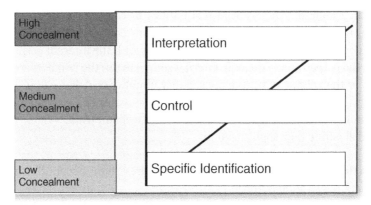

FIGURE 3.2   Fraud Concealment Strategies

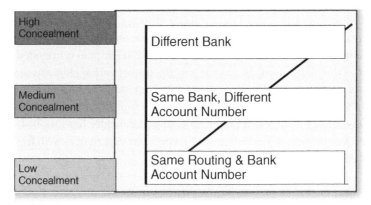

FIGURE 3.3   Illustration Bank Account Number

Figure 3.1 illustrates how to correlate the sophistication of concealment to the examination of data.

Figure 3.2 illustrates how to correlate the sophistication of concealment to the fraud data analytics strategies.

Figure 3.3 illustrates how to correlate the sophistication of concealment to a specific data field.

The fraud auditor must consider how the level of concealment impacts the fraud data analytics plan's ability to identify transactions that have a higher probability of being fraudulent versus a red flag caused by a data error. The concept is also important to understand how a fraud data analytics plan may have a false negative. To explain how a false negative can occur within your fraud data analytics plan, consider the duplicate bank account test:

The test is perfect for low sophistication because the bank account numbers result in an exact match. However, at the medium level, the exact match can only occur on the bank routing number, and at high sophistication of concealment the strategy will fail to have any match on bank account number. It is that simple.

SHRINKING THE POPULATION THROUGH THE SOPHISTICATION FACTOR

To explain the concept of shrinking the population, the fraud auditor needs to understand that there is a direct correlation between the degree of sophistication of the concealment strategy and the number of transactions meeting the data profile requirements. In low sophistication, the pattern recognition is specific (exact match on a street address), whereas in high sophistication, there is no exact match; therefore, more vague criteria must be used to narrow the population (all entities created in a time period within a postal code radius).

The resulting impact is the ability to shrink the population of possibilities. Highly sophisticated concealment strategies tend to have a larger number of transactions meeting the fraud data profile. By contrast, low-sophistication concealment strategies tend to have a smaller number of transactions meeting the fraud data profile. Understanding how the sophistication of concealment impacts the number of transactions meeting the profile is critical to using the inclusion and exclusion theory discussed in Chapter 4. Shrinking the population is one way to minimize the impact of the general concealment conditions (see Figure 3.4).

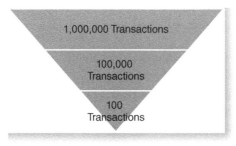

FIGURE 3.4   Improving Your Odds of Selecting One Fraudulent Transaction

The goal of fraud data analytics is the selection of transactions that have a higher probability of linking to a fraud scenario. Clearly, fraud data analytics is not about a random selection of transactions. The following guidelines should be considered in understanding how the sophistication of concealment will impact the fraud auditor's ability to identify the right transactions for audit examination.

Low Sophistication:

- Specific identification strategies are used for both entity and transactional data.
- Entity identifying information links to the perpetrator's known identifying information, for example, a specific street address.
- The false entity structure will match to another entity in either the same database or a different database.
- False entity will also reveal missing identifying information in order to reduce someone else's ability to contact the false entity.
- The patterns associated with the transaction data will typically be overtly obvious to the naked eye.
- The pattern recognition for the transaction data allows for specific identification.
- Sample size is determined by the number of transactions that match the data profile. The sample size can be either zero because no transactions link to the data profile or a very large sample because the match criteria are not sufficiently defined.

Medium Sophistication:

- Internal control avoidance strategies tend to be more effective.
- Specific identification routines are less effective because there is no direct match to the entity's data.
- Specific identification will allow for a match on some aspect of the entity information.
- Specific identification is more effective when there is an allegation that focuses on a person or department.
- Entity identifying information relates to some aspect of the perpetrator's known identifying information, for example, a postal code versus a physical street address.
- Internal control avoidance strategies should be used for transactional data.
- Outliers' patterns tend to be effective for transactional history analysis.

- Creating smaller homogeneous data groups, referred to as cluster patterns, will facilitate the auditor's ability to spot an anomaly.
- Filtering techniques based on dollar magnitude are effective in reducing the number of transactions fitting the data profile. The difference between filtering and red flag identification is discussed in Chapter 4.
- Sample selection is based on the entities or transactions that avoid the internal control after all relevant filtering.

High Sophistication:
- Data analytics at this level is like code breaking. There is no finite criterion that serves as identification criteria. The process tends to be judgmental selection versus criteria selection. The key is to understand how the fraud scenario occurs in your business systems.
- The specific concealment strategies used by the perpetrator tend to be more deliberate and planned.
- Direct matches seldom occur.
- Entity identifying information has no relationship with the perpetrator's known identifying information.
- Entity identifying information may relate to a mailbox service or an out-of-area address that has a mail forwarding feature, providing the illusion of a real business.
- Transactional data are more effective at identifying fraud scenarios versus entity data.
- The process of creating smaller homogeneous data files based on geography, transaction types, transaction codes, and cost centers facilitates the data interpretation.
- Filtering techniques like drill-down analysis are effective in reducing the number of transactions fitting the data profile, thus allowing data interpretation to be more effective.
- Sample selection relies on data interpretation skills.
- Sample size tends to be judgmentally determined based on the data interpretation.
- Selection process is based on understanding how the scenario operates, money trail, fraud theory, concealment theory, and professional experience of the auditor.

 ## BUILDING THE FRAUD SCENARIO DATA PROFILE

The fraud scenario data profile is all the identified red flags associated with the fraud scenario. The red flags need to be calibrated to the level of fraud sophistication. The following guidelines should be considered in building a fraud data profile:

1. Red flags are both data items logically identified either through data inter-rogation or through audit examination of documents.
2. Most data red flags are contained in the underlying documents support-ing the transaction.
3. Red flags that exist in public records should be incorporated into the selec-tion process or audit examination, whenever possible.
4. Using multiple red flags for sample selection will reduce the number of false positives.
5. Each red flag should have a weight assigned to the importance of the red flag: low, medium, and high. Clearly, not all red flags have the same value.
6. A composite score of all the red flags associated with the entity or trans-action should be the basis for sample selection.
7. Please do not rate everything high; it defeats the purpose of ranking the red flags.
8. Most red flags have both a fraud tendency and a logical business explana-tion. It is important to understand the distinction of good or bad.
9. False entity scenarios start with entity red flags based on the type of false entity and then search for the transaction red flags that link to the fraud scenario.
10. Conflict-of-interest entities have similar characteristics to false entities.
11. Real entity scenarios seldom use entity criteria for selection except for real entities operating under different names.
12. Real entities scenarios tend to focus on the transactional red flags associ-ated with the specific fraud scenario.
13. The fraud data profile is a set of specific identifiable criteria for specific identification, internal control, and number anomaly strategies. The fraud data profile is relevant for the data interpretation strategy but the strategy tends to be more judgmental for sample selection.
14. Transactional red flags correlate to false entities, conflict-of-interest enti-ties, and real entity scenarios.
15. Entity red flags will match the perpetrator at low- and medium-concealment strategies but not at high-concealment strategies.
16. Transactional red flags usually contain a footprint of the perpetrator.
17. Remember, these are guidelines, not absolute rules.

Precision of Matching Concept on Red Flags

The concept of identifying red flags seems relatively simple until the fraud auditor factors into the equation the following types of matches:

- *Exact match.* The two data elements are an exact match. An easy example is invoice date. Two invoices from the same vendor are dated July 24. From an address field, two or more vendors have the same street address; city, state, and postal code are an exact match.
- *Close match.* The data elements are in close proximity to another transaction. Two invoices from the same vendor are within three days of each other. From an address field, two or more vendors have the same city, state, and postal code, but different street address in the street field.
- *Related match.* The data elements are within close proximity but exceed the close match test. From an address test we would focus on postal code or all postal codes within a geographic radius.

As a guideline, the fraud data analytics should start with exact match followed by close match. The related match tends to be used for high sophistication of concealment or a specific allegation of fraud. The allegation allows the data analytics to reduce the population of entities and transactions, which allows data interpretation strategies to be more effective.

FRAUD DATA ANALYTIC STRATEGIES

There are four basic strategies in developing a data interrogation routine. Within each strategy, we need to identify the associated pattern and consider the frequency of the event. Each strategy has strengths and weaknesses for fraud detection:

1. Specific identification of a data element or an internal control anomaly
2. Internal control avoidance
3. Data interpretation
4. Number anomaly

Specific Identification of a Data Element or an Internal Control Anomaly

The design of the test is exactly as it sounds; it focuses on identifying a specific data pattern. The process starts with a fraud scenario and then specific data pattern that is associated with the fraud scenario. The following fraud scenario illustrates the concept:

A real supplier overbills the company by intentionally overcharging within the payment tolerances for matching a purchase order to an invoice in the accounts payable system, resulting in the loss of company funds.

The specific identification is all supplier invoices that exceed the original purchase order amount within the tolerance levels. The frequency analysis would highlight those suppliers committing the fraud scenario with a higher frequency versus a pattern that occurs with a low frequency.

The following types of data interrogation tests are usually associated with the specific identification strategy:

1. The specific identification strategy focuses on the following types of tests for entity data:
    a) Match: searches two different databases for the same data element. The matching concept is also used in the internal control avoidance.
    b) Duplicate: searches within one database for the same data element in two different entities. The data analytics should use data elements that are more difficult to conceal or would cost the perpetrator money—i.e., telephone number or email address.
    c) Missing: searches for a data element that should exist in the data file. With missing searches it is the totality of the missing information versus a missing data element.
    d) Changed: searches for a change to a data field through examination of the change file or comparing two database files at the beginning and end of the scope period.
    e) A specific anomaly in a specific data field.
    f) Address and bank accounts tend to be critical data fields because the transfer of funds requires an electronic transfer or the mailing of funds. If both data fields are blank, this is an example of a specific data anomaly.
2. The specific identification strategy focuses on the following types of tests for transactional data:
    a) The identification process starts with a specific fraud scenario.
    b) A specific pattern in the data—i.e., a sequential pattern of vendor invoice numbers.
    c) A group of transactions that can be identified based on a specific data criterion—i.e., excessive overtime or invoices applied to a dormant purchase order.
    d) Missing: invoices with no purchase order.

e) Change analysis should focus on a transaction being changed, deleted, or voided—i.e., an employee's time report changed by a supervisor or payroll supervisor.

f) Duplicate transactions. Supplier invoices with a duplicate invoice number or two invoices with the same date and amount.

g) Manual transactions. These are transactions that are not created through the automated systems and are instead recorded through a manual process.

h) Data anomaly in a specific data field that correlates to a fraud scenario or a concealment strategy.

i) Data anomaly associated with your company's normal business practices—i.e., speed of payment is searching for a vendor that is paid faster than normal company payment terms.

3. Specific identification tends to be more effective by starting with a cluster pattern and then using specific attributes to refine the selection process. The use of multiple criteria reduces the number of false positives.

Illustrative Examples of Specific Identification Strategy:

1. Employee that is missing a user ID for access to the building.
2. Employee that is missing emergency contact information.
3. Employee with a change to bank account near termination date.
4. Two employees with different last name, same bank account for direct deposit.
5. Employee's name matches a contract employee name in the vendor file.
6. Employee claiming exemption from income taxes and the gross wages would indicate the employee could have a tax liability if there is no tax withholding.
7. All employees with no voluntary withholding for fringe benefits, such as 401(k) plan and health insurance.

Guidelines for Use of Specific Identification Strategy:

1. The specific identification is used when the concealment of the fraud scenario is at a low level.
2. The focus of the strategy for entity information is to locate false entity scenarios.
3. The focus of the strategy for transactional information is to identify specific data pattern associated with a fraud scenario.
4. To illustrate, I would use the specific identification strategy to identify open purchase orders with multiple invoices, or I would identify all invoices that are greater than the original purchase order.

5. Obviously, a vendor invoice being greater than the purchase order is not a reason to call in the investigators. However, history has also taught us that override or change orders are associated with fraud scenarios.
6. Do not have a myopic view of the test words. *Missing* can be used in many different ways for testing purposes. *Missing* could mean internal controls require the data element to be populated or may simply mean that the data field is blank.
7. The goal of the test is to identify a specific entity or a set of transactions that link to a specific entity that meets the specific identification criteria.

Consider the Following Scenario

Budget owner causes an employee who terminates employment (employee stops going to work) not to be removed from the payroll system, and the budget owner submits time and attendance records in the name of the terminated employee for a temporary period of time, causing the diversion of funds.

Since the statement indicates the scenario is temporary, we can identify all terminated employees as our first specific identification test. The reason for selecting all terminated employees is based on the temporary criteria and the fraud that the budget owner is committing over a period of time.

The second test is based on payment method. If the employee is paid with direct deposit, then through our data analytics we could identify all terminated employees that had a bank account change during their employment period. Since the scenario could not occur without a change to bank account, the analysis provides a sample that has a higher probability of being consistent with the specific fraud scenario.

If the employee is paid through a manual check, then the specific identification identifies a group of employees that fit the profile but requires manual examination of records to see if red flags exist on the endorsement side of the check.

 INTERNAL CONTROL AVOIDANCE

The concept focuses on transactions that either avoid internal controls or attempt to circumvent internal controls. The strategy is based on the concept that when an individual is intentionally avoiding internal controls the person may have evil motives. The audit examination determines whether the control avoidance is linked to a fraud scenario or to a cavalier attitude toward internal controls.

The Fundamental Strategies for Internal Control Avoidance

1. Avoidance of the dollar levels:
   a) Structuring transactions to avoid a control level. This is the process of splitting one transaction that would exceed the control level into two or more transactions to avoid a control level. The tests are designed to locate duplicate transactions or to identify multiple transactions in the aggregate that exceed a control level. This concept goes by many different names, such as split transactions.
   b) All transactions are below a control level. All transactions associated with a specific entity are below the control level. The aggregate dollar volume with the transaction is a key criterion in the selection process.
2. Off-period transactions:
   a) Creating or changing an entity during non-business hours or days.
   b) Creating, changing, voiding, or deleting transactions during non-business hours or days.
   c) Creating, changing, voiding, or deleting transactions from a remote location.
   d) Create or change a transaction that originated from someone who did not typically process the transaction. The controller recorded the invoice versus the accounts payable function.
   e) Create or change a transaction by someone that is absent from work due to some form of personal leave.
   f) Create or change a transaction by someone responsible for the custody of an asset.
3. Illogical order of transactions; every business system has a logical flow of documents. In purchasing, there should be a requisition, followed by a purchase order, a receipt transaction resulting in a vendor invoice. Comparing the purchase order date to invoice date would indicate the transaction that avoided the purchasing internal controls.
4. Reclassification, changes, transfers, reversals, voids that occur within a short duration after the initial recording of the transaction or occur in two different operating periods.
5. Speed of transaction; the transaction is processed more quickly than policy or normal business practice. The technique compares the date of one transaction to the date of another transaction. A simple example is comparing the vendor invoice date to the payment date, searching for vendor invoices that are paid faster than normal terms.
6. Use of aged documents or system codes that provide open authority.

7. Manual transaction is a transaction that is created and processed external to the automated system and then is recorded manually in the database.
8. Override transactions; many systems have codes that allow a transaction to bypass computerized controls for logical business reasons. These override features allow a perpetrator to circumvent internal controls. A manual transaction can also be viewed as override transaction.

Illustrative Examples of Internal Control Avoidance

1. Requesting a vendor to split an invoice so that both invoices only require one approval but in the aggregate would have required two approvals.
2. A dormant vendor's address is changed on Saturday night at 11:00 PM from a remote computer that links to the controller.
3. Purchase order is created after the receipt of the vendor's invoice.
4. Payroll manager issues two payroll checks to herself; the first is through the automated system, the second is a manual payroll check.

Guidelines for Use of Internal Control Avoidance Strategy

1. The internal control avoidance strategy is used when the concealment of the fraud scenario is at a medium level.
2. The false entity has limited linkage to the perpetrator's identity.
3. Locating false entities can still occur at this level when we have identified a person or a group of persons who are the focus of the data analytics.
4. The frequency number must be established for each test.
5. The pattern recognition is based on the design of the internal control.
6. All off-period entity transactions should be selected. With business operating 24/7, the design of this test becomes more challenging.
7. Retrospective analysis of a contract or bid is an effective method to detect corruption.
8. The concepts of exact match, close match, and related match are critical to assess internal control avoidance.
9. The goal of internal control avoidance is to identify a transaction that has the appearance of avoiding an internal control.
10. The difference between specific identification and internal control avoidance is sometimes a blurred line. I encourage the reader to stay focused on the intent of strategy.

Consider the Following Scenario

Budget owner in collusion with a supplier splits invoices to stay below a control level for the purpose of overbilling the company based on price, resulting in the diversion of company assets (impact statement) or budget owner receives a kickback from the supplier (conversion statement).

In contrast, this scenario involves a real entity; therefore, entity testing is not relevant. The transaction testing will start with exact match on vendor invoices based on invoice number and date. The second criterion is based on the aggregate amount of the invoice match exceeding the control amount. While a frequency of one split transaction is sufficient for sample selection, a regular frequency of the invoice splitting for one vendor or one department would improve the odds of establishing intent. The next test would be to compare the selected transactions from the first test to the line items on the invoice to previous transactions for the same line item, searching for a pattern of price increases.

If no transactions are identified in the exact match test, the second level of testing would use a close match on invoice number and invoice date.

DATA INTERPRETATION STRATEGY

This strategy requires the selection of entities or transactions through visual examination of data on a report designed by the fraud auditor. Data interpretation is very similar to the standard audit step that states: Review the journal for unusual transactions. The difficultly of performing a manual review of the journal is that the journal tends to list transactions in date or control number order. The manual review requires the auditor to assimilate all that information as part of the process of selecting a transaction. In fraud data analytics, we are able to create a report that summarizes all transactional data related to an entity into one line. In this way, auditors can focus their energy on the selection process.

Guidelines for Use of Data Interpretation

1. The data interpretation strategy is used when the concealment of the fraud scenario is at a high level.
2. In my opinion, high concealment generally exceeds the requirements of an audit but would be included in fraud investigation. I also believe that data interpretation would be included in a whistle blower allegation in which the corporation has deemed the allegation to have merit. My comment is based on audits providing reasonable assurance versus absolute assurance.
3. The first step is identifying which fraud scenarios are included in the audit scope due to high concealment.

4. The selection of the fraud scenario could occur simply because the auditor is conducting a fraud audit or the fraud risk assessment has rated residual risk as high.
5. The advantage of planning at the high concealment is that it creates the opportunity for locating all fraudulent activity related to the fraud scenario.
6. The disadvantage of not planning at the high level is the opportunity for false negatives. In essence, the auditor missed the fraudulent activity because the perpetrator was more sophisticated than the audit procedure.
7. Once the fraud scenarios are identified, the process starts with identifying the population of data that relates to the fraud scenario. The transactions should be summarized in a high-level format. The inclusion/exclusion theory is the next step.
8. The exclusion is intended to eliminate the lines, whereas the inclusion is the lines being considered within the data interpretation strategy. The key is to document your judgment for both the exclusion and inclusion. Since the process is judgmental, the decision process will also be high-level explanations.
9. The exclusion theory is to exclude those records or lines that are not consistent with the fraud theory that links to the specific fraud scenario.
10. The goal of the exclusion step is to reduce the size of the report requiring manual review.
11. The last step is the inclusion theory, or the basis for selecting a line for audit examination.
12. For expenditure or revenue audits, I typically use a format that summarizes transactions by aggregate dollars, aggregate record, maximum record, minimum record, and average record. Depending on the analysis, the report should include data from entity file that will assist in the review. I have found entity creation date to be useful.
13. For payroll, I typically summarize the payroll transactions: number of payroll payments, gross payroll, and net payroll. I find the grade level or job description to be useful.
14. The goal of the visual review of the report is to reduce the size of the report through the use of data-extraction routines that filter out those lines that are not consistent with the fraud theory associated with the fraud scenario. This is a critical step in making the process a success. Imagine a 100-page report with each page having 50 lines, which would require the auditor to examine 50,000 lines of data. Clearly, this is not a practical approach.

15. Using the data fields I have summarized, we make judgmental decisions about the inclusion/exclusion process. Using the columns of summarized data, we make judgments that are based on fraud theory and the mechanics of the fraud scenario. These judgments are not based on scientific studies but, rather, auditor judgment is based on experience.

16. We also use other external databases or Internet searches to support our decisions in selecting an entity for audit examination.

Consider the Following Scenario

Budget owner acting alone or in collusion with a direct report/causes a shell company to be set up on the vendor master file/processes a contract and approves a fake invoice for goods or services not received/causing the diversion of company funds (Figure 3.5).

Using the report of summarized data, we ask questions about the data to exclude certain vendor lines to reduce the report size to a number of lines that can be reviewed through visual examination:

Basis for Exclusion:

1. *Aggregate number of records.* Using the frequency concept we would ask how many false invoices the budget owner would submit in a one-year period. Using the frequency of 52, we would exclude all vendor lines with greater than 52 records. The number 52 correlates to once a week.

2. *Aggregate dollar value.* In this exclusion process, we would first focus on eliminating small-dollar vendor lines. I must caution that the perpetrator might use multiple shell companies to keep a low visibility. I also caution that you do not make any judgments in which you will not be able to eliminate any lines, which defeats the purpose of the process.

3. *Maximum dollar amount.* The budget owners typically do not want to submit a fake invoice to their supervisor. Therefore, we could exclude any vendor line when the maximum amount would require the approval of the budget owner's supervisor.

4. *Minimum dollar amount.* The exclusion factor for the minimum is more of a judgment than on the maximum dollar amount. I believe most auditors would see the logic in the exclusion factor. As a starting point, we could say, if the minimum is a negative number, denote a credit; we could exclude those vendor lines. What if the minimum is $2.49; would that indicate a real or a false invoice? One perspective is that the perpetrator would submit a low-dollar invoice amount to allow the vendor to be set up. Another perspective is that a budget owner committing a false billing scheme would not submit an invoice for $2.49. Remember, I said the strategy is based on auditor's judgment.

DIV_NUM	VEN_NUM	SHORT_NAME	NO_OF_RECS	VEN_NUM_SUM	VEN_NUM_MAX	VEN_NUM_MIN	VEN_NUM_AVERAGE
5	74600	ST ELECTRI	4714	351,664,400.00	74,600.00	74,600.00	74,600.00
6	32330	K R ELEC S	3026	97,830,580.00	32,330.00	32,330.00	32,330.00
5	55000	N E ELECTR	2716	149,380,000.00	55,000.00	55,000.00	55,000.00
6	1060	A P ELECTR	2635	2,793,100.00	1,060.00	1,060.00	1,060.00
5	51400	M DISTRIBU	2436	125,210,400.00	51,400.00	51,400.00	51,400.00
5	9150	CAP ELECTR	1686	15,426,900.00	9,150.00	9,150.00	9,150.00
6	87840	WE CO DIST	1420	124,732,800.00	87,840.00	87,840.00	87,840.00
5	88737	WW INDUSTR	1345	119,351,265.00	88,737.00	88,737.00	88,737.00
5	26501	GB ELECTRI	1293	34,265,793.00	26,501.00	26,501.00	26,501.00
3	2000	AN, INC.	1079	2,158,000.00	2,000.00	2,000.00	2,000.00
5	8960	C / R	998	8,942,080.00	8,960.00	8,960.00	8,960.00
3	100	A-TECH COR	888	88,800.00	100.00	100.00	100.00
6	2110	A R INC	723	1,525,530.00	2,110.00	2,110.00	2,110.00
6	21210	GR ELECTRI	718	15,228,780.00	21,210.00	21,210.00	21,210.00
1	80925	U RENTALS	706	57,133,050.00	80,925.00	80,925.00	80,925.00
5	54900	N CORPORAT	638	35,026,200.00	54,900.00	54,900.00	54,900.00
6	21120	GR ELECTRI	551	11,637,120.00	21,120.00	21,120.00	21,120.00

FIGURE 3.5 Maximum, Minimum, and Average Report Produced from IDEA Software

DIV_NUM	VEN_NUM	SHORT_NAME	NO_OF_RECS	VEN_NUM_SUM	VEN_NUM_MAX	VEN_NUM_MIN	VEN_NUM_AVERAGE
1	7420	C CONSOLID	542	4,021,640.00	7,420.00	7,420.00	7,420.00
6	8265	C D INC	493	4,074,645.00	8,265.00	8,265.00	8,265.00
1	72180	T OIL CO.,	466	33,635,880.00	72,180.00	72,180.00	72,180.00
1	24070	HOME DEPOT	464	11,168,480.00	24,070.00	24,070.00	24,070.00
6	76180	IN CHILD S	446	33,976,280.00	76,180.00	76,180.00	76,180.00
1	22740	HZ EQUIPME	443	10,073,820.00	22,740.00	22,740.00	22,740.00
5	2230	A EQUIPMEN	420	936,600.00	2,230.00	2,230.00	2,230.00
5	4740	B F S	406	1,924,440.00	4,740.00	4,740.00	4,740.00
6	23520	HOME DEPOT	379	8,914,080.00	23,520.00	23,520.00	23,520.00
6	31490	KE ELECTRI	371	11,682,790.00	31,490.00	31,490.00	31,490.00

FIGURE 3.5 (Continued)

5. *Average amount.* Once again, the exclusion factor is judgmental. Typically, the smaller the average, the more likely we would eliminate the vendor line.

Basis for Selection:

1. The report after applying the exclusion theory provides a listing of vendor lines that meet the high-level criteria of our fraud data profile for the fraud scenario.
2. One selection theory is that all perpetrators have a risk comfort level. The level might be high or low, depending on the perpetrator's fear of detection. Therefore, as the gap between the maximum amount and the average amount gets closer, it is one indicator of the perpetrator comfort zone for the dollar amount of the fake invoices. It may also indicate a perpetrator who has a predictable pressure for an income stream.
3. Whatever the selection criteria, the fraud auditor needs to identify the selection criteria before reviewing the report.

▦ NUMBER ANOMALY STRATEGY

The strategy is exactly as it sounds. We identify anomalies by focusing on numbers. The strategy is a blend of specific identification and data interpretation. The best part of the analysis is the ease of use. The summarization feature of audit software uses the amount field as the key and summarizes the aggregate dollar value and frequency of occurrence of the amount. The analysis could perform the same summarization by entity by amount. In a large database, the report may become unwieldy.

1. *Bedford's law.* The search for an anomaly in the first, second, etc. integers of an amount. The anomaly is based on Bedford's distribution table. The explanation of the concept is beyond the scope of this book. In fact, entire books have been written on the topic.
2. *Even number transaction.* The goal of the strategy is to locate a frequency of an even number occurring with a frequency greater than one transaction that links to the same entity structure. The analysis typically focuses on round amounts, such as $1,000 or $5,000.
3. *Repeating number transaction.* The goal is similar to even number analysis but focuses on any number that repeats with a frequency greater than a predetermined number and links to the same entity structure.

4. *Contra-entry transaction.* The search for a negative number when the number should be positive or for a positive number when the number should be negative.

Guidelines for Using the Number Anomaly Strategy

1. In the number anomaly analysis, the data analysis starts with the data anomaly of the test, a pattern, and frequency of an even amount or recurring amount that links to one entity. The fraud auditor then needs to use data interpretation skills to determine which fraud scenario is most likely occurring.
2. The strategy is the least impacted by the sophistication of concealment.
3. The strategy does not work when the perpetrator continually changes the amount field.
4. The anomaly is the frequency of even numbers or a recurring number to one entity. The contra number is the anomaly.
5. The strategy is highly effective in locating false entity schemes based on the theory that a real vendor would normally have invoices of varying amounts.
6. The strategy is also useful in searching for pass-through schemes involving equipment rental. Since rental amounts are often the same, the drill-down review on the amount field would easily identify vendors.
7. In one project, a vice president created three shell companies and submitted invoices for $1,100 six times for each shell company.
8. In one project, a project manager created a shell company called BR Equipment. All the invoices were for $5,500.
9. In one project, the controller was concealing bad debt on the financial statement by concealing the rebill credit as a contra entry in the sales register. He would issue a credit for the old invoice and record the credit in the sales journal versus the sales adjustment general ledger account. The controller would then issue a new invoice, with a current date replacing the old invoice. The contra entry in the sales journal was the clue.
10. Contra-entry schemes are immediately flagged. In one case, we identified negative adjustments in a deduction field that was increasing net pay versus decreasing net pay. In another case, the controller was increasing incurred cost for percentage of completion; the red flag was the size of credits existing in accounts payable. The largest was a negative $420,000.

Consider the Following Scenario

Project manager creates a shell company; he leases equipment under the shell company's name from a real equipment leasing company and then causes the company by which he is employed to lease the equipment from his shell company at an inflated price, resulting in the diversion of company assets.

In the number anomaly strategy, the analysis would identify a high frequency of a recurring invoice amount paid to the same supplier. Since the supplier is an equipment rental company, the next-level analysis would focus on the invoice number pattern, most likely a sequential pattern, and the description field would be vague by normal industry standards. Referencing BR Equipment, one of the clues in the description field was the fact that the description field referenced a brand name of equipment that could have been leased directly from the brand-name company.

 ## PATTERN RECOGNITION AND FREQUENCY ANALYSIS

The science of pattern recognition is very broad, with many different methodologies ranging from the use of the science of mathematics to various classification identification systems. The International Association of Pattern Recognition was formed to fill a need for information exchange among research workers in the pattern recognition field. Pattern recognition is used in fields ranging from medicine to physical security. Within the context of this book, we will use it to describe red flags that are typically associated with a specific fraud scenario.

The use of frequency analysis is combining fraud theory to a number of instances that would correlate to a fraud scenario. The frequency analysis may focus on a specific number or use greater-than or less-than analysis. Frequency analysis may allow us to exclude a grouping from our analysis or require the inclusion of the grouping. Remember, perpetrators seldom steal once.

Frequency Analysis

Frequency analysis is the process of assigning a record count that correlates to the number of transactions that are attributable to an entity that links to a fraudulent action, in essence attributable to a fraud scenario. The frequency analysis focuses on either over or under a predetermined record count. The record count number is judgmental, based on the auditor's professional experience and the relevant fraud theory. It should be noted that the record count is not relevant to every fraud scenario. In establishing a record count, we suggest the following guidelines:

1. The frequency count is based on the expected occurrence rate associated with the specific fraud scenario or the fraud pattern.
2. Frequency analysis is typically associated with the transaction analysis versus the entity analysis.
3. The number of transactions associated with false entity schemes is determined by the perpetrator.
4. In payroll, the number of transactions is typically associated with the payroll cycle.
5. Record count should be based on a logical interval whenever possible—that is, daily, weekly, monthly, quarterly, semiannually, or annually.
6. Specific identification strategies associated with transaction analysis should be sufficient to indicate an intent factor versus a normal error rate for the population.
7. Internal control avoidance strategies focus on the number of records avoiding a control threshold if the scenario is a false entity scenario.
8. Internal control avoidance strategies for real entity schemes can be a frequency of one or more.
9. Data interpretation for the frequency of the pattern is a critical aspect of the selection process.
10. Number anomaly frequency should be sufficient to indicate an intent factor versus a normal error rate for the population.
11. Remember, with every guideline there is a logical exception.

Pattern Recognition

Pattern recognition is the process of searching for a predefined condition in a data set. The pattern either is implied through the four strategies or is defined as an attribute to a fraud scenario. Every data interrogation routine uses pattern recognition. The key is to know what you are looking for versus identifying a data pattern that does not correlate to a fraud scenario. There are five general categories of pattern recognition for fraud detection:

1. Creating groups of data for further study, often called *cluster analysis*. The cluster is typically associated with a business process or transaction type within a business system. Based on the first cluster, the goal is to create a micro-cluster within the primary cluster. The goal is to identify a discrete number of transactions that conforms to the fraud scenario data profile.

2. Anomaly pattern is the identification of transactions that do not conform to an expected pattern or deviate from the norm. The various patterns are: nonconformance with a process or procedure; event occurs at an unusual date or time; and illogical order of events or outliers analysis based on frequency, individual amount, aggregate amount, percentage, or range.

3. Outlier pattern is focused on the transactions that exist outside of the bell-shaped curve.

4. Entity pattern is based on all the known permutations of the shell entity, conflict of interest, and real entity structures that are associated with fraud scenarios.

5. Transaction pattern is a form of predictive analysis that suggests a pattern of data within transactions is more likely to be fraudulent than nonfraudulent. It is a lot like building a hypothesis and testing the hypothesis through data examination.

Correlating the pattern recognition between entity and transaction is the key to fraud detection. When the transactional data associated with the entity fit the fraud action pattern, the likelihood of fraud detection increases dramatically.

Strategies for Master File Data

The first step is to understand that there are three primary categories of entities; the applicability will vary based on the nature of your organization. In each primary category, there are different types of entities that create different fraud scenarios and require unique search routines to locate the entity. The three primary categories of entity structures are shell companies, conflict of interest, and real entities. For vendors and customers, the following provides a list of the secondary type of entities within the primary category. Employees follow a similar pattern, but due to the nature of employees, the description would be different, whereas the concept would be the same.

Through understanding the different permutations, the fraud auditors can improve their pattern recognition. The following provides a list of entity patterns associated with fraud scenarios.

Shell Company:

1. Stand-alone company.
2. Pass-through stand-alone company created by an internal source.
3. Pass-through stand-alone company created by salesperson at real company.

4. Assuming the identity of dormant vendor.
5. Temporarily assuming identity of the same active vendor.
6. Temporarily assuming identity of the random active vendor.
7. Causing a real vendor not on your master file to be added to master file, in essence, assuming the identity of a real entity.
8. Hidden entity
   a) Look-alike name.
   b) Real vendor with multivendor numbers or names.
9. Temporary or one-time entity.

Conflict of Interest:
1. Real company has one customer.
2. Pass-through stand-alone has one customer.
3. Real company with hidden ownership.
4. Real company with multiple customers has no hidden ownership that corrupts the internal selection process.

Real Company:
1. Real entity is complicit in corrupting internal source.
2. Real entity is extorted by internal source.
3. Real entity operates as a pass-through, typically in collusion with an internal source.
4. Real entity operates under multiple names.
5. Real entity operates as temporary or one-time entity.
6. Real entity is not complicit.
7. Subcontractors to a general contractor can function in the same manner; however, since the subcontractor is not within the master file, it is beyond the scope of this book.

Guidelines in Building Data Interrogation Routines for Entity Types

1. The first step is to decide which primary entity category is within the audit scope.
2. Data interrogation routines should be designed for each secondary type of entity in the primary category.
3. The description of the secondary entities will vary by revenue, payroll, and expenditures.
4. For shell companies, the data interrogation should search on missing information, anomalies in the identifying information, and matching to

other company data files. If the shell company is a vendor, then matching to human resources or customer database would prove to be useful.

5. For multiple shell companies operated by the same individual, search on duplicate address, bank account, telephone number, or email address.

6. Shell companies operating as a pass-through shell company by an internal source are similar to shell companies for false billing schemes.

7. For shell companies operating as a pass-through by a salesperson from a real company, the data interrogation should search on duplicate address, bank account, telephone number, or email address.

8. Conflict-of-interest entity with one customer has a similar analysis to the shell company.

9. Assume identity schemes always search on change of address or bank account. The caveat occurs when the perpetrator is able to manually control the payment for expenditures or change or delete a customer's transaction after shipment.

10. Real companies operating under multiple names: Search on duplicate identifying information. The permutation typically is associated with corruption schemes.

11. For real companies, the analysis should focus on the transactional activity that links to the fraudulent action.

▓ STRATEGIES FOR TRANSACTION DATA FILE

The inherent scheme has two components, the entity structure and the fraud action statement, which links to the transactional files. This section will explain our methodology for building data interrogation routines for transactional data. Chapters 7 through 15 explain how to apply the methodology to the specific core business systems. Our methodology for using transactional data needs to address the following six questions:

1. What data are available for the business transaction?
2. What patterns could occur within the specific data item?
3. What pattern would normally exist in the database?
4. What would cause a pattern to be a data anomaly versus a red flag of fraud?
5. Which patterns link to the fraud scenario?
6. How do we develop a data interrogation routine to locate the links to the fraud scenario?

What Data Are Available for the Business Transaction?

Data is data. Maybe that's a philosophic statement, but for most data items used in fraud data analytics the concept is that basic. Finding the data in your databases is a different challenge. Most transactions have a core set of data that is necessary to initiate, process, and record the transaction. There is no magic here; the starting point for transactional fraud data analytics centers on the auditor's ability to use the following information:

1. Control number: purchase order number, vendor invoice number, payment number, sales order number, sales invoice number, remittance number, etc.
2. Date of the transaction: purchase order date, vendor invoice date, etc.
3. Amount of the transaction: vendor invoice amount, discount amount, payment amount, etc.
4. Alpha description of the transaction: words used to describe what was purchased, inventory description, etc.
5. Numeric description of the transaction: product number, sku number, etc.
6. General ledger account number.

Specific data elements that relate to a specific fraud scenario are discussed in later chapters.

Depending on the business system the auditor will need to change the generic term, control number, to a business-specific number. We have vendor invoice numbers, customer order numbers, transaction numbers; the list goes on and on. What is important is to understand is how the control number or any other data element can be used in transactional fraud analysis. To explain the methodology we will use the control number to illustrate how to answer the six questions listed earlier. The chapter will address the remaining data items by providing the necessary guidance on how to use the data element versus illustrating the application of the six questions.

What Control Number Patterns Could Occur within the Specific Data Item?

The pattern question is not a fraud question but rather a logic question: What are all the logical patterns that can exist within the specific data element? Remember, many control numbers in your database are created by another organization (vendor or customer). That organization decides on the control pattern versus your company. Using permutation analysis, a listing of logical patterns associated with a control number follows:

1. No number.
2. Sequential number.
3. Duplicate number.
4. Random ascending numbers.
5. Random descending numbers.
6. Mix of ascending and descending numbers.
7. All alpha or alpha right-justified or alpha left-justified.
8. Date format numbers.
9. Project numbers.
10. Project number with hyphen sequential number.
11. Illogical range—the pattern focuses on the beginning control number and ending control number based on the date range in the scope period. The illogical question is whether the control number range makes sense for the perceived size of the vendor or customer. The determination is subjective and based on limited range. With the right professional experience, the analysis can be very effective to detect someone who knows not to use a sequential pattern but did not think about the range of numbers over a period of time.
12. Hidden number is a number that is intentionally disguised to avoid data detection. The number might have a letter added to avoid duplicate number testing, it might be created by selecting a number that was not used, or it might exceed the known range or a dormant number.

Practical Suggestion

Interview the function responsible for entering the transaction and determine their administrative practices for entering documents. If there is no control number, is the field blank or is a created number entered into the field? If the document has overt data errors, what are the administrative practices? If the control number has 15 integers, are all integers entered into the field? The time allocated to the question will save an enormous amount of time resolving transactions that appear to have red flags.

What Control Number Pattern Would Normally Exist in the Database?

False positives are an interesting problem in fraud data analytics. One of the reasons for false positives is a lack of understanding of the data. There was an oil commercial years ago in which the tagline was, "You can pay me now or you can pay me later." The tagline is on point with understanding your data before you create reports. Most data patterns that we use in fraud data analytics are either a normal business pattern for an organization or an anomaly that might indicate a fraud scenario. The most bizarre story I have seen was a company that reverted back to control number 1 when it reached control number 100,000. Confused? Well, so was I, but that is the reality of the type of patterns your analysis might find attached to an entity structure.

In the pattern-recognition stage, we need to understand both our business practices and our suppliers' and customers' business practices. If my suppliers are large public corporations, I would expect ascending direction of invoice numbers. If my suppliers are small, nonpublic companies, I would not be surprised to have invoices with no invoice number. This step is about creating realistic expectations as to the quality of the data for data-mining procedures. In Chapter 4, the concept of data availability, reliability, and usability will be discussed.

Typically, a sequential pattern of vendor invoice numbers would be a red flag of a shell company. However, in certain industries, the sequential pattern is a normal business pattern. In a project-based industry, invoice numbers are sometimes a customer's project number hyphenated for the project billing cycle (i.e., 0604-19). Assuming that the supplier submitted 19 invoices with a range of 0601-01 through 0604-19, then the supplier invoice pattern is a sequential pattern. However, the sequential pattern identified in this example correlates to normal business practice versus a fraud scenario. The fraud auditor needs to understand the patterns that exist in the company's database and the patterns that correlate to a fraud scenario.

So, here is the million-dollar question: Should the data analytics be further refined to mitigate the false positive, or should the audit team resolve the false positive through performing audit procedures? This should be a definitive decision within the fraud data analytics plan. The only wrong answer is to ignore the question.

What Would Cause a Pattern to Be a Data Anomaly versus a Red Flag of Fraud?

There are four categories of data anomalies in your database that will affect the success of your fraud data analytics plan:

1. *Data entry errors.* A digit is added to a vendor invoice number, the control number is entered as 19250 versus the correct control number of 1925, and the list goes on and on. Data reliability is further discussed in Chapter 4.

2. *Changes in society.* In payroll for years, having a duplicate bank account number with two different names would be a red flag of a ghost employee, or if the area code of the telephone number did not correlate to the physical location of the business, then maybe we found a shell company. Societal changes have changed the traditional red flags.

3. *How your customer or suppliers use the five data elements on their documents.* If a vendor includes letters in its invoice number, then the fraud auditor's ability to calculate an invoice number range via a control number is impacted.

4. *False positives.* The data anomaly matches the pattern for the fraud scenario; however, the pattern has a logical business explanation.

Which Patterns Link to the Fraud Scenario?

The fraud auditor needs to understand that selecting the pattern is an educated guess; however, without selecting the pattern, you will not be able to write the program to search for a pattern that is associated with a fraud scenario. Chapters 7 through 15 will provide examples of patterns that link to specific scenarios.

Data interrogation routines are designed to search for a pattern that correlates to a fraud scenario. There are no absolutes as to which pattern correlates to which fraud scenario. However, without careful consideration, the data interrogation step will search for data anomalies caused by errors or natural anomalies that simply exist in every database.

Let's select three patterns and correlate the control number to the most likely fraud scenario:

1. *Sequential pattern of vendor invoice numbers* is useful to locate shell companies or conflict-of-interest companies because the sequential pattern suggests that the vendor has only one customer.

2. *Duplicate numbers* is useful in searching for a real vendor operating in collusion with an internal person who is structuring invoices to avoid control levels or to search for intentional duplicate payment schemes.

3. *Limited range* is useful in searching for pass-through entities operated by an outside salesperson who has more than one customer participating in the scheme or a shell company where the perpetrator was sophisticated enough to avoid a sequential pattern but not sophisticated enough to make the range of numbers consistent with the perceived size of the company. Pass-through schemes are discussed in detail in Chapter 7.

How Do We Develop a Data Interrogation Routine to Locate the Links to the Fraud Scenario?

In this step, the fraud auditor becomes the programmer. Using the available software routines, the fraud auditor develops reports to identify the noted pattern for either audit examination or further refined data interrogation routines. This step requires both skill and imagination. The skill is associated with the use of the software. The imagination is associated with finding creative ways of working around the data issues that will exist in every database.

Practical Guidance on How to Use the Remaining Data Elements

The Date Field As with the control number, the starting point is to identify the date patterns based on logic versus fraud. The logical date patterns are:

1. Blank or no date
2. Duplicate date: exact, close, or related
3. Document date
4. Transaction date
5. System-generated date
6. Creation date
7. Termination date
8. Reactivate date
9. Change date
10. Recorded date
11. Date anomalies

The date field allows the auditor to develop a timeline for a business transaction. We can use this timeline to search for speed of transaction, circumvention of an internal control, off-period transaction, or an illogical sequence of events. The following illustrates the concept:

- Speed of transaction is always a critical test because it indicates someone is taking a special interest in the business transaction. The starting point is to understand the normal processing time for a business transaction. If your company policy is to pay vendor invoices in 60 days, then why are the Fraud Auditing Corporation invoices paid in 3 days?
- Circumvention of internal controls should always be a red flag for the fraud auditor. In payroll, there is an automated system that calculates payroll on

a periodic basis. Knowing those dates, the fraud auditor would search for payroll payments that do not coincide with the automated dates, thereby identifying all manual checks. The last phase is summarizing the number of manual checks by employee number, identifying all employees receiving more than one manual check. In one investigation, the controller was receiving his biweekly payroll check from the automated payroll system. Then in the off-week, he would issue himself a manual check and record the check to a professional services account versus a payroll account. A second test in payroll using the date field is comparing the dates on manual checks to termination dates. In this scenario, the controller was diverting the final manual check.

- Off-period analysis is identifying the date and time a transaction was recorded in the business system. Obviously, off-period analysis is dependent on the organization. The anomaly occurs when the transaction is recorded after hours, on a holiday, or at the end of a reporting period. In one case involving the theft of inventory through the revenue system, the sales transactions were consistently voided after the goods left the warehouse on a Sunday morning. Combining the use of frequency analysis with the off-period analysis, pattern and frequency of voiding sales would have been highlighted and the fraud scenario discovered.
- Illogical sequence is identifying transactions where the date order of the transactions does not follow a normal transaction. In one sense, the test is similar to the speed of transactions and circumvention of internal controls, but the difference is in the intent of the illogical sequence of the events. In a sales transaction, if the ship date is before the customer order date, the illogical order of the transactions may indicate improper recognition of revenue.

The transaction type will determine how the date is used in the fraud data analysis. The same six questions listed earlier need to be asked and answered as part of building the fraud data interrogation routine for the selected transaction.

Illustrative Examples of Using the Date Field:

- Asset misappropriation—the invoice date and the payment date are equal. Illustrates the speed of transaction.
- Internal control circumvention—the invoice date is before the purchase order date.

- In corruption schemes, the invoice date is before the purchase order date, which indicates that the acquisition most likely circumvented the purchasing process.
- In financial reporting, the receiving report date is after the inventory posting date, indicating an overstatement of inventory.

The Amount Field   There are a lot of theories and fraud stories about amounts. The most common story is that a fraud scenario starts out small and gets bigger over time. Or that fraud amounts will typically correlate to the upper spheres of control levels. While these have some semblance of truth, they also can be misleading as it relates to fraud data analysis.

I believe that the amount of a fraudulent transaction or the aggregate amount of the fraud is far more complex than the interesting stories. I think there is a direct correlation to a person's risk tolerance as related to the person's perception of detection, pressures facing the individual, and at what stage the person believes there is a higher likelihood of detection. Most of this requires the auditor to know the perpetrator on a personal basis. As a reminder, the focus of this book is searching for fraud without predication or a target.

The dollar amount of the transaction is what fraud is all about. How much did the person steal? How much was revenue overstated? There are nine logical amount patterns:

1. A single amount is below or above a control threshold.
2. Duplicate amount, linking to control number, date, or description.
3. Two or more in aggregate exceed the control threshold, which then links to a specific to date or control number.
4. Even amount.
5. Odd amount.
6. Recurring amount.
7. Amount embedded with a lucky number. (Yes, in one case, the perpetrator embedded his high school football jersey number in the amount.)
8. Contra amount is a negative or positive, which is inconsistent with the expected value.
9. Aggregate amount.

The Description Field: Alpha and Numeric Considerations   The alpha and numeric field is critical for both false entity and real entity analysis. In false entity schemes we search for alpha or numeric descriptions that are not consistent with our business expectation. In real entity analysis, we use the description field to search for overbilling and corruption schemes. There are nine logical patterns:

1. Tangible good descriptions generally contain an alpha description and numeric description referred to as the product number.
2. Illogical product description. A product number that has an insufficient number of numeric positions as related to industry standard or no alpha description.
3. Service transactions tend to be an alpha description, but may refer to a contract number.
4. Duplicate descriptions.
5. Duplicate product numbers.
6. Missing alpha description.
7. Missing product number.
8. Grade level in payroll.
9. Grade title in payroll.

General Ledger Account Numbers   The general ledger account number is what I call the home of the fraud transaction. The home is going to have a division number, department number, and expense code. For the budget owner scenarios, the fraudulent transactions are recorded in an account the budget owner controls and monitors. By contrast, the direct input function needs to find a home to record the fraudulent transactions. The home for the direct input function needs to be recorded where the transaction will avoid scrutiny by the budget owner. The senior manager has many homes for the fraudulent transaction. Understanding the general ledger numbering system is important in fraud data analysis. The primary categories are as follows:

- Financial reporting: The entire fraud data analytics is centered on the transactions recorded in a general ledger account.
- Asset misappropriation: The beginning analysis is not dependent on the general ledger account number until the fraud auditor starts to find suspicious transactions.
- Corruption: In favoritism analysis or targeted expenditure analysis, the general ledger account number is a key element of the fraud data analytics.

In addition to the data created from business transactions, data systems also create logs of when transactions were created, changed, or deleted.

The use of logging information follows the same guidelines as information from documents:

- Control number
- Date of transaction
- Time of transaction
- User ID creating transaction
- IP address

Practical Guidance for Master File Data and the Transaction Data

As a matter of style, the last step before beginning the fraud data analytics is the process of linking the transactional data to the master file data. When a pattern is identified in the transactional data, the next logical step is to link the transactions to the entity data file. Therefore, as a practical suggestion, link the entity file to the transactional file at the beginning of analyzing transactions versus after transaction analysis. Obviously, the size of files may make this process not feasible.

Practical Guidance for Transactional Data Associated with a False Entity

Transactional data associated with a false entity is different in many ways from transactional data with real companies. The perpetrator is creating the documents; he is creating the control number, date, amount, and description, and deciding where to record the fraudulent transaction. The transaction in some way is a reflection of the perpetrator's personality. (No, I have no intention of incorporating behavioral analysis into my fraud data analytics.)

The key is to recognize that the control data associated with a false entity is less likely to reflect being created by a real business and more likely that a person created the false data. The control number may be sequential because the small business software simply increments the control number after creating the next document. All the amounts may be even. The date field may be all Saturdays because the perpetrator is creating the document on the weekend. The same error may exist in multiple documents for different entities. The description field on a created vendor invoice most likely will not reflect the product description of a real wholesale company in the business of selling widgets. The widget product may only have four integers, which is not consistent with a large company selling millions of items. As a general guideline, for false entity schemes, search for the absence of what would normally exist for a real company.

Illustrative Example of Transactional Data and False Entity

In one fraud data analytics project, an internal manager created three shell companies. The companies all had different addresses, in different states, and different telephone numbers. The only common pattern in the master file was that all three companies were created in the database on the same day, but at different times of the day. However, in the transactional file, the vendor invoices were all the same amount, the same date, and the same description, and the control numbers for all three companies had the same pattern: $0001, 020506$, $0003, 071806, 0005$, and 0006. Most likely, the pattern was intended to be a sequential pattern, but note that the same data error occurs in the control number for all three companies. If you believe in coincidences, then pass on further review. If, however, you do not believe in coincidences, then start your fraud investigation, because you have just found three shell companies that all link to the same individual because of the general ledger account.

Practical Guidance for Transactional Data Associated with the Real Entity

In real entity scenarios, analyzing the entity data for the most part is an obvious waste of time. Yes, there are exceptions to all rules. I learned that in third grade. The obvious exception is the hidden entity scheme. Therefore, we need to build the fraud theories around whether the real entity is committing the fraud scenario alone or the real entity is in collusion with an internal source or external source. Transactional data becomes the focus of real company analysis:

- **An external entity with no internal collusion** submits transactional data that either exploit the vulnerabilities within the internal controls or create the appearance of conforming to internal controls, but the volume or frequency exceeds business norms. To illustrate the concept, many payments systems will automatically pay the invoice if the invoice is below a certain dollar amount, referred to as a *small-dollar invoice*. The dishonest supplier continually submits small-dollar invoices, knowing that accounts payable will pay the invoice. The specific identification strategy or internal control avoidance is generally the right strategy.
- **An external entity in collusion with an internal source** means the transaction generally conforms to internal documents; therefore, exception analysis generally will not detect this permutation. The use of data interpretation strategy as the prime strategy, coupled with a secondary strategy, is the most effective approach. The secondary strategy

might be outlier analysis, historical change analysis, timing analysis, and targeted analysis. The previous example would occur in the same manner, but the internal budget owner is approving the small-dollar invoice and the budget owner is receiving a kickback.

SUMMARY

This chapter is about the science of fraud data analytics. It is a systematic study of fraud scenarios and fraud scenarios' relationship to data. Like all scientific principles, the continual study of the science and the practical application of the science are both necessary for the success of the fraud data analytics journey in the discovery of fraud scenarios that are hiding in core business systems. As stated in Chapter 1, fraud data analytics is both a science and an art.

CHAPTER FOUR

How to Build a Fraud Data Analytics Plan

ontinuing with the house analogy, we will now create the blueprint for your house based on the building code from Chapter 3 and the fraud scenarios identified from Chapter 2. In this chapter, we will design each room of the house based on the fraud scenarios identified in your fraud risk assessment. Hopefully, we will avoid change orders, although I believe the nature of fraud data analytics is an evolving process.

In this chapter, we will discuss the methodology for building a fraud data analytics plan. There are eight stages to building the plan. Initially, you may feel the process is bureaucratic or redundant. In some ways the reader is right. However, it is critical to ask as many questions as possible before creating the data interrogation routine. Otherwise, the plan may result in either excessive false positives or, worse yet, false negatives (a missed fraudulent transaction). In time, the process of developing a fraud data analytics plan will become intuitive.

Asking the right questions, in the right order, is critical from a logic perspective. However, for my free thinkers, I offer the list not to constrain you but to give you a checklist of questions you need to consider. Within each step there will be many considerations. The decisions should be understood and documented as part of the workpaper process. So, what are the steps or questions to building a fraud data analytic plan?

1. What is the scope of the fraud data analysis plan?
2. How will the fraud risk assessment impact the fraud data analytics plan?
3. Which data-mining strategy is appropriate for the scope of the fraud audit?
4. What decisions will the plan need to make regarding the availability, reliability, and usability of the data?
5. Do you understand the data?
6. What are the steps to designing a fraud data analytics search routine?
7. What filtering techniques are necessary to refine the sample selection process?
8. What is the basis of the sample selection?
9. What is the plan for resolving false positives?
10. What is the design of the fraud audit test for the selected sample?

To illustrate the use of the questions, you should imagine you are assigned to an audit. You are required to implement a fraud data analytics plan. This is the first time your department will use fraud data analytics. The scope of the assignment is the expenditure cycle. So, what are the answers to the 10 questions? Later chapters will discuss the actual routines for procurement and disbursement fraud.

PLAN QUESTION ONE: WHAT IS THE SCOPE OF THE FRAUD DATA ANALYSIS PLAN?

The starting point of the plan is to understand what is and what is not included in the scope of the project. The concept of searching for fraud is too broad. It provides no realistic boundaries or sense of direction. The auditor without a roadmap will be found wandering around the desert without any hope. To be clear, you can search for the entire fraud risk structure in one audit, assuming you have a roadmap for all the fraud scenarios.

The starting point is the purpose of the assignment. Are we performing an audit or an investigation? In an investigation, the project scope is determined by the allegation or the legal action. In an audit of financial statements, the scope is determined by Generally Accepted Auditing Standards. For internal audits, the scope of the fraud analysis needs to be determined by the chief internal auditor. Regardless of the scope, the fraud risk structure is the basis for defining the beginning and ending points for the fraud data analysis project.

The fraud risk structure in Chapter 2 discussed the concept of a fraud risk structure as a basis of defining the project scope. The audit team needs to define the parameters of the audit scope by starting with the primary fraud categories of financial reporting, asset misappropriation, or corruption. The second step is to understand which secondary types of fraud categories are included within the scope.

The time period of the fraud data analysis is the next step. Will the analysis include one, two, three, four, or more than four years of data? I prefer the fraud data analysis to use full-year data sets and avoid partial-year data sets. The exception to that rule is investigations or specific audit tests. In financial statements audits, there may be a need to include the next year's data up to the opinion date or use last year's data for retrospective analysis. The next step is to identify the primary table and secondary tables. The scope establishes the date parameters for the primary table; the time parameters for the secondary tables are driven by your desire to match transactions.

To illustrate the concept, your audit scope is the expenditure cycle for the year 2015. In order to match the vendor invoice table to the purchase order table, the data analytics will need to select both the 2015 purchase orders and purchases orders prior to 2015. As a practical tip, identify the lowest-number purchase order number in the expenditure table, then go to the online system and find the date of the lowest purchase order number. The payment table will need to go beyond 2015 to find the date when all 2015 vendor invoices were paid.

The last step is to identify the primary table and the secondary tables. Databases are composed of a series of tables that link together based on a common identifier. In fraud data analytics, the fraud scenario defines the primary table and the associated tables. In false entities, the primary table is the table with entity information: name and address, and so on. In real entity scenarios, the primary table is the transactions associated with the fraud action. To illustrate the table concept in a speed-of-payment analysis, the vendor invoice table is the primary table and the payment table is the secondary table. The vendor number will be the common identifier linking the two tables followed by the invoice number and purchase order number.

Scope Concept for the Corruption Project

The following is an illustration of the expenditure project, which we will call the Corruption Project. The audit project is the fraud scenarios that reside in the expenditure cycle. For practical purposes, I divide the cycle in half. The first half is the procurement and the second half is the payment. As a soft guideline, in the purchasing process the fraud auditor should focus on corruption fraud in the procurement cycle and for the payment process the fraud auditor should focus on asset misappropriation. Within the scope of the illustration, the fraud auditor has decided to focus on corruption in the procurement process. Therefore, the purchase order file is the primary table.

 PLAN QUESTION TWO: HOW WILL THE FRAUD RISK ASSESSMENT IMPACT THE FRAUD DATA ANALYTICS PLAN?

The purpose of the fraud risk assessment is to identify all the relevant fraud scenarios within the audit scope and determine the extent of residual risk. The timing and extent of the audit procedures and determining residual risk is beyond the scope of this book. Within the scope of this book, the fraud risk assessment provides the audit team with a comprehensive listing of fraud scenarios for the fraud data analytics plan.

The decision to use fraud data analytics to search for evidence of a fraud scenario is based on auditor judgment. Obviously, a fraud scenario with a high-residual risk rating should be a candidate for fraud data analytics. The auditor's judgment could be based on fraud scenarios that have occurred in the past, fraud scenarios that commonly occur in the industry, or simply a focal point of the chief auditor. The fraud data analytics plan should have a direct cross-reference statement to the fraud risk statement.

Continued Illustration of the Corruption Project

The fraud risk assessment has indicated two corruption fraud scenarios that have a high-residual risk. Corruption by definition has two or more parties. One party is committing the required fraud action, and the other party is conspiring with the primary party. In the *first scenario*, the internal party is corrupting the bidding process by issuing a series of small-dollar purchase orders throughout the year to avoid the bid process. The supplier in collusion with the internal person inflates pricing and pays the internal source a bribe. In the *second scenario*, a supplier is intentionally operating under different names, which facilitates the internal person to split the purchase to what appears to be different vendors, thereby avoiding the bidding process. The vendor inflates pricing and pays a bribe to the internal person.

PLAN QUESTION THREE: WHICH DATA-MINING STRATEGY IS APPROPRIATE FOR THE SCOPE OF THE FRAUD AUDIT?

This is like the expression, Which comes first, the chicken or the egg? The fraud data analytics strategy is connected to the fraud concealment, but the auditor needs to determine what level of concealment will be considered within the scope of the audit. At a minimum, audits mostly consider low sophistication up to medium sophistication. In an investigation, the team should consider low to high sophistication.

In Chapter 3 guidelines are provided for using each strategy. The fraud auditor needs to apply the guidelines in the selection of the right strategy for the fraud data analytics plan. One strategy could be used throughout the audit, or the strategy could be on a fraud scenario basis. What is most important to understand is the purpose of each strategy—how to use the strategy and how the strategies correlate to the fraud concealment sophistication theory.

Continued Illustration of Corruption Project

Split Purchase Orders Fraud Scenario

Internal person is in collusion with a supplier, the internal person issues purchase orders below the control threshold to the supplier and inflates pricing on the item, the supplier then pays the internal person a kickback, resulting in the corruption of the purchasing process.

The fraud scenario is composed of a real entity that is complicit in the scenario and the fraud action is issuing multiple purchase orders to ensure no purchase order triggers the bidding requirements. The fraud data analytics strategy is the internal control avoidance. Therefore, the fraud data analytics plan focuses on the fraud action versus the entity. The first analysis would summarize purchase orders by vendor using stratification by dollar level associated with bidding levels. Vendors with no small-dollar purchases and only large-dollar purchase orders that required bidding procedures would be excluded from further analysis. The second analysis would summarize the remaining purchase orders by line item. The second report would provide a frequency count, aggregate dollars, and average purchase order. The sample selection is based on vendors with annual purchases that exceed the dollar level for bidding or a vendor with a high frequency of purchase orders and a high average purchase order amount. To further refine the process for vendors meeting the first selection process, the analysis would focus on line items on the purchase order. Remember, we are continually shrinking the haystack.

Hidden Entity Fraud Scenario

Internal person in collusion with a supplier, the supplier is in the vendor file under different names with different identifying information, purchase orders are intentionally spread to the different vendor names to avoid bidding requirements, and the supplier pays the internal person a kickback, resulting in the corruption of the purchasing process.

The inherent scheme is composed of a false entity, referred to as the hidden entity, and the fraud action is issuing small-dollar purchase orders to multiple vendors. The fraud data analytics plan will focus on the false entity versus the transaction. The search for hidden identities will use specific identification strategy focusing on duplicate testing on address, telephone, bank account, email address, and contact person. The testing will start with exact match and consider close match depending on the initial results. If the duplicate data interrogation routine identifies entities, then the transactions for those specific entities will be linked for analysis.

The second report would provide a frequency count, aggregate dollars, and average purchase order. The second scenario is very similar to the first scenario. The difference between the two fraud scenarios is the entity structure, not the fraud action statement. Once you realize the similarity and differences between all the fraud scenarios in your scope, the idea of building a comprehensive fraud data analytics plan will not be overwhelming.

PLAN QUESTION FOUR: WHAT DECISIONS WILL THE PLAN NEED TO MAKE REGARDING THE AVAILABILITY, RELIABILITY, AND USABILITY OF THE DATA?

The purpose of assessing the availability and reliability of the data is to determine if the data are usable for fraud data analytics. The availability focuses on the completeness of the data, whereas reliability focuses on the overt accuracy of the data for the planned tests. The word *overt* is used with intent. Most data are derived from a document. The reliability test cannot determine if the data are entered correctly, but rather, searches for an overt data error. To illustrate, the scope period is 2014, but the vendor invoice date in the database is 1925. Clearly, 1925 is not the correct date on the vendor invoice.

The reliability of data depends on the planned tests. As in this project, the fraud auditor is searching for circumvention of bid levels. So, the invoice date is less critical. If the scope is searching for a duplicate payment scenario, then the date field is critical to the plan.

The completeness test is simple because the fraud data analytics test counts the number of blanks or quasi-blanks (i.e., a dash versus a blank) in the fields to be used for testing. The tough part of the analysis is to determine what impact blank data fields will have on the success of our planned fraud data analytics testing. At a minimum, the fraud data analytics workpapers and final audit report should provide the reader with the relevant statistics as to the total number of the items and the total number of blanks in each field.

The outcome of the completeness analysis will depend on the size of your database and the degree of error. If the company has 500 employees, and three employees are missing telephone numbers, the auditor could perform manual research procedures to identify the telephone numbers. If population is 100,000 active employees, with 10 percent of the telephone fields being blank, then a manual research procedure would consume an extensive amount of time.

As a reminder, fraud data analytics always reveals false positives. False positives occur from the design of the test or data integrity issues. The key strategy question is how much effort we should expend in data analytics to eliminate overt false positives resulting from data integrity or whether we should allow the auditor to resolve the false positives through audit procedures. The false positive question is a tough question, but an important one. If you do not consider these questions before data interrogation, you will need to address the questions later in the audit.

Entity Availability and Reliability

The entity availability analysis should determine what percent of each entity data field is populated. In small databases, an easy test is to sort on each data column that is included in the test. Then count the number of fields that are blank or contain a dash. In large databases use the count feature to determine the number of blanks or dashes in each column. The important step is to determine the availability of data for planned tests. The reliability testing for the entity data does not lend itself to fraud data analytics.

The purpose of the usability analysis is to determine what impact the lack of data integrity has on planned tests. For shell companies, missing data become an audit trigger. In hidden entity testing, which uses a duplicate test, missing data reduces the effectiveness of the test.

Transaction Availability and Reliability

The availability analysis for transactions is designed to ensure the completeness of the data. In Chapter 3 we discussed that most business or computer transactions typically contain a control number, date, amount, and description. The first step is to ensure that the critical fields are populated. Similar to the entity availability analysis, the workpapers should document the degree of error.

The second part of the availability analysis is matching the various tables to ensure that we have completed transactions. To illustrate, in the expenditure cycle we have a purchase order, a vendor invoice, and a payment transaction. In the availability analysis we need to ensure that we have purchase order, invoice, and payment information for the transaction. There may always be a few transactions that are missing purchase order or the payment transaction due to timing and aging reasons. However, prior to data interrogation we should know how many uncompleted transactions are within our audit population.

The reliability test for transaction is critical for fraud data analytics. Control numbers originating from source documents are not typically verified; therefore it is my experience that a control number has a higher degree of error than an amount field. Data entry errors that are typically associated with a control number are: adding numeric integers, data entry operators entering a portion of a long number, documents that do not have a control number, substituting a different control number, and an error in entering the number. Although these types of errors usually have no impact on the business process, the error can create false positives associated with fraud data analytics testing which uses the control number.

Date errors create problems with sequence testing or speed-of-processing tests. A simple test is to ensure the year in the date field is consistent with the scope of the audit.

Amounts are typically correct although reversal transactions may provide the illusion of duplicate transactions or inflated record counts. In the data-cleaning phase, we can search for reversal transactions using exact reversal search techniques to mitigate false positives associated with the amount field.

The description field is critical for most transaction analysis. When the description field is populated based on internal systems, the field is usually reliable. Examples of internal systems are sales systems that populate a sales invoice from a product description file or the payroll system that populates earning type from an earnings code table. In these systems, the analysis should search for codes that are not consistent with the known codes in the tables.

Description fields that are created from a manual entry process or description fields created from a vendor document or customer document may have a high degree of error or inconsistency as to the information contained in the database.

The outcome of the availability and reliability analysis is to determine the usability of the data for the planned tests. The fraud data analytics project should try to anticipate the type and frequency of errors that will occur in your fraud data analytics plan.

The Usability Analysis

The usability analysis is a byproduct of the availability and reliability analysis. The purpose of the usability analysis is twofold. First, does the data have sufficient integrity to ensure the fraud data analytics will provide a meaningful sample? Second, provide a conclusion on how to go forward with the sample results. There are four usability conclusions from the availability and reliability analysis:

1. Should the fraud data analytics plan be postponed until a later date until management improves the internal controls over data entry or enforces adherence to existing internal controls?
2. The transactions containing obvious data errors will be extracted from the specific test to eliminate false positives originating from overt data integrity.
3. The degree of error is acceptable and will have minimal impact on the success of the test.
4. The degree of error may create false positives; however, the fraud auditor can resolve the false positives in the audit test phase of the fraud audit.

Second, assuming the data are deemed usable, the next step is to clean the data consistent with the usability conclusions. The cleaning process includes data formatting and excluding overt data integrity items. A word of caution: I have seen and heard of many interesting data-cleaning techniques, and while many of these techniques are quite clever, the cleaning technique does change the original data, which could have an impact on your sample selection or create false positives. One step to avoiding errors is to include the original data next to the clean data so visual examination process is able to detect false positives created from the data cleaning.

Continued Illustration of Corruption Project

What availability and reliability issues should the fraud auditor anticipate?

- How many vendor invoices do not have a purchase order?
- How reliable is the line item description on purchase orders and vendor invoices?
- How many entities are missing data that would be used in the hidden entity analysis?
- What impact will the usability question have on our project?

PLAN QUESTION FIVE: DO YOU UNDERSTAND THE DATA?

The word *anomaly* is defined as an extreme deviation from the norm. The understood data question is all about understanding what is the norm of the data. In each later chapter, we will discuss the types of planning reports.

The goal in this stage is to understand both gross numbers and transaction type numbers. To illustrate gross numbers in payroll, how many employees are on the database? How many are active? How many are inactive? To illustrate transaction type numbers, how many are paid via direct deposit versus paid with a check? How many are salaried employees versus hourly paid employees?

This stage should create statistical reports summarizing transactions by entity number, by control levels, by transaction types, or by internal codes that are relevant to the business system and planned audit tests. The reports should provide aggregate dollar level, number of records, maximum dollar, minimum dollar, and average dollar.

The auditor should study these reports to understand the norm of the population and the various subgroups created through internal codes before creating and designing fraud data analytic routines.

Continued Illustration of Corruption Project

The purchase order is the key document followed by the vendor invoice. The first report is a summary of purchase order issuance by vendor number. The report should provide the frequency of purchase order, aggregate dollar value, and the maximum, minimum, and average purchase order. This type of report is always my first type of summary report. This report will point me to the split purchase transaction through data interpretation.

A second report is a summary by line items on purchase orders in the scope period, providing the same information as the first report. An enhancement of the report would be by line item by vendor. This report would point you directly to the hidden entity.

A third report would be the comparison of the purchase order date to the invoice date. The purpose of this report is to determine the frequency of budget owners that procure the item first and then submit the invoice for payment. I would expect to find a difference in purchases associated with inventory and administrative purchases.

As a matter of style, I prefer to start with the same report structure for all projects and all companies. It provides a common baseline for me in fraud data analytic projects. In addition, it avoids being overloaded with lines of data. Once I see the data pattern, I refine the report based on my first review. Sometimes, I may be refining the report within minutes of seeing the data. Once again, my personal style is to start high level and continually refine the data. Sometimes it takes several iterations of drilling down to create the report that points to the fraud scenario.

PLAN QUESTION SIX: WHAT ARE THE STEPS TO DESIGNING A FRAUD DATA ANALYTICS SEARCH ROUTINE?

The following eight steps are necessary to build the data interrogation routines:

1. Identify the components of the fraud scenario—the person committing, the type of entity, and the action statement.
2. Identify the data that relates to the fraud scenario.
3. Select the strategy consistent with the scope of the audit, sophistication of concealment, degree of accuracy (exact, close, or related), and the nature of the test.
4. Based on the data availability, reliability, and usability of the data, clean the data set for overt errors.
5. Identify the logical errors that will occur with the test.
6. Create your homogeneous data sets using the inclusion and exclusion theory.
7. Establish the primary selection criteria, followed by the remaining selection criteria.
8. Create the test using the programing routines to identify all entities or transactions that meet the testing criteria.

The following provides guidance in using the fraud data analytics questions for developing your data interrogation routines.

Step 6.1: Identify the Fraud Scenario

The person committing the scenario identifies whether the fraud data analysis is searching for direct access, indirect access, or override capacity to the database. From a data function, there are two fundamental issues. The person committing the fraud scenario needs the ability to record a transaction and a location to record the transaction. If the person has direct access, then the summary will focus on the record creator; when the person has indirect access, the summary will focus on the location. Remember, this is about data analysis versus internal controls.

The direct access is generally referred to as the input function. The person performing the input function can create, change, delete, or void a transaction. In the simplest of environments, the input function is vested with one individual, so the analysis is easy. However, in most large companies, many individuals will have input capacity. Therefore, the data analysis will need to summarize transactions by creator. What the input function does not have is a budget to record the fraudulent transactions. Therefore, the fraud auditor will need to consider logical locations where the fraudulent charge could be recorded without detection.

The indirect access causes the direct access function to update the record based on the budget owner's authorized action. The authorization action is either valid or a forgery. However, the advantage the budget owner has over the direct input function is that the budget owner has a home to record the transaction. The summary of transactions must occur through the budget owner code versus the direct input function.

The override capacity has the best of all worlds in one sense. They have the ability to cause the transactions to be recorded in the database and they have several budgets to record the transaction.

As a reminder, entity analysis is for false entity scenarios, whereas real entity scenarios tend to focus on the transactions file. The exception is when searching for real entities operating under different names, referred to as hidden entities. In theory, entity analysis functions as a form of cluster analysis. The goal is to create three categories of entity structures: false entity, conflict of interest entity, and real entities.

The fraudulent action requires the linkage of the entity to the transactions meeting the profile. In the corporation illustration, the purchase order file and the invoice file are the basis for our fraud data analytics.

Step 6.2: Identify the Data That Relates to the Scenario

In one sense, this is the most important aspect of the plan because fraud data analytics is all about interrogating data. However, in another way, this stage is the most predictable.

In the Appendix at the end of this chapter, there is an example of a generic data request form for an expenditure fraud data analytics plan. In reviewing the list, the reader should see that the data are rather obvious. We need purchase order information, invoice information, receipt information, and payment information. As a starting point, the plan will need control number, date, amount, description, and the general ledger account number.

Using the exhibit, review the online systems to identify the name of the data on the screen. Compare the generic list to the data on the screen to determine additional data that would help in the fraud data analytics plan. Once the list is created, the auditor will need to identify where the data reside in the database. A third column should be created, cross-referencing the table and column name of the data field.

Step 6.3: Select the Fraud Data Analytics Strategy

The correct strategy has several considerations. The starting point is the objective, the scope of the audit, and the fraud scenarios included in the scope. The next consideration is the level of sophistication of concealment, whether the plan will search for low, medium, or high sophistication. The concealment decision will be a key factor in the selected data-mining strategy, or how, when, and where to use the strategy:

- The specific identification strategy is a good place to start because of the ease of use.
- The control avoidance strategy should be used when the fraud scenario is based on a direct input function. For indirect access the strategy becomes an inference analysis.
- The data interpretation strategy should be used to search for high-concealment or real entity scenarios.
- The number anomaly strategy is the easiest way to search for even numbers and recurring number patterns.

Step 6.4: Clean the Data Set: Data Availability, Data Reliability, and Data Usability

The procedures for performing this step are somewhat dependent on the software used by the fraud auditor and how the data are extracted from the database. The first step is always the availability of data; the second step is the reliability of data. The last step is to prepare the data for the interrogation routine. To illustrate, if the report will contain a date range, what format is the date range, as to month, day, and year? Depending on the country, the date field will have a different format. The second question is the field alpha numeric format or numeric format. Many of the steps are housekeeping procedures, but without consideration, the data interrogation process will be fraught with errors.

Step 6.5: Identify Logical Errors

Errors in this stage are defined by data that will cause a false positive. Data integrity errors were discussed in the availability and reliability section. Three main sources of data errors are caused by the way external parties create their documents, how the input function enters the data, and what I call true anomalies.

External parties, customers, and vendors create documents that contain information that is entered into the database. An example is a vendor invoice number. Some vendors use alpha in their invoice numbers. In computing an invoice range report, the alpha in the invoice number will create an error in the calculation. In searching for duplicate addresses, a false positive is created because two different vendors occupied the same space at different times (a true anomaly).

Fortunately or unfortunately input functions often focus on getting the transaction processed through the system, versus after-the-fact fraud data analytics. The way an input function enters a transaction may have no impact on proper reporting of the financial statements or cause an improper payment to a vendor; however, the way the data are entered will create false positives.

To illustrate how an input function creates false positives, a vendor invoice may have no invoice number. However, the accounts payable system requires a vendor invoice number. Therefore, the input function may create a unique number or use a date for an invoice number. In one project, operations staff would frequently submit an invoice without a purchase order. The accounts payable function, instead of creating a line item purchase order to support the invoice and provide the actual items purchased, would create a purchase order with a quantity of one; the unit price was the total of the invoice and the description was the invoice number.

True anomalies are a byproduct of an ever-changing society. Telephone numbers are either a mobile number or a land line. The Telephone Portability

Act allows a person to retain their telephone as they change geographic location. Therefore, there is no correlation between area code and physical location. In payroll, the search is for duplicate bank accounts under different names. Married couples may keep their own name, causing a false positive with the duplicate bank account number test for different last name.

Data are not perfect. There are anomalies caused by many factors; the goal of this stage is to anticipate the types of errors that will occur. The plan should either determine if the false positives can be minimized through the data interrogation routine or whether the auditor will need to resolve the false positive through document examination. Lastly, the report should offer recommendations on improving the quality of data for management monitoring processes.

Step 6.6: Create the Homogeneous Data Files Using the Inclusion and Exclusion Theory

The inclusion/exclusion theory is a critical step in building the fraud data analytics plan. The inclusion is the data that are consistent with the fraud data profile and the exclusion is the data that are not consistent with the fraud data profile. The theory is consistent with shrinking the haystack. Whether or not the fraud auditor actually creates separate files is a matter of style, whereas the concept of inclusion/exclusion is necessary in identifying anomalies.

The reason for this step is the size of company data files and has nothing to do with hardware storage or speed of processing. It has to do with understanding what data relate to the fraud scenario and what data do not relate to the scenario. First, it is a mental exercise in defining the scope of the fraud data interrogation routine. Second, it is about identifying an anomaly. *Whether or not the fraud auditor creates separate files is a matter of style.* Yes, I emphasize this because style is dependent on the auditor. However, without going through the mental exercise, the fraud auditor is bound to increase the number of false positives or miss the anomaly.

The importance of the inclusion and exclusion step varies by the nature of the inherent fraud scheme, the fraud data analytics strategy, and the size of the data file.

Let's assume the vendor master file has 50,000 vendors; 5,000 vendors are inactive. The first homogeneous data set would be only active vendors. The fraud scenario is a shell company created by an internal source. The data interrogation procedure focuses on missing data as the primary selection criteria. This test identifies 100 vendors meeting the search criteria.

The transaction file contains a million vendor invoices. Should we test all million invoices for shell company attributes, or only those invoices that meet the shell company missing criteria test? The inclusion theory would only select those transactions for the 100 vendors identified in the missing analysis.

The inclusion and exclusion theory is a critical thought process in the building of fraud data analytics. By ignoring the thought process, the size of the reports becomes an obstacle in identifying the fraud scenario that reduces the effectiveness of the fraud data analytics methodology.

Step 6.7: Build the Fraud Data Analytics Test through Identifying the Selection Criteria

In the selection criteria, there are two fundamental strategies. The first is to identify all entities or transactions that meet the criteria. The purpose of the test is to exclude all data that do not meet the criteria. Since that test operates on one set of criteria, the sample population tends to be large, although much smaller than the total population. The auditor then can use either a random selection or auditor judgment on selecting the sample. The advantage is that the auditor has improved the odds of selecting a fraudulent transaction.

The second strategy is to select all data that meet the testing criteria, referred to as the *fraud data profile*. The selected strategy is a key criterion on selecting the sample:

- *Specific identification.* The sample should be the transactions that meet the criteria.
- *Control avoidance.* The sample should be the transactions that circumvent the internal control.
- *Data interpretation.* The sample is based on the auditor's judgment.
- *Number anomaly.* The sample is based on the number anomaly identified and auditor judgment.

So, what is the difference between the two strategies? The first strategy uses an exclusion theory to reduce the population, whereas the second strategy uses an inclusion theory as a basis for sample selection. Remember, after identifying all transactions meeting the criteria, data filtering can be used to shrink the population.

Step 6.8: Programming Routines to Identify the Selection Criteria

It is interesting to see how different individuals program the software to create the data interrogation routines. Since programming is software dependent, I offer the following strategies to avoid faulty logic in the design of the search routine:

- Flowchart the decision process prior to writing the search routine. The order of the searching criteria will impact the sample selection process.
- Create record counts of excluded data and then reconcile the new control count to the calculated control count. It is easy to reverse the selection criteria, thereby excluding what should have been included. The reconciliation process helps avoids this error.
- Perform a visual review of the output. Ask yourself, does the result seem consistent with your expectations?
- Create reports that can function as a workpaper. Remember, there needs to be sufficient information to locate the documents. Reports with too many columns are difficult to read on the screen and are difficult to read in a printed format.

PLAN QUESTION SEVEN: WHAT FILTERING TECHNIQUES ARE NECESSARY TO REFINE THE SAMPLE SELECTION PROCESS?

At this stage, the data interrogation routine has identified entities or transactions that meet the criteria of the test. Filtering of the identified transactions can occur through the software or through manual observation.

Filtering and creating homogeneous data files may sound like the same process but in fact they are very different. Creating the homogeneous data file is the process of normalizing the data file in order that all the transactions have a commonality before the data interrogation routines. In the filtering stage all the transactions met the testing criteria but in the fraud auditor's judgment all the selected transactions should not be included in the final sample for fraud testing. The reasons vary, but the common reasons are materiality, frequency, and overt data errors.

So, why not filter out the small-dollar transactions as part of the inclusion and exclusion process? The answer is simple; fraud in the aggregate. Not all perpetrators commit one large fraud scenario; many perpetrators simultaneously commit several small frauds. Create the report, look at the report, and decide how and what to filter from the report.

Continued Illustration of Corruption Project

Since the specific identification included all purchase orders meeting the criteria, the plan would filter:

1. Purchase orders where the aggregate of the matched purchase orders does not exceed the bidding level.
2. Average amount of the purchase orders is low. There might be an efficiency comment lurking in the data but most likely not a bid avoidance issue.

PLAN QUESTION EIGHT: WHAT IS THE BASIS OF THE SAMPLE SELECTION PROCESS?

The sample selection process is dependent on the data interrogation strategy and the intent of the data interrogation routine.

The specific identification strategy is designed to identify all entities or all transactions that meet a specific attribute or attributes. Therefore, in theory all transactions meeting the specific identification test should be part of the sample.

Another use of the specific identification in conjunction with the inclusion and exclusion theory is to reduce the size of the population to increase the probability of a random sample selecting a fraudulent transaction.

Let's assume in a payroll audit that your company has 100,000 active employees. The fraud scenario is a fictitious employee. One of the tests is a duplicate bank account number. In today's world, finding two different employees with the same bank account number is not unusual. The test has 5,000 employees that meet the duplicate bank account number test. If the auditor randomly selects 25 employees, the odds of finding a fictitious employee are 1 in 5,000 versus 1 in 100,000.

The internal control avoidance theory is that an internal person is intentionally avoiding an internal control for the purpose of committing a fraud scenario. The sample selection is based on all transactions that meet the internal control avoidance theory.

Data interpretation is used when the sophistication of concealment is high. The items selected and the number of items selected is judgmental based on the fraud auditor's judgment.

Number anomaly the sample selection should be based on the definition of the number anomaly. That is, recurring number anomaly is a number that recurs six or time times attached to the same entity.

Continued Illustration of Corruption Project

The sample selection would be based on the selected fraud data analytics strategy.

 PLAN QUESTION NINE: WHAT IS THE PLAN FOR RESOLVING FALSE POSITIVES?

The first step is to identify the types of false positives that will occur based on your data interrogation routine. To illustrate the problem, we will use the duplicate test to locate hidden companies; the search routine examines the address field on the master file. So, what could cause a duplicate test to identify a duplicate address that does not link to a shell company?

1. A dormant vendor on your master file that ceased doing business and a new vendor that has moved into the address.
2. Merging of different company files.
3. An inherent weakness in the new vendor procedures that allows the same company to be added to the master file.
4. A real company that operates different businesses under different names.

There are two fundamental strategies: Minimize the false positives through the data analytics plan, or allow the fraud auditor to resolve the false positives through the audit procedure. The only wrong answer is no answer to the question.

Continued Illustration of Corruption Project

In the purchase order analysis, a false positive may occur through the lack of a proper description in the line item. Through visual examination, the fraud auditor will review the description and determine if the match is based on a data integrity issue based on input error.

In the entity analysis for the hidden entity, the previous reasons for a duplicate address will be considered.

PLAN QUESTION TEN: WHAT IS THE DESIGN OF THE FRAUD AUDIT TEST FOR THE SELECTED SAMPLE?

The last step of the plan is to design the audit procedure that will corroborate or refute the transactions identified through the fraud data analytics plan. The fraud audit procedure has four considerations (see Figure 4.1).

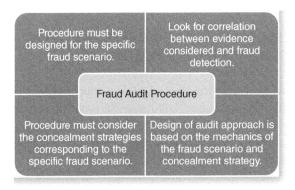

FIGURE 4.1 Audit Procedure Design to Detect Fraud

In Chapter 1, the concept of degree of certainty was discussed. For the fraud auditor, in the fraud test our degree of certainty statement is the "is or is not statement," as follows:

There "is or is not" credible evidence that the following scenario is occurring.

It is important to reflect on the different conclusions of a fraud auditor and a fraud investigator. The fraud auditor's job is to find transactions for investigation, whereas the fraud investigator's job is to refute or corroborate whether the fraudulent act occurred.

Continued Illustration of Corruption Project

The audit procedure for the hidden entity scenario would use the procedure described in Chapter 6.

The split purchase order test would need to determine if the price increase was consistent with industry price inflation or consistent with a kickback scheme.

Illustrative Example of a Fraud Data Analytics Plan Using Payroll Fraud Scenarios

Finally, we are at the stage of building the fraud data analytics plan. Starting with Chapter 2, our fraud scope is the primary category of asset misappropriation, and the secondary category is the theft of monetary funds. The following fraud scenarios are identified as a byproduct of the fraud risk assessment:

1. Budget owner/causes a fictitious person to be set up on the employee master file/the budget owner submits false time and attendance records for the fictitious person/causing the diversion of funds.
2. Payroll function/causes a fictitious person to be set up on the employee master file/the payroll function creates false time and attendance records for the fictitious person/causing the diversion of funds.

The following illustration is designed to provide the fraud auditor with an example of the thought process outlined in Chapters 2 and 3. The two fraud scenarios are very similar from a fraud data analytics perspective. From a *how the fraud scenario is committed* perspective, though, they are very different. Remember, fraud data analytics is all about the data versus the inherent control weakness that would allow the scenario to occur in your company.

1. Identify the components of the fraud scenario:
   a) Person committing in the first scenario is a budget owner, which indicates that the person committing the scheme has indirect access versus direct access to the master file. The budget owner does have a home for the fictitious person scheme and a budget where the false payroll expense can be recorded. How the budget owner causes a false employee to be added is an internal control issue, not a data issue.
   b) Person committing in the second scenario is the payroll function, which means they have direct access but no budget where the false payroll can be recorded. The payroll function challenge is to record the payroll expense in a department where the payroll expense will not be noticed. For the payroll function, the fraud auditor's knowledge of the company and those departments where a fictitious employee would go unnoticed becomes part of the thought process.

   c) Type of entity is a falsely created employee, which means the false employee must be added to the payroll with a disguised identity. The second possibility is that the created employee only appears in the payroll register versus in the human resources master file.

   d) The action statement is paid for services not performed. The time sheets are part of the concealment strategy and a necessary false record to cause payroll to calculate a payroll payment. For the budget owner, the fraud action statement is easy. Budget owner creates the time record. The user ID for the time record should link to the budget owner. For the payroll function, the ease or difficultly will depend on whether the timekeeping is manual or automated. In manual systems, the payroll function has direct access, therefore the payroll function has the ability to enter false hours. Whether the timekeeping is directly integrated into payroll system and whether payroll has override capacity on the timekeeping or payroll system are the important questions. The answers to these questions will determine how to search the data.

2. Identify the data that relate to the scenario:

   a) Master file will contain the identity information: name, address (street, city, state, postal code, country), bank account, government identification number (key information), telephone number, emergency contact information, email address, birthdate, hire date, position code, marital status, beneficiary information associated with health insurance or life insurance benefits, and tax withholding information (value of tax information varies by country).

   b) Time record file contains the hours submitted for payment. Time stamp for hours submitted might be useful depending on internal processes. In an automated system, creator ID and approval ID will be part of the time record, although the physical device in which the time record was created will be the key data element.

   c) Payroll records as to employee: gross payroll, deductions, and net payroll.

3. Select the fraud data analytics strategy:

   a) Specific identification.

     i. Missing data analysis would search for employee records that are missing normal identifying information. The availability analysis to determine what is the norm within your company for missing information would tell the fraud auditor the effectiveness of this test.

    ii. Duplicate information regarding: government identification number, bank account, or street address. Since most audit software has predetermined duplicate tests, the duplicate test should always be considered.

    iii. Specific anomaly:

        1. No address or bank account information.

        2. No tax withholding.

        3. Employee on the payroll is a prior employee.

        4. Bank account is external to country of origin for the company.

        5. A lack of voluntary deductions.

        6. Human resource records do not indicate that an employee evaluation was submitted.

    iv. Match to vendor file to determine if employee was a prior contract employee. This would explain valid government registration number. Second, test to determine the country of residence. The third test is to search for a change or different bank account number between accounts payable and payroll.

  b) Internal control avoidance:

    i. Budget owner—user ID of budget owner linked to creating the time record versus the employee ID.

    ii. Physical device creating the time record is a duplicate for the creator and approver of the time record.

    iii. Payroll function—after-hours creation of employee record.

    iv. Payroll function—user ID of payroll function linked to creating the time record versus the employee ID.

  c) Data interpretation—fictitious employee schemes seldom require data interpretation analysis. A caveat to that rule is when the fictitious person was created by senior management to pay bribes.

  d) Number anomaly—time records or reported hours are often even or round numbers, so the test would produce a lot of false positives.

4. Clean the data set:

  a) Availability is an important test before using the missing analysis.

  b) Reliability—time records do not typically have the data errors found in vendor payments or the revenue cycle.

  c) Usability—the availability test on the employee record will determine the usability.

5. Find logical errors:

  a) Employee records—the duplicate test would expect to create false positives regarding bank account, address, and telephone number if the company allows family members to work for the company.

b) Time records and payroll records are not anticipated to create false positives.

6. Create two homogeneous data files. One of the difficulties in fraud data analytics for payroll is that different groups of employees have different data and payment processes. That is, hourly employees are paid via the number of hours on a time record, where salaried employees' gross pay is based on annual salary divided by the number of pay periods. Therefore creating homogeneous data sets is required to perform effective data analysis.

   a) The inclusion theory for hourly employees would include:

      i. Hourly employee who works a full-time schedule.

      ii. Hourly employee who works a part-time schedule.

      iii. Temporary employee whose sole purpose is to cover planned absences.

   b) The exclusion theory for hourly employees would not include:

      i. Terminated employees, because they would have no time record or payroll register record.

      ii. Salaried employees.

   c) The inclusion theory for salaried employees:

      i. Include all active salaried employees, assuming time attendance records are submitted.

      ii. Terminated employee within the scope period. Note if the scenario was a temporary employee scheme, then the inclusion/exclusion theory would be different.

7. Select criteria for each test designed. There must be criteria for selection:

   a) Missing test—the number of missing data fields would be based on the frequency of missing data by employee. The scoring sheet concept.

   b) Duplicate test—the key fields would be address and bank account, depending on the method of payment.

   c) Specific anomaly test—all employees meeting the specific anomaly are selected.

   d) Match to vendor file, based on government identification number—all employees meeting the match criteria are selected. Data filtering might be used to reduce the number matched.

   e) Off-hours creation of employee record, all is selected.

8. Identify programming routines. The programming would be dependent on the audit software, which is beyond the scope of this book.

9. Select filtering techniques. No filtering of ghost employees will be used due to the fraud scenario.
10. Select sample. Based on the reports created and the selection criteria, all transactions meeting the criteria are selected.

SUMMARY

The fraud data analytics plan is based on the fraud scenario, the sophistication of concealment, usability of data, and the selected data-mining strategy. The fraud data analytics plan must be created for each fraud scenario included in the scope. Yes, there will be overlap between the fraud scenarios. But the plan is all about the thought process in building the data interrogation routines.

APPENDIX: STANDARD NAMING TABLE LIST FOR SHELL COMPANY AUDIT PROGRAM

VENDOR MASTER FILE

1. Vendor Number
2. Company Number
3. Division Number
4. Active or Inactive Code
5. Vendor Creation Date
6. Vendor Creation Time
7. Last Update File Date
8. Last Update Time
9. Vendor Record Creator ID
10. Vendor Record Authorizer ID
11. Vendor Update ID
12. Vendor Update Authorizer ID
13. Vendor Name (If both a full name and short name are recorded, provide both fields.)
14. Vendor Address Street (If multiple fields, provide each field as a separate column.)
15. Vendor Address City

16. Vendor Address State
17. Vendor Address Zip Code
18. Vendor Country
19. Vendor Federal ID #
20. Vendor Telephone Area Code (If multiple telephone numbers, provide each as separate columns, i.e., cell number.)
21. Vendor Telephone Number (seven-digit number)
22. Vendor Contact Person
23. Vendor Contact Telephone Number
24. Vendor Email
25. Vendor Website
26. Minority Business Code
27. Electronic Payment Field
28. Bank Routing Number
29. Bank Account Number

VENDOR INVOICE FILE

1. Vendor Number
2. Company Number
3. Division Number
4. Vendor Name
5. Invoice Number
6. Invoice Line Number
7. Invoice Date
8. Invoice Amount
9. Item Number
10. Item Unit Price, if information is recorded
11. Item Unit of Measure, if information is recorded
12. Item Quantity, if information is recorded
13. Item Description
14. Transaction or Journal Number
15. Transaction or Journal Recording Date
16. Transaction or Journal Recording Time
17. User ID or Name of Record Creator
18. Approval Code or Name
19. Approval Department
20. Purchase Order Number
21. Purchase Order Date

22. Original Purchase Order Amount
23. Amended Purchase Order Amount
24. Purchase Order Issuer ID
25. Receiving Number
26. Receiving Date
27. Receiving Time
28. Receiving Amount
29. Check/ACH/Wire Payment Indicator
30. Check/ACH/Wire Number
31. Check/ACH/Wire Date
32. Check/ACH/Wire Time
33. Check/ACH/Wire Amount
34. Check Address
35. Bank Account Number
36. Bank Routing Number
37. Electronic Approval
38. Manual Check Indicator
39. General Ledger (Typically the accounts payable, inventory, or work-in-process account. The expenditure code is captured from the purchase order file. In case of no purchase order file, determine how general ledger expense classification is linked to the expenditure transaction.)
40. Job Number
41. Contract Number
42. Commodity Code
43. Bid Code

PURCHASE ORDER DATA

1. Vendor Number
2. Vendor Name
3. Company Number
4. Division Number
5. Purchase Order Number
6. Purchase Order Date
7. Purchase Order Amount
8. Transaction or Journal Number
9. Transaction or Journal Recording Date
10. Transaction or Journal Recording Time
11. User ID or Name of Record Creator

12. Approval Code or Name
13. Buyer Code or Name
14. Revised Purchase Order Amount (Information will depend on how information is stored. Typically either the new total purchase order amount is recorded or the change amount to the purchase order. Please advise if multiple fields for purchase order change fields.)
15. Buyer Code or Name responsible for the purchase order change
16. Revised Purchase Order Date
17. Commodity Code Standard classification code for the item purchased
18. Bid Code (Describes the method for obtaining competitive bidding for the item purchased.)
19. General Ledger Account (All fields necessary to post to proper expenditure code, including but not limited to division, company, department, expense G/L, and any other codes for responsibility reporting.)
20. Job Number, if expense is coded to a specific job

DISBURSEMENT FILE

1. Vendor Number
2. Vendor Name
3. Company Number
4. Division Number
5. Check Number, ACH Number, Wire Number
6. Check Date, ACH Date or Wire Date
7. Check Amount, ACH Amount or Wire
8. Bank Account Number
9. Bank Routing Number
10. Vendor Invoice Number
11. Vendor Invoice Date
12. Vendor Invoice Amount

MASTER FILE CHANGE FILE

1. Vendor Number
2. Vendor Name
3. Company Number
4. Division Number
5. All Other Fields in Change Record (Each field should be retained in its own column.)

CHAPTER FIVE

Data Analytics in the Fraud Audit

F raud auditing is truly searching for a needle in a haystack. To illustrate the concept, someone in a business system may be misstating the financial statements, stealing assets, or committing a corrupt act. However, at the beginning of the fraud audit we do not know who, what, or when. Yet there is an expectation that an auditor should be able to detect who, what, and when. So, where or how should the auditor start searching for the fraudulent transaction?

While the fraud auditor may not know who or how or when, the fraud auditor does know what fraud scenario someone can commit in a business system. The fraud auditor does understand how perpetrators conceal their footprints. The fraud scenario approach is designed to even the playing field between the auditor and the perpetrator. Yes, the perpetrator does have an advantage because of how he conceals his footprints. However, the auditor has the advantage because fraud data analytics is an integral part of fraud auditing. Whether the fraudulent act causes a misstatement of the financial statements, a misappropriation of assets, or a corrupt act that is a violation of law or policy, fraud data analytics is intended to uncover the fraud scenario hiding in the haystack.

The fraud scenario approach is based on a methodology of how to write a fraud risk statement. The fraud scenario statement becomes the basis for building the fraud audit program. The sampling technique is driven by the fraud scenario statement. The audit procedure is driven by the fraud scenario statement. The audit conclusion is either credible evidence exists that a fraud scenario has occurred or there is no credible evidence of a fraud scenario. In summary, uncovering the fraud scenario is the objective of the fraud audit.

The fraud scenario approach is based on the fraud theory that there is a common set of fraud scenarios for every business system. The predictability factor provides the auditor with a logical starting point. Yes, the common scenarios need to be adapted to the vulnerabilities that naturally exist in every company. Once adapted, the audit is designed around the three elements of the fraud scenario. The quality of evidence gathered is then calibrated to the level of fraud concealment sophistication.

There needs to be a fraud audit program for each fraud scenario. There will be overlap between the listing of fraud scenarios in the audit scope and the audit program. Said differently, one fraud audit program may link to several fraud scenarios. The important step is for the auditor to understand the mechanics of the scenario and to ensure that each fraud scenario has a fraud data analytics plan.

HOW FRAUD AUDITING INTEGRATES WITH THE FRAUD SCENARIO APPROACH

The purpose of fraud auditing is to uncover fraud in core business systems. It is not about proving fraud—that step is for the fraud investigator and a court of law. This is an important distinction in understanding the difference between fraud auditing and fraud investigation. So, how does fraud auditing relate to the professional practice of auditing?

Generally accepted auditing standards (GAAS) require the auditor to detect a material error in the financial statements caused by fraud. Internal auditors should perform audit procedures to determine the operating effectiveness of fraud prevention and detection controls. The bottom line is that there is an expectation that auditors will detect fraud in core business systems.

The next question that needs to be considered is how to integrate fraud auditing or fraud testing into the audit program. The answer requires two discussions. The first discussion is, how should the auditor design the sampling plan to locate a fraud scenario? That is easy—the fraud data analytics plan. The second discussion is, how should the auditor design the nature, timing, and extent of the audit test? This question is beyond the scope of this book; however, it is an integral part of the fraud audit program. Said differently, it makes no sense to design a sample to locate a fraud scenario if the audit procedures do not recognize the fraudulent transaction.

Fraud data analytics is about creating a biased and focused sampling plan to search for a fraud scenario. Fraud data analytics is not intended to help the auditor to offer an opinion concerning the operating effectiveness of internal controls. The auditor uses a random, unbiased sampling technique to accomplish that objective. Yes, if we uncover fraud, then we can state that fraud prevention controls or fraud detection controls failed to mitigate the fraud risk.

So what is a biased, focused sampling plan? It starts with the fraud scenario. It builds a data profile for the scenario using the person committing the scenario, the type of entity structure, and the fraud action statement. The fraud data analytics identifies transactions consistent with the fraud data profile. It effectively excludes all transactions that do not meet the fraud data profile, meaning the sample only includes transactions consistent with the fraud data profile. We refer to this as the inclusion and exclusion theory of selecting a sample for the fraud audit.

HOW TO USE FRAUD DATA ANALYTICS IN THE FRAUD AUDIT

The use of fraud data analytics is to assist the auditor in responding to the risk of fraud consistent with the applicable auditing standards. At the risk of repeating the opening statement of the book, the world's best auditor using the world's best audit program cannot detect fraud unless their sample includes a fraudulent transaction. This is why fraud data analytics is so critical to the auditing profession.

Fraud data analytics is a sampling methodology. While the methodology examines the entire database, fraud data analytics is a sampling methodology. You can debate that fraud data analytics is an audit tool; however, the fallacy of the argument is that after creating the report, the auditor stills needs to examine documents, hence the argument that fraud data analytics is a sampling tool. It simply identifies transactions that need to be examined by an auditor.

Fraud data analytics is the best tool to uncover fraud in core business systems. If properly used, I believe fraud data analytics would become the number-one reason for fraud detection. Yes, I believe it would outpace the proverbial whistleblower. The use of fraud data analytics in the audit process is only limited by the auditor's imagination and available resources. There is no specific way to use fraud data analytics. The following list illustrates different ways to use fraud data analytics. My goal is to cause you to think differently about how to use fraud data analytics. I have intentionally not written the list in any specific order:

1. Fraud data analytics can be used for specific identification of transactions that link to a fraud scenario profile, the most common way auditors view fraud data analytics.
2. Summarize data to identify outliers. Using the data interpretation strategy, the fraud auditor would use their business knowledge and fraud knowledge to identify transactions that require fraud audit procedures.
3. Shrink the population of transactions using the exclusion theory, thereby increasing the odds of randomly selecting a fraudulent transaction.
4. Automate the process of searching for internal control avoidance.
5. Create a sample of zero. In this way, fraud data analytics indicates that the specific fraud scenario did not occur within the scope period.
6. Improve the quality of a company's data for fraud monitoring purposes. The first step in creating a robust fraud data analytics plan is to improve the quality of the data for fraud monitoring.
7. Identify data that should be added to the database to allow for fraud monitoring. In procurement the addition of a bid code would allow for identifying the competitive purchasing practice followed in awarding the purchase order—that is, sole source or preferred supplier or three written bids.
8. Identify a type of transaction that, in the auditor's judgment, has a higher risk of being linked to a fraud scenario. The auditing standards have already created this expectation by requiring auditors to test journal entries.

Understanding How to Use Data from a Fraud Perspective

I have always said that data is data. For the most part, regardless of the operating system, data is data. Sure, there are technical issues in locating and extracting data from different operating systems. Those are the technical IT issues associated with obtaining data and extracting the data.

From a fraud perspective, is data just data? An address field in the vendor master file, customer database, or your human resources system is still just an address field. The field is alphanumeric; it contains a number and a description of a physical location. The issue is not the address field; the issue is how to use the address field in the search for fraud scenarios.

The false vendor, false customer, or false employee created by the internal person has an address field. The address field in the database may be a street address, a PO box, a mailbox service address, or a mailbox forwarding address. In reality the person creating the shell company has many options. Each different type of address requires a different type of fraud data analytics:

- Search for the vendor with no street address, excluding overtly obvious vendor with no address—that is, government vendors because payments are wired versus mailed and the street address most likely provides no control value.
- Match the street address in the vendor master file to the employee address field.
- Perform a duplicate address search on the master file, searching for the false hidden entity.
- Download all public mailbox service companies from the Internet and perform a duplicate address procedure.
- Identify the method by which the public mailbox service company labels their box number and perform an alpha search on address field one and address field two for the applicable alpha string.
- Combine related fields with the address field. In the payment cycle, we either mail the payment or send the payment electronically. The absence of a street address and bank account is a red flag that payment was hand delivered.

Yes, data is data. What the fraud auditor needs to understand is how to use data in each field in the search for a fraud scenario.

As discussed in Chapter 4, a key strategy is creating homogeneous data sets based on a specific data field. Using the above examples, we will identify all vendors using known mailbox service companies. The mailbox service address field is the basis for the homogeneous data file for fictitious vendors. The next step is to attach the transactions to the vendor file. Using transactional data, the fraud auditor continues the search for the identified fraud scenario.

Step by step, the fraud auditor shrinks the population using the data consistent with the search for a fraud scenario. The goal of the methodology is to develop a sample of transactions using data associated with a specific scenario versus a sample of data errors.

Using Data in the Exclusion and Inclusion Theory

Using the needle-in-the-haystack analogy, as the size of the haystack shrinks, the ability to see the needle becomes easier. Business systems contain a diverse set of transactions, and all of these transactions are associated with different fraud risks. Using the expenditure cycle as an example, there are transactions with purchase orders, without purchases orders, or with open purchase orders. The purchase order may have been issued before the invoice or after the receiving the invoice. Expenditures are for services, supplies, inventory, construction, research, and so on. While all of these transactions follow the same set of internal controls, all of the transactions have different susceptibility to all the fraud scenarios facing the expenditure cycle. The concept of creating homogeneous data sets correlates to shrinking the haystack to improve the odds of the auditor seeing the anomaly associated with the fraud scenario.

Homogeneous data sets created by data elements is an important step in all forms of fraud data analysis. In change analysis, the homogeneous data set is the before and after on the data field. In outlier analysis, it is ensuring the data in the analysis has a high degree of commonality. For favoritism analysis in a corruption fraud audit, it is comparing apples to apples versus apples to oranges. Creating the homogeneous data set through data fields is just one critical step in building a targeted fraud data analytics plan.

Disaggregated analysis is becoming a new buzzword within the auditing world. The concept is consistent with creating homogeneous data sets. It is also consistent with creating a focused and biased sample. Using the homogeneous data set, disaggregated analysis shrinks the data set to its lowest finite point based on the fraud scenario. In this way, the anomaly becomes more apparent to the auditor and becomes the basis for the sample selection.

In summary, the inclusion and exclusion theory is a valuable technique in the fraud data analysis plan. You start with the entire data file; you exclude those transactions that are not relevant to your fraud scenario or fraud data profile. Now you have a data set that is consistent with your fraud scenario. Let the data interrogation procedures begin.

FRAUD DATA ANALYTICS FOR FINANCIAL REPORTING, ASSET MISAPPROPRIATION, AND CORRUPTION

In this section, it is the intent to discuss the nuances or challenges of fraud data analytics for each primary fraud category. Future chapters will provide specifics of fraud data analytics for core business systems.

The starting point of all fraud testing is to understand the nuances of each primary fraud category and the subsequent secondary category. An important concept is that one size does not fit all. There is no one specific fraud data analytics routine because there is no one fraud risk. Every fraud category has several subsets, inherent schemes, and eventual fraud scenarios. How we develop our fraud data analytics plan will vary by the category of fraud risk. Hence, one fraud data analytics plan does not fit all fraud risks.

Financial reporting is the easiest of the three categories. I did not say *easy*; I said the easiest of the three categories. GAAS provides the auditor with guidance on how to design the audit but it provides minimal guidance on asset misappropriation and no guidance on corruption schemes.

Financial reporting fraud data analytics starts with the search for a material error that causes a material misstatement of the financial statements. If a material error has occurred, the error is either overstatement or understatement of an account balance. *Overstatement* means that the fraud scenario is recorded in the general ledger for the year under audit. *Understatement* means that the fraud scenario is not recorded in the general ledger. These are not meant to be absolute statements but rather general guidelines.

There are two clear homogeneous data files. Financial activity is recorded through a manual journal entry or the fraudulent transaction is recorded through a source journal. The manual journal entry or the source journal create two separate and distinct homogeneous data files. The inherent scheme structure then links to each homogeneous data file to create secondary discrete homogeneous data. Therefore, creating the fraud data analytics plan is predictable.

The predictability factor is based on all fraudulent transactions overstating the balance sheet or income statement are recorded in the general ledger. Overstatement could also occur through the failure to write off or write down an asset—therefore, the search would be for the absence of an entry. Understating the balance sheet or income statement generally indicates that the transaction is missing from the general ledger for the year under audit. Understatement occurs the same way, through the general ledger, through source journals and manual journal entries. The difference is that the transaction is recorded in the year before or the year after. In the final analysis, all the data are available in the general ledger. Lastly, the misstatement can also occur through the misclassification of a transaction, the proverbial above or below the line.

The second predictability factor for financial reporting is the concealment factor. Fraud concealment in financial reporting is intended to create the illusion of meeting the GAAP or meeting the financial statement assertions. Fraud data analytics can be developed to search for the fraud concealment because the concealment is recorded in the general ledger. To repeat earlier statements, fraud data analytics is not for all fraud scenarios or all fraud concealment strategies.

To illustrate the concept of fraud auditing in financial reporting, we will start with the presumption that the audit program has indicated misstatement of revenue is an identified fraud risk; the audit is focusing on revenue overstatement versus revenue understatement. The scenario is a false customer and false revenue.

The first homogeneous data file is all revenue recorded in the sales journal versus revenue created from a journal entry. The second data file is the customer master file. Within the source journal all sales transactions are linked to either a false customer or a real customer. The fraud audit can either search for a false customer and false revenue or for the fraud concealment strategy used to hide the false revenue.

To illustrate the concept, we will assume that the controller has recorded false revenue to a fictitious customer. The fraud auditor has two choices:

1. The fraud data analysis would use the specific identification strategy to identify customers meeting the profile of a created customer or sales transactions meeting the profile of a created revenue transaction.
2. The fraud data analytics would use specific identification to identify customer accounts through cash receipts journal. Therefore, the data analytics using the concealment approach will focus on customer payments versus false revenue.

Using the concealment strategy, the disaggregated analysis would create two groups of customers. One group of customers has postings from the sales journal but no postings from cash receipts journal. The second group of customers has postings from a sales journal and credits from cash receipts journals. The customers with no cash receipts postings would be the first focus of finding false revenue to a created customer.

The customers with cash receipts postings would require a second analysis because the concealment technique to conceal the fraud scenario is a temporary posting of a real customer's payment to the fictitious customer's account, and then the cash receipts transaction is transferred back to the real customer's account after aging analysis. Therefore, the customers with cash receipts postings would have two groups, customers with no cash receipts transfers and customers with cash receipts transfers.

Asset misappropriation fraud data analytics is about finding the person who is stealing company assets. The person is either internal or external to the company. The asset theft is either a monetary asset or a tangible asset. The loss may also occur through sale of an asset below fair market value or purchase above fair market. The business system, revenue, expenditure, or payroll will change the nature of the fraud data analytics. Each scheme in each business system provides different challenges. To illustrate the nuances of the different schemes:

1. Theft of assets through a company credit card provides a direct link of the misappropriated assets to the perpetrator.
2. A shell company can be identified through fraud data analytics; however, the linkage to the perpetrator occurs through the investigation process.
3. Theft of revenue before the revenue is recorded, referred to as skimming, starts with the purchasing file versus the revenue file.
4. The scope period for the three examples can be a one-year period. Obviously, once a theft is discovered, the scope period will be based on the fraud investigation plan.

Fraud data analytics for corruption scenarios is the most difficult of the three fraud categories. Corruption is about corrupting the decision process. The secondary categories of corruption are similar but are very different (e.g., price fixing, FCPA violation, or discrimination in hiring). The scope question becomes the first challenge. It is common for auditors to include the same fraud scenario in either the asset misappropriation category or the corruption category. From a fraud theory discussion perspective, these can create interesting discussions, but are not critical to fraud data analytics, except for the audit scope question. To illustrate the concept using the following fraud scenario:

A budget owner in collusion with a vendor causes increases to the unit price after the bidding process (resulting in the loss of assets) or the internal person receives a kickback to corrupt the payment process.

The loss of assets implies asset misappropriation, whereas kickback implies corruption. Which is it, corruption or theft of assets? This is why the scope question is the first challenge.

The second scope question is, who is corrupting? Corruption fraud data analytics will differ by whether your company is the corrupting agent or whether your company is being corrupted. Similar to asset misappropriation, the business system of revenue, expenditures, or payroll will change the nature of the fraud data analytics for the corruption scheme.

When the fraud audit is focusing on corruption schemes, the definition of the scope requires critical consideration before building data interrogation routines. The second critical issue is that corruption involves collusion that further increases the difficulty of the fraud audit.

Corruption schemes require collusion—typically an internal person and an external person. Data that reside at the external source are not available to the fraud auditor. Data systems vary on the amount of data that may exist in data files that is useful for the fraud data analytics plan. The lack of available data will cause the fraud auditor to use inference analysis to select a sample.

Corruption schemes can also occur solely through external parties. In this regard the ability to identify the scheme becomes more difficult because the majority of the red flags exist in the documents versus your data files. Obviously, companies that maintain extensive procurement data in their database may provide a different result to the use of fraud data analytics.

Fraud data analytics for corruption schemes usually require two or more years. In contrast, fraud data analytics for asset misappropriation and financial reporting can operate effectively on one year of data.

Understanding the nuances of creating a fraud data analytics plan for each primary category of fraud is important for the fraud auditor. Each category has different data, different approaches, different scenarios, and different fraud data analytic plans.

IMPACT OF FRAUD MATERIALITY ON THE SAMPLING STRATEGY

The discussion of materiality cannot be avoided in fraud detection. Nor should the discussion be avoided. All auditors use materiality in some way in the conduct of an audit. GAAS recognizes that errors individually or in the aggregate may have a material impact on the financial statements. The standards further discuss the concept of reasonable assurance and the gathering of evidence from both a quantitative and qualitative perspective. Although each professional set of standards may express the concept differently, all of the standards address the concept of quantitative and qualitative evidence.

The primary category of fraud will clearly impact the sample selection decision regarding materiality. From a financial statement perspective the dollar amount is based on the material error concept. Asset misappropriation is based on dollar amount of theft that the audit should detect. Corruption materiality will depend on the type of corruption and whether the corrupt act is a violation of law.

In Chapter 3, we discussed the concept of filtering in the data interrogation routine just before the sample selection. Starting with the easy materiality concept, the dollar value of the fraudulent activity individually or in the aggregate directly correlates to the sample selection criteria. In fraud data analytics, we can also use frequency of occurrence, percent of change, dollar amount of change, number of records, and aggregate dollar value of activity by entity as a materiality factor in the sample selection.

HOW FRAUD CONCEALMENT AFFECTS THE SAMPLING STRATEGY

The qualitative aspect of evidence correlates to the sophistication of the concealment strategy used by the perpetrator. There is a direct correlation between the design of the audit plan and the sophistication of the concealment. If the strategy used by the auditor is less sophisticated than that of the perpetrators, then the audit plan will fail in the fraud detection. Conversely, if the audit plan is more sophisticated than the concealment strategy, the audit plan should detect the fraud scenario. The decision to calibrate the audit plan should be based on the audit standards used by the auditor, the objective of the audit program, and the qualitative aspects of the evidence the auditors deem necessary to formulate an opinion.

The decision process to calibrate the audit program is a little more complicated than simply picking low, medium, or high. It is not my desire to write a treatise on how auditors should design their audit plan to meet the associated professional standards as related to fraud concealment. However, all audit standards require auditors to exercise due professional care in the design of an audit plan. This includes an understanding of the fraud risks consistent with the audit scope. Part of exercising the due care standards requires that auditors understand how fraud can occur in a business system. The fraud scenario approach describes how the fraud scenario can occur in a business system. The fraud concealment describes how the perpetrator hides the fraud scenario in the business system.

The purpose of fraud auditing is to uncover transactions that meet the profile of a fraud scenario. In fraud auditing, the sampling technique is to create a focused and biased sample that links to a fraud scenario. At a minimum, the design of the sample must consider the level of fraud sophistication. It should understand what the fraud data analysis is designed to accomplish and what the design cannot accomplish. While the standards do not provide direct guidance on the concept of sophistication of concealment, ignoring the concept will ensure that auditors do not understand what they can uncover and what they cannot uncover.

In Chapter 3, we discussed the four different fraud data analytics strategies. The strategies provide a direct link to the level of sophistication of concealment. By default, the auditor calibrates the audit through the selection of a fraud data analytics strategy. By default, the sample size also correlates to the level of sophistication of concealment.

PREDICTABILITY OF PERPETRATORS' IMPACT ON THE SAMPLING STRATEGY

Perpetrators generally have a comfort zone in committing a particular fraud scenario. They tend to commit the same scheme or a similar fraud scenario many times. They tend not to stop until they are caught. This is why pattern and frequency analysis is critical to fraud data analytics.

Since the fraud scenario is committed over an extended period of time, at some point perpetrators tend to make a mistake or some event out of their control happens, causing their concealment strategy to fail to hide the fraud, hence the predictability factor of perpetrators committing a fraud scenario.

If they have set up a shell company, they tend to use the same shell company on multiple occasions. While they may use more than one shell company, they tend not to use hundreds of shell companies. In payroll fraud, the fraud scenarios tend to occur in a small group of employees that perceive some level of trust among the group of perpetrators.

They need to have some sense of control over the fraudulent activity. Therefore, the fraudulent act links to their job position. Greed is a weakness of most perpetrators. While being a motive for committing the fraud scenario, it also means the fraud will most likely grow over time.

As a reminder, we never know what fraud scenario a perpetrator is going to commit or how they will conceal the fraud scenario. However, by understanding the logical permutations and incorporating the concealment theory, we can build a fraud audit program that should be able to detect the fraud scenario, hence the predictability factor of the fraud scenario permutation analysis.

IMPACT OF DATA AVAILABILITY AND DATA RELIABILITY ON THE SAMPLING STRATEGY

In the perfect audit world, we have all the data; the data are reliable and formatted in a manner that allows for fraud data analytics. Yes, in the perfect world.

Unfortunately, data are not always available, the business system may not capture data, and data contain errors and require extensive effort to format for fraud data testing. As a result, we have false positives or reduced effectiveness of planned tests.

The data dilemma requires a decision for the auditor among four choices:

1. Allocate additional time to the fraud data programming to minimize the false positives. In reality, audits operate under time constraints. Trying to achieve the perfect fraud interrogation routine is not reality. Therefore, the goal should be to clean the data with a reasonable effort. The audit examination will need to resolve the remaining red flags.
2. Do not minimize the false positives in the data analytics phase and allow the auditor to resolve the red flag through audit testing. The yin and the yang of data analytics. The auditor should strive to find balance between options one and two.
3. Exclude all transactions from testing that contain overt data integrity issues. I am sure this concept bothers many auditors. If the plan has only one report, then this approach is fraught with many problems. However, if the fraud data analytics plan has many reports, using different approaches, then this plan has many merits.
4. Identify data integrity issues as an inhibitor to fraud prevention and fraud detection internal controls. This approach is more of an internal control testing approach versus a fraud detection approach.

CHANGE, DELETE, VOID, OVERRIDE, AND MANUAL TRANSACTIONS ARE A MUST ON THE SAMPLING STRATEGY

In reading about fraud scenarios there is a common theme; these words are *change, delete, void, override,* and *manual transactions.* The fraud data analytics plan should understand how these transactions occur in business systems and have the ability to identify the transactions.

Change can occur in many ways. It may start with changing a data element in an entity file, allowing the perpetrator to take control of the entity on either a temporary or permanent basis, which suggests an asset misappropriation scenario. It might involve changing business activity, which suggests a corrupt act might be occurring. From a financial statement perspective, a new account may result in false transactions being booked to overstate income.

In using the fraud triangle rationalization theory, a person's change in their behavior or motives to commit a fraudulent act is a red flag. In fraud data analytics, *change* is one of the operative words in searching for fraud scenarios.

Deleting a transaction should not occur in a business system. However, many times fraud scenarios have occurred or have been concealed because an internal control weakness allowed someone to delete a transaction. Since most business systems have a control number, searching for gaps in sequence numbers or control numbers out of sequence with dates is a fundamental fraud data analytics routine.

Voiding is different from a deleting a transaction because the transaction is still recorded in the business system. The transaction is recorded but typically with a zero value.

Override of internal controls is identified as one of the key internal control failures. In essence it inhibits the design of the internal control to operate as planned by management. We need to think of override in many different ways. The most common override is when a manager instructs a subordinate to process a transaction in a manner inconsistent with internal controls. Management override correlates to all three primary fraud risk categories. Business systems have codes incorporated to allow a transaction to bypass traditional computer controls. Typically, these require approval of a manager that may be involved in the fraud scenario. The use of a contra entry tricks the traditional controls or calculations by causing a reverse transaction. Understanding the inherent weakness in an internal control allows the perpetrator to process a transaction contrary to the intent of internal controls.

Manual transactions are those transactions or calculations that do not occur in the automated business systems. The perpetrator records the transaction and bypasses the internal controls in the automated business systems.

The concept of change, delete, void, and manual transactions must be understood by the fraud auditor and incorporated into the fraud data analytics plan.

⬚ PLANNING REPORTS FOR FRAUD DATA ANALYTICS

The fraud audit should start with a set of reports that are designed to inform the auditor about the frequency of transactions and the dollar value of transactions. In each chapter, we will discuss specific types of reports for each business system. The planning reports should be linked to the concept of homogeneous data sets and the fraud scenarios within the audit scope. The essence of the planning reports is to help with the likelihood question.

The fraud data analytics planning reports are designed to tell the fraud auditor at a high level of the probability that the fraud scenario is occurring in the business systems. The reports are generally not sufficiently detailed to identify a fraud scenario. The probability is based simply on the fact that transactions exist in the data set that on a high level are consistent with the fraud data profile for the scenario.

To illustrate probability concept, ghost employees who are false and created by the internal person tend to have a high percentage of net payroll to gross payroll. One of the first fraud data analytics reports in payroll fraud audit is a comparison of gross payroll to net payroll by employee with a percentage calculation. The high percentage of net-to-gross points the fraud auditor to an employee with a high net-to-gross payroll. This statistic is consistent with a fictitious ghost employee, a contra adjustment scheme in the deduction field, or a false adjustment scheme to net payroll. In one project, the controller's net payroll was 150 percent of gross payroll. I may not know what fraud scenario is occurring, but I am sure selecting the controller will reveal something.

The likelihood question is designed to ask where fraud scenarios may exist in core business systems. Traditionally, the profession relies on the internal control approach to answer the likelihood question. The theory is based on internal controls that prevent or detect fraud. The likelihood question would focus on fraud scenarios with a high residual risk. Therefore, the search for fraud scenarios is focused where internal controls are deemed not to be adequate.

The data question is based on searching for patterns and frequencies consistent with the fraud scenario. In essence, if no data exist consistent with the fraud scenario data profile, then the likelihood answer is that the fraud scenario is less likely to be occurring in the audit scope.

Yes, both approaches have inherent weaknesses. The internal control approach does not recognize that fraud scenarios can occur and comply with all the internal controls. Internal control inhibitors can create the illusion of compliance with internal controls, although the fraud scenario is hidden with in the data file. The data approach may fail to identify a fraud scenario because the level of sophistication of the concealment strategy exceeds the design of the fraud data analytics plan.

The data approach is designed to point the fraud auditor in the right direction based on data versus residual risk, which focuses on opportunity. It is not my desire to debate which approach is appropriate. I will let the profession debate the question. What is critical is to ensure that fraud auditors focus their resources at the fraud scenarios that have the highest likelihood of occurring within your audit.

HOW TO DOCUMENT THE PLANNING CONSIDERATIONS

In the audit world, we document objectives, scope, decisions, sample selection procedures, evidence gathered, and conclusions in our working papers. A key aspect of the documentation process is the linkage factor. The linkage factor was first introduced in Chapter 1. The fraud scenario circle is intended to illustrate the concept of how all audit work links to the fraud scenario (Figure 5.1).

Consider the following scenario in relation to the fraud scenario circle:

Budget owner or payroll function causes a fictitious person to be set up on the employee master file. The budget owner or payroll submits time and attendance records for the fictitious person, resulting in the loss of company funds.

1. Scope: Primary category is asset misappropriation and the secondary category is theft of monetary funds.

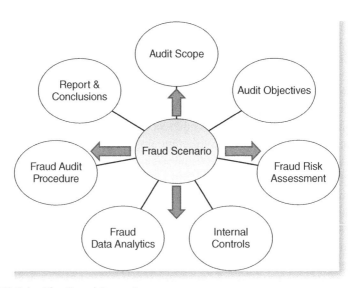

FIGURE 5.1 The Fraud Scenario

2. Objective: Determine if a budget owner or payroll function causes a fictitious person to be set up on the employee master file, and the budget owner or payroll submits time and attendance records for the fictitious person, causing the diversion of funds.
3. Fraud risk assessment: Assessment is a listing of fraud scenarios and the decision process of determining residual risk.
4. Internal controls: A listing of internal controls, both fraud prevention and fraud detection, link to the fraud scenario.
5. Fraud data analytics: The fraud data profile and the methodology for selecting a sample designed to locate employees on the master file that meet the fraud data profile.
6. Fraud audit procedure: The procedure performed to test for evidence of the fraud scenario—that is, perform a payoff procedure to determine if a budget owner or payroll function causes a fictitious person to be set up on the employee master file.
7. Report or conclusion: No credible evidence exists indicating that a fictitious person exists in the employee master file, or credible evidence does exist that the budget owner or payroll has submitted time and attendance records in the name of a fictitious person.

KEY WORKPAPERS IN FRAUD DATA ANALYTICS

The following four workpapers are required documentation to support the fraud data analytics plan:

1. The fraud risk assessment, which includes a listing of all fraud scenarios in the audit scope.
2. A fraud risk assumption memo. The fraud assumption memo is used to define all the assumptions that the auditor has used in developing the listing of fraud scenarios.
3. Fraud data analytics plan. The purpose of the plan is to document the thought process used in creating the fraud data interrogation plan. Since many software packages provide an audit trail of the programming logic, the audit trail report could function in this capacity. At the end of Chapter 4, a sample workpaper was prepared illustrating all the decisions made in the development of a fraud data analytics plan for one scenario.
4. The sample selection criteria are always a critical workpaper in all audits. Was the intent to shrink the population and use a random sample technique, or was the intent to test all transactions meeting the search routine?

SUMMARY

In the first five chapters, the fraud data analytics methodology using the fraud scenario approach to uncovering fraud in core business systems was explained. While I am sure some readers want to jump to the remaining chapters to read about how to discover shell companies, ghost employees, or fake journal entries, auditors need to be able to explain their judgment in their workpapers. The first five chapters were written to guide you through all the questions that arise in the real world of fraud data analytics.

Fraud data analytics can be depicted by the inverted triangle or, as some call it, the funnel. Whatever you think the picture looks like, remember that fraud data analytics is about finding one suspicious transaction that cannot be resolved through the audit examination. When a suspicious transaction is identified, the inverted triangle is flipped over and the fraud data analysis expands versus contracts.

CHAPTER SIX

Fraud Data Analytics
for Shell Companies

oards of directors, stockholders, management, and the professional
standards are expecting auditors to respond to risk of fraud in core
business systems. Within a company's accounts payable file, shell
companies are being used to steal millions of dollars from companies or the
shell company is used to conceal bribe payments that violate anti-bribery laws.
The purpose of this chapter is to explain our methodology and experiences in
detecting shell companies within the fraud audit.

In your customer database, internal employees have set up shell companies to sell to themselves at large discounts. We call this a *front customer scheme*.
Internal employee then sells the goods to your customers at a markup. The
internal employee then skims off the profit. In your vendor database, internal
employees have created shell companies to misappropriate company funds or
management has created a shell company to conceal the payment of bribes.
In payroll, the internal employee has created the proverbial ghost employee.

The fraud scenario approach to uncovering fraud in core business systems
recognizes that every secondary category of the fraud risk structure has one
or more inherent fraud schemes. Every fraud scheme has two parts—an entity
and a fraudulent action statement. This chapter will discuss fraud data analytics to search for the entity structure of the inherent scheme. In particular,

FIGURE 6.1 Categories of Shell Companies

this chapter will discuss fraud data analytics for locating the shell company. Starting with the homogeneous data concept, Figure 6.1 illustrates the concept of three groups of shell companies.

From a fraud data analytics perspective, there are three homogeneous categories of shell companies. A fourth category is a subset of the first three. The shell company describes the vendor or customer. How the list relates to employees will be discussed in Chapter 8.

1. Category one: The traditional shell company
   a) The traditional shell company is an entity that is created by the internal or external person to perpetrate the fraud action statement. The following list provides examples of the permutations:
      ▫ Stand-alone company legally created.
      ▫ Stand-alone nonlegally created, a DBA filed in the county of record.
      ▫ Pass-through stand-alone company created by an internal source.
      ▫ Pass-through stand-alone company created by salesperson at real company.
      ▫ False minority entity in the USA.
      ▫ False government preferred entity outside the USA.
      ▫ For a more sophisticated perpetrator, there are companies that sell legal shell entities. The company was legally created many years ago and has been dormant. The incorporation date provided the illusion that the company has been in business for years.

2. Category two: The assumed entity shell company
   a) The assumed entity is a real company where the perpetrator takes over the identity by changing the address, banking information, telephone number, or email addresses. The assumed entity is similar to the real entity that is not complicit. However, the key difference is that the assumed entity did not process the transaction, whereas the real entity that was not complicit did process the transaction through their books and records.
   b) Assume the identity of dormant vendor or customer.
   c) Temporarily assume identity of the same active vendor or customer.
   d) Temporarily assume identity of the random active vendor or customer.
   e) For a more sophisticated perpetrator, assume a real vendor or customer's identity that is not in the master file and the perpetrator causes real vendor or customer to be added to master file.
3. Category three: The hidden entity shell company
   a) In the hidden entity shell there are a minimum of two companies in your database that have a common ownership. The purpose of the hidden entity is typically to circumvent dollar control levels. The companies usually have different names but may have a common identifier. The primary test is to search for duplicate master file data: addresses, bank accounts, telephone numbers, and email accounts.
   b) Other purposes of the hidden entity are to function as a subcontractor, create false bids, meet government quotas for preferred vendors, or whatever scheme the perpetrator needs two or more organizations. On the revenue side, bad-debt customers place orders under a new name; customers reaching a credit limit may create a second organization to avoid control levels.
   c) The hidden entity scheme is a real company operating under two or more numbers or names. The companies may be two real standalone companies with a common ownership or two or more companies that operate under one roof.
   d) The hidden entity scheme may also be a shell company where the sole purpose of the second company is to create the illusion of a second company for whatever purpose.
   e) Hidden entity using a variation of a real company's name; however, unlike the other hidden entity schemes there is only one entity in your master file; the real entity is not involved and the duplicate test will not reveal the permutation.

f) Real vendor with multivendor numbers. For some reason, it is very common to find the same vendor or customer in your database two or more times. When a real company has two or more numbers it creates opportunities that should not exist with good master file internal controls.

4. Category four: The limited-use shell company

a) The limited-use shell company is a *subset of categories one, two, and three.* The only difference is the frequency that the shell company is used in the fraud scenario.

b) One-time use of a shell company. Many companies' procedures for one-time payments are not as robust as the internal control procedures for a permanent company.

c) Temporary use of a shell company. The perpetrator processes a few transactions through the entity to stay below the control radar before moving on to a different entity. In one fraud audit project, the perpetrator using the one-time payment procedure would submit one invoice under a company name, then another company name,when in fact the companies did not legally exist. The fraud scenario was committed over a two-year period.

WHAT IS A SHELL COMPANY?

A shell corporation is a legally created entity that has no active business or is to conceal the true identity of the real company operating through a shell company. In essence, a shell corporation exists mainly on paper, has no physical presence, employs no one, and produces nothing. Within more sophisticated concealment strategies the perpetrators may employ the use of an office or employees to provide the illusion of a legitimate business entity. Shell corporations are frequently used to shield identities and/or to hide money in cases of money laundering, bankruptcy, bribery, and fraudulent conveyances. Scandals range from thousands to millions of dollars and always result in embarrassing moments for the corporation and management. Shell companies are called different names in different industries and different continents. Common names are *paper company, fictitious company, nominee company, front company, dummy corporations,* and *numbered companies.* Shell companies can also occur in nonlegally created companies, meaning in name only.

From an internal perspective of asset misappropriation in category one, the shell company is used for false billing schemes or a pass-through scheme, which is discussed in Chapter 7. In category two, the assumed identity shell companies are also used for false billing and pass-through schemes. Category three shell companies are used to circumvent payment internal controls and procurement internal controls. Category four shell companies are used in asset misappropriation schemes and internal control avoidance. All four categories are also associated with corruption schemes.

Shell companies are also used in financial statement fraud scheme where management is recording false revenue or transferring liabilities. The data analytics for shell customer is the same as the data analytics for shell vendor, except the data profile would need to be tailored for attributes associated with a customer versus a vendor.

 ## WHAT IS A CONFLICT-OF-INTEREST COMPANY?

The conflict-of-interest entity is a legally created company and provides the services or goods as described on the invoice. The conflict of interest is based on an undisclosed legal or beneficial ownership of the company. In Chapter 8, we will discuss conflict of interest in the purchase decision. The conflict-of-interest entity may operate as a shell company or as a real company with an undisclosed legal or beneficial ownership conflict-of-interest company. In first situation, the conflict of interest may have only one customer. In the second situation, the conflict-of-interest entity is in the business of providing services to the entire business community.

 ## WHAT IS A REAL COMPANY?

I know this sounds silly, but there are two types of real companies. The first type is a real company that is complicit with the fraud action statement. The second type is a real company that processed the transaction through their books and records but was not complicit with the fraud action statement.

 ## FRAUD DATA ANALYTICS PLAN FOR SHELL COMPANIES

The plan starts with recognizing the homogeneous grouping of companies in the vendor master file or the customer master file. Using disaggregated analysis the fraud data analytics plan recognizes the subcategories within the homogeneous group of shell companies. The fraud sophistication concealment theory understands that at the low level the analysis of the master file should disclose the false entity, whereas, as the sophistication rises to medium to high, the ability to identify shell companies diminishes. The medium to high levels require the analysis of the transactions that link to the entity structure. At the high level, the search will start with the transactions and link back to the entities that have the transaction anomaly.

FRAUD DATA ANALYTICS FOR THE TRADITIONAL SHELL COMPANY

The search for the shell company starts with the specific identification strategy. We use the matching search routines, missing search routines, and the data anomaly testing. The matching test is comparison of two databases for a match. The most common test is the vendor database to the employee database. However, the same test should be performed for employee and customer database.

The matching test is highly effective because the match provides direct evidence of the linkage between the two entities. The matching should focus on address, bank account, telephone number, government identification number, and email address. The matching test is effective for low-sophistication concealment but loses its effectiveness when the perpetrator ensures that the two entities have different identities. Figure 6.2 illustrates the impact that concealment theory has on the address field when using the matching test.

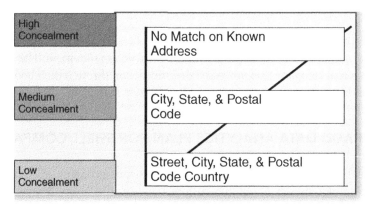

FIGURE 6.2   Address Field

The missing analysis is an inference analysis that suggests that missing information is an indicator of someone with something to hide. The missing analysis should focus on address, bank account, telephone number, government identification number, and email address. It is the weight of all the missing information versus the lack of one element.

The anomaly testing uses the data in the master file to identify attributes associated with a shell company (e.g., P.O. box) or compares data for illogical data patterns (e.g., vendor has no address or bank account in the master file). The types of anomalies are:

- Addresses that match to mailbox service companies or mailbox forwarding companies.
- Email addresses that use public email addresses—such as Gmail or Hotmail.
- Time and date the entity was added to the master file.
- Lacks both an address and a bank account number.
- Company names that only contain initials.

The person committing the scenario must be considered in designing the data interrogation routine for traditional shell companies. When the person creating the shell company has direct access to the master file, then the internal control avoidance strategy of searching for off-period updates is a critical test. If the fraud scenario involves a department manager, then the off-period analysis is not a valid routine. Unless the fraud scenario involves collusion with the direct input function, then the off-period analysis should also be considered.

FRAUD DATA ANALYTICS FOR THE ASSUMED ENTITY SHELL COMPANY

The assumed entity shell focuses on the change analysis. The key fields for vendors are address or bank account, because your company either electronically transfers the payment or mails the payment. For customer shell companies, the address tends to be critical due to the shipment of inventory. Other fields may also be changed to control the flow of information: telephone number, email address, and contact person name.

In change analysis we must consider both temporary and permanent change analysis. In the temporary change, someone is taking over the identity and processing one transaction and then changing the identity information back to the original data. The key is to search for a frequency of change by the internal person who has the ability to change the data. In permanent change, the first step is to identify entities with a change to address or bank account. Then attach the transactional history for anomalies in the transactional history.

If the company maintains a change file, the fraud data analysis is a matter of summarizing the change file by type of change for the permanent changes. If the change is a temporary change, then there should be two changes for the entity number. If no change file is maintained, then the analysis must compare two master files. The comparisons should be the first master file at the beginning of the scope period and the last master file at the end of the scope period. This analysis is not effective for the temporary change. In that case, the analysis would need to focus on the transaction file. To illustrate the concept of using the transaction file:

Using false customer refunds for dormant customers with a credit balance, the fraud data analytics plan would search the payment table for duplicate addresses with different customer names.

In the vendor file involving false invoices, the fraud data analytics plan would search the payment table for a vendor number having payments going to two or more addresses or bank accounts. The key in both data elements is using the payment table.

In the rare cases where a perpetrator takes over the identity of a real company that is not on the master file and is not complicit in the fraud scheme, the data interrogation would use the missing or data anomaly testing. The key difference would be in the audit testing. The address in the master file would not match the address of the real not-complicit vendor.

FRAUD DATA ANALYTICS FOR THE HIDDEN ENTITY SHELL COMPANY

The hidden entity focuses on the duplicate test because the shell company is operating under two or more different names or operating under the same name but different vendor or customer numbers. The hidden entity shell company might be two or more legal entities or one legal entity operating under different names. The duplicate analysis would first focus on address, bank account number, telephone number, government issued number, contact person, or email address. The hidden entity typically correlates to the same general ledger accounts or the same budget owner.

The use of fuzzy logic on name fields is also useful. Once the fuzzy logic identifies a match on names, the second analysis should use the duplicate testing or go directly to the transaction testing.

FRAUD DATA ANALYTICS FOR THE LIMITED-USE SHELL COMPANY

Typically, companies have codes or numbers to tag one-time vendors. In one company, all one-time payment vendors had the same vendor number. In another company, the company assigned all temporary vendors with a vendor number starting with nine. The key is to understand how your company tags one-time vendors. The first report for one-time vendors is an aggregate dollar and a record count analysis to determine the dollar materiality and frequency of use. The second level of analysis is anomalies in the transactional data.

LINKAGE OF IDENTIFIED ENTITIES TO TRANSACTIONAL DATA FILE

Within the shell company fraud data analytics an exact match to the payroll database or an exact duplicate match by itself is sufficient to cause the auditor to select the entity for fraud testing. However, linking the transactions to the entity number is the convincing piece of information.

Let's assume we perform a duplicate address test in the vendor master file. We identify two vendors with a duplicate address and two different names. As a general rule, once your shell company testing has identified an entity of interest, attach the transactional history to the vendor or customer number and summarize the activity by dollar and record count. Let's look at two different situations:

1. Vendor one has a spend level of $1 million and vendor two has a zero spend level. Obviously, there is no current fraud risk when the vendor spend level is zero.
2. Vendor one has a spend level of $1 million and vendor two has a spend level of $750,000. The transactional history should be analyzed for duplicate transaction history or transactional anomalies—that is, the $750,000 invoice number pattern is a sequential pattern.

FRAUD DATA ANALYTICS SCORING SHEET

The scoring sheet is a valuable tool in analyzing entities or transactions for the red flags associated with the fraud scenario. It is based on the totality of the red flags associated with the fraud data analytics plan versus one red flag. Seldom is there one red flag which is strong enough to suggest that a fraud scenario is occurring in a core business system.

The scoring sheet should weight each red flag on a score of one, two, and three. The evidence of the red flag would cause a score for the red flag. The scoring sheet would then total all of the red flags. The higher the score, the more persuasive the evidence is for sample selection purposes.

 ## IMPACT OF FRAUD CONCEALMENT SOPHISTICATION SHELL COMPANIES

In Chapter 3, we discussed the three levels of concealment. The level of sophistication has a direct impact on the type of data interrogation routine, as described in this section.

The exception to the rule is the assumed entity shell company. Impact of fraud concealment sophistication shell companies operating as an assumed identity is not critical on the fraud data analysis routine. In the permanent takeover, the change to the critical field causes the sample selection. In the temporary takeover, it is the pattern and frequency of the event linked to a person that should cause the sample selection. Yes, the data field can have the same sophistication in hiding the entity, but the change to the critical field causes the sample selection.

Low Sophistication and Internal Perpetrator

There is a direct linkage between the perpetrator identity and the shell company identity. The fraud data analytics should compare the employee database to the vendor or customer database using the specific identification strategy using an exact match. Using the address field, the match would occur on street, city, state, and postal code.

Low sophistication should always start with exact match because of the simplicity of designing the test. If the exact match test does not provide a sample, then consideration should be provided to using the close or related match testing. The close match may focus on the postal code or the area code of a telephone number. The related match may identify all entities within a radius of the corporate office using the postal code field.

Medium Sophistication and Internal Perpetrator

There is a limited linkage between the perpetrator and the shell company. Some aspect of the identity will match; however, the matching information by itself is not sufficient to cause a sample selection. That is, the vendor and employee use the same bank but have different bank account numbers or the vendor and employee have the same city, state, and Zip Code but have a different street address. When the fraud data analytics is focusing on a specific person, there may be sufficient linkage for a sample selection at the medium sophistication.

To illustrate data interrogation at the medium level, there is an allegation that someone in the accounts payable function has created a shell company. The employee payroll records indicate that the employee has direct deposit at bank XYZ. The human resource records also indicate a start date of April 1, 2016. The fraud data analysis plan then would identify all vendors using bank XYZ that were added to the master file on or after the employee start date.

High Sophistication and Internal Perpetrator

There is no linkage between the perpetrator and the shell company. The use of the matching technique does not work. The fraud data analytics plan should focus on the fraudulent action statement and then link back to the entity structure.

Low Sophistication and External Perpetrator Permutation

This is either a hidden entity or a pass-through scheme. Pass-through fraudulent action is discussed in Chapter 7. Fraud data analytics should compare vendors to vendors, customers to customers, or vendor and customer using the exact match. If exact match is not successful, then the close match or related match should be considered.

Medium Sophistication and External Perpetrator

This is similar to the medium sophistication and internal perpetrator fraud data analysis.

High Sophistication and External Perpetrator

This is similar to the high sophistication and internal perpetrator fraud data analysis.

BUILDING THE FRAUD DATA PROFILE FOR A SHELL COMPANY

The process of building a fraud data profile starts with identifying the data that links to the fraud scenario. Typically, this is the easy part of the process. The second step is to identify how the data element links to the fraud scenario. The third step is to describe the characteristics of the data in a manner that allows a fraud data interrogation routine to be developed. The last step is to program the search routine. I want to stress that step three is critical to designing the search routine.

My goal in this section is to illustrate the types of data red flags that the auditor could search for. In reality, the profile must be built for the company and country where the business is located. With a red flag test, there are always going to be exceptions. This is why the weight of all the red flags is more indicative of a fraud scenario versus one red flag. This is why the scoring sheet concept is so important.

To illustrate, in the email field, we will indicate that email addresses using a public email service versus a company designation is a red flag. Just before I started writing this book, I received an email from a prominent attorney who was using AOL as his email address. Hey, you never know.

Shell Company Profile Information

Name

Shell companies often have nondescriptive names. Nondescriptive names tend to have a limited number of alpha positions, and contain abbreviations or initials:

- One search is to look for names with a limited number of consonants in the name. Obviously depending on where in the world the search is performed will impact the variable. In the United States we use five consonants. We strip out the "Inc.," spaces, vowels, or special symbols and then count the alpha string.
- Shell companies often use initials in the name. In this case, we strip out all the alpha and numeric positions and count the special symbols. Since

abbreviations use periods, the count should focus on periods versus all special symbols.

- In a second test for initials, we strip out the "Inc.," spaces, vowels, or special symbols, and then count the alpha string.
- From a data interpretation strategy, search for company names that are nondescriptive of what products or services the company provided. Publicly traded companies are generally not considered within this test.

Street Address

The street address field typically has two fields, street address one and street address two. Some databases have a physical address, a payment address, and salesperson contact information. Since address is a critical field in searching for shell companies, it is important that the auditor understand the categories of addresses that can be identified in the fraud data analytics:

- Street address, which has a number and a street name.
- P.O. box, which is either a bank lockbox or a postal address.
- A public mailbox service company, such as UPS.
- A private mailbox service company. These addresses are either a high-profile address, such as Park Ave, NYC, or CPA firms that provide bookkeeping services for companies.
- A mail forwarding address. To illustrate, Regus advertises that they have over 3,000 locations around the world that can function as a virtual office. A second company, My US, advertises they are the most trusted consolidation company in the world, operating in over 220 companies worldwide. USA2ME advertises that you can have all your USA mail sent to your USA2ME address and then have the mail forwarded to you. Mailbox Forwarding advertises that since your mailbox will be a real physical street address, not a PO box, you can receive mail and packages from carriers such as UPS and FedEx, use the address with financial institutions, and portray a more professional image. I am not questioning the business integrity of these companies but rather, pointing out how a physical address, street and number, may be a mail forwarding company. The first step with mailbox service companies or mailbox forwarding companies is to understand the address format used by the company. The second step is to identify all customers or vendors using that category of address.
- Missing address is a test designed to search for shell companies in category one. In reality, vendor database address field might be blank because the

vendor requires electronic payment. Government vendors' address fields often blank.

▪ Duplicate address is a test designed to search for the hidden entity.

▪ Anomaly—when the vendor address links to a public mailbox company, a private mailbox company, or a mail forwarding company. As a word of caution, small companies or companies operating from their home use these types of services.

▪ Programming these search routine requires the fraud auditor to use creativity in building the search routines. The following are examples of using creativity to search for the address anomalies:

    ▪ Strip out all alpha, spaces, and special symbols and search for duplicate numeric strings in the vendor database or between payroll and vendor databases. In searching for duplicate numeric strings the Zip Code field should be linked to street number to minimize false positives.

    ▪ Mailbox forwarding companies often embed a customer number in the street address. Therefore, strip features on the address field from right to left. First, strip the numeric, then the alpha; this should leave a numeric string.

Country, City, State, and Postal Code

One belief is that the shell corporation would be within a radius of the corporation or within the state to avoid crossing state or country lines. We believe this is more likely with low- to medium-sophistication perpetrators than high sophistication. The search routine could identify entities within the defined geographic location. The routine is enhanced when it can be linked to a person and a creation date.

Telephone Number

Shell corporations often use mobile lines when no physical office exists. Hidden entities may not want the expense of a second line. Salespeople know that their telephone number is their lifeline to their sales effort. The following tests are useful in the telephone number field:

▪ Missing telephone number is indicative of a shell company because the perpetrator is trying to control the flow of information or the shell company does not have a telephone number.

▪ Matching telephone number between payroll database and the vendor or customer database is indicative of a shell company.

▪ Duplicate telephone number is indicative of the hidden entity or a pass-through scheme involving a salesperson at a real company.

Bank Routing Number

Payments are transferred either by wire or address. The routing number can be used to correlate to prospective individuals. The theory is simple; the perpetrators are smart enough not to use their personal bank account but would use the same bank for their shell corporation bank account.

- Missing—indicative of a shell company because the perpetrator is trying to avoid a match between the shell company and the perpetrator.
- Matching testing—searching for a match between two different master files. The most common test is between vendor and employee. The test should also be performed between employee and customer to identify a pass-through when a salesperson is committing a pass-through scheme.
- Duplicate testing—searching for duplicate bank account numbers in the master file.
- Anomaly—an entity that has no address or bank account number. If the data analysis is focusing on a specific person, then identifying all vendors that use the same bank may be useful.

Government Registration Number

The government registration number is indicative of one company using different names or a hidden entity shell company. I should mention operating as a DBA is an acceptable process, although the DBA should be registered. The duplicate search routine would also detect the hidden entity.

- Missing—the lack of government registration numbers is common in the USA because until recent years there was no need to collect the information. In Europe and other parts of the world, a missing government registration number would be a glaring red flag.
- Matching—searching for a match between two different master files.
- Duplicate—searching for a duplicate government registration number in the master file.
- Anomaly—a partnership or corporation and the government registration number is in the format of an individual's government registration number.

Email Address

Almost everyone has at least one email address. Individuals may use their business email and their personal email. Personal emails are attached to a business.

- Missing—the lack of an email address is not common and should be considered an important red flag.

- Matching—searching for a match between two different master files.
- Duplicate—searching for a duplicate email address in the master file.
- Anomaly—a business using a public email system such as AOL or Gmail.

Create Date

Most fraud scenarios are disclosed within four years or less according to most fraud studies. The theory is simple: If the company has been active on the master file for greater than 48 months, then it would suggest the company is a real company. No, I would not give this a high rating, but it is a useful guide. Create dates on weekends and holidays are useful for off-period analysis.

Create Time

This is useful for off-period analysis. The search is for an entity created during nonbusiness hours, which is a red flag.

ID of Record Creator

There are two categories of individuals. The user ID that by job description is responsible for creating or changing entities, and individuals who may create an entity but this is not part of their normal duties. In the vendor master file, these duties are typically limited to a small group of individuals. In the customer master file, depending on the company and industry, the number of individuals that can create or change a customer master file can be large. The missing, matching, and duplicate test is generally not very useful on this data element. The importance of the data element is linking the event to a person and the search for individuals accessing the master file where that is not part of their normal job duties.

Shell Companies Operating as Customers

Shell companies are usually associated with vendors; however, shell companies can also be used to commit asset misappropriation schemes, discussed in Chapter 12, and financial statement fraud, discussed in Chapter 14. The same identifying information should be interrogated for shell customers using the same types of tests. In addition the credit code or credit amount should be included. For material financial statement fraud, the credit code would be high for a new customer. For asset misappropriation, the credit code will determine the amount of false invoices.

Shell Companies as Employees

Payroll shell companies are referred to as ghost employees. The category description of ghost employees is similar to the preceding categories; the categories' names need to be changed to employee names. Ghost employees are discussed in Chapter 11.

FRAUD AUDIT PROCEDURES TO IDENTIFY THE SHELL CORPORATION

The primary purpose of this book is to explain a fraud data analytics methodology for fraud scenarios versus fraud auditing procedures to examine documents. However, understanding how the fraud links to the fraud data analytics is also critical. In this chapter, we will illustrate the type of evidence gathering procedures necessary to link to your fraud data analytics program.

Before reading, some will believe the procedures are audit related and some will believe the procedures are investigative. Just ask yourself the following question: Would your test of the new vendor procedures reveal a shell company? If not, continue reading. For those still undecided, consider the rules of audit evidence as it relates to qualitative evidence. The highest form of qualitative evidence is externally created and externally stored. The steps described in entity, legal, physical, business capacity, and reference checking fit that bill. One more example: In a financial audit of accounts receivable, auditors send confirmations, which is externally created and externally stored evidence. Remember, it makes no sense to identify a fraudulent transaction in your sample if your audit procedure cannot identify the fraud scenario.

The four entity verification procedures are: legal creation, physical location, business capacity, and reference checking. The first step in entity verification is to determine that the control procedures were adhered to in recording the entity into the business system. Identification of the people associated with establishing an entity structure must be performed for comparison purposes in future fraud audit procedures. The intent is not control testing, but the gathering of information to establish a basis for entity verification.

Entity Verification

The order of verification is: analyzing the legal existence, verifying physical existence, evaluating business capacity, and reference checking. The first three procedures can generally be performed in a covert manner; however, reference checking tends to be overt, and so the procedure is generally performed last.

Verify Legal Existence

- Government registration. All entities have a legal registration. Employees have birth records and corporations have registration requirements with an applicable government office. The first step is to establish whether the entity is legally created, then gather identifying information that can eventually be linked to other pertinent information. Names of registrars; officers' addresses; and dates related to entity creation, dissolutions, or changes tend to be the critical information. In one case, the name on a government registration document matched a name on a packing slip for a shell company. This was the first red flag that eventually led to a three-million-dollar pass-through fraud scheme.
- Government registration date. Compare the government registration date to the date of the first business transactions. For vendor invoices, compare the first invoice date to the government registration date.
- Trade associations. When an entity is a member of a trade association, a business's membership provides evidence that the entity is a real one or provides a lead to the true ownership. The failure of the business to be a member of any logical trade group is a red flag because most real companies belong to at least one trade organization.
- Use of Internet search companies such as Lexus Nexus, which gathers public record information that is made accessible to clients. A search of a company on Lexus Nexus can find if any public records exist on the company and what types of records they are.
- **Conclusion:** The Company is legally created. We are looking for a linkage on the government database to internal employees, linkage to known vendors, or the absence of identifying information. We are also focusing on dates, addresses, and formation companies.

Verify Physical Existence

- Telephone verification. By contacting the entity, you verify physical existence by the mere fact of the call being answered. Then it becomes a question of how the call is answered. How the call is answered is part of the evidence associated with the audit judgment of whether the entity is real or false. By calling, the possible outcomes are: the telephone is disconnected; someone answers in the name of a different entity; or someone answers in the name of the entity in question. Interview skills are the critical skill to ensure the success of the procedure. Here a few practical tips:
    - Use a telephone in the area code of the company you are auditing. Area codes from out of the area may create a suspicion of why you are calling.

- Be prepared to provide an explanation as to why you are calling. Possible explanations are updating records, resolving internal problems, or tracking down misplaced original documents. Try not to raise suspicion at this stage of the audit.
- Have the documents readily available to ask questions or provide answers.
- Avoid calling multiple times, as a second telephone call raises suspicions.
- Remember, the entity you are calling may have Caller ID. Therefore, do not indicate that you are someone other than the person associated with the number identified.
- The manner in which a call is answered must be consistent with the anticipated business size.
- Internet search engines like Google can determine what physical structure is located at the known address, and whether the address is consistent with the entity structure. Often, the created entity scheme will use a personal residence address. Remember that many small businesses operate from the owner's personal residence, so, in this case, reference checking may be preferred in order to reveal that the entity does not conduct business.
- Site visit. By visiting the site, it can be determined what physical structure is located at the known address, and whether the address is consistent with the entity structure. Private detectives often will perform the procedure for a nominal charge, so the use of one may be useful for verifying entities that are not located in your geographic area. A significant international fraud was revealed by visiting the physical location, which determined that the business was a beverage store versus an international food brokering company.
- Public records can determine whether a government or business recognizes the entity as a real entity, and that the address is recognized by other entities. A legal instrument filed by banks securing a loan indicates that the bank believes the entity is real. The loan instrument may provide clues that link to the perpetrator.
- The IRS website can provide federal identification verification, which will determine whether the federal identification number or Social Security number matches the name associated with the ID number. In many parts of the world, corporations will have a VAT number, which can be confirmed with a government ministry and provide a source of data intelligence.
- The Internet has extensive databases and search engines to gather information. At the simplest level, Google is an excellent starting point. At the

advanced level, there are research companies that have made an art of how to navigate the Internet.

- **Conclusion:** Is the known physical location of the business consistent with the business on the vendor invoice?

Business Capacity Test

- Proof of insurance. Real companies tend to have insurance. The fraud testing procedure would consist of a request of the certificate of insurance. Fortunately, such a request is a normal control procedure in many companies, but for fraud audit purposes, the need is to examine the certificate to note the date of coverage and types of coverage. The lack of workers' compensation might indicate that the company has no employees. Caution: Workers' compensation can be purchased through payroll companies.
- Employees. A company telephone directory provides evidence that the company has employees. By calling the company, you are often referred to the company telephone directory when you do not know an employee's extension. The lack of a telephone directory might be a clue.
- A public record filed by a bank or a financing company can indicate a lien has been filed against the described asset. It also indicates that the bank recognizes the entity as a real company.
- Shipping documents, such as a bill of lading, indicate the source of the shipment, therefore providing the name of the company that shipped the goods.
- Vendor invoices. What software produced the document? Was it Excel or consistent with a known database accounting software? Is the product description consistent with industry standards as to sku numbers or alpha descriptions?
- Websites. If a company has a website, does such a site provide matching information about the businesses and services offered? An examination of a website determined that the goods purchased from the company were not consistent with the website, revealing a real company involved in a pass-through scheme with an internal employee.
- **Conclusion:** We believe the business capacity test is the most important analysis. The determination is simple: Does the company listed on the invoice have the capacity to provide the goods or services listed on the invoice?

Reference Checking

- Professional associations. Is the entity recognized by a trade association? Such organizations can also provide useful information on trade practice and trends, which in turn can be used to corroborate representations made by individuals.
- Competitors. Contact competitors to establish that the entity conducts business consistent with the goods and services described on the invoice. Competitors may also provide other information regarding ownership and business conflicts.
- Media searches. Information published regarding the entity may provide names, services, and legal actions regarding the entity. Advertisements by the entity would suggest the existence of the entity and describe the type of services provided by the entity.
- **Conclusion:** Is the business known by the industry?

Summary of Intelligence Information Regarding Shell Companies

The legal, physical, business capacity, and reference checking provides a sound methodology for gathering evidence that an entity is a shell company versus a real company. The process is not one-dimensional, but rather a process of collecting and analyzing information that correlates to the fraud scenario. The identification of red flags in both the entity structure and the transactional data provides the auditor with sufficient circumstantial evidence to recommend an investigation process through the legal system.

 SUMMARY

Shell companies are widely used by people who want to steal company assets, ranging from internal persons to organized crime groups. Management may create a shell company as a way to disguise bribe payments. Banks search for shell companies in their AML programs. From a fraud data analytics perspective, once a shell company is found, there is no question that someone is committing a fraudulent act. As a personal recommendation, I suggest starting your fraud data analytics journey with the search for shell companies. By using the fraud data analytics methodology on something as simple to understand as shell companies, the fraud auditor will improve the art form of the methodology.

CHAPTER SEVEN

Fraud Data Analytics for Fraudulent Disbursements

For the perpetrator, fraud in the disbursement cycle is like a child in a candy store. The child has a favorite candy, and the child seldom takes one piece of candy. For fraud data analytics, the favorite candy is the fraud scenario, and frequency analysis is the amount of candy. Just like the candy store, the choice of candy is limited to the candy in the store; for the perpetrator, the number of fraud scenarios is limited to the number of fraud scenarios in the fraud risk structure that links to the perpetrator.

INHERENT FRAUD SCHEMES IN FRAUDULENT DISBURSEMENTS

The inherent scheme fraud theory states that the number of inherent schemes and scenarios are finite and predictable. The fraud auditor will need to convert the generic inherent scheme to a company-specific fraud scenario, and if a targeted expenditure audit, to the language of the expenditure area.

The inherent scheme comprises an entity structure that is a supplier and a fraudulent action. The following fraudulent actions comprise the list of inherent disbursement schemes. To create the fraud scenario, the fraud auditor will need to link the person committing the scheme and the entity structure to the action statement. The auditor should write the scenario statement consistent with the approach described in Chapter 2.

1. *False billing* is the process of paying a shell company for goods or services that are not received.
2. *Pass-through billing* is the process of paying for goods and services that are received when three entities are involved. The three entities are described later in the chapter.
3. *Overbilling* is the process of paying for goods and services that are received from a real vendor. There are three major categories of overbilling based on the person committing the scenario and the method of overbilling:
   a) Vendor alone by exploiting weaknesses in the internal controls.
   b) Vendor in collusion with an internal source, with the overbilling occurring before the procurement process. This permutation is discussed in Chapter 8.
   c) Vendor in collusion with an internal source with the overbilling occurring after the procurement process, avoiding the procurement process or through the false administration of the purchase order or contract.
   d) The methods of overbilling are:
      i. Overcharging on price.
      ii. Charging:
         1. For a higher quantity than delivered.
         2. For a higher quality than delivered (product substitution).
         3. For goods/services that are not needed by the company.
      iii. False charges on real invoices.
      iv. False add-on charges.
      v. Intentional duplicate payment.
      vi. Intentional overpayment and divert refund.
4. *A personal expense* is the process of paying for personal expenses that are inuring to the benefit of the internal person.
5. *Disguised expenditures* occur when an internal person purchases goods with the intent of committing a theft scheme.
6. *Conflict of interest* is the process of paying for goods or services that are received from the vendor but an internal employee has an undisclosed ownership in the vendor. Conflict of interest in the selection process, with no ownership, is discussed in Chapter 8.

The easiest way to explain the process of converting the inherent scheme to a fraud scenario for a targeted expenditure is to illustrate the concept.

For purposes of illustration, we will assume internal collusion with an internal budget owner, the expenditure area is professional consultant fees, and the consultant is a real supplier that is overbilling on the contract:

1. The internal budget owner operating in collusion with the consultant charges a higher hourly rate on the invoice than the hourly rate in the contract, resulting in the loss of company funds. The reason for the higher hourly rate is the concealment strategy.
2. The internal budget owner operating in collusion with the consultant charges for more hours worked than the number of hours originally authorized in the contract, resulting in the loss of company funds. The internal person approves the invoice knowing that hours are overstated, which is part of the concealment strategy.
3. The internal budget owner operating in collusion with the consultant charges for hours worked by a para-professional at the consultant's rate, resulting in the loss of company funds. The internal person approves the invoice knowing that hours were performed by someone else, which is part of the concealment strategy.
4. The internal budget owner operating in collusion with the consultant lists fictitious services on the invoice, resulting in the loss of company funds. The internal person approves the invoice knowing services were not performed, which is part of the concealment strategy. Also, in all four examples the internal person receives a kickback from the consultant.

IDENTIFYING THE KEY DATA: PURCHASE ORDER, INVOICE, PAYMENT, AND RECEIPT

The expenditure cycle comprises a purchase requisition, purchase order, vendor invoice, receiving document, and the payment, which can occur through a paper check or electronic transfer. The understanding of the information on these documents becomes the basis of fraud data analytics for the fraud action. Consistent with Chapter 3, the documents all have a control number, a control date, an amount, a line item description, and are recorded to a general ledger account.

As part of the planning process, the fraud auditor should understand when the document is issued, by what function, and the true internal control effectiveness. Issuing purchase orders after receiving the vendor invoice implies that the purchasing function was circumvented; therefore, the internal control effectiveness is reduced to a low level. If separation of duty concepts is not enforced, then control effectiveness must be considered low. The use of internal control avoidance testing can provide a good barometer as to the true internal control effectiveness.

The requisition might be initiated through a document or through an automated reorder process. The requisition is more critical in the search for procurement fraud scenarios versus payment fraud scenarios.

The purchase order is intended to create a contract between the vendor and your company. The placement of the purchase order is what causes the vendor to supply the goods or services. It is important to understand when purchase orders are issued within your company. Is the purchase order created before the vendor invoice, is the purchase order issued after the invoice, or is no purchase order issued? The use of disaggregated analysis on when the purchase order was issued may provide a clue to fraud opportunity.

The receiving document is created upon the receipt of the tangible goods to signify both the quantity and quality of the goods are consistent with the description on the purchase order. It is important to understand what tangible goods are received through the receiving function and what tangible goods bypass the receiving function.

The proverbial three matches occur when the vendor invoice matches the purchase order and the receiving document. This process initiates the payment to the supplier.

The payment occurs through a paper check or through an electronic payment. It is important to understand what causes a payment to occur. Is it through a three match or through an internal approval signature? If the payment occurs through electronic payment, then we know what bank account received the funds. If the payment occurs through a paper check, then all we know in data analytics is the payee listed on the check.

DOCUMENTS AND FRAUD DATA ANALYTICS

Fraud data analytics for the fraud action statement is the process of examining the purchase order, the vendor invoice, the receiving document, the payment, and the general ledger account for red flags consistent with the specific fraud scenario. The fraud auditor has two approaches: the compliance approach or the fraud scenario approach.

The first approach assumes the auditor is performing a compliance-based audit. In the compliance approach, the auditor searches for noncompliance with a procedure. Then the auditor searches for a pattern or frequency of noncompliance associated with a person or entity. In the compliance approach, the auditor must link the noncompliance to a fraud scenario either through additional fraud data analytics or through audit testing procedures. In the compliance audit the fraud data analytics is based on the internal control avoidance strategy.

The second approach is based on the fraud scenario approach, which is the basis of this book. In this approach, we build fraud data profile of the fraud action using the control number, date, amount, and description on the purchase order, vendor invoice, payment, and the general ledger account. In the scenario approach, the fraud data analytics strategies of specific identification, internal control avoidance, data interpretation, and number anomaly are the basis of the fraud data analytics approach.

 ## FDA PLANNING REPORTS FOR DISBURSEMENT FRAUD

The first step is to gather data to identify homogeneous data sets within the expenditure data file. The second step is to use disaggregated analysis to further shrink the homogeneous data set based on specific fraud scenarios. The homogeneous data sets are created based on the scope of the audit. A few illustrations are:

1. Major expenditure categories within the company.
2. Number of records in one year for purchase orders, invoices, receiving reports, and payments.
3. Number of vendors on master file, as to active and inactive.
4. For vendor master file testing, how many fields are blank versus populated.
5. Purchase order—compare purchase order date to invoice date summarizing by dollar and frequency purchase orders issued before, equal to, or after the invoice.
6. Vendor invoice summary—providing aggregate spend level, number of records, maximum invoice amount, minimum invoice amount, and average invoice amount.
7. Number of payments that occur through paper check and electronic payment by vendor.
8. Vendor invoices with and without a purchase order or vendor invoices with no independent receiving document.
9. Identify nuisance—nuisance vendors are those vendors that will create false positives by the nature of the vendor or the type of expenditure

(e.g., in a duplicate date test a delivery service company may have many invoices on the same date). The plan should attempt to identify these vendors before running the test. This concept is offered from a practical perspective versus a fraud concept.

FDA FOR SHELL COMPANY FALSE BILLING SCHEMES

The inherent scheme structure has two components for fraud data analytics plan. The shell company is discussed in Chapter 6. The fraud data profile for the false billing action statement can be characterized by these nine tendencies:

1. Invoice amount has the following tendencies:
   a) Invoice amount is below a threshold, requiring a second approval.
   b) The minimum invoice is greater than $1,000. An exception to this guideline is the first invoice, which may be a small amount to avoid scrutiny on setting up a new vendor.
   c) The amount may be an even amount or a recurring amount. The type of expenditure impacts the use of even number theory or recurring amount theory.
2. Invoice number has the following tendencies:
   a) Invoice number is a sequential pattern.
   b) The first number is a low number, often 1,100 or 1,000.
   c) If not a low number, the invoice will be an even number.
3. Invoice date has the following tendencies:
   a) The invoice date field by itself is not a critical date; it is possible that there could be a tendency to create the invoice the same day of the week.
   b) Invoice dates consistent with a regular pattern of being created on non-business days.
   c) The invoice date is critical in the comparisons to purchase order date and payment date. For purchase order date, when the purchase order is issued after the invoice, it may indicate circumvention of purchasing. For payment date, we are searching for speed of payment.
4. Invoice description has the following tendencies:
   a) Tends to be for services.
   b) If for tangible goods, the anomaly is based on the lack of a numeric or alpha description consistent with the tangible goods.
   c) Description on the invoice is vague (e.g., professional services).

d) General ledger accounts are an easy way to identify service-based invoices.

5. Other tendencies of the false billing scenario:
   a) The number of invoices is 52 (one a week) or less.
   b) The aggregate spend level with the vendor is in the bottom third of all vendors.
   c) There is no purchase order; purchase order is an open purchase order or the purchase order is issued after the invoice.
   d) If the scheme is perpetrated by someone in accounts payable, they may use a dormant open purchase order.
   e) Speed of payment is faster than normal customer payment terms.

6. Specification identification:
   a) As a reminder, specification identification is the process of identifying a specific attribute of a purchase order, invoice, or payment that would cause the selection of a vendor for testing. While some scenarios have some great red flags, it is the weight of all the red flags that should cause the selection of the transaction or entity for audit examination.
   b) The fraud data analytics scoring sheet is a critical tool within the specific identification strategy. To illustrate how the scoring sheet would highlight a vendor transaction history of expenditures:
      i. There are no purchase orders associated with the invoices.
      ii. Number of invoices is 12 over a 12-month period.
      iii. Invoice total amount is an even amount.
      iv. Invoice amount is a recurring amount for the 12-month period.
      v. Invoice number pattern is a sequential pattern.
      vi. First invoice number is a low number.
      vii. The aggregate of attributes causes the selection of the vendor versus one specific attribute.
   c) The following red flags should be ranked the highest for the search for a false billing:
      i. A sequential invoice number pattern. At a minimum, it appears the vendor has one customer. That customer would be your company.
      ii. All invoice amounts are below a control threshold. The person committing the scheme wants low visibility.
      iii. General ledger category associated with services.

7. Internal control avoidance:
   a) Structuring vendor invoices is the process of splitting one vendor invoice that would exceed the control level into two or more invoices to

avoid a control level. In vendor invoice structuring, the fraud auditor needs to decide if fraud data analytics will focus on total invoice amount or line items on an invoice. The matching then occurs on invoice date and/or the line item description. The second consideration is whether the structured invoice is associated with one vendor number or two or more vendor numbers.

b) Using one vendor number, the invoices are structured to stay below the control threshold. Structuring is when two or more transactions in the aggregate exceed a control level. The FDA should search for two invoices associated with a common vendor number which have a match on invoice date or invoice number and that each invoice is below a control threshold; however, in the aggregate the invoices exceed the control threshold.

c) Using two or more vendors, each vendor invoice is below the control threshold; however, in the aggregate the invoices exceed a control level. The testing for hidden entities in Chapter 6 is the start point. Then search for duplicate pattern associated with invoice number, invoice date, or invoice amount.

d) The challenge is linking the two or more vendors to a common person. The linkage could occur through the person that created the entity, department number, or project number.

e) Layering invoices is similar to structuring invoices; however, in layering the split invoices are recorded in multiple cost centers or companies where an individual has management control.

f) Off-period analysis is used when the person committing the fraud scenario works in the accounts payable function.

g) Illogical order of purchase order and invoice is not typically found because the person wants to maintain a low visibility around their activity.

h) Speed of payment is an excellent analysis especially if the motive for committing the fraud scenario is associated with a personal vice.

i) Manual transaction analysis is not critical unless the scheme is being perpetrated by someone in accounts payable.

8. Data interpretation:

a) The data interpretation strategy is required when the perpetrator conceals the false billing scheme at a high level.

b) The fraud auditor needs to make certain assumptions in their analysis that may or may not be supported by an authoritative study. Stated differently, the fraud auditor will make assumptions based on their professional experience.

c) The first assumption I make is that the vendor's revenue is equal to 5 percent of the aggregate spend level in accounts payable. I use this assumption to interpret whether the patterns in the specific identification and internal control avoidance are consistent with my expectations of a company operating at a certain revenue level.

d) To provide an easy illustration:
   i. Annual spend level with the vendor is $100,000.
   ii. Using the 5 percent, I would project revenue at $2 million.
   iii. The number of invoices submitted recorded in accounts payable is eight.
   iv. Average invoice amount is $12,500.
   v. The vendor should have issued 160 invoices, assuming the $12,500 is representative of vendor's average invoice amount.
   vi. The range of invoice numbers in accounts payable is 125. The first invoice is 1119 and the last invoice number is 1244 for a range of 125 invoices. Therefore, the assumed range of 160 is greater than the range in accounts payable of 125.
   vii. Since the range is not consistent with my expectations, the transactional history would suggest the vendor is a false entity.
   viii. Reminder: I am also considering attributes identified in the shell company analysis as the basis of the sample selection.

e) Sample selection in the data interpretation strategy is not for the faint of heart. It requires a high degree of judgment. However, using the fraud data analytics scoring sheet, it is the weight of the attributes versus a specific attribute.

9. Number anomaly:
   a) In vendor invoice number anomaly we summarize invoices based on the invoice amount. The report has three columns, the invoice amount, the frequency of the amount, and the aggregate amount associated with the invoice amount.
   b) The first test is for round number analysis. The auditor needs to define which round amounts are included in the analysis. Based on the selected round number amounts, the second analysis is the frequency of a vendor number occurring within the round number. Once the low frequency has been excluded, the fraud data analytics should search for a pattern in the invoice number, date, or description.

c) The recurring number analysis is similar to the even number test, except the first trigger is any invoice amount that occurs more than once. The second test is to identify vendors in the recurring number that have at least five occurrences. Once again, the auditor should look for a pattern in the invoice number, date, or description.

UNDERSTANDING HOW PASS-THROUGH SCHEMES OPERATE

Pass-through schemes provide the illusion of an arm's-length business transaction with a real company. The goods and services are received, the internal three-way match is in full compliance, and the internal person has committed the fraud scenario, either alone or in collusion with an external party. To further complicate the matter, the middle company, which is the pass-through company, is either a shell company or a real company. There are six permutations of the pass-through entity scheme.

The pass-through schemes are similar in structure, but very different in the fraud data analytics. The fraud auditor will need to build a separate plan for each version of the pass-through scheme. The starting point is to understand how the entity structure operates:

- The shell company pass-through scheme is composed of three companies. There are two permutations of the shell company pass-through. The first company is your company, the second company is the shell company, and the third company is a real supplier. The shell company is controlled either by an internal person or by a salesperson at the third company, which is the supplier of the goods. Each version has a similar but different fraud data profile. In the false entity scheme both the entity and transaction analysis maybe effective in locating the shell company (Figure 7.1).
- The real company pass-through scheme is also composed of three companies. The first company is your company, the second company is a real supplier that is currently providing your company with goods or services, and the third company is also a real supplier and either is or is not currently providing your company with goods or services. There are four versions of the real pass-through scheme. The first three versions are similar; the fourth version is difficult to detect with fraud data analytics because the scenario occurs through the general contractor versus your internal database (Figure 7.2).

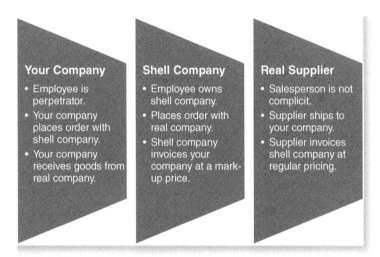

FIGURE 7.1 Pass-Through Entity: Internal Person

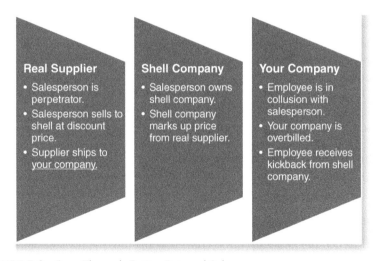

FIGURE 7.2 Pass-Through Entity: External Salesperson

Version One Description

The shell company pass-through scheme when the internal person creates the shell company.

The first version is when the shell company is created by an internal person. The internal person causes a purchase order to be issued to the shell company. The shell corporation has no assets or employees, so the shell corporation in essence purchases the goods from a real company. The real company ships the goods directly to your company. The real company invoices the shell company and the shell company invoices your company at a markup from the real invoice. Thereby, the scenario complies with the three-match procedure of a purchase order, invoice, and receipt. The fraud profit for the internal person is the difference between what the real company charges and what the shell company charges your company. The conversion cycle occurs by the internal perpetrator controlling the shell company bank account.

Version Two Description

The shell company pass-through scheme by the external salesperson from real company.

The second version is when the shell company is created by a salesperson at the real company. In the salesperson version the salesperson pays a bribe to the internal person to purchase from the shell company versus the real supplier. The internal person issues a purchase order to the shell company. The real company ships directly to your company, the real company invoices the shell company, and the shell company invoices your company. The conversion cycle occurs when the salesperson that created the shell company pays a kickback to the internal person.

The fraud data profile for both shell company pass-through schemes is similar but both schemes have a few unique attributes. Using the pass-through company invoice, the fraud auditor would interrogate the data as follows:

1. Invoice amount has the following tendencies:
   a) Unlike the false billing scheme, the invoice amount does not need to stay below a control threshold. The amount of the invoice is based on the internal order versus the false billing perpetrator's desire to remain below a control threshold.
   b) When the pass-through is created by the internal person, the invoice amount has a higher tendency to be an even amount.
2. Invoice number has the following tendencies:
   a) Similar to the false billing, the invoice number pattern starts with a low invoice number.
   b) Version one has a sequential pattern of invoice numbers.
   c) Version two has a limited range pattern, or an illogical pattern of invoice numbers. The reason is that the salesperson from the real supplier might be perpetrating the scheme with more than one customer.

d) When the perpetrator is sophisticated, the perpetrator starts the invoice number with a high invoice number. The audit procedure of comparing the incorporation date to the first invoice date would be the red flag.

3. Invoice date has the following tendencies:
   a) The invoice date is compared to the purchase order date for speed of processing.
   b) The date is used for speed of payment analysis.

4. Invoice description has the following tendencies:
   a) Tends to be for supply items versus inventory items.
   b) Equipment rental charges also are related to the pass-through scheme.
   c) The use of the general ledger account number is useful in identifying invoices that are associated with the pass-through scheme.
   d) For tangible supply items, the description field should have both an alpha and a numeric description.
   e) The numeric description should be tested for the number of integers in the numeric description. The fraud theory is based on real companies that have product description files. The item sold is assigned either as product number or sku number. Real company product numbers tend to be nine integers or greater. In reality, the number of integers will vary by large or small suppliers. Therefore, when the product number has fewer integers than the normal supplier for your company, the numeric string becomes a useful red flag.
   f) The alpha description follows the same logic as the numeric string. The first test is for invoices having a missing alpha description. The test for the number of alpha positions may also be used but tends to be less effective.

5. Other tendencies associated with the pass-through scheme:
   a) The aggregate spend level with the vendor is in the middle third of all vendors.
   b) Unlike the false billing scheme, the number of invoices per year is not a critical item.
   c) Speed of payment is faster than normal customer payment terms. In the early stages of the scheme, speed of payment may mirror a real vendor; however, as the duration of the scheme goes beyond the six-month period, typically a faster pay pattern will occur.
   d) The purchase order is typically issued before the invoice and is most likely an open purchase order.
   e) The general ledger account tends to be an expense account, although recently reported cases have indicated that companies operating as a manufacturing representative have occurred for inventory items.

f) The new vendor is a government-preferred supplier where the original supplier did not have preferred government status.

Version Three Description

A real company operating as a pass-through scheme

In version three, the middle company is a real company and operates as the pass-through company. However, the real middle company is not in the business of selling the item that your company requires. The internal person conspires with the real middle company to purchase the real item from another supplier. Since the real middle company does not supply the item, the real middle company must purchase the item from another real company. The shipment of the item to your company typically occurs from second real company. However, the second real company may ship directly to real middle company, and the real middle company would ship to your company. The fraud scheme requires a markup on the price to your company and the middle real company paying the internal person a bribe. The final investigation may determine that the third company was either complicit or not complicit in the scheme.

FDA Plan

There is no entity analysis because the supplier is real.

The fraud data analytics must focus on the line-item description on the invoice or the purchase order. The analysis is searching for a vendor that the majority of purchases are within a specific expenditure area; therefore the anomaly is line item purchases that are not consistent with the primary expenditure associated with the supplier.

When a company uses a commodity code within its purchasing file, the identification of the anomaly is simple. The fraud data analytics summarizes purchases by vendor by commodity code. Vendors that have only one commodity can be excluded. The fraud auditor then uses data interpretation to review the remaining list for anomalies. If your company does not maintain commodity codes, the use of general ledger account number may provide a similar analysis. The final approach would be a summary by vendor, by line item. The last approach would require the most extensive manual effort by the fraud auditor.

The first audit step should be to review the selected vendor's website to determine if the vendor advertises the anomaly purchase on its website. If the item is not advertised, the fraud auditor has credible evidence to perform an investigation.

Version Four Description

A real company operating as a hidden entity operates as a pass-through scheme

The scheme operates exactly as version three, except the middle and real company have a common ownership. The entity is referred to as a hidden company, which was discussed in Chapter 6. In this scheme, your company will purchase from both the middle and the real company. The true purpose of the hidden pass-through is to avoid dollar control levels by splitting the purchase. In this scheme, the internal person may or may not be complicit in the scheme.

FDA Approach

The entity testing relies on the duplicate analysis, which was discussed in Chapter 6.

If the entity testing reveals hidden entities, the first step of the transaction analysis is linking the transactions to the vendor numbers identified in the hidden entity testing. In this way, instead of summarizing all transactions by vendor number, we are able to shrink the population to those transactions that link to the hidden entity number. The transaction analysis searches for duplicate line items between the two companies. If exact matches do not occur on the line item, using a general ledger number may provide a commonality for analysis. If line-item analysis is not effective, search for duplicate invoice number or invoice date between the two companies. Once the duplicate purchases are identified, summarize the transactions based on dollars and frequency to determine if the combined purchases exceed key control thresholds.

If entity analysis does not reveal hidden entities, then we need to search on all transactions. The first step is finding a common denominator between the transactions. Start with the general ledger code, department code, or cost center. Based on the common denominator match, search for a secondary match for duplicate information between the transactions such as invoice number, invoice date, line-item description, or purchase order number. The secondary match would be a duplicate test using a duplicate date and common line item between two different vendor numbers or a duplicate invoice number and common line-item description between two different vendor numbers.

One of the complexities associated with the scenario is how the supplier uses the two companies. In one situation, the second company's sole purpose is to facilitate the structuring of purchases to avoid your company's internal dollar levels. In essence, the second company is similar to a shell company. If this is true, then the fraud data analytics for one of the hidden entities would meet the profile of the false billing shell company.

If the second company is a free-standing company selling to multiple customers and various product lines, then we will search for duplicate line items between the two vendors and the secondary criterion would be date of purchase. As a practical suggestion, in the data usability analysis determine the quality of the line item descriptions in your files.

Version Five Description

Real business acts like a shell company but operates as a pass-through scheme

There are a number of businesses that operate as a legal pass-through company. Examples are manufacturing representatives, product brokers, and minority suppliers or government-preferred vendors. These types of suppliers are real and provide a necessary service to the business community. Unfortunately, there are suppliers in this category that are legally created, may have an office, but in essence function like a shell company because your company is actually procuring the item, and the real supplier is actually shipping the item to your location. The supplier in the middle simply functions as a legal pass-through.

FDA Plan

The entity analysis would first focus on those codes that may help identify a government-preferred supplier. Since the other vendors in this category may be operating from home offices or small offices, the address field may be of use. The fraud data analytics could focus on street addresses or known mailbox service addresses.

The transaction analysis would focus on invoice number and line-item descriptions. The invoice number pattern would most likely be a sequential pattern or a limited range pattern. The amount of the invoice would not be critical because the supplier was most likely selected on a sole source basis. In my experience, the invoice amount tends to be an even amount.

When the real pass-through company operates as a shell company, the invoice description tends to be vague or provide limited line-item descriptions as with a real supplier. The data interrogation should focus on the lack of alpha and numeric in the description. The numeric description may also have limited integers.

Version Six Description

FDA for prime contractor and subcontractor

The internal person directs the prime contractor to select a specific subcontractor and the internal person directs the prime contractor to pay the subcontractor a specific amount. The subcontractor then pays a bribe directly to the internal person. Generally there is no effective fraud data analytics plan to search for version six, unless there is a change order reflecting the subcontractor's identity or a line item on the general contractor's invoice, which provides a subcontractor's name.

Overbilling: The Vendor Alone by Exploiting the Vulnerabilities of the Company's Internal Controls

In this category, the basic assumption is that the internal source is not complicit in the overbilling. However, for whatever reason the internal controls do not prevent or detect the vendor from overbilling your company.

A vendor understands a company's receiving and payment internal controls in some ways better than the company itself. With this knowledge, the vendor exploits the vulnerabilities in the receiving and payment process. Although the illustrations are for tangible goods, the concept is similar for services. Typically the invoices are considered small dollar for the organization. The concept of small dollar is relevant to the organization versus the concept of a small number. The reason for the small-dollar invoice is the reduced visibility concealment concept, and often the internal controls are less robust for small-dollar invoices. Due to the volume of transactions in this analysis, filtering of activity is paramount to the success of the analysis. The more common scenarios perpetrated under this category of overbilling are:

1. Submitting an invoice where the amount or unit price on the invoice exceeds the purchase order. However, the price increase is within the acceptable tolerances that exist in a company's payment system. The fraud data analytics compares invoice amount to purchase order amount searching for invoices that exceed the purchase order amount within tolerances. The analysis may occur on line item or total invoice. The report should provide three columns of data. Each column of data will provide a frequency and aggregate dollar value of the vendor invoices. The first column is frequency and aggregate dollar value of vendor invoices that are equal to or less than the purchase order. The second column is the frequency and aggregate dollar value of invoices exceeding the purchase order within tolerance. The third column is the frequency and aggregate dollar value of vendor invoices exceeding the purchase order tolerance. The first selection process is based on frequency of occurrence of invoices exceeding purchase order within the tolerance and the dollar impact. The second selection is the invoices exceeding the purchase order tolerance level. If internal controls are operating effectively, then invoices exceeding

the purchase order should not be paid without a change order, or the overbilling scheme would indicate someone is overriding internal controls, which then indicates collusion between an internal and external party.

2. Submitting small-dollar invoices that are fictitious and are matched to an open purchase order. The first step is to identify open purchase orders. The attribute is a purchase order than has more than one invoice. The fraud data analytics summarizes by vendor by purchase order the invoices by small dollar and large dollar. The dollar value is based on what is large and small for your company. The report should provide both the aggregate dollar value and frequency of invoices by the two categories. The sample selection is based on data interpretation focusing on the line item descriptions, which tend to be vague, nondescriptive, or illogical for the noted vendor.

3. Submitting small-dollar invoices that are fictitious and do not require a purchase order. The first step is to identify invoices that have no purchase order number. The fraud data analytics summarizes by vendor the invoices by small dollar and large dollar. The dollar value is based on what is large and small for your company. The report should provide both the aggregate dollar value and frequency of invoices by the two categories. The sample selection is based on data interpretation focusing on whether the frequency and aggregate dollar value of the item on the small-dollar invoice is logical for the vendor and your company. The sample selection is based on data interpretation focusing on the line item descriptions, which tend to be vague, nondescriptive, or illogical for the noted vendor.

4. In scenarios two and three, the data interpretation is the challenge because of the sheer volume of transactions. The use of inclusion and exclusion theory is important when the analysis has a large number of transactions. So a few thoughts in refining the process:

   a) The starting point is to exclude vendors that have a low number of small-dollar invoices, based either on frequency or aggregate dollar amount.

   b) Exclude the nuisance vendors from the analysis.

   c) Use the number analysis on the remaining vendors. Exclude large-dollar invoices because the scenario is searching for a high frequency of small-dollar invoices. The number anomaly is searching for the vendor submitting small-dollar invoices of the same amount for goods or services not provided.

   d) Using the description field on the invoice, search for a description that has no numeric integers in the description line. The lack of integers indicates that the line item description was created manually versus from a customer's product database.

5. Submitting an invoice with a false add-on charge. The false charge might be either a line item on a real invoice or an invoice with just the false add-on charge. These charges range from shipping to restock charge. The difficulty is how to search and isolate the add-on charge. The following techniques have been helpful to identify the scenario:

   a) Start by summarizing the line-item description field on the vendor invoice and provide the frequency of occurrence of the line-item description. The report, while voluminous, will identify all line-item descriptions and variations of spellings in your database. The intent of the report is to act as a reference tool more than a sample selection tool.

   b) Establish a table of common names used to describe an add-on charge. The previous report is useful in identifying common names for add-on charges. The fraud data analytics creates a table of common names and performs an alpha string search for the common name in the line-item description. The report should summarize by vendor number by the common name providing the frequency of the line item and aggregate dollar value of the line items. The last line for each vendor should be all line items not on the table of common names. The sample selection is based on data interpretation focusing on whether the frequency and aggregate dollar value of the add-on charge are logical for the vendor or whether the add-on charge itself is logical.

   c) A second approach is to summarize by vendor number, by invoice number identifying the invoices having an add-on charge, and the invoices that do not have an add-on charge. The report should provide the frequency and aggregate dollar value of vendor invoices for both the have and have-not occurrence. The sample selection is based on data interpretation based on the anomaly of why some invoices have an add-on charge and other invoices do not have an add-on charge. The nature of the line-item description will be the first clue.

   d) A third approach is to search the invoice line for add-on charges through the quantity field on the line item. Line items on a vendor invoice tend to have a quantity of zero, blank, or one in the quantity field. The correct answer for the search depends on how accounts payable records line-item add-on charges in the database. The fraud data analytics is to identify by vendor invoice by invoice line all invoices that have blank, zero, or one in the quantity line. The sample selection is based on data interpretation focusing on whether the frequency and aggregate dollar value of the add-on charge are logical for the vendor.

6. The quantity on the invoice is greater than the quantity delivered. This scenario typically occurs for tangible goods that no physical inventory exists for the item—that is, supply items. The fraud data analytics should first identify all tangible goods. Using the general ledger codes is an easy but not perfect way to isolate tangible purchases. The analysis will exclude all purchases associated with inventory because the variance between book and count should reveal a theft scheme occurring. The key is to summarize the quantity purchased from the vendor by line item. The sample selection would start with outlier analysis and then switch to data interpretation based on whether the aggregate quantity for line item is logical for your company.

7. Submitting invoices for items that are not ordered but delivered. The first level of identification is all invoices with no purchase order. The transactions should be summarized by vendor, by line item. Each line item should have the aggregate quantity and aggregate dollar value. The sample selection is based on data interpretation on whether the line item quantity is logical for your company.

8. Vendor invoices that have one line item and a quantity of one. This may be an indicator that the invoice was entered with the line item being one, the unit price is the total value of the invoice, and the extended total equal to the unit price. This would indicate the invoice was entered in a manner to circumvent the three-way match. In reality, this might be an indicator of either vendor alone or vendor in collusion. If nothing else, it is indicator that something is wrong with your internal controls.

9. Submitting real invoice that one or more line item is a false charge. For invoices with purchases orders, the data interrogation should match line item on invoice to line item on the purchase order. The sample selection would be for invoice line items with no corresponding match to the purchase order.

Overbilling: By Submitting Duplicate Invoice via the Vendor Alone or Vendor in Collusion Accounts Payable or by Accounts Payable Alone

The scheme occurs by intentionally submitting an invoice twice for payment of the same goods or services. Duplicate payment test depends on how the vendor or accounts payable clerk is submitting or recording the second invoice. The test examines the invoice number, invoice date, invoice amount, and invoice line-item description. The test is designed to search for the true duplicate with no concealment or a duplicate invoice that uses concealment by a change in the second invoice: invoice number, invoice date, invoice amount, or line item description. For clarification, the concept of first or second invoice is not intended to describe the order the invoice was submitted but rather, the concept of two vendor invoices for the same goods or services. Also, the discussion will describe duplicate testing when there is no purchase order or an open purchase order. The testing could also be relevant when the purchase order is issued after the receipt of the invoice and the purchase order transaction is created by accounts payable. The fraud auditor will need to understand the fraud opportunity question, person committing, as it relates to their organization to properly address the possible combinations of opportunity.

1. The first test should be to search for invoices with an exact match on a duplicate invoice number, duplicate date, and duplicate amount. The test could also focus on duplicate invoice number, date, and amount alone. The analysis could also focus on one data element (e.g., duplicate date); unfortunately, this approach requires the fraud auditor to use data interpretation searching for the duplicate pattern versus specific identification. Remember, always perform the easiest test first and then perform tests in the order of difficulty.
2. Hidden duplicate invoice number occurs when the invoice number on the second invoice, the duplicate invoice, is changed to avoid the internal edit for duplicate invoice number. The typical variations are where a letter, special symbol, or a numeric digit is added or subtracted from the second invoice to avoid the duplicate test or second invoice number has a transposition in the invoice number. In the hidden duplicate invoice number test, the data interrogation plan will need to create a virtual invoice number field and strip out the alpha, special symbol on the beginning or end of the string or embedded somewhere in the invoice string. The report should place the virtual invoice number and the actual invoice number next to each other for easy visual comparison.
   a) If the alpha or special symbol technique is added to the second invoice, the duplicate test on the virtual invoice number should find the duplicate invoice number.
   b) If an extra numeric digit is added, there should be a significant gap between the last and first invoice number. The report should calculate an invoice number range and a date range. Unfortunately, this report

may produce a high number of false positives due to data integrity issues.

c) If an extra digit is added or subtracted from the second invoice number, the anomaly would be the number of digits in the invoice number by vendor number. By vendor number, create a frequency analysis of the number of integers in the invoice number. The report is searching for a vendor that has multiple lines of frequency by integer (e.g., five integers, six integers).

d) If the approach is a transposition of integers within the invoice number, then there should be an anomaly between the invoice number sequence pattern and the sequence of invoice dates. Assuming the vendor follows an ascending pattern of invoice numbers the dates should also follow an ascending pattern. The report is searching for vendors with invoice numbers and invoice dates that do not follow a logical ascending pattern.

3. Different vendor invoice number with a duplicate date or duplicate line item or duplicate amount or any combination of the three other items. The first problem with the test is described earlier in this chapter as the nuisance vendor. These vendors by their nature submit multiple invoices per day for the same type of service or goods. The different invoice number duplicate payment analysis should create two groups of vendors for the test: the list of nuisance vendors and the list of non-nuisance vendors. Data interpretation by the fraud auditor will be required for both data sets.

4. Different invoice number, date, and amount. The second invoice contains an additional charge (add-on charge) that provides the illusion of two different invoices. See the previous section regarding vendor alone exploiting the vulnerabilities of internal controls for discussion of add-on charges.

5. The accounts payable function may be in collusion with a vendor and the accounts payable function is intentionally paying a vendor invoice twice. The accounts payable function is receiving a kickback from the vendor. The data pattern is a high frequency of duplicate payments to one vendor.

6. In smaller accounting organizations, the accounts payable clerk can commit the duplicate payment scheme alone by intentionally paying a vendor invoice twice. The accounts payable clerk then contacts the vendor, indicating the invoice was paid twice in error. When the vendor remits the refund for the duplicate payment, the accounts payable clerk diverts the refund to a bank account that the accounts payable clerk controls. The data pattern is a regular frequency of duplicate payments to different vendors.

Overbilling: Understanding the Fraud Risk Structure When Collusion Occurs between the Vendor and the Internal Person without the Involvement of the Procurement Process

The concept is simple: The vendor operating in collusion with a budget owner or senior manager overcharges your company. Overcharging that occurs through the procurement function is discussed in Chapter 9. In this chapter, overcharging does not involve the procurement function but is linked to the approval process, receipt process, or payment process. *Collusion* is the key word in this scheme. The internal person is a control owner. The variables in overcharging are the expenditure category, the industry, responsibilities of the control owner participating in the scheme, and where the scheme occurs in the expenditure cycle. It would be impossible for anyone to describe all the overcharging permutations by industry, so this book will focus on the methodology and allow the fraud auditor to adapt the methodology to the industry and expenditure category.

The first step is to understand the inherent scheme structure of how overbilling occurs:

1. Overcharging on unit price occurs through a change in price after procurement, or the unit price is inflated. If inflated, the approach is to use either trend analysis, outlier analysis, or benchmarking a vendor unit price to another source.
2. Charging for a higher quantity than delivered—the methodology should differentiate between inventory items and supply items. Inventory items should eventually reflect a variance or excessive adjustments, whereas non-inventory items will use outlier analysis by identifying a quantity that exceeds business use.
3. False charges on real invoices simply stated—either the service was not performed or the tangible item was not received.
4. Intentional duplicate items on real invoices—the test focuses on duplicate description field. For tangible good expenditures, obviously this will create an extensive list of false positives. For services, the test may not be as effective because of the nature of service descriptions on invoices.
5. Intentional duplicate payment of an invoice—the fraud data methodology will focus on duplicate date, invoice number, or amount for exact matches.
6. False add-on charges will vary by services and tangible goods. The fraud data analytics searching for falsely added charges should have two homogeneous data sets: service expenditure and tangible good expenditures.

For service, using keyword searches that relate to the service will prove effective. For tangible goods, search line items that have no quantity or a line-item description that does not have a numeric string.

7. Charging for a higher quality than delivered (product substitution). The nature of product substitution does no lend itself to fraud data analytics because the fraud is in the tangible item versus the data. However a line item description that does not provide standard industry information may be a red flag.

8. Charging for goods/services that are not needed by the company. In this scheme the goods and services are received. The nature of the scheme does not lend itself to fraud data analytics. Outlier analysis may help, but without an allegation, finding a starting point is difficult.

Fraud data analytic routines need to be designed around the opportunity to commit the scheme and the method of overbilling. The fraud data analysis starts by creating homogeneous data files based on the opportunity to commit the scheme, then the search for the overbilling techniques. The analysis typically requires creating multilayers of files to identify the specific fraud scenario. The reason for the opportunity analysis is to establish the intent factor through frequency analysis. The technique analysis is to identify the method of overbilling. In this book, we will discuss opportunity analysis from three perspectives:

1. False administration of the properly issued purchase order. The starting point is the change order.
2. Budget owners circumventing purchasing but providing the illusion of compliance. The starting point is to identify all invoices with no purchase order, open purchase orders, small-dollar invoices, and invoice splitting.
3. Budget owner that purchases directly from the supplier by design of purchasing policies. The starting point is invoices with no purchase order or the purchase order is issued after receipt of the invoice.

Once the opportunity homogeneous data files are created, the second step of the analysis is to search for the various overbilling techniques. Based on my experience, the fraud auditor should start with an inflated unit price, false add-on charges, and excessive item purchases scheme.

To avoid confusion, within the context of this chapter, the term *purchase order* includes either a purchase order or a contract. In regard to bidding procedure, the approach described will not distinguish between oral quotes, written quotes, or sealed bid procedures.

The basic assumption in this overbilling category is that procurement controlled the acquisition and the procurement function is not involved in the scheme. A purchase order is issued and the overbilling occurs through falsely approving changes to the purchase order, overriding the purchase order with invoice approvals, or the budget owner provides advance communication of a future change of the purchase mix and no change to the purchase order.

The overbilling in this scheme occurs after procurement through the false administration of the purchase order. So, do not be fooled by the evidence of written bids, written quotes, purchase orders, and contracts. The bidding process provides the illusion of sound internal controls, which effectively conceals the budget owner's intent to corrupt the procurement process.

The good news is that overbilling after procurement leaves an audit trail of change. Now the bad news: Since most vendors on your master file are real vendors, the sheer volume of data is a general concealment condition. Furthermore, changes to purchase orders are common, and changes to projected needs do occur. Whatever the reason, the key word is *change*.

The change fraud data analytics methodology in the false administration scenario is the search for change through the purchase order file or through the invoice file. This is not a matter of style but the search for different types of changes.

 ## IDENTIFY PURCHASE ORDERS WITH CHANGES

The change fraud data analytics strategy based on the purchase order file searches for the changes to the unit price, quantity, and dollar value of the purchase order. The goal is to identify a high frequency of change by vendor or department or changes that have a material impact on the dollar value.

The first step is to create two homogeneous data files: purchase orders with changes and purchase orders without changes. First, summarize the two files by vendor number, providing frequency, aggregate dollar value, maximum, minimum, and average. The first report is intended to provide gross statistical information. The second report would summarize by vendor number, providing frequency and aggregate dollar value of purchase orders with changes and without changes. The second report is to identify vendors with a higher frequency of purchase order changes.

The purchase order change report should also summarize by the person committing the scenario. The person committing the fraud scenario could be a buyer, department, or any other meaningful business grouping. The purpose of the summary report by person committing the scenario is to link the purchase order changes to a person.

Now that the planning reports are complete (remember the understand data step) the next step is to interrogate the data.

FDA: Changes to the Purchase Order

The types of purchase order changes that typically occur are

- Change to the original purchase order as to price, quantity, or specific line items.
- Purchase order extension.
- Add-on purchase order.
- Changes to the quantity received or changes to the product description.
- Changes to the mix of items procured.
- Increase in the total dollar amount of the purchase order.

Specific identification strategy is initially used to create homogeneous data sets. In this scenario category purchase orders with no change would be excluded from the fraud data analysis because change is the key criterion. So, the first homogeneous data file is purchase orders with changes. In the second step, the purchase order should be disaggregated into two separate files, purchase orders with one invoice and purchase orders with multiple invoices. The reason for two files is because the change between one purchase order and one invoice is simply easier to see than when there are multiple invoices.

Using the purchase order change files, the fraud data analytics should search for the type of change, or change by buyer, or by general ledger category. The goal of the analysis is to identify a pattern and frequency of change that correlates to an internal person or a vendor.

As a reminder, our goal is to shrink the haystack in order that an anomaly becomes more visible to the naked eye. At this point, the fraud auditor could filter out the changes with an immaterial dollar change and use a sample selection methodology to select purchase orders within the change category, or the fraud auditor could continue with their fraud data analysis.

 ## FALSE ADMINISTRATION THROUGH THE INVOICE FILE

The change fraud data analytics strategy based on the invoice file is to summarize actual purchases described on the vendor invoice by line item and prepare the same summary for the purchase order. Then the next step is to search for change between vendor invoice summary of actual purchases to the line items on the original purchase order. The goal is to identify changes on a line item between the invoice summary and purchase order summary. There are two outcomes. The first outcome is a change to the total purchase order amount and a change to the mix. The second outcome is no change to the purchase order total amount but a change in the mix of the items purchased. The change in the mix provides the vendor with more favorable margins. In both approaches, the goal is to recreate the purchase selection process by comparing actual purchases to each vendor's bidding information to determine if the lowest-cost vendor was in fact selected or if the change allowed the vendor to commit an overbilling scheme.

By purchase order number, summarize the vendor invoices by line item that links to each purchase order. Then summarize the purchase orders by line item. Compare the invoice summary to the purchase order summary and search for change on the line item. The goal is to identify changes in the mix of the actual items purchased to the mix of items on the original purchase order. The purchase orders with no change to the mix should be excluded from the fraud data analytics in this scheme. Now the fraud auditor has created a homogeneous file of changes.

FDA: Change through the Invoice File

Using the purchase order change file, link the invoices to the purchase orders that had the change criteria. The analysis follows the retrospective analysis introduced in the auditing standards.

The fraud data analysis in the invoice file is searching for a change in the mix of items purchased from the vendor. The change in mix is purchasing different quantities of items, different quality, or different items than described on the original purchase order. The change in mix can occur through one vendor in collusion with the budget owner or two vendors operating in collusion without the budget owner. Start with the budget owner permutation and one vendor.

The change in mix is the first indicator of a vendor and internal person operating in collusion. The fraud data analysis by itself will identify the change in the mix; it is the fraud auditor's job to determine if the change occurred through normal business evolution or the change occurred through intent to commit the scheme.

Change in the mix can also occur between two vendors. When you place an order for the item, the vendor indicates that it is out of stock for the item.

Since the item is time critical, you purchase the item from the next-lowest-cost vendor in the bid file. The goal of the vendors is to sell only those items with the highest margins. In the procurement chapter, this scheme would be referred to as *vendor bid rigging*.

A good red flag of the two vendors operating in collusion is searching for a zero quantity purchase of a line item on a purchase order. In this scheme the vendor awarded the purchase order avoids selling those items with low margins and the vendor not awarded the purchase order fulfills your needs of the zero purchase line item selling the item at a high price.

The specific identification strategy using the invoice file would identify purchase orders by vendor that have a zero quantity of a purchase line item. The zero quantity item purchase order lines become a homogeneous data file. The next step is to determine if the zero purchase line item was procured from a different vendor. Using the line item, perform a duplicate test for duplicate line items but different vendor number. If the zero line item file is small, use the general ledger account as a common dominator for linking purposes, and perform the old hunt-and-peck approach.

The fraud auditor then must examine the facts and circumstances of the zero purchase line-item schemes. Caution: The obvious criterion is a significant unit price difference between the two vendors. However, it is possible that both bid prices were inflated; therefore, no significant unit process changes are evident.

Overbilling: When the Budget Owner or Senior Manager Operates in Collusion with the Vendor to Avoid Bidding Levels but Complies with Purchasing Procedures

In the circumvent scheme, the budget owner circumvents the procurement function by creating requisitions below the bidding level and recommending a preferred vendor, or the budget owner purchases directly from the vendor through small-dollar purchases; however, the purchases in the aggregate would require bidding procedures. The key word is *circumvention* through compliance with purchasing procedures.

The *circumvention fraud data analytics strategy* is based on small-dollar purchase orders, small-dollar invoices, and split invoices. The circumvention is how the internal source avoids the intent of procurement controls and provides the illusion of full compliance with procurement. A second avoidance strategy is the time extension of the purchase order, which effectively allows for avoidance of the procurement procedures. Circumvention can also occur when a real supplier operates under multiple names.

FDA: Circumvention through Small-Dollar Purchases

Specific identification strategy is used to create the file of vendors or buyers that meet the criteria of the scheme. The data interpretation strategy is used to identify the circumvention of the procurement process through small-dollar transactions. The pattern was established through the specific identification strategy. The frequency of occurrence or the dollar magnitude of the small-dollar transaction will be the basis of the data interpretation. The linkage factor starts with a vendor number and then on the line item, project number, department number, general ledger code associated with the purchase order, and the small-dollar invoices.

The first step is to create two homogeneous data files based on bidding levels. The first file is all purchase orders below the bid level and the second file is all purchase orders above the bid level. If invoices are processed without purchase orders, then the same process would need to occur. The purchase orders and invoices above the bidding level are excluded from the next analysis.

Starting with the small-dollar purchase orders, summarize the small-dollar purchase orders by vendor, providing the frequency and aggregate dollar value of purchase orders. By vendor number, summarize the frequency and dollar value of small-dollar invoices with no purchase order. Then create one report with three columns of data: small-dollar purchase orders, invoices with no purchase order, and the aggregate of the two columns. Filtering of small-dollar activity is critical because of the abstract nature of the data interpretation in the next phase. The fraud data analysis reports by their nature might be voluminous, which makes data filtering critical.

The concept of testing for splitting invoices is searching for split invoices by vendor number using the exact match in the duplicate test using invoice date and/or line items on invoices. These concepts were already discussed in the book.

Overbilling When the Vendor Is in Collusion with an Internal Source (Budget Owner) and the Internal Source Negotiates the Purchase and Administers the Contract, Effectively Bypassing Procurement

In this scenario, the entity is real, the fraud profit is embedded in the invoice or purchase order, and no change is required to the documents. Therefore, the red flags are not visible in one transaction but would be visible over a period of time. A caveat: If the fraud auditor has superior knowledge about a specific purchase, the fraud auditor would be able to see the anomaly in a transaction. In a classroom setting, using one invoice from an equipment rental fraud scheme, a gentleman with 25-plus years in the equipment rental business was able to see the fraud in two seconds. For the fraud auditor without superior knowledge, fraud data analytics is the methodology for identifying overbilling.

Fraud data analytics is a multi-tiered approach, starting with internal control circumvention, use of change analysis followed by specific identification, and then the use of data interpretation through the use of change, trend analysis, or benchmarking to similar purchases. The fraud auditor will need to make a few assumptions in the analysis based on fundamental fraud theory. For example, the greed factor will cause the perpetrators to want more money. The fraud will continue until some event stops the fraud. The supplier and internal person are friends.

The first step in the circumvention strategy is to identify purchase orders that avoided procurement. By avoiding procurement, it means that no meaningful procurement procedures were performed on the selection of the vendor. The mere fact that a purchase order is issued does not indicate that meaningful procurement procedures were performed. The problem becomes how to identify such acquisitions. In this analysis, the fraud data analytics plan will need to make assumptions regarding how to identify circumvention. So, any invoice issued on the same day as the purchase order, or the purchase order is issued after the invoice date, becomes the first homogeneous data file. Therefore, all invoices where the purchase order is issued first are excluded from the analysis. The assumption in this decision is that procurement selected the vendor versus a budget owner.

In those companies that have bid codes in their procurement systems, the fraud data analysis would start by identifying which purchase orders were issued with a code, which indicates the purchase order was issued without a bidding process (e.g., sole source selection). Unfortunately, most companies do not have such a code. Therefore, your first internal control recommendation is for your company to require that a bid code become part of your data files.

The next step is to filter out what I have referred to as distraction vendors. To illustrate, payments to utilities, office rental, and mail delivery services usually match the data selection assumption. Since these vendors are not what the fraud data analysis is searching for, the vendors should be excluded from further analysis.

The next step is to summarize the purchases that circumvented purchasing by person, department, or line item of purchase, searching for the following change patterns:

- Change of internal person and change to vendor for a specific line item.
- Change of vendor for the specific line item and no change to the internal person.
- No change of internal person and no change to vendor.

Searching for change in vendors in large companies sounds good, but in reality is very difficult. The use of general ledger categories can facilitate the process because the general ledger category does create a common denominator of like purchases.

A second approach to search for vendor changes is to summarize by line item, sort the line items in date order, then by vendor number. The first record and last record analysis in the software is a great tool for this analysis. The process is searching for a change in vendor on a line-item basis. Data filtering should be considered after the data summarization.

Using the change analysis, we now have two homogeneous data files: purchase orders with a change to supplier or internal person and purchase orders with no change to supplier or internal person.

The next step for both files is specification identification using a form of trend analysis by searching for increases in price or quantity of a line item over a period of time.

Using the exclusion theory, exclude from your analysis all line items that had no change in price or quantity consistent with your fraud theory. The next step is to determine the size of the resulting file. If the resulting files are large, data filtering based on the dollar size of the line item may be an effective technique to further reduce the size of the file.

Searching the Opportunity Files for Specific Overbilling Techniques

The sample selection is based on data interpretation strategy based on the aggregate dollar value and the increase in unit price. A similar process is followed for add-on charges and excessive purchases. Fraud data analytics for add-on charges are discussed in the vendor alone section of the chapter. The excessive purchase scheme uses the quantity field and summarizes by line item. To be clear, this analysis is not easy; it is time consuming and requires patience. If the analysis results from an allegation, the process is easier because the analysis has a starting point as to vendor or internal person.

Disguised Expenditures: Internal Person Purchases the Goods with the Intent of Committing a Theft Scheme

In this scenario, the internal person purchases items with the intent to commit a theft scheme for the purpose of selling the item. In some ways, this is one of the most difficult fraud scenarios to detect, because where does the fraud auditor start? The auditor's experience and knowledge of the company is paramount to selecting the starting point. It becomes an educated guess.

The good news about the scenario is that the frequency of purchase and aggregate dollar value are the best clues. If the item is inventory based, variances or write-offs may provide a clue. Maybe the frequency and aggregate can be linked to a person.

Data interpretation is the best strategy for this fraud scenario. The fraud data analytics will start with the data summarization by expenditures, followed by the use of outlier analysis. The first summary is all about creating homogeneous data sets. The second summary is all about data interpretation. The sample selection is based on the fraud auditor's knowledge of the business. The fraud auditor is encouraged to select a department, expenditure area, a specific item to summarize. Trying to summarize all company data for this fraud scenario is too overwhelming. There are three overall strategies for data summarization:

1. Identify tangible items in which the consumption exceeds company requirements.
2. Identify tangibles items that have an easy resell value.
3. Identify assets recorded in the balance sheet—inventory or equipment that have known shortages—or focus on asset write-off schemes.

The fraud data analytics should summarize purchases by a category by specific line items in the category. The analysis should focus on aggregate quantity of the specific item and aggregate dollar value of the purchase. The use of disaggregated analysis is critical to identify items that fit the theft pattern versus normal internal consumption. The sample selection is based on the quantity of the item purchased consistent with company needs.

For recorded assets, the data summarization should focus on the frequency and aggregate value of the write-off. Hopefully, the fraud data analysis can link the write-off to a person.

Service expenditures do not fit the concept of theft; however, services paid by the company that inure to the benefit of a company employee would fit the parameter of theft. The fraud auditor should consider expenditures that would have a personal benefit.

In one project, a factory supply manager was purchasing all supply items from one supplier. Closer examination of all the supply purchases revealed a high quantity of ladders. The supply manager was selling the ladders. To further illustrate expenditure areas involving theft-for-resale schemes based on my experience: copy paper, copper cabling, IT supplies, and small tools.

Personal Expenses: Paying for Personal Expenses That Inure to the Benefit of the Internal Person

The first place to look for this scenario is in the procurement card purchases. Chapter 10 will cover these expenditures. The difficulty associated with the personal expense analysis is that by the nature of the scenario, the expenditure is typically small dollar and low frequency.

The targeted expenditure approach is effective for finding personal expense scenarios. One approach is to subjectively identify departments that by the nature of the department purchase items in the normal course of the business that would also have a personal nature to the expense. To illustrate the concept, think about the types of items purchased by IT or marketing.

Conflict-of-Interest Entities Conflict of interest is the process of paying for goods or services that are received from the vendor but an internal employee has an undisclosed ownership in the vendor. In Chapter 6, we discussed that conflict-of-interest entity has either one customer or multiple customers. The transactional analysis will vary based on the number of actual customers that the conflict-of-interest entity serves.

The transactional profile of a conflict-of-interest entity with one customer is similar to the transactional profile of a false billing shell company. When the conflict-of-interest entity has a few customers, the transactional profile is similar to the pass-through scheme operated by the salesperson. When the conflict of interest has many customers, the fraud data analytics would follow the over-billing scenario.

▓ SUMMARY

Searching for fraud in the disbursement cycle is like fishing for trout in a fully stocked pond. It is only a matter of time before you catch a trout. The analogy is the same for performing fraud analytics in the payment cycle. It is only a matter of time before you find fraud.

There are more than 50 common fraud scenarios in the disbursement cycle. When considering company-specific, internal control inhibitors, expenditure, or industry-specific, the numbers of fraud scenarios become staggering. However, by understanding the power of the fraud scenario methodology, the search for fraud in the trout pond becomes easier.

If there is a limited time budget, what are the three fraud data analytics tests the fraud auditor should perform, and why should the fraud auditor perform the analysis?

1. Shell company analysis, because once the supplier is identified as a shell company, the fraud auditor has found either a false billing scheme or a pass-through scheme.
2. Vendor invoice number analysis, because a sequential pattern or a low invoice number is easy to identify. The sequential pattern is an indicator that the vendor has one customer. Why does the supplier have only one customer?
3. The number anomaly test searching for round numbers or recurring numbers, because the test is easy and has produced results.

CHAPTER EIGHT

Fraud Data Analytics
for Payroll Fraud

F raud scenarios occur in payroll for a variety of reasons. First, employees are motivated to increase their net payroll. A supervisor is
motivated to increase the net payroll of a good employee or the supervisor is motivated by receiving a kickback from the employee. Human resources
payroll grades are unreasonable. Senior management is motivated for personal
enrichment or to disguise a bribe, which is an FCPA issue. Whatever the internal person's motivation for committing the fraud scenario, payroll systems
are vulnerable to internal employees committing fraud scenarios through the
payroll system.

On first appearance, internal controls in most payroll systems seem
sound. Separation of duties between payroll and human resources functions
are deemed adequate. The company has a form for every step of the process.
Approval controls are abundant throughout the entire system. However,
fraud auditors should not be fooled by the evidence of an internal form, the
appearance of separation of duties, and approval signatures in planning their
fraud data analytics plan.

The predictability or vulnerability of the payroll system to a specific fraud
scenario is how the internal control works in the real world. I refer to this as the
difference between control theory and control reality.

In the legal system, there is a phrase, "form over substance or substance over form." Payroll systems definitely have a "form over substance" from an internal control perspective. There is a form for every step. There is a form for new hires, a form to change your profile, and a form for termination. The question is, does our payroll process have "substance over form"? The key to understanding where payroll systems are vulnerable to fraud is by understanding how robust your internal controls are at each key control. The fraud auditor needs to understand the answers to who, what, where, how, and when the internal control is performed. The fraud auditor must understand the substance of the process over the form of the process.

The *who* question correlates to the trust factor of fraud opportunity. Supervisors and employees develop personal relationships. These relationships may cause a less robust approval process. *Who* relates to who actually causes the employee master file to be updated. Are human resources a true control function or an update function? Are human resources or payroll a "form" control or a "substance" control?

What is the span of internal control? How many employees does a supervisor monitor? Do employees work on staggered shifts? Does this work environment create opportunities for time reporting fraud?

Where does the hiring process occur? In a retail environment, hiring occurs at a store level. The manager interviews the employee and submits the necessary paperwork to human resources. The manager is perfectly situated to place a fictitious employee on the payroll. An employee quits work, but the supervisor continues to submit time sheets for the employee and diverts the employee's payroll check.

How is human resources notified of a change or an addition? Is the employee required to go to human resources, or does a supervisor forward the necessary paperwork?

When is the procedure performed? Is the procedure performed during normal business hours or after hours?

The intent of these questions or statements is not to suggest that internal controls are not operating as intended by management, but rather, the concept of understanding where your company is vulnerable to fraud.

 INHERENT FRAUD SCHEMES FOR PAYROLL

The inherent fraud scheme structure is the starting point for fraud data analytics in payroll. The inherent scheme structure for entities is similar to vendors, except in payroll the entity structure is an employee. There are three entity structures in payroll fraud scenarios:

1. *Fictitious employee* occurs by creating the identity for a person that does not exist in real life. The person committing the scenario in essence creates an identity for the fictitious employee.
2. *Assumed identity employee* occurs by taking over the identity of a person either for a temporary time period or on a permanent time period. This entity structure is similar to the assumed identity for shell companies.
3. *Real employee* is complicit in the fraud action. In payroll, *complicit* is defined as the real employee receives the payroll payment.

The fraud action statements for payroll are:

1. Payment for services not performed; often called the ghost employee scheme. The entity structure of the inherent scheme for the ghost employee is a false entity (employee), a noncomplicit employee, or through a complicit employee.
2. Overtime fraud is payment for services not performed that are in excess of the standard hours.
3. False adjustment scheme occurs to the gross pay, deductions, or net payroll. A supervisor, the payroll function, or corporate controller is the typical perpetrator of the fraud scenario. The internal person creates and processes a payroll transaction that inflates gross or net payroll.
4. Manual payroll disbursements are payroll payments that are initiated, calculated external to the automated system, and the payroll data are manually entered into the automated system. Manual payroll payments occur for many reasons: final payroll payments, bonus payments, to correct an error, and to commit a fraud scenario.
5. Theft of stale payroll checks occurs when an employee does not receive their final paycheck, for whatever reason, and an internal person diverts and negotiates the check.
6. Inflated sales commissions or sales bonuses occur by intentionally manipulating performance statistics.
7. Disguised compensation occurs when management overrides human resource policies and provides am employee with additional compensation. While the employee is not complicit in the scheme, the employee benefits from the fraud scenario.
8. Payroll-related expenditures are those expenditures that relate to employee benefits that are not considered wages in the traditional sense. That is,

employees working in a foreign country are eligible for allowances such as tuition reimbursement plans. The fraud scenarios in these areas would depend on the nature of the benefit.

9. Employer fraud involves a company that intentionally is underpaying employees. These schemes require the fraud auditor to understand the labor law, which is beyond the scope of this book. However, with the frequency of these cases reported in the media, I would be remiss in not listing the scheme.

Understanding How Payroll Is Calculated

The good news is that fraud data analytics is easier in payroll than in vendor payments. The payroll system tends to have less data integrity issues, so data cleansing routines are less critical. The payroll calculation tends to be accurate, which is different from authorized and consistent with company policies. Therefore, most payroll data interrogation procedures and sample selection criteria are specific identification strategies versus data interpretation strategies. Now the bad news: Because of all the subsystems that are required to calculate net payroll, more time is required to understand all of these systems and gather the data.

In payroll fraud, there are two key numbers: gross payroll and net payroll. Understanding how both numbers are calculated, stored, and reported will become the basis of your fraud data analytics plan. The planning for the fraud data analytics plan requires the fraud auditor to understand the data that resides in the following files:

- Human resources database.
- Time and attendance reporting database.
- Payroll registers record the data used to calculate gross payroll and net payroll.
- Annual payroll summary table—the annual summary of one year's payroll registers.
- Change files for human resources, time, and attendance and payroll registers.

Starting with the human resources database, identify what information can be used for fraud data analytics. In human resources, there is the obvious information, name, address, and so on; the other relevant items of information are:

- Employee hire date
- Last update

- Employee classification systems as to job titles
- Salary grade as to the maximum salary within the grade
- Employment status: regular full time, contract employee, temporary status
- Country of residence

The time and attendance system starts the payroll calculation. For hourly employees, time and attendance system is the basis of their gross payroll; for full-time employees, it indicates whether the employee is using personal time. The fraud auditor should understand how the information is created, changed, and reported. Other necessary information is the creator ID, the approver ID, the computer ID, job duties if employee performs different jobs and different rates, date, and time records for creating and changing the time record.

The table structure for payroll has two primary tables for fraud data analytics, the payroll register table, which has the results of the payroll calculation, and the payroll summary table that is used for tax reporting and various fringe benefit requirements. The fraud data analytics should be based on the payroll register table; however, the payroll summary table is useful because the table size is small in comparison to the size of all the payroll registers for the year.

The net payroll calculation is gross payroll minus deductions equals net payroll. The gross payroll is based on a salary grade, divided by the number of pay periods. Hourly employees are paid based on the number of hours multiplied by an hourly rate. Gross wages are classified based on an internal earnings code; the fraud auditor should obtain a copy of the earnings code as part of the planning.

Within the payroll system, there can be many earnings codes that mirror how the business operates. Some of these earnings codes are for classification of wages, such as vacation time. Other earnings codes are designed to increase gross payroll, such as a one-time bonus payment. Within fraud data analytics the earnings codes are an integral part of searching for fraud in payroll.

There are two types of deductions from gross wages. Those deductions required by the government and voluntary. The fraud auditor should obtain a copy of the deduction codes as part of the planning.

Now that regular gross payroll is calculated, the next step is to understand how adjustments to gross payroll, deductions, and net payroll are reported and where the adjustment transaction is recorded in the database.

Lastly, how is net payroll calculated? Within some companies, employees are reimbursed for expenses through payroll. The company includes the reimbursement as an adjustment to net payroll.

PLANNING REPORTS FOR PAYROLL FRAUD

The first report that should be created is a gross payroll and net payroll by employee. The difference between net and gross should be calculated and percentage of employee net payroll to employee gross payroll. The informational items on the report should be the number of payroll payments, the employee number, the employee grade, employee title, and department number.

There should be summary reports on payroll information:

1. By payment code, the number of employees paid through direct deposit versus manual payroll check.
2. By earnings code, a summary of gross wages also includes the frequency of the earnings code occurring in the payroll registers.
3. By deduction code, a frequency count of employees using the deduction code.
4. By employee, the total number of automated payroll payments and the total number of manual payroll payments. The start date and termination date are critical to determine if the number of payroll payments is consistent with your expectation (payroll payment frequency report).
5. By employee, the total number of hours reported for hourly employees.

Each of these reports can be further refined based on what the reports reveal. Summarization and filtering routines are useful in allowing these reports to be user friendly. Using the payroll frequency report:

- Summarize the total number of automated payments and the total number of manual payments.
- Filter out all employees when the number of payroll payments is consistent with their employment period.

Remember, the planning reports are intended to assist the auditor in the likelihood analysis versus the sample selection process. Using the payroll frequency report, if no manual payroll payments were issued, then no fraud scenarios could occur through manual payments. Before you start creating fraud data analytics reports, study the planning reports to ensure you understand the data.

FDA FOR GHOST EMPLOYEE SCHEMES

The term *ghost employee* is widely used throughout the audit profession. It generally is defined as payroll payments to a person who does not exist in real life. Using the inherent scheme approach, there are 11 ghost entity types. The fraud action statement is the same for each entity type: payment for services not performed.

Fictitious Employee That Does Not Exist

The fictitious employee is added to human resources file by someone with direct access or through indirect access. In many organizations, the hiring process occurs remotely from corporate human resources. For example, in retail, the store manager performs the hiring function and then submits the necessary paperwork to human resources, causing the fictitious employee to be added to the master file.

FDA Plan for Fictitious Employee That Does Not Exist

The plan can focus on the entity data, payroll register, or cross-match to other data files to ascertain evidence of work performance. The entity data can focus on missing data and specific identification of data. The duplicate test can search for common linkage between two employees. The payroll register may have anomalies in the gross, deductions, or net payroll calculation.

Generally, employees on a world basis have a government identification number. The critical question becomes how sophisticated are the local government business systems in identifying an invalid government number for the citizen or foreign national. If yes, then an invalid number would soon be detected by government reporting; if no, then government identification numbers are not problematic for the person committing the fraud scenario.

So, where can we find a government identification number?

- When a person dies, the government identification number becomes inactive. However, in the year of death, the number will remain active for payroll reporting.
- If the government does not make a government identification number inactive, then perpetrator can use a dead person's number.
- Accounts payable—the person may have started working as a contractor.

- Foreign nationals who leave the country and return to their home country.
- In the United States, an employee may also have an ITIN number. These numbers start with the number nine and are also nine digits.

The employee master may search for employees missing normal employee information or perform a duplicate test to link two individuals together, one real and one fictitious. The first step is the data availability analysis to determine which fields are typically populated by human resources. The missing analysis should be based on information that would normally exist for a real employee. The scoring sheet concept is critical to using the missing data approach in that some information is simply more important than others.

1. Missing government identification number or an invalid number
2. Missing address or bank account. (In the missing test, an employee without a street address would be considered missing address.)
3. Employee is in payroll register but no record in the human resources database
4. No health insurance code
5. No retirement code
6. No emergency contact person
7. No personal telephone number
8. No employee personal email address
9. No last evaluation date, assuming information is recorded in human resources
10. Creation date
11. Grade level and job title
12. Department number

The duplicate test searches for a common linkage between two employees. The test can result in many false positives if the sample selection criteria are based on one criterion. The first test is a duplicate government identification number. System internal controls should not allow a duplicate number, but better safe than sorry. The second duplicate test would focus on duplicate bank account number and duplicate address. Now, depending on the person committing the scenario, the second attribute is a duplicate department number. The reason for duplicate department number is that the payroll charge needs to be recorded to a general ledger account. Assuming the person committing the scheme is a budget owner, then the budget owner's account number is the most likely place to avoid detection. If the person committing is in payroll, then a judgmental identification of departments with ghost employee payroll charges would not be as evident. If the scheme is committed as part of a bribe scheme, FCPA violation, then the budget number may not provide a logical connection.

The payroll register provides the gross payroll, deductions, and net payroll for the fictitious employee. The payroll register anomalies are:

- No voluntary deductions.
- No voluntary government tax withholdings.
- Net payroll is a high percentage of gross payroll.
- Gross payroll is above the 50 percent tier for the grade level.
- Employee is not recorded in the human resources database.

The best test to identify a ghost employee is evidence of work performance, the ability to match an employee in the payroll registers to an employee in a security database. Common databases are building access, parking garage access, computer access, or internal telephone system. The first level of the test is to determine if the employee in the payroll register is listed in the security database. The second level of the test is to determine if the listed employee is showing activity in the security database.

While evidence of work performance is the best test for identifying ghost employees, there are challenges with the fraud data analytics test. The first challenge is matching an employee's name between two unrelated databases. If employees are assigned an employee number, the match is relatively simple. If the match occurs on name, then the match will have spelling issues, much like the address field. The second challenge is associated with the diversity of the workforce. Finding one database for a diverse employee workforce may not be possible. The retention of access security might be limited. Lastly, how robust is the enforcement of the security program? With this aside, matching your employee database to a secondary database is the best tool to identify ghost employees.

Real Employee, Not Complicit, Temporary Takeover of Identity

In this scenario, the employee departs the workplace and the supervisor does not notify human resources of the employee's departure until weeks later. The scenario typically occurs in entry-level positions or positions that have regular turnover. During the employee absence the supervisor submits the necessary time and attendance reports to cause a payroll payment. The person committing the scenario is typically a department manager, and the employee is receiving a manual check. While the supervisor could submit a change to the employee's bank account, the action seems less likely. If the person committing the scenario is a payroll person, the fraud data analytics should search for a change to bank account close to the termination date.

FDA Plan for Real Employee, Not Complicit, Temporary Takeover of Identity

The first criterion is all employees who have a termination code because the scenario is a temporary takeover. We then create two homogeneous databases of terminated employees: employees paid with direct deposit and employees paid with a manual check. If the employee is paid with direct deposit, there needs to be change to bank account. If the bank account is changed, then the employee is selected for testing. If the employee is paid with a manual check, then there is no further data analytics. The sample selection is based on judgmental criteria. If the time and attendance records are automated, then examine the record to determine who created the record.

Real Employee, Not Complicit, Permanent Takeover of Identity

In this scenario, the employee departs the workplace and the supervisor does not notify human resources of the employee's departure. The supervisor submits time and attendance reports to cause a payroll payment. The scenario can occur either with a manual check or by causing a change to the direct-deposit bank account. The key with this scenario is to understand the wage and tax reporting within the country. If the terminated employee is not notified of wage and tax withholding, then this scheme could occur forever. If the employee is in a country where wage and tax reporting is reported to the employee, then concealing the scheme is more difficult but not impossible. This is why country code is important. If the employee is a foreign national and the employee leaves the country on a permanent basis, then wage reporting is not a robust detection control.

FDA Plan for Real Employee, Not Complicit, Permanent Takeover of Identity

The fraud data analytics plan should search for change to either the employee master file or the net payroll calculation. In the employee master file, the fraud data analytics should search for change to banking information or the address.

In the payroll calculation, the change would be a decrease in withholdings or an increase in the net payroll. The employee's country of residence may also help. Nonresident employees would have a higher likelihood of having their identity assumed because government wage reporting for that person is less critical. If the time and attendance records are automated, then examine the record to determine who created the record.

Real Employee, Not Complicit, Employee Who Is Reactivated

In this scenario, the employee departs from the workforce and human resources are notified. However, at a later time, someone causes the employee to be reactivated on the payroll. In essence someone is taking over the identity of the employee.

FDA Plan for Real Employee, Not Complicit, Employee Who Is Reactivated

The first step is to identify all employees who are reactivated. The second step is to determine if there were any changes to banking information or address information. If the time and attendance records are automated, then examine the record to determine who created the record.

Real Employee, Not Complicit, Pre-Employment

In this scenario, a supervisor or payroll causes a payroll payment to occur in the employee's name before the employee actually starts working for the company. The first payment is diverted. The payment is usually associated with a manual check.

FDA Plan for Real Employee, Not Complicit, Pre-Employment

While this scheme sounds unlikely, the scheme has occurred. The likelihood depends on the nature of the workforce. The fraud data analytics for the fraud scenario will most likely not be able to identify those employees where this scheme has occurred. Remember, fraud data analytics is not designed for all fraud scenarios. The fraud data analytics for this scenario is the process of comparing the first payment to the second payment and identifying change—that is, change from manual check to direct deposit, change in voluntary deductions from gross payroll.

Real Employee Who Is Complicit and Performs No Services: Asset Misappropriation

In this scenario, the employee is a real person and typically in collusion with a manager. The employee has a personal relationship with the manager. The employee is often referred to as a no-show employee. The employee is typically hired with the intent of being a no-show employee.

FDA Plan for Real Employee Who Is Complicit and Performs No Services: Asset Misappropriation

The previous routines are generally not effective because the person is real person and there is no change. Matching to a security database is the best opportunity to identify the no-show ghost.

Real Employee Who Is Complicit and Performs No Services: Corruption

In this scenario, the employee performs no services and the payroll payment is a bribe. This scenario is typically associated with a senior manager who is in a position to override normal internal controls. While the employee is in essence a no-show employee, the intent of the payroll payment is associated with corruption versus asset misappropriation.

FDA Plan for Real Employee Who Is Complicit and Performs No Services: Corruption

The fraud data analytics will need to search for PEPs (politically exposed persons) as defined by FATF (Financial Action Task Force). There are various government and commercial databases that might be used as the matching database.

Another approach, although more time consuming, is to create a report of all new hires within the scope period, providing start date, gross salary, job title, date job title created or changed, and department code. Create a second report of contracts that link to customers that are considered government customers under the FCPA or other relevant bribery laws. Compare the hire dates to relevant customer contract dates. The sample selection is judgmental based on correlation to start date and customer contract date. The second consideration is job title and department code.

Human Resources Error Resulting in a Real Employee to Continue Receiving Direct Deposit after Departing from the Workforce

Throughout the years, I have heard that an employee who terminates employment notifies human resources; however, through an error the employee is not removed from the active payroll. The employee continues to receive a regular payroll payment and does not notify payroll of the ongoing error. While the scenario is not a true fraud scenario, I would be remiss in not mentioning the scenario.

FDA Plan for Real Employee Who Is Complicit

The previous routines are generally not effective because the person is real and there is no change. Matching to a security database is the best opportunity to identify the no-show ghost.

Real Person Who Is a Temporary Employee

The temporary scenario can occur through a fictitious person or through a real person. The reason I have listed the permutation is the temporary employees tend not to have the same rigid human resource controls because the person is temporary. Oftentimes, the hiring supervisor has a high degree of control, which is what causes the scenario to occur.

FDA Plan for Real Person Who Is a Temporary Employee

The first step is to identify all employees with the code. The next step is a summary step as to gross wages and the number of payroll payments. The sample selection will be judgmental. If your company has a large seasonal employment force, the fraud data analytics will need to apply all of the previously described ghost employee schemes to the temporary employee.

Real Person in Payroll Register but Not in the Human Resources Database

This scheme is typically committed by someone in payroll. The person is paid through an override feature, manual check, or poor internal controls.

FDA Plan for Real Person in Payroll Register but Not in the Human Resources Database

Create a list of all employees in the payroll register and match the list of employees to the human resources database. The sample selection is all employees in the payroll register, but not in the human resources database. A second test is a record count of all active employees to the number of employees listed on the payroll register. It is important to know how employees on leave are listed in human resources; otherwise, the reconciliation procedure will result in a false positive discrepancy.

FDA FOR OVERTIME FRAUD

Overtime fraud is simple; an employee falsifies the number of hours the employee actually works. Most overtime schemes are not complicated; the employee determines that no one is monitoring the hours submitted on a time card. Overtime fraud is a crime of opportunity. To understand the concept of opportunity, the fraud auditor needs to understand the permutations associated with the person committing the fraud scenario:

- Employee alone overstates her hours worked and the supervisor unknowingly approves overtime. This opportunity can occur in a staggered work-day or by the supervisor not carefully checking time cards or not being present during the overtime hours or just a general neglect of their duties. Remember, how robust are your internal controls?
- Employee operates in collusion with another employee to falsify their payroll hours. Once again, this will occur without the knowledge of the supervisor. In a manual card system, the employees enter arrival or departure information for each other. In an automated system, an administrative employee with access to the time reporting system changes the time record after supervisor approval.
- Employee and supervisor operate in collusion. The supervisor may be receiving a kickback from the employee or for some motivating reason, providing the employee disguised compensation.
- Employee and payroll employee operating in collusion. The payroll person may be receiving a kickback from the employee or providing the employee disguised compensation for whatever motivation. The payroll person overrides the properly reported hours. To conceal their actions, the time card is altered, destroyed, or a new version is created.

- Employee forges the approval of the supervisor. In an automated time card system, this would occur through a weak password control procedure.
- Employee working in payroll overstates his own hours worked.

FDA Plan for Overtime Fraud

The initial search for overtime abuse is simple; the fraud data analytics searches for all employees reporting overtime. I would encourage the use of the year-to-date summary table as a starting point for total hours. Overtime wages can be earned by both full-time employees and part-time employees. Using the specific identification strategy identify all employees reporting overtime wages. For large databases, I would create two summary databases, employees having overtime and employees that do not have overtime.

The created database should contain employee number, employee name, hire date, total hours reported, gross payroll, overtime wages, and department codes. Summarize the two files by department code as total employees by department having overtime and employees in the same department not having overtime. If your company operates multiple shifts, it may be necessary to summarize by department by shift. The purpose is to identify how prevalent overtime wages are within the company and by department in the company, which is an example of understanding the data report.

The second stage of the fraud data analytics is to search for patterns of abuse. To accomplish this step, the fraud data analytics will need to access either the time record system or the payroll registers. The patterns of overtime that are consistent with overtime fraud to search for are as follows:

- Excessive hours for an employee. There are two approaches: First judgmentally select a number of overtime hours and then identify all employees exceeding the number of hours. A second approach is to compute the average number of overtime hours reported by employees; exclude all employees who did not report overtime hours from the calculation. Then use the mean or median for excessive hours.
- Cluster of employees reporting overtime hours in one operating unit. It may be an indicator of employees operating in collusion or employees in collusion with a supervisor. The two preceding databases are useful for this analysis. Summarize by department the employees not receiving overtime and summarize by department employees receiving overtime. The report of employees having overtime should also have total hours of overtime, total dollars of overtime paid. Link the two reports by department number. Review the report for a department which only has a few employees receiving overtime.

- Pattern of recurring overtime hours reported (i.e., four hours every day). This analysis is a form of number anomaly analysis.
- High number of overtime hours in one day. Similar to the excessive total hours, the analysis should select a number of hours.
- Off-period overtime is hours reported on a nonscheduled workday.
- Leave and overtime. Search for employees on paid leave, vacation time, or other paid leave who are receiving overtime wages.
- Changes in the time reporting system would indicate an override by someone, either a department administrative employee responsible for department time reporting or someone in the payroll function.
- Compare the hours reported in the time and attendance system, assuming system is automated to the hours in the payroll register. The purpose of the test is to identify a payroll person changing the hours reported to the hours paid.
- The use of access security databases might be effective, assuming that the company requires all employees to log in and log out. The fraud data analytics would compute the hours worked through the access security log and then compare the hours reported for payroll purposes. It is difficult to find one database for all employees. Many times, the analysis may only be applicable to a limited number of employees.

As a caveat, the number of overtime hours a person may work might be attributable to personal behavior traits, family issues, or supervisor rules.

FDA FOR PAYROLL ADJUSTMENTS SCHEMES

There are three categories of payroll adjustment schemes: adjustments to gross pay; adjustments to deductions fields; or adjustments to net payroll. The key to understanding false adjustment schemes is to understand how payroll is calculated within your database system. In the database, there are a series of earning codes for gross payroll. The payroll system automatically calculates the "regular earnings" and the system automatically classifies payroll based on time and attendance records—that is, regular earnings or regular earnings classified as vacation wages for purposes of benefits. However, there are other earnings codes to increase an employee's wages (e.g., bonus payments) or to classify a wage as a benefit (e.g., vacation pay).

In the gross pay false adjustment scenario, an employee receives an adjustment to gross payroll. The employee supervisor may have initiated the adjustment as a form of disguised compensation or a payroll person may have recorded the adjustment to receive a kickback. Whatever the motivation for the scheme or internal control deficiency the adjustment is easy to find.

In the false adjustment deduction scenario, there are two methods. The first is to enter a contra number in the deduction field, which increases net payroll. The second false adjustment scheme is when a deduction does not occur within the payroll calculation but later is added to the employee's year-to-date earnings record through a false transaction. To illustrate, at the time of gross pay and net pay calculation, there are no taxes withheld from the employee's net payroll calculation. Later, an income tax adjustment transaction directly updates the employee's year-to-date table by increasing the employee's income tax withheld on the annual wage reporting statement to the government.

In the net payroll false adjustment scenario, the employee's net payroll is increased through an adjustment to net payroll. Many companies will reimburse employees for out-of-pocket expenses through payroll versus accounts payable. The indicator of this scheme is a journal posting to a non-wage account or a reclassification entry transferring the payroll charge to a non-wage account.

In one investigation, the controller gross payroll was $60,000 and his net payroll was $120,000. The documentation supporting the adjustment to net payroll was to reimburse the controller for out-of-pocket expenses ranging from office supplies to purchase of office equipment.

FDA Plan for False Adjustments to Gross Payroll

In the planning stage, the fraud data analytics plan created a report of gross wages by employee by grade. Employee's gross wages exceeding her grade level is the first clue that a false adjustment scheme is occurring.

The first step is to summarize an employee's earnings for the year by the earning codes. The exclusion theory would eliminate all employees with only earning codes of zero or normal earning codes associated with benefits. For the remaining employees, we would summarize by employee by earnings code to provide the gross dollars by earnings code and frequency of occurrence of the earnings code. I would include the employee's grade level in the report. In this way, we could also determine if any of the employees in the test have exceeded their salary range. The sample selection is based on an employee who has a frequency of earnings codes other than normal earnings or a large adjustment to gross payroll.

FDA Plan for Contra Entry Deduction Scenario

The contra entry test is simply the process of searching for a contra entry in the employee's earnings record. The contra entry is a negative number in a field that all the deductions should be a positive number. By entering a negative number, gross pay less deductions actually increases net payroll. Once the contra entry is identified, summarize the dollar impact and the frequency of occurrence.

FDA Plan for False Transaction Deduction Scenario

The fraud data analytics will require two sets of data. The first data set is the payroll registers for the calendar year. The second data set is the internal database table used for wage reporting to the government. Using the payroll registers, the fraud data analytics would calculate the annual earnings record from the payroll registers. Then the recomputed earnings record would be compared to the summary table used for government earnings reporting. The sample selection would be all employees where there is a difference between recomputed table and the internal table of annual earnings.

The approach could also search for manual adjustments to an employee's year-to-date earnings records. If there are only a few employees with manual adjustments, the fraud auditor would review the employee's earnings records through the online system. If the number of manual adjustments is high, then it may be necessary to calculate the net payroll for those employees with manual adjustments.

FDA Plan for False Adjustments to Net Payroll

The planning report of comparison of gross payroll to net payroll is the first report that will flag abuse in this area. A second planning report is to summarize journal entries originating from the payroll system. The predictability factor would be the dollar value of debits to general ledgers other than wages. Yes, the initial posting could be a debit to wages with a subsequent reclassify journal entry.

 ## FDA FOR MANUAL PAYROLL DISBURSEMENTS

There are many reasons why an employee may receive a manual payroll payment versus an automated payroll payment ranging from bonuses to final payment resulting from termination of employment. The planning report that counts the number of payments should highlight this fraud scenario. Care must be taken to ensure the summary report captures all payroll payments. Questions to ask are:

1. In what data tables are manual payroll payments stored?
2. Do manual payroll payments have a different sequence of control numbers from the automated payroll payments?
3. How are manual payroll payments recorded in the general ledger? Is the entry automated, or is the posting a manual entry?
4. What is the process for final payments to employees after their final workday?
5. What is the company policy on paying employees for unpaid vacation time, personal time, and sick time?

FDA for Manual Payroll Payments

The fraud data analytics approach will depend on the answers to the previous questions. One approach is the frequency of payroll payments by employee. A second report should search for journal entries originating from a payroll payment to a nonsalary general ledger account. A third report would search for the control number sequence associated with the manual payroll payments. The reports described in the false adjustment section may also highlight the scenario.

Another category is the search for payroll payments after termination date. The scenario would need to identify whether the employee or payroll is complicit in the payroll. If the employee is not complicit and is paid with direct deposit, then we would search for a change to bank accounts. The scenario is easier to commit when the employee receives a paper check.

The fraud data analytics creates a file of all terminated employees through the termination date. The terminated employee file would then search for all payroll payments to an employee in the terminated employee file. The termination date is compared to the payroll register, for both automated and manual payments; the resulting report should identify the frequency and dollar value of all payments after termination date. The sample selection is based on the answers to the manual payroll payments questions. So, if it is normal for an employee to receive one final payroll payment after termination date, then a frequency of two or more would be the sample selection criteria. Second criteria would also be the dollar value of the final payments.

FDA FOR PERFORMANCE COMPENSATION

Employees paid based on performance can be motivated or can rationalize their behavior to falsely increase their performance. A manager may assist the employee through a disguised compensation scheme or to receive a kickback from the employee. The key to building a fraud data analytics plan is to first read and understand the performance criteria plan. The fraud auditor should then identify the methods that an employee could falsify their performance statistics. The most common techniques are to:

■ Decrease the performance criteria during the year when it becomes evident that the employee cannot achieve the target. The fraud data analysis would create two files: the performance criteria at the beginning of the year and the performance criteria at the end of the year. The sample selection is based on a reduction of the performance criteria and the employee receives a performance bonus.

■ Record false sales transactions at the end of the reporting period to achieve the performance level. There are two approaches, search for false sales recorded in the final quarter or search for reversal of false sales in the next quarter. The starting point is to identify all employees who achieved their performance bonus. The report should identify both the performance target and the total sales for the performance period. The analysis should identify total dollars the sales exceeded the target and a percentage calculation. The second file is sales returns and adjustments for all customers associated with the sales representatives. I would stratify the report by the week or month that the credit was posted. This can be tricky, because following the logic of the analysis, there will be types of credits, credits for real sales and credits for false sales. The low-sophistication approach is to cause the credits immediately after the year end; the more sophisticated approach is to cause the credits to be posted later in the preceding quarter, but before an aging analysis would identify the false sales.

 ## FDA FOR THEFT OF PAYROLL PAYMENTS

Believe it or not, sometimes employees do not pick up their final payroll check. The scenario occurs because the final payroll check is provided to someone, either human resources or an operations manager. At some point, the person holding the check falsely negotiates the check.

Employees are often entitled to final paycheck for reasons other than hours worked (i.e., unused vacation pay). Believe it or not, employees are not always aware they are entitled to a final payroll payment. How the scenario occurs in your company will depend on your organizational structure. The scenario can occur through a direct deposit, if payroll changes the bank account number either on a temporary basis or final basis. The scenario can occur through the theft of a manual check and false negotiation.

Using the speed of payment test, compare the payment date to the bank clearing date. Since payroll checks are usually negotiated quickly, the speed of payment testing is actually searching for checks that are not negotiated quickly.

SUMMARY

Fraud in payroll happens in large companies and small companies. While the traditional ghost employee seems to be the popular fraud scenario to discuss, the ghost schemes involving noncomplicit real persons is a more likely scenario. Overtime fraud most likely occurs in companies that have a base of hourly employees. False adjustment schemes as a form of disguised compensation occur with a greater frequency than fraud statistics would suggest.

In one fraud data analytics project, we identified an employee who was receiving an additional $200 per week in net payroll. When the employee's supervisor was questioned, not only did he admit it was false but he justified his actions as the best way to keep a good employee. Rationalization of events in payroll fraud scenarios by employees and supervisors should be expected by the fraud auditor.

If you have a limited time budget, what are the three fraud data analytics tests the fraud auditor should perform, and why should the fraud auditor perform the analysis?

1. The gross-to-net payroll report will identify anomalies in the relationship of gross-to-net payroll. It may not tell the fraud auditor what scenario is occurring, but it will tell the fraud auditor where to look.
2. Summarize journal entries posting the payroll register to the general ledger searching for debits to nonwage accounts. Also look for reclassification journal entries. The person committing the scheme needs to hide the

payroll scheme. Since comparison of wages to budget is a common management control, the perpetrator needs to hide the payroll scheme in a general ledger account that is not as visible as the salary account.

3. Search for the ghost employee that links to a bribe scheme. My recommendation is not based on the ease of locating but rather the impact that occurs if your company is investigated for violation of the bribery acts around the world (notably, the FCPA and the UK Bribery Act).

CHAPTER NINE

9

Fraud Data Analytics for Company Credit Cards

The general consensus is that fraud does and will occur within your procurement card system. This is not a reflection on the internal controls but rather the fraud triangle, which indicates that opportunity, pressure, and rationalization is present when fraud occurs. The opportunity is created by the fact that when an employee is assigned a procurement card, the employee can use the card for legitimate business needs or for fraudulent needs. Yes, we can implement many internal controls, but the bottom line is that we cannot prevent an employee from using the card for non-business purposes. However, we can detect the employee that uses the card for non-business purposes. Through our fraud response practices we can deter employees who may consider using the card for non-business purposes, but cannot simply stop an employee.

The purpose of the chapter is to identify the fraud scenarios associated with procurement card fraud and provide data interrogation routines that will facilitate our sample selection process. The good news is, most of the common scenarios are widely known. The bad news or difficult news is that the sheer volume of small-dollar transactions that are processed through the system on an annual basis functions as a general concealment strategy.

The starting point is to realize that the inherent fraud scenarios confronting the procurement card are the same inherent fraud scenarios described in Chapter 7. Procurement cards are a disbursement system for the company. An employee could create a shell company and then obtain a credit card account and use a company procurement card to purchase false goods or services. An employee could collude with a vendor in an overbilling scheme and the employee would receive a kickback from the vendor. The important point is to understand that the same inherent fraud scenarios confronting your accounts payable function are confronting your procurement card system.

However, the predictability factor indicates that personal purchases disguised as legitimate business expenses or purchase-for-resell fraud scenarios are the most recognized fraud schemes perpetrated by employees. External crime groups are also confronting procurement card systems, but fraud schemes perpetrated by external hackers are beyond the scope of this book.

ABUSE VERSUS ASSET MISAPPROPRIATION VERSUS CORRUPTION

The starting point of the fraud data analytics plan is to identify the types of illicit procurement card activity to be included in the audit scope. Is the plan searching for abuse, theft, or corruption? Within each category, what fraud scenarios are included in the audit scope? This is important for both the fraud data analytics and the fraud audit procedure.

1. Abuse is submitting expenses that are not consistent with company policy. The abuse may range from circumvention of internal controls to incurring expenses that are not viewed as normal and customary by the company.
2. Asset misappropriation scenarios occur when the employee receives an economic benefit that is concealed through a false representation or false receipts.
3. Corruption scenarios or FCPA violations could also be at the core of the procurement card scheme. The intent of the charge is to pay an economic gratuity or bribe to obtain a corrupt benefit.

If the plan is searching for abuse, the search criterion is company policies. If the plan is searching for asset misappropriation, the criterion is locating a transaction on the credit card statement for which the primary purpose is personal conversion. If the plan is searching for corruption, the criterion is a disguised bribe. The purpose will define how the fraud auditor judges the validity of the credit card charge.

INHERENT FRAUD SCHEME STRUCTURE

The inherent fraud scheme structure for procurement cards is similar to fraudulent disbursements described in Chapter 7. There are fraudulent vendors, complicit vendors, and non-complicit vendors. The person committing the fraud scenario is the cardholder. The fraudulent action, while similar to fraudulent disbursements, needs to be tailored to the predictable fraudulent actions known to be used in procurement card scenarios.

The fraudulent action can be written in a generic format or a specific type of expenditure format. The following illustrates the two different formats:

- Cardholder through a non-complicit vendor commits a disguised expenditure scenario, resulting in the loss of company funds.
- Cardholder through a non-complicit vendor procures gasoline for her personal vehicle, resulting in loss of company funds.

The fraudulent action defines the search routine in procurement card fraud. The action statement is critical in creating the homogeneous data file for the fraud data analytics plan. Using the generic scenario, the plan is searching all charges, whereas in the specific fraud scenario the plan is interrogating one type of charge. By combining the fraud action statement to the fraud data analytics approach, the scope of the project will become clear to the fraud auditor.

REAL VENDOR SCENARIOS WHERE THE VENDOR IS NOT COMPLICIT

The disguised expenditure fraud scheme is the most common fraud scheme described in professional literature regarding procurement cards. The scheme is easy to understand: The employee purchases an item on the company procurement card, the company pays the credit card, and the employee diverts the item for his personal use or consumption.

The legal pass-through scheme occurs when an employee uses a real vendor (e.g., PayPal) to purchase personal items on the card and the employee diverts the item for their personal use or consumption.

The purchase-for-resell fraud scheme is exactly the same as the disguised expenditure fraud scheme, except that the employee resells the purchased item and converts the sales proceeds to his own personal funds.

Abusive or excessive purchase scheme occurs when an employee purchases an item that has some business purpose but the cost of the item procured is excessive for business purposes.

Questionable business purpose scheme occurs when an employee purchases an item that does not have a true business purpose as defined by accounting policies or the contract terms and conditions.

Travel-related purchase scheme occurs when an employee purchases travel-related expenses with a procurement card and circumvents travel expense reporting procedures or seeks reimbursement for the same expenses through the travel reimbursement system.

Cash equivalent purchase scheme occurs when the employee purchases gift certificates or uses convenience checks and converts the funds to her own personal funds.

Refunds or credits scheme occurs when an employee procures an item or service with the credit card and returns the items or cancels the service. The employee then convinces the merchant to provide a refund through currency or check. The merchant could be complicit in the scheme or the merchant is simply trying to appease the customer.

Duplicate purchase scheme occurs when the employee purchases an item via the procurement card and then seeks reimbursement for the same item through another payment system such as accounts payable through employee reimbursement. In this scheme, the employee obtains two receipts from the merchant for the same item.

Duplicate purchase scheme also occurs when an employee purchases an item and the employee already receives reimbursement through an allowance program. The distinction is that the allowance program typically is controlled by human resources, whereas the previous reimbursement is controlled through accounts payable.

Supervisor fraud scenario occurs two ways. The first way is the supervisor requires an employee to purchase the item, knowing that the supervisor will approve the statement. The second approach is when the supervisor uses a terminated employee credit card, once again knowing that the supervisor approves the credit card charges.

REAL VENDOR SCENARIOS WHERE THE VENDOR IS COMPLICIT

The cash conversion scheme is when a vendor and employee collude to commit the scheme. The vendor charges the company procurement card for a sum of money, such as $500, and the vendor kicks back a portion of the $500 to the employee. The company does not receive the goods or services. This scheme occurs for personal gain or to obtain funds to pay for a bribe or economic gratuity.

The vendor overbilling scheme is when a vendor and employee collude to overbill the procurement card through higher prices, less quantity, product substitution, and false charges. The vendor provides the employee with a kickback.

An example is credit card charges that appear to have a legitimate business purpose but the event was never going to occur. To illustrate: A meeting planner schedules an event with a hotel. The contract has a cancelation clause. The employee then cancels the event, the hotel charges the credit card the cancellation fee, and the vendor pays a kickback to the employee. There is a big distinction between wasteful expenditure and a charge that occurs with the intent to misappropriate funds. The scheme can also occur when the event is planned at a higher-expense level and the procurement card is charged before the event at the higher rate. Then the meeting planner reduces the size of the event and the vendor provides a refund through a check reimbursement to the employee versus a credit to the procurement card.

Conflict-of-interest scenario occurs when a cardholder purchases from a related party and the vendor overbills the cardholder.

FALSE VENDOR SCENARIO

The employee creates a legal corporation that in fact is a shell company and contracts with a credit card company to set up a credit card account. The employee then uses the company procurement card to incur charges with the shell company. The fraud action is most likely a false billing scheme, although a variation of the pass-through scheme is possible.

IMPACT OF SCHEME VERSUS CONCEALMENT

In Chapters 1 and 3, we discussed the distinction between the fraudulent act (fraud scenario) and fraud concealment strategy. In Chapter 3, we discussed the impact of the sophistication of the concealment strategy on the proper fraud data analytics strategy. Within this chapter, we also need to stress the difference between data red flags and document red flags. These reminders are important to understand the role of the fraud data analytics plan and the fraud audit program. The following fraud scenario will be used to illustrate how the calibration of the sophistication of concealment impacts the fraud data analytics:

Using the disguised expenditure scheme, the employee purchases an item on their procurement card and converts the item to personal use.

Situation One: Low Sophistication of Concealment

The employee purchases goods from a vendor for which the merchant code is not consistent with the employee's job duties, the vendor name is a recognizable vendor in the retail community, the purchase occurs weeks before a significant holiday where giving of gifts is normal, and there are two charges on the same day at the same store, both below the control threshold, but in the aggregate the charges exceed the control threshold. There is no receipt attached to monthly statement, but the employee approves the statement of charges. Clearly, the employee assumes no one is looking at her monthly expenditures.

Situation Two: Higher Sophistication of Concealment

The employee purchases goods from a vendor where the merchant code is consistent with the employee's job duties; the vendor on the credit card statement is a legal pass-through (e.g., PayPal). The actual supplier of the goods is a retail store with multiple sites. The employee splits the purchases over many stores over different days. The expenditure does not occur around a significant holiday, the expenditure is below the control threshold, and a falsified receipt is attached to the statement. Clearly, the employee assumes he has effectively concealed his fraud scheme from management review.

Fraud data analytics in procurement cards must incorporate both the fraud scenario and the predictable concealment strategies associated with the fraud scenario into the fraud data analytics plan. So what are the concealment strategies associated with the previous illustration?

1. The sheer number of transactions and the number of cards throughout the company.
2. The use of a legal pass-through, PayPal, to hide what was purchased, and the true identity of the vendor that supplied the item.

3. The use of a vendor that has multiple retail sites.
4. Splitting the total acquisition between multiple retail sites on multiple days.

The plan must also understand the inherent limitations of the data available in a procurement card system as it relates to the fraud scenarios. In the theft-for-conversion scheme, the fraud data analytics can identify a pattern and high frequency or expenditures with a specific vendor. However, a fraud data analytics plan alone would not be able to identify the theft-for-resale scheme. The fraud auditor through examination of vendor slips would identify the anomaly in the quantity of an item purchased.

 ## FRAUD DATA ANALYTIC STRATEGIES

In Chapter 3, we discussed the four fraud data analytics strategies. The following illustrates how the strategies would correlate to a disguised expenditure scheme.

- Specific identification strategy:
  - Vendors with merchant codes inconsistent with the company or merchant codes inconsistent with the employee's job duties
  - Charges from an employee on leave
  - Charges for a terminated employee
- Internal control avoidance:
  - Pattern and frequency of split charges associated with a vendor
  - Off-period purchases that are not consistent with an employee's job duties
  - Charges during periods of vacation
  - Employee charges that are for the benefit of the supervisor
- Data interpretation:
  - Excessive or questionable expenditures
  - Charges that have questionable business purpose
  - Duplicate purchases that occur through procurement card and other payment systems
- Number anomaly:
  - Cash conversion scenarios
  - Refund scenarios
  - Pattern and frequency of split charges associated with a vendor

LINKING HUMAN RESOURCES TO CREDIT CARD INFORMATION

Employee information is useful in our ability to identify expenditure patterns that are not consistent with an employee's job duties, job position, and expenditures that occur during paid leave. The first step is to link the human resources data to the credit card information.

- Department number and job title—useful in targeted expenditure reviews.
- Compensation grade—useful to identify expenditure amounts that are excessive or exceed an amount typically associated with a grade level.
- Address information—search for purchases that are associated with an employee's personal residence.
- Hire and termination date—search for purchases that occur before hire date or after termination date. A supervisor purchases items using the terminated employee's credit card versus her own credit card. The supervisor then approves the expenditures on the terminated employee's credit card statement, avoiding her supervisor's review and approval.
- Birthdate—search for purchases that occur around an employee's birthdate.
- Vacation—personal time or extended leave; search for expenditures that occur when the employee is not working.

PLANNING FOR THE FRAUD DATA ANALYTICS PLAN

Planning reports are intended to provide the auditor with summary information by key data elements. The reports are not intended per se to identify an employee that might be committing a fraud scenario, but rather to establish statistical information regarding procurement card use:

1. Purchases by employee—providing total expenditures, count of charges, maximum, minimum, and average. The report should also include relevant human resources data.
2. Purchases by MCC code—providing total expenditures, count of charges, maximum, minimum, and average.
3. Purchases by commodity code—providing total expenditures, count of charges, maximum, minimum, and average.

4. Purchases by vendor ID number—providing total expenditures, count of charges, maximum, minimum, and average.
5. Purchases by vendor country code—providing total expenditures, count of charges, maximum, minimum, and average.

 ## FRAUD DATA ANALYTICS PLAN APPROACHES

The search for fraud in procurement cards may use different strategies to build a sample for the fraud auditor. The plan may have a single focus or may start with a primary strategy to create a homogeneous data set, then use a secondary strategy as the basis of the sample selection process. The following strategies are useful in developing the fraud data analytics plan:

1. Fraud scenario—the plan focuses on transactions that are consistent with the fraud scenario.
2. Fraud concealment—the plan focuses on the identified concealment strategies. In the concealment strategy approach, the first step is to identify transactions that link to the concealment strategy. Once transactions are identified, the fraud auditor will need to be able to link the transactions to the fraud scenario. The typical fraud concealment strategies are:
   - Split purchases at same vendor location
   - Split purchases with same vendor different location
   - Use of legal pass-through vendors to disguise the purchase
   - Purchases from an organization that provides a wide range of goods
   - Card sharing—two employees split a purchase
   - High frequency just below control threshold
   - Supervisor requires direct report employee to procure item
3. Targeted purchases—the plan focuses on specific expenditures searching for patterns and frequencies associated with an employee. Targeted purchase scenarios should focus on:
   - Expenditures that also have a personal use, such as gasoline purchases
   - Expenditures by specific departments that may have a disguised expenditure capacity (e.g., IT department where IT employees are operating a side IT business)
   - Expenditures in industries that have a high corruption index
   - Expenditures in industries that can provide personal services as a form of kickback (e.g., meeting planners booking an event and receiving free services at the location beyond normal and customary in the industry)

4. Keyword searches—the plan identifies keywords and searches for them in the description field. The analysis is useful in FCPA compliance audits.

5. Matching credit card expenditures to other databases—using the time reporting system, identify employees using procurement card while on paid leave. Identify expenses that are paid through accounts payable. Identify employees who are reimbursed for expenses through accounts payable. The focus of the strategy is to match procurement card charges to the same expense that is paid or reimbursed through other disbursement systems.

6. Employee job function—employee's job duties correlate to the type of expenditures that would be normal and customary for the job function.

FILE LAYOUT DESCRIPTION FOR CREDIT CARD PURCHASES

To illustrate the fraud data analytics plan, we will use the following file layout of data as the basis for creating the fraud data analytics plans.

1	CARD_LAST_4_DIGITS
2	MCC
3	TXN_NUMBER
4	POST_DATE
5	PURCHASE_DATE
6	AMOUNT
7	CREDIT
8	DEBIT
9	PAYMENT_AMOUNT
10	ITEM_DESCRIPTION
11	ITEM_PRICE
12	CARD_EMPLOYEE_ID
13	CARD_EXPIRE_DATE
14	CARD_PROFILE_SINGLE_TXN_LIMIT
15	ORIG_SRC_CURR_CODE
16	ORIGINAL_AMOUNT
17	ORIGINAL_CRD_AMT
18	ORIGINAL_DBT_AMT

19	ORIGINAL_PMT_AMT
20	ORIGINAL_PURCH_DATE
21	ORIGINAL_SRC_AMT
22	PURCHASE_COMMODITY_CODE
23	PURCHASE_DESTINATION_COUNTRY_CODE
24	PURCHASE_DESTINATION_POSTAL_CODE
25	PURCHASE_DISCOUNT_AMOUNT
26	PURCHASE_DUTY_AMOUNT
27	PURCHASE_ID
28	PURCHASE_ORDER_DATE
29	PURCHASE_ORGIN_COUNTRY_CODE
30	PURCHASE_ORIGIN_POSTAL_CODE
31	PURCHASE_SHIPPING_AMOUNT
32	PURCHASE_TAX_AMOUNT
33	PURCHASE_UNIQUE_INVOICE_NUMBER
34	TERMINAL_ENTRY_CODE
35	VENDOR_CITY
36	VENDOR_COUNTRY
37	VENDOR_ID
38	VENDOR_STATE
39	VENDOR_ZIP
40	POST_DT
41	PURCHASE_DT
42	PURCHASE_ORDER_DT

The starting point for fraud data analytics is to understand what data are available and how to use the data in the data interrogation phase of the analysis. Obtain the file layout from your company procurement card. Line by line, make sure you understand what data are available. Compare the actual data to the file description. Perform a limited walk-through comparing the data to an actual statement and the attached receipts to confirm your understanding.

MCC Codes

A *merchant category code (MCC)* is a four-digit number assigned to a business by a credit card company. The code reflects the primary category in which the merchant does business. The first step is to download the file and link the description to the credit card transaction file. The second step is to identify the MCC codes that are consistent with the fraud data analytics plan.

Commodity Code

The term *commodity code* refers to classification numbers for goods system developed by the World Customs Organization. It provides universal descriptions for commodities. The first four digits specify a product category and the last two digits specify a subcategory in the product category. I should caution the reader, there are different commodity code systems, so the first step is to understand which system is embedded in your data. The second step is to download the code table to add the alpha description into the data set.

FDA FOR PROCUREMENT CARD SCENARIOS

Disguised Expenditure Fraud Scenario

The fraud scenario is when a procurement card charge is personal versus business. The purchase-for-resell scenario and the legal pass-through scenario are similar to the disguised expenditure scenario; however, the fraud data analytics for the resell and legal pass-through scenarios is different due to the attributes of the scenarios.

The easiest fraud data analysis is to search for charges by employee, by MCC code, or by commodity code. The analysis focuses on those codes that would have a high degree of personal versus business. Obviously, personal versus business will depend on the employee's job duties and the industry.

The next analysis is to summarize charges by employee by vendor. The review of the report would focus on vendors that do not correlate to the employee's job duties. In some cases, the vendor name is sufficient to question the business purpose, such as a dating service vendor—unless the employee is a researcher studying the impact of online data services on society. This is why the employee's job title is critical to the analysis.

Summarize employee purchases, providing aggregate expenditure and frequency of charges. Sort by department code, searching for the employee in the department with unusually high spend levels in the department.

The sample selection is either specific identification regarding an MCC code or a commodity code or data interpretation based on the frequency and aggregate dollar analysis. The item description field is useful in the data interpretation phase of the selected analysis to identify charges for the fraud auditor's expenditure review.

The Purchase-for-Resell Fraud Scenario

The purchase-for-resell fraud scenario is exactly the same as the disguised expenditure fraud scenario, except that the conversion is for resell versus personal consumption. The key criteria are the volume of purchases by employee by vendor ID or by employee by merchant code.

The first step is to create the reports by vendor ID or by merchant code, then to exclude those lines of the report in which the dollar volume is not significant. The sample selection is either specific identification using dollar aggregate and frequency or data interpretation using the human resources data to identify a pattern not consistent with job duties.

The second report is to use the purchase destination data to identify a pattern of purchases by employee that has a high frequency of different destination codes. This would indicate the employee is ordering the item and having the item ship to the resell point.

The third report is to use the purchase destination data to identify a pattern of purchase by employee with a high frequency of the same destination code, but the location differs from the employee's home address or business address. The search is for a destination code that links to a mailbox service or mailbox forwarding address.

Legal Pass-Through Scenario

The legal pass-through scenario occurs when an employee uses a real vendor such as PayPal to purchase personal items. The starting point is with the summary of charges by vendor ID code. The fraud auditor should review the report and identify the legal pass-through scenarios that have charges in the scope period. The first homogeneous data file is all transactions linking to the identified vendor ID code for the legal pass-through entities.

The first report is a summary of all transactions for the selected vendor ID number by employee by vendor ID number. The first two columns summarize the transactions by aggregate dollars and frequency of charges. The purpose of the report is to identify the use of legal pass-through entities by employee. Data filtering should be used to reduce the size of the report based on frequency and aggregate dollar expenditures.

The next report identifies all credit card transactions for the employees on the previous report. The first column provides total charges, the second column is all charges for a non-pass-through, and the third column is all charges for pass-through vendor codes. The fourth and fifth data column is dollar difference and percentage of expenditures associated with legal pass-through vendors. The purpose of the report is to identify employees that use legal pass-through vendors with regular frequency or high aggregate dollars.

Using the specific identification strategy, the sample selection can use high aggregate dollars or frequency of charges by employee to a legal pass-through vendor.

Using solely the legal pass-through file, the second sample selection approach is using the internal control avoidance searching for split transactions, off-period transactions, round-number transactions, or transactions that occur during periods of paid leave. The focus of the review is by employee and internal control avoidance technique.

Using the data interpretation strategy, the human resources data will be useful to identify patterns and frequency that are not consistent with the employee's job duties.

Abusive or Excessive Purchase Scenario

Abusive or excessive purchase scenario occurs when an employee purchases an item that has a business purpose but the cost of the item procured is excessive for business purposes. The concept of abusive or excessive charges is relevant on a company-by-company basis. So, the starting point is to identify what charges would be viewed as excessive or abusive within your company. Examples of abusive purchases would be:

- $5,000 for a Day-Timer calendar. A calendar might be a valid business expense, but $5,000 is excessive.
- Broadway show tickets. Although some expenses are justified to entertain clients, this would be worth checking out.
- Big-screen TV. It's possible the office needs one—it could also be a personal item.

The sample selection is based primarily on data interpretation using the item description. The MCC code or commodity code is also useful in identifying abusive or excessive expenditures.

Questionable Business Purpose Scenario

Questionable business purpose scenario occurs when an employee purchases an item that has limited business purpose. Questionable business charges are a subset of abusive or excessive; however, the difference is that for a questionable charge, the event does not have a true business purpose. The charge tends to be an actual charge where the organization receives the goods and services at a fair and reasonable price. So, the first step is to define the concept of a questionable charge for your organization. I need to stress that a questionable charge in one organization might be a normal and reasonable charge in another organization. Second, in contracts, depending on the contract terms, the charge may be considered a fraudulent charge. Without establishing the concept of questionable business purpose, the fraud auditor will not have a basis for questioning the charge.

To start, let's consider the types of expenses that may occur within this scenario:

- Charges at the end of an operating period that are incurred to use the budget versus an actual need.
- An actual charge that does not relate to the contract terms and conditions.
- An actual charge that does not benefit the contract.
- Services charges exceed necessary business purpose.

The fraud data analytics is based on your definition of questionable charge. Using the concept of charges at the end of an operating period, identify all charges that occur within 30 days of the end of the operating period. Summarize the charges by employee and employee department. The sample selection is based on high frequency of charges or the aggregate dollar level.

Charges that do not benefit the contract would start with the general ledger by identifying expenditures the match a contract number originating from the procurement card. Link the general ledger charge to the procurement card data. Then summarize by contract number using the merchant code or the commodity code. The sample selection is based on the merchant code or commodity code that is not consistent with the purpose of the contract.

Travel-Related Purchase Scenario

Travel-related purchase scenario occurs when an employee purchases travel-related expenses with procurement card and circumvents procedures for reporting travel expenses.

The starting point is to understand whether procurement cards are allowed to be used for travel expenses. If not, the analysis is easy. If procurement cards are allowed to be used for travel, then the first step is to compare the credit card charges to the general ledger travel codes to exclude those charges reported through travel expense reporting.

The fraud data analytics plan should use the merchant code, 3000 series, to identify employees using the procurement card to purchase travel-related items. Other MCC codes that would useful for fraud data analytics are: Travel agency and Tour operators and Restaurant codes and other codes that provide food such as a drugstore. A third level of review are those MCC codes that could be used to circumvent travel reporting. Here are some code examples:

- Drugstores and Pharmacies
- Grocery Stores or Supermarkets
- Bakeries
- Candy Stores (my personal favorite)

The first report would be a summary of charges by employee, by MCC code based on the targeted MCC codes. The second report is matching travel expenses by employee. The key here is whether your company captures dates within the travel expense reporting. If so, then comparing travel expense dates to credit card date would identify an employee who is double dipping.

If exact dates of travel expenses are not recorded, then the travel week may be used to create two homogeneous date files: credit card charges incurred in travel status and credit card charges not incurred in travel status.

Cash-Equivalent Purchase Scenario

Cash-equivalent purchase scenario occurs when the employee purchases gift certificates or purchases convenience checks.

Gift certificates or gift cards can be purchased through many different MCC codes. At low or medium sophistication, these transactions tend to be round numbers. Therefore our first homogeneous data file would be all transactions that are an even number and a round number. The first step is to divide the charge by two; any transaction that has cents would be eliminated. The search for round numbers would be based on the number of zeros in the remaining number.

Using the number anomaly strategy, we could summarize by charge amount, by employee by charge amount, or by vendor by charge amount. Using the data interpretation for sample selection, the employee or vendor that has a high frequency or high aggregate dollar value of round number charges would be selected for audit examination.

Duplicate Purchase Scenario

Duplicate purchase scenario occurs when the employee purchases an item via the procurement card and then seeks reimbursement for the same item through another payment system, such as accounts payable through employee reimbursement.

The fraud data analysis starts with all payments to an employee through the accounts payable system. If no payments, then the scenario did not occur. In some companies, this is a unique vendor number. If not, then match vendor names to the human resource file. The general ledger code is critical to be able to use the commodity or merchant code to identify like codes. The starting point with the credit card purchases is to summarize credit card charges by employee by merchant code. Then create a second file to summarize the expenditures extracted from the general ledger code by employee and general ledger code. The last step is to match the credit card charges to the general ledger expenditures. In reality, the ability to perform this match depends on the quality of the description in the line item.

The fraud data analysis is easier to perform in the use of a targeted expenditure review, for two reasons: First, the quantity of data in a targeted expenditure review is less, and second, the expenditure data already have a commonality that can be more easily linked to a merchant code. The nature of the analysis will depend on the fraud auditor's manual review of the like expenses.

Duplicate purchase scenario occurs when an employee purchases items and the employee already receives reimbursement through an allowance program. The fraud scenario is similar in nature to the previous duplicate analysis; however, due to the nature of the allowance program, the merchant code identification is an easier match.

Supervisor Fraud Scenario

Supervisor fraud scenario occurs when supervisor requires employee to purchase item with the intent of the supervisor approving the charge.

The starting point is to link supervisor card number to employee card numbers. The department code in the human resources file is useful for this test. The next step is to summarize the expenditures by employee by vendor or by employee. The next challenge is to identify which scenario the analysis is searching for: disguised expenditures, excessive expenditures, and so on. The next challenge occurs in the fraud audit phase by obtaining a statement from the employee that he was directed by the supervisor to procure the item.

Supervisor fraud scenario also occurs when a supervisor continues to use a terminated employee's card. The first step is to match the human resources termination date to employee card number. The search is for charges that occurred after the employee's termination date.

Real Vendor Scenarios and the Vendor Is Complicit

The Cash Conversion Scenario

The cash conversion scenario is when a vendor and employee collude to commit the scheme.

The fraud scenario is usually found in travel expenses, but the fraud scenario does occur in procurement cards. The number anomaly strategy is useful to identify recurring numbers or even-number transactions by vendor by employee. The report would summarize by vendor by the amount field, providing aggregate dollar amount and frequency. The first report will be extensive. The next step is to exclude all amounts that are not even or occur with a low frequency. In searching for this vendor, it might be useful to exclude vendors that would not fit the profile of a vendor willing to commit this scenario. The sample selection is based on the frequency of the even or recurring numbers by vendor by employee.

The Vendor Overbilling Scenario

The vendor overbilling scenario is when a vendor and employee collude to overbill the procurement card. In this fraud scenario, the company is receiving goods or services from the vendor except for false charges. There is typically a valid receipt attached to the statement. Therefore, the analysis will rely on outlier analysis based on aggregate dollars. The fraud auditor will need to be knowledgeable about the purchases to be able to identify what is reasonable and what is inflated. Here are three possible approaches:

1. Compare employees in the same department and the same vendor or same merchant code to identify outliers.
2. Compare employees in a different department and the same vendor or same merchant code to identify outliers.
3. Make a detailed examination of vendors that have a high aggregate dollar value with one employee.

The vendor overbilling scenario requires extensive detailed examination of the supporting documentation by the fraud auditor to identify the overbilling scenario.

Conflict-of-Interest Scenarios

Conflict-of-interest scenario is when the cardholder purchases from a related party and the vendor overbills the cardholder.

The fraud scenario is the same as the vendor overbilling scheme with a kickback, except in this scenario, the vendor is related to the employee. Fraud data analytics most likely will not identify this scenario, but the fraud auditor should be aware of the scenario in the process of performing fraud audit procedures. The audit approach discussed in Chapter 6 for shell companies should be used to detect this scenario.

Another source of fraud is credit card charges that appear to have a legitimate business purpose but are in fact for an event that was never going to occur.

The fraud data analysis should focus on events, such as meetings, training, consulting, and service-related expenditures. The employee is in collusion with the vendor and the vendor provides a kickback to the employee. More than likely, at least one of the charges is for a real event. Usually, the first few events are real; that is how the illicit relationship started.

Use the merchant code to identify expenditures that are consistent with the type of charges fitting the profile. Sort the charges by date order. The frequency of the charge to a specific vendor in the category is the first analysis. Exclude those vendors who only have one event. Review the charges occurring from newest to the oldest, looking for an anomaly. The newest charge is when the trust relationship starts. The oldest charge is where the fraud occurs. The number anomaly strategy searching for round numbers may also be useful.

False Vendor Scenario

The employee creates a legal corporation, which in fact is a shell company, and contracts with a credit card company to set up a credit card account.

Shell companies are usually found in accounts payable. The internal employee submits invoices for goods or services not provided. However, the same scheme occurs in procurement cards. While similar to the shell company described in Chapter 6 and false billing scenarios discussed in Chapter 7, the use of a shell company in a procurement card system does have a different fraud profile.

The credit card layout used in the book has some of the information found in accounts payable files, but is not as extensive as the analysis discussed in Chapter 6. Therefore, the entity analysis is not useful as described in Chapter 6. The frequency of charges described in Chapter 7 is less critical, for two reasons. First, the visibility factor of using the procurement card is not a factor as in submitting an invoice to accounts payable. Since most procurement cards have a dollar limit on a charge, the dollar limit per charge may cause the cardholder to process more fraudulent charges. Therefore, a higher frequency of charges to a vendor that links to one cardholder number is a clue. There may be duplicate charges on the same date to stay below a control threshold.

The first analysis is to identify vendors used by one employee. The second step is to eliminate those vendors with a low frequency or low aggregate dollar level. The vendor city and Zip code can be useful as a match to the employee's home city or Zip code.

The second analysis will focus on the transaction as to purchase amount, purchase date, and purchase description. The sample selection is judgmental based on the frequency of transactions, aggregate dollar amount, and the vendor name. The purchase description may have limited information or a vague description because the shell company has no product file. It is also more likely that the transactions will have a post date or time associated with nonworking hours.

In examining the receipts, it is also likely that the transaction would have no tax amount, unless of course the employee is reporting the sales on a tax return.

SUMMARY

Fraud in procurement cards has become so commonplace that the question is not whether someone is committing a fraud scenario, but rather, if you will find the fraud scenario. Through the use of fraud data analytics driven by the fraud scenario approach, the fraud auditor should be able to locate the scenarios on the mounds of data in a procurement card system.

So, why should the fraud auditor allocate resources to a fraud scenario in P-cards that most likely will not be significant in terms of dollars? It is true, in one sense the dollar losses are not material. Depending on the industry, the adverse publicity can cause greater harm than the dollar loss. Maybe we use the examination of P-cards as a tool to identify other fraud scenarios that are occurring in your company.

Using the fraud audits or investigations performed by my company, it seems that all fraud committed by management also involved fraud through travel expenses or P-cards. In one investigation, the manager in the risk department misappropriated more than $500,000 through false claims. However, in examining his travel expenses, we found a taxi receipt he changed from seven dollars to nine dollars. Maybe we use procurement card fraud data analysis to stop the person early in the fraud cycle, or we use it to identify on which managers we should perform an extensive investigation of their operations.

CHAPTER TEN

Fraud Data Analytics for Theft of Revenue and Cash Receipts

T he opportunity to commit theft in the revenue and cash receipts cycle is greatly dependent on a number of factors ranging from quality of internal controls to management override and nature of the industry—the list goes on and on. With that said, I believe theft in the revenue cycle occurs with greater frequency than in many of the published reports regarding fraud.

The fraud scenarios in the revenue cycle occur through the theft of revenue, theft of inventory through the revenue cycle, theft of customer remittances, theft of other cash receipts, theft of customer credits or false sales returns, or false sales adjustment or credit scenarios. Also, there are conflict-of-interest schemes called pass-through customer schemes and bribery scenarios associated with preferential terms. The primary focus of this book is theft committed by an internal source and bribery involving an internal person. Fraud scenarios committed by organized crime groups or customers are not a primary focus of this chapter.

The difficulty in providing a framework for fraud data analytics in the revenue and cash receipts cycle is that business systems vary in this cycle depending on the nature of the industry, type of cash receipts, billing, and accounts receivable systems. Is the customer an individual or a multinational corporation? Is the industry a retail location or international steel manufacturer? There are so many variables that it almost seems like an impossible task to write a chapter on this topic. Readers of this chapter may need to work a little harder on seeing the applicability of the methodology to their specific industry or their company's business systems.

In this chapter, I will discuss the types of information the fraud auditor needs to understand regarding company policies and procedures. To illustrate the concepts, examples are provided on different variations of typical business processes. In revenue systems more than standardized systems like accounts payable and payroll, the fraud auditor will need to understand the business process as to how the fraud action would occur and the opportunity provided to the internal person to commit the scenario.

INHERENT SCHEME FOR THEFT OF REVENUE

The inherent fraud scheme structure is the starting point for fraud data analytics in revenue. The inherent scheme structure for entities is similar to vendors, except that in revenue, the entity structure is a customer. There are three entity structures in customer fraud scenarios. From a fraud data analytics perspective, there are three homogeneous categories of shell companies in the revenue cycle:

1. The traditional shell customer, used for the pass-through customer scheme
2. The assumed entity shell customer, used for theft of customer credits
3. The hidden entity shell customer, used for bad-debt scenarios

From a fraud data analytics perspective, there are two types of real customers:

1. Real customer that is complicit in the scheme
2. Real customer that is not complicit in the scheme

The fraud action statements are:

a. Theft of revenue before the revenue transaction is recorded
b. Theft of revenue after the revenue transaction is recorded
c. Pass-through customer scenarios
d. False adjustment and return scenarios
e. Theft of customer credit scenarios

   f. Lapping scenarios
  g. Bad-debt write-off scenarios
  h. Currency conversion scenarios or theft of sales paid in currency
   i. Other miscellaneous revenue scenarios
      a) Theft of scrap income or equipment sales
      b) Inventory theft for resale
      c) Bribery scenarios

IDENTIFYING THE KEY DATA AND DOCUMENTS

Building a fraud data analytics plan for fraud scenarios in the revenue system starts with understanding what your company sells. Do you sell inventory, services, or inventory and services? How the fraud scenarios occur is driven by the nature of your industry, how your customer places orders, and how the goods and services are delivered. How does the customer remit funds? Does the customer remit funds directly to an internal person, or are the funds remitted directly to a bank? The answers to these questions will determine how to build the fraud data analytics routines for each fraud scenario.

More importantly, will the fraud data analytics search for the theft of revenue through the sales records, inventory records, or by searching for the theft of the customer payment? As a general guideline, first the fraud data analytics searches for a missing customer invoice or a missing customer payment and then links the missing item to an internal person.

Lastly, the misappropriation of revenue occurs before the revenue transaction is recorded or after the revenue is recorded. It is that simple. Both scenarios require a concealment strategy to hide the misappropriation of the revenue, inventory, and customer payments.

Customer Sales Records

For sales orders, the revenue process starts with either a customer placing an order or a salesperson placing an order. Customer orders can originate from a customer (a purchase order), a salesperson using an internal sales order form, or via a customer appointment. The importance of the sales order transaction is that it is the first recorded event that a sales transaction may have occurred. These records are useful in the theft of revenue before the revenue is recorded or the theft of customer remittances.

Sales invoices are recorded in a sales journal, and the invoices typically have an invoice number, invoice date, invoice amount, description of the item sold, and are recorded in a general ledger account. The sales invoice is the record indicating that a sales transaction occurred between a customer and your company. These records are useful in the theft of revenue after the revenue is recorded.

Inventory records indicate that something was purchased and something happened to the inventory. It was sold, stolen, or written off.

Shipping records indicate where the item was shipped and the method of acceptance by the customer. The shipping records establish that the inventory was removed from your company for some purpose. These records are useful for pass-through scenarios.

Service records indicate where a service was provided, who provided the service, what service was provided, and whether the service provided labor or labor and parts. These records are useful in the theft of revenue before the revenue is recorded or the theft of customer remittances.

Customer Payment Records

Customer payments are in the form of currency, checks, credit card, electronic transfer, or a financing payment. Customer payments are recorded in a cash receipts journal and a customer account. Typically customer payments in the form of currency or checks are the most prone to theft.

Customer accounts receivable records reflect all recorded customer activity as to customer invoices, customer payments, and customer adjustments or returns. Accounts receivable records provide a history of all customer activity. These records are useful for false adjustment scenarios, theft of credit balances, lapping scenarios, and bad-debt write-off scenarios.

Understanding how customer master file data, sales order data, sales invoice systems, and customer remittance files relate to each fraud scenario is the basis of developing the fraud data analytics plan.

Planning Reports for the Theft of Revenue and Customer Remittances

In theft of revenue scenarios the starting point is the margin analysis when focusing on the revenue transaction. The follow-up to margin analysis is the use of disaggregated analysis to the lowest finite point possible. When focusing on the theft of customer payment, it is the composition of cash receipts as to the type of cash receipts or those transactions that cause the customer balance to reflect a zero balance due. The fraud data analytics plan should start with summary reports by transaction type, by customer, and by an internal person.

Remember, the planning reports are not intended to find the fraud scenario but are intended to assist in the likelihood question of which fraud scenarios are more predictable.

THEFT OF REVENUE BEFORE RECORDING THE SALES TRANSACTION

The attributes of theft of revenue *before* revenue as recorded for purposes of this chapter is defined as:

- Goods or services were provided to the customer.
- Customer initiated an action, either a customer order or a customer appointment.
- Customer is either complicit or not complicit.
- Customer payments are not mailed to a lockbox or electronically transferred to the bank.
- Customer payments are received directly by an internal person.
- For inventory, the internal person either diverts the customer payment or sells the inventory.
- For services, the customer payment was diverted by the internal person providing the service or by an internal person in a position of receiving a customer payment.

Starting with theft of inventory, the item is removed from the premises before a sales transaction is recorded. In one sense, the scheme is an inventory theft scheme. In one sense, the scheme is a theft of revenue. The answer to the question depends on the person committing the scheme. Is the scheme being perpetrated by a warehouse employee or someone in the sales function? The bottom line is there is no entry in a sales journal. The lack of a recorded sales transaction allows the internal person to misappropriate the customer payment or the inventory for resale.

There are scenarios that involve theft of revenue before creating the sales invoice by initiating a sales order that causes the necessary documents to be created to allow the removal of inventory. The sales order then is voided or deleted, resulting in no sales invoice being created, or the sales invoice is changed to a zero invoice. The internal documents allow for the inventory to be removed from the premises without detection.

The fraud data analytics for the previous scenario needs to search the sales order file for deleted or voided sales orders or search the sales invoice file for a zero dollar invoice or a missing sales invoice number. The frequency of the event by customer or the internal person is the first clue. Off-period analysis linking the change to an internal person that is changing the sales order is also useful.

There are scenarios that involve theft of revenue before creating a sales invoice that occur by simply accepting the customer payment and providing the customer with the inventory. The fraud data analytics starts with summarizing sales by product and the number of units sold. The fraud audit procedure is to identify a supply item that correlates specifically to the sales unit. In one project, the theft involved the selling of cakes. The purchased item for comparison to the sales records was the cardboard round used under the cake. The analysis projected that over 2,000 cakes sales were misappropriated in one year, resulting in the loss of over $200,000.

The fraud data analytics through inventory records needs to compare purchase records for inventory to the sales records associated with the inventory record. The initial analysis is focusing on purchase-units (adjusted for inventory balances) that exceed the corresponding revenue units, which indicates missing revenue. If the inventory was shipped, then link the missing items to shipping address. The sample selection will focus on the frequency of the missing item to a common address. If the item was not shipped, the sample selection is based on purchase units exceeding sales units.

Theft of revenue for services indicates that the customer ordered the services, the services were provided, and the customer payment was diverted. The fraud data analytics starts with the customer appointment records, followed by matching to a customer invoice. The sample selection is based on the frequency of sales orders with no sales invoice. The sample selection is then refined based on the frequency of no sales invoice that links to an internal service provider.

The theft of customer payment is typically currency. The first data analytics is to summarize customer payment by the type of customer payment: currency, credit card, check, electronic transfer, or financing. Since credit card payments, electronic payment, and financing occur through an independent party, the most likely theft is customer payments in the form of currency or customer checks. Theft of customer checks is not as challenging as many people believe. The check can be negotiated by a forged endorsement, check-cashing companies, night deposits, or conspiring with a dishonest banker.

The fraud data analytics for the theft of customer payments should start with a summary of cash receipts by type of cash receipts over an extended period of time. The analysis is looking for a downward trend in the percentage of currency. Once identified, the fraud data analysis is similar to theft of revenue before the revenue transaction is recorded.

THEFT OF REVENUE AFTER RECORDING THE SALES TRANSACTION

Theft of revenue *after* the revenue is recorded means that there is an entry in the sales system indicating a sales transaction. In this scenario, the internal person must cause the sales invoice to be voided or deleted, change the sales invoice to a zero amount, or cause the customer invoice to reflect payment. The fraud data analytics should search the sales invoice file, the cash receipts journal, or the customer's accounts receivable records.

In the theft of revenue scenarios, the fraud scenario will occur either with a repeated pattern to a customer or a random pattern of customers. The repeated pattern indicates the internal person is in collusion with that customer. In the repeated pattern scheme, the customer forwards the payment to the internal person or the internal person is motivated by a personal relationship with the customer. In the random pattern scheme, the internal person is not in collusion with the customer and the internal person is diverting the customer payment.

The fraud data analytics on the sales invoice file will use the specific identification strategy searching for gaps in the sequential pattern of sale invoice numbers or search for zero dollar invoices. If a change record is available, then search for changes to customer invoices. If there are gaps in the sales invoice number or zero dollar invoices, the fraud data analytics has found the theft after recording.

If no gaps in the invoice numbers, the fraud data analytics will search the customer accounts to determine how the customer account was caused to show a zero balance:

- Pattern and frequency of adjustments to a specific customer with an occurrence rate that exceeds normal business standards.
- Pattern and frequency of adjustments associated with an internal person with an occurrence rate that exceeds normal business standards.
- Pattern and frequency of adjustments to a random customers account indicates transfer of dormant customer credit balances or dormant credits transactions to cause the customer balance to reflect a zero balance.

PASS-THROUGH CUSTOMER FRAUD SCENARIO

The pass-through customer scheme is composed of three entities. The first company is your company, the second entity is a shell company (shell customer), and the third entity is a customer to the shell customer (real customer).

The shell customer is controlled by an internal person, typically someone in the sales function. The internal person uses their position of authority to sell to the pass-through customer at deep discounts, which enables the pass-through customer to sell the item in the marketplace.

The pass-through customer purchases the goods from your company with the full intent of reselling the goods or services to the real customer. Your company ships the goods to the real customer versus the front customer. In more advanced scenarios, the shipping address is a freight-forwarding company. The real customer remits funds to the pass-through customer. The pass-through customer remits the funds for all purchases to your company. In real life, there may be different variations; however, fundamentally, all pass-through customer scenarios operate in a similar manner. In Chapter 7, there is an extensive discussion of pass-through vendors. Use that discussion to adapt the pass-through customer scenarios for the potential permutations of entity type.

FDA for Pass-through Customer Scenarios

The fraud data analytics starts with the entity because the entity structure is a false entity. The false customer testing follows the same logic as followed in Chapter 6 for shell companies.

- Match to employee database for address and telephone. Change analysis for dormant customers as described in Chapter 6.
- Specific identification testing using the missing information analysis.
- Specific anomaly testing:
  - Credit limit is higher-than-normal standards for a new customer or rapid increase of the credit limit.
  - Email address that uses a public email address.
  - No bank account information.
  - Company name is nondescriptive (i.e., initials only).
  - Creation date of customer is within a maximum of 48 months of audit scope date. Most likely, I would start the analysis at 24 months and then review the results.
  - Duplicate shipping address for two or more customers.
  - Shipping address links to freight-forwarding address.
  - Multiple shipping addresses for one customer in a common geographic area.

The fraud data analytics for the transaction analysis starts with the cash receipts journal for the pass-through customer payments:

- Search for a sequential pattern of check numbers from the customer in the cash receipts journal.
- Search for a limited range of customer check numbers from the customer in the cash receipts journal.

The fraud data analytics for the sales invoice file for the pass-through customer follows:

- Compare unit price on customer invoice to product file, searching for a pattern of deep discounting.
- Search customer invoices with a line-item discount.
- Search customer accounts receivable file for a frequency of sales adjustments.
- Search for customers within the 48-month period that are receiving preferential terms (e.g., no shipping charges).
- A common tendency is the customer aging becomes more delinquent over time.

FALSE ADJUSTMENT AND RETURN SCENARIOS

In this scheme, a fictitious sales return or sales adjustment is posted to a customer's account by an internal person. To illustrate the concept:

In retail, the store clerk provides a refund to a customer credit card for a return that never occurred.
In retail, a customer commits a shoplifting scheme by first stealing the item, then returning the item for a credit to his or her account.
In the telecommunication industry, customer service personnel are authorized to provide credits to customers that complain of service-related issues.
In the health food or vitamin industry, the sales force is authorized to provide credits for items that were not sold before their expiration date.

The fraud data analytics brainstorming starts with understanding how an internal person can cause a false adjustment or false return to be posted to a customer's account. The second aspect is to understand how the internal person benefits from the fraud scenario. The use of frequency analysis associated with either a customer or internal person is a good starting point.

FDA for False Adjustment and Return Scenarios

The starting point for the fraud data analytics is to identify the internal person that initiates the sales return or sales adjustment. The second aspect is to understand whether the return and adjustment is matched to a sales transaction or is posted to the customer balance. The last aspect is to understand whether the internal person enters the transaction, as in retail, or whether the internal person's actions cause another noncomplicit internal person to enter the transaction. The information is critical to develop the right scenario for the industry and your company.

When the internal person can enter the transaction, the starting point is a summary of transactions by internal person by customer. Assuming the coding for a sales adjustment is different from a sales return, the summary of transactions should be by type of transaction. The summary report should be by internal person by customer, providing frequency of transaction and aggregate dollar value. The key data element is the frequency analysis by internal person by customer. If the internal person cannot enter the transaction, then the frequency analysis is by customer with greater attention to the aggregate dollar value by customer.

Since the volume of data is extensive, the use of the inclusion and exclusion theory is critical to reduce the size of the initial report. The sample selection is based on the frequency of adjustment to one customer account. If no high frequency is noted, the use of data interpretation becomes necessary in reviewing the data for an anomaly that links to a customer or an internal person.

THEFT OF CUSTOMER CREDIT SCENARIOS

In this scenario, a valid sales return or sales adjustment is posted to a customer's account. Typically, the credit transaction becomes dormant. In the scenario, an internal person steals the dormant credit by transferring the credit to a customer account that is under the control of the internal person. The under control concealment theory indicates the internal person is linked to the customer address or customer bank account number. The concept of dormant credit may have different meanings, depending on how credits are applied to a customer's account. The dormant credits are:

- Customer is a dormant customer with a credit balance.
- Open credit that the customer has not used for whatever reason.
- Open credit that has not been applied to an invoice.

The second scenario is to change the dormant customer address to an address that the internal person controls either directly or in collusion with a third party. The fraud data analytics starts with changes to customer addresses or bank account information. The second step is to search the accounts for refunds. The sample selection is based on the frequency of refunds to an address or the frequency of the transfer of a dormant credit by the internal person.

The conversion of the theft of customer credits can occur through accounts receivable or accounts payable. In accounts payable the goal is to have a refund issued to a customer that effectively is under the control of the internal person. In accounts receivable, the goal is to provide a real customer with a credit that belongs to another customer. The motivations to falsely transfer the customer credit might be a kickback from the real customer or a family or personal relationship with the customer.

FDA for Theft of Customer Open Credits through Accounts Payable

In the accounts payable approach, there are two general approaches:

1. Create an FDA file of dormant customer accounts with a recent refund. In Chapter 6 on shell companies, we provide an FDA for vendors; the FDA for customers would be similar:
   a) The customer master file should have a code indicating that the customer is inactive. Search the change file for changes to the activity code from inactive to active.
   b) If there is a change file, search for a change to the address or bank account.
   c) If no change file is maintained, then compare a customer master file from two years ago to the current year, searching for changes to the activity code. There is nothing magic about the two-year point. In your company, you may decide to shorten or expand the duration.

    d) Using the accounts receivable file from two years ago, summarize the debits and credits. Any customer that has no activity is a dormant customer. Then perform the same summary for the current year, searching for customers with activity. Then match the two-year-old customer file with no activity to the current-year file customer file and identify any customers that were dormant and no have current-year activity.

2. An internal person causes a change to the customer's address or bank account for a dormant customer account to an address or bank account that the internal person controls. The second step for the fraud perpetrator is to initiate a refund request on behalf of the dormant customer. Accounting then issues the refund and either mails or electronically transfers the refund to the fraud perpetrator. The fraud data analytics should create a homogeneous data file of all customer refunds and search for a duplicate address or bank account in the refund address.

3. Using the list of dormant accounts, the goal is to search for transfers of dormant customer credits. Summarize the transfer of credits focusing on the recipient of the credit. If the scenario is occurring, the report should show multiple credits from multiple customer accounts going to one customer account. The customer account receiving the multiple transfers would have multiple refunds.

4. The internal person in collusion with a real customer may transfer credits from a dormant customer, and the real customer may request a refund. This item is different from the previous item because the focus point is the transfer of credits versus the change of an address.

FDA for Theft of Customer Open Credits through Accounts Receivable

In the accounts receivable system, the common data element is the transfer of credits to a customer account. The motivation is not a critical element to the fraud data analysis, except for the frequency analysis associated with the customer receiving the credit. In this scheme, the internal person is in collusion with a customer.

The fraud data analysis starts with identifying the transfer of all customer credits, whether payments, sales returns, or sales adjustments. The next step is a summary of transfers by internal person, then by customer. The summary report should provide both frequency and dollar aggregate of the transfers. The sample selection is based on the frequency of transfers to a customer. The person making the transfer is the secondary criterion of the sample selection.

LAPPING SCENARIOS

In this scheme, an internal person misappropriates a customer's payment for a recorded sale. To hide the theft of the customer payment (first customer), the internal person applies another customer's payment (second customer) to the first customer's account. The scheme continues with the theft of another customer's payment with the application of another customer's payment. Eventually, the fraud scheme becomes so large that the sheer weight of the fraud scheme becomes too difficult for the internal person to hide. There are many variations of the scheme. The scheme can apply to various industries, although the mechanics of the scheme is the same.

The key to the scheme is the ability to steal a customer's payment and apply a credit to the customer's account. The credit to the customer's account is the audit trail for the fraud data analytics plan. It is important to understand if the customer payments are applied to a specific invoice or a customer balance. The fraud data analytics will vary depending on the how customer payments are applied.

FDA for the Traditional Lapping Scenario: Applied to a Balance

The fraud data analytics should start with the cash receipts journal. The analysis is simple. Using the cash receipts journal, identify the customer number, customer name, cash receipt amount, date of customer's remittance, and the control number on the remittance. The fraud data analytics will create monthly columns of the customer remittance number by customer. The fraud data analytics will compare the remittance control number on the first month to the remittance control number on the second month, etc. The report should subtract the control number from the first column from the control number on the second column, and so on. Since control numbers are typically ascending, the fraud data analytics is looking for a negative change in the calculation. The reason for the negative change is the perpetrator is applying any customer's payment to any customer account balance.

FDA for the Traditional Lapping Scenario: Applied to Customer Invoice

The fraud data analytics should start with the cash receipts journal. The fraud data analytics will depend on the extent of detail captured in the cash receipts journal and depend on whether the perpetrator is posting both the cash receipts journal and the accounts receivable records. The weakness in concealing the scheme for the perpetrator is finding a customer's payment that matches the customer's payment that was stolen. The fraud data analytics is searching for a customer payment that is applied to more than one customer's account. If the remittance amount is posted in total, then the cash receipt transaction may have more than one customer's account number. If a customer remittance amount is split in the cash receipts journal, then search for a duplicate control number, duplicate date, and more than one customer number. The key in both situations is the multiple customer account numbers.

FDA for the Traditional Lapping Scenario: Use of Dormant Credits

The theft of a customer's payment may also be concealed by applying a dormant credit from one customer's account to the account with the customer's remittance that was stolen. The fraud data analytics should search for transfers between two customers' accounts. The date of the credit that is transferred is the key data element for sample selection.

 ## ILLUSTRATION OF LAPPING IN THE BANKING INDUSTRY WITH TERM LOANS

Loan officers have been known to issue loans to fictitious customers and then divert the bank funds. I use the term *loan officer* loosely to mean any bank official who has the authority or capacity to issue a loan. To illustrate the concept, we will assume the loan is a 90-day term loan. At the end of the 90 days, the loan is due. To conceal the fraud scenario, the loan officer must find a way to repay the loan or ensure the loan does not appear on the delinquency report. The first way is to issue a new loan to repay the old loan. The new loan is either in the same customer's name or in a different customer's name. The second way is to divert funds from a dormant bank account or a bank account that has minimal activity and minimal monitoring by a customer. The last way is to use a variation of the lapping scheme to keep the loan from appearing on the delinquency report.

FDA for Lapping in the Banking Industry with Term Loans

Starting with a new loan, the fraud data analytics should summarize loan activity by customer over an extended period of time. The FDA is searching for a pattern of customer loans with term loans that are consecutively issued by using the dates of the term loan. Each term loan should have an increasing balance because the new loan is used to pay the old loan plus the interest.

The second approach occurs when the second loan used to pay the first loan is in a different fictitious customer's name. Using the cash receipts journal, the search is for a customer name or customer number on the cash receipts journal that is applied to a different customer loan balance.

The third approach is when the loan officer diverts funds from a dormant customer to pay off the fictitious customer loan balance. The loan officer may either transfer the funds to a bank account in the fictitious customer's name to repay the loan or transfer the fund directly from the dormant customer to the fictitious loan balance. Using the cash receipts journal, the search is for a customer name or customer number on the cash receipts journal that is applied to a different customer loan balance. If the payment is directly from the dormant bank account, the FDA starts with first identifying dormant accounts that have become active. The FDA is similar to the cash receipts journal test, searching for payments of a loan balance that match a withdrawal from a dormant account.

Bad-debt scenarios occur through either a customer or an internal person

There are three primary variations of the bad-debt scheme. The variation is caused by the person committing the scheme, which is explained below. The fraud action is the same: The customer balance is written off based on false reasons. The second aspect is whether the customer remains active after the false write-off. The conversion occurs through a kickback to the internal person, or the internal person commits an asset misappropriation scheme by diverting the customer payment. Many companies have internal procedures that require delinquent customer payments to be directed to the internal collection person. The internal collection person could also advise the customer to wire the funds to a special bank account, thereby diverting the customer payment. Remember, desperate people will do desperate things to conceal the fraud scenario.

1. Customer intentionally does not pay for goods and services. At some point, your company stops selling to the customer and eventually the customer balance is written off. However, the customer creates a new company and starts the process all over again.
2. An internal person accepts a kickback from a customer that is in a severe collection status to write off the balance of the account. Typically, the internal person causes a new customer file to be established for the customer, and the delinquent customer is complicit.

3. An internal person working in collections diverts payments from customers that are in severe collection status. The internal person writes off the remaining customer balance and causes a new customer file to be established for the customer. In this scheme, the customer is not involved.

4. An internal person working in collections diverts payments from customers who are in severe collection status. The internal person then uses dormant credits from another customer account to offset the theft of the customer payment. In this scheme, the customer account remains intact.

The common element in the scheme is that the delinquent customer is reinstated into the active sales file with a different identity. The fraud data analytics starts by identifying delinquent customers; that is the first data criterion. The second criterion is to identify the delinquent customers that are closed or have become dormant as to sales activity. Using the homogeneous data file the fraud data analytics performs a duplicate test by comparing the delinquent customers to the active customers. The duplicate test is based on address, shipping address, bank account, telephone number, government identification number, email address, and contact person. The first analysis is using the exact match followed by the close match.

In the use of dormant credit scheme the fraud data analytics starts with the homogeneous data file of delinquent customers. A key data element is the date the customer was classified as delinquent. The fraud data analytics then searches the customer account for transfers of credits or payments to a delinquent account.

CURRENCY CONVERSION SCENARIOS OR THEFT OF SALES PAID IN CURRENCY

In this scheme, an internal person is misappropriating currency received from customers. The internal person is concealing the theft of currency by holding back customer checks or using checks from miscellaneous sources for future deposit to conceal the theft of currency.

In theft of revenue scenarios, currency is usually the first form of cash receipts that is misappropriated. From an internal control perspective, the accounting system should categorize cash receipts as to the form of cash receipts: currency, customer check, credit card, etc. A report should be prepared periodically summarizing cash receipts as to the form of cash receipts. If currency is being misappropriated, then currency as a percentage of total cash receipts will decrease. In my experience, in one case currency as a percentage of cash receipts went from 25 percent to 1 percent. The internal person misappropriated over a quarter of a million dollars in a two-year period.

The first FDA is to summarize by the form of cash receipts for a 12-month period; in this way, all the cycles of the year are reflected on the FDA report. The search is for downward trend of currency as percentage of total cash receipts. The fraud auditor may also want to benchmark changes to changes in personnel.

If the cash receipts journal does not capture the form of cash receipts, then the FDA should search for the absence of an event associated with the receipt of currency. The key in the analysis is comparing the amount of cash receipts to an income production statistic that the perpetrator cannot control or alter.

To illustrate the concept, a medical practice receives copays from patients. The FDA would create a homogeneous data file of copays and patient billings. The first report would be a summary of copays by day, providing frequency and aggregate dollar. The second report should be able to match all billings for office services to copays, understanding that not all visits require copays. In a professional service business associated with tax preparation, the FDA would reconcile customer's payments to the number of tax returns filed. The key is to use a second file that the perpetrator cannot alter or change.

THEFT OF SCRAP INCOME OR EQUIPMENT SALES

Theft of scrap income or miscellaneous equipment sales is a common scheme primarily because of the ease of committing the scheme, and lack of formalized procedures for controlling the sale and the receipt of scrap income. The fraud scenario is a crime of opportunity. The scenario is on point with the theft of revenue before the revenue transaction is recorded. From an internal control perspective, scrap income should be recorded in a miscellaneous income account for easy monitoring. Unfortunately, in my experience scrap income is posted in an expense account associated with the expense associated with the scrap sale.

The first step is to summarize scrap income over a period of time. Since scrap sale scenarios have been known to occur over long periods, the scope of analysis may be greater than two years. The first red flag is no scrap income. The second red flag is scrap income that is less than expected.

In most scenarios, the audit trail for fraud data analytics stops at this point. However, if the scrap income is associated with a project involving the replacement of a tangible asset, the next step is to compute the amount of tangible product purchased and compare the amount purchased to the dollar value of the scrap income. To illustrate the concept, consider the following:

In one project, the theft of scrap income was associated with the replacement of water pipe. Based on the footage of the replacement water pipe, we calculated the amount of scrap water pipe. We used actual scrap water pipe to determine the weight of the scrap pipe and then estimated the total amount of scrap pipe in yards. Then the fraud audit procedure compared the projected scrap income to the scrap income deposited in the company bank accounts.

 ## THEFT OF INVENTORY FOR RESALE

Theft of inventory scenarios is not truly a *theft of revenue* scenario. The crime is associated with weak physical inventory controls or weak internal controls over disposal of inventory. However, it would seem remiss not to at least mention the scheme.

Similar to the theft of scrap income, the theft of inventory does not provide an audit trail, except for something is missing. Missing red flags are associated with inventory shortages or a frequency of inventory adjustments associated with inventory write-off.

If the scheme involves theft between two locations, the fraud data analytics would focus on matching transfers between the two locations. For those transfers that do not have a match, the second step is to match the missing transfers to someone. If the theft scheme is simply removing the inventory, then there is no audit trail.

If the tangible good is not recorded in an inventory account, then the fraud data analytics would use the summary tool to determine the quantity of an item purchased. Using data interpretation, the sample selection is based on whether the quantity purchased is reasonable for the business operation.

One last approach is based on understanding what inventory or supplies are purchased and would have easy resell value. The fraud data analytics for this approach is similar to a targeted expenditure review. This approach requires the fraud auditor to truly think like a thief.

 ## BRIBERY SCENARIOS FOR PREFERENTIAL PRICING, DISCOUNTS, OR TERMS

The mention of bribery generally causes auditors to focus on the procurement cycle. However, bribery also occurs in the sales cycle when a customer wants favorable pricing or favorable terms. As indicated in the procurement chapter, the fraud data analytics uses inference analysis. If it is too good to be true, then it most likely is false. The starting point is to understand policies and procedures for customer pricing and customer terms and conditions. The second aspect is to identify the internal person who has the authority to provide customer pricing and terms. I suggest the fraud auditor review the concept of internal control inhibitors in developing the permutations of the person committing the scheme. While the fraud action is the critical aspect, the internal person committing the scenario will assist the fraud auditor in the interpretation of the results.

The third aspect will depend on the nature of your industry. In banking, it is the issuance of a loan to a customer that is not creditworthy. In the manufacturing or wholesale industry, bribery occurs by providing a customer with favorable pricing. The fraud auditor needs to understand the likely benefits for which the customer would be willing to a pay a bribe.

The fraud data analysis is by pricing, specific sales or payment terms, or customer acceptance. The pricing is either based on differences between book price and sales invoice price or customer discount. Terms relate to those items that provide the customer a benefit such as credit limit or payment terms. The sample selection will use the data interpretation to select a sample based on anomalies for your company.

SUMMARY

To repeat, fraud data analytics in the revenue cycle more than any other core business systems must be adapted to the industry and the company's internal revenue systems, policies, and procedures. The selection of the three fraud data analytics every audit plan should include is impossible. With that said, the single fraud data analytics routine is based on the fraud scenario that has a common occurrence in the industry:

- In the banking industry, the fraud data analytics should search for fictitious term loans.
- In industries selling a tangible good, the fraud data analytics should search for the pass-through scheme.
- In industries in which the customer pays for goods or services with currency, the fraud data analytics should search for the theft of currency.

CHAPTER ELEVEN

Fraud Data Analytics for Corruption Occurring in the Procurement Process

C orruption in the purchasing function is all about creating the illusion of compliance with purchasing procedures and competitive purchasing practices. In reality, the selection of the supplier was predetermined and the process was rigged to ensure the favored supplier was selected. Sounds simple! In reality, corruption in the purchasing function is the most difficult to identify and prove for the fraud auditor. Therefore, our goal for isolating our fraud anomaly is to search for circumvention of the selection process or for the appearance of favoritism in the selection process. The fraud auditor through document examination and interviews will need to determine if the selection of the supplier was corrupted with an evil motive.

In fraud data analytics, it is important to understand the scope of the project and what fraud scenarios can be realistically identified with the fraud data analytics plan. In the expenditure cycle, corruption can occur at the selection process or at the administration process. This chapter is solely for the selection process; supplier overbilling was covered in Chapter 7. The realistic goal of fraud data analytics for corruption in the selection process solely depends on the technique used to corrupt the process.

WHAT IS CORRUPTION?

Corruption is the act of doing something with the intent of giving some advantage inconsistent with the official duty and rights of others. The corrupt influence occurs at either of the following:

- Contract award—the bribe
- Execution of a contract—the kickback

The intent of the corrupt act is to obtain an undue advantage. The corrupt influence occurs by:

- Overt influence—directly impacts purchase process or the bid documentation.
- Covert influence—information provided to the advantage of one supplier.
- Indirect influence—uses management position or personal integrity to influence others to award purchase to supplier.

Understanding how and where corruption occurs in the purchasing process will help the fraud auditor in interpreting the data consistent with the corruption theory. The second step is to understand who corrupted the process: purchasing function, budget owner, or supplier?

INHERENT FRAUD SCHEMES FOR THE PROCUREMENT FUNCTION

The fraud scenario methodology starts with understanding the inherent scheme component of the corruption fraud risk structure. Then the fraud auditor needs to convert the inherent scheme structure to a fraud scenario consistent with the scope of the audit project and company procedures.

In procurement, the fraud auditor starts with the assumption that the supplier that is awarded the purchase order is a real supplier or a pass-through supplier and the supplier is complicit in the fraud scenario. I should clarify that I will use *purchase order* throughout the chapter to indicate either contract or purchase order.

The supplier is either in collusion with an internal person or in collusion with other suppliers, referred to as supplier bid rigging. The suppliers named on the bid documents are a real supplier that is complicit, a pass-through supplier, or a real supplier that is not complicit in the scenario. However, the complicity aspect is for the fraud auditor to determine through document examination phase of the fraud auditor. The importance of understanding the person committing the scenario is to understand who is corrupting the process. The typical permutations of persons committing the scenario are as follows:

1. Real supplier operating with one name is complicit with an internal source.
2. Real supplier operating under multiple names (hidden entity) is complicit with an internal source.
3. Real supplier is operating under a false government preference classification.
4. Real supplier is complicit with an external source (real supplier).
5. Subcontractor to a general contractor is complicit with an internal source.
6. Internal source has an undisclosed ownership in a shell company or a subcontractor, which is a pass-through supplier.
7. Internal source has an undisclosed ownership in a real supplier or subcontractor, referred to as an ownership conflict of interest.

While the fraud data analytics focuses on the fraud action statement, understanding the entity structure is important in the data interpretation phase of the fraud audit. In procurement, the fraud action statement has two parts: the primary action statement and the secondary action statement. The primary action statement is the scope of the project and the secondary fraud action statement is the basis of the fraud data analytics plan. The ability to identify the secondary category depends on the data within your procurement database. The fraud audit procedures must follow the fraud audit approach for the secondary fraud category that is explained later in the chapter.

The fraud risk structure starts with the primary category followed by the secondary categories:

■ Bid avoidance is the method used by the internal person to avoid the bidding process. The internal person uses the following techniques to avoid the bid process:
  ■ False sole source statement
  ■ Splitting the purchase order
  ■ False justification for purchase order extension
  ■ Management override
  ■ Limiting the time for suppliers to respond to the bid request

- Internal person corrupts the need phase or specification phase of procurement by:
  - Creating a need that exceeds company requirements as to specifications or quantity
  - Market timing to allow for higher prices
  - Future changes not disclosed
  - Hidden defect not disclosed
  - Specification favors awarded supplier: restrictive specifications
  - Specification favors awarded supplier: vague specifications
  - Specification or quantity favors awarded supplier: advance communication
  - Selection criteria favor awarded supplier
- Internal person facilitates the corruption of procurement by allowing false statements regarding the suppliers requested to bid on the project:
  - Unqualified supplier—financial
  - Unqualified supplier—capacity or capabilities
  - Unqualified supplier—experience
  - False statement of capacity or capabilities
  - False statement of experience
  - False statement of financial capacity
  - False statement of certifications
  - Exclude a qualified supplier from the bidding process
  - Supplier has a history of poor performance
  - Unreasonable "pre-qualification" procedures
  - Failure to advertise bid to entities consistent with policy
  - Supplier is in the proper industry but the supplier is not equipped to provide the goods or service
- Internal person corrupts integrity of the receipt, opening, and control of the bid documents by:
  - Acceptance of late bids
  - Awarded supplier: allows changes during the bid evaluation
  - Creates false bids
  - Discards bids
  - Revealing bidder information to other bidders
  - Intentional withdrawal of bidder
  - Acceptance of nonresponsive terms in bid
  - Insufficient documentation submitted or retained

- Internal person allows the negotiation of the terms and conditions after the opening of the final bids to the benefit of one supplier. It should be noted that in some organizations for some purchase orders there may be multiple submissions of bid documents; therefore, the word *final* is critical to the scenario.
  - Preferred terms or conditions
  - Speed of payment considerations
- Internal person creates bid criteria that favor one supplier.
  - Selection criteria favor awarded supplier
  - Acceptance of nonresponsive bids
  - False evaluation of bid
  - False benchmarking
- Internal person simply corrupts the selection process used in awarding the purchase order to the supplier by management override of internal controls:
  - Award to nonlowest supplier
  - Award to unqualified supplier
  - Change of selection criteria after bid opening
  - Scoring system favors selected supplier
  - Supplier is allowed to resubmit bid
  - False disqualification of a qualified supplier
  - Withdrawal of qualified supplier and supplier becomes a subcontractor to the purchase order
- Change order is the process of managing the changes that occur throughout the life of the project. The following are common red flags of corrupt intent:
  - Multiple change orders
  - Changes for unforeseen items
  - Prior bidder becomes a subcontractor
- Post-administration, which is the payment process and change order process. (See Chapter 7.)

Remember the analogy in Chapter 2 of the fraud auditor who is running the marathon? Fraud by itself is the marathon; the primary fraud risk category is the first way of establishing the mile markers of the race. The second fraud risk category serves as a diagnostic tool in reviewing data patterns and documents identified in the planning stage of the fraud audit. Once bid avoidance or favoritism is identified, the next step is to search for the secondary fraud action statement.

Process of Converting the Inherent Scheme to a Fraud Scenario for a Targeted Expenditure

The fraud scenario comprises the person committing the scenario, the type of entity, the action statement, and the impact. Fraud scenarios in procurement fraud as described in this chapter include collusion. The collusion either occurs between an internal person and a real entity or between a real entity and a real entity. The fraud scenario statement starts with describing the person that is corrupting the decision process followed by the real entity. Therefore, in corruption scenarios the second person committing the scenario is also the complicit real entity. The fraud action statement typically starts with the secondary action statement followed by the primary action statement. The following three scenarios illustrate how to write a fraud scenario statement for the fraud data analytics plan.

Internal Person and Real Entity with a Generic Statement (Bid Avoidance)

Procurement officer in collusion with/a real supplier/makes a false statement regarding sole source supplier/thereby avoiding the bidding process/resulting in higher project costs.

Real Entity and Real Entity Targeted Statement for Construction (Favoritism)

Architects and engineers in collusion/with a construction manager/fail to disclose known conditions at the job site in the blueprints/thereby corrupting the need phase of the acquisition/resulting in higher project costs.

Internal Person and Real Entity for Retrospective Analysis (Favoritism)

Budget owner in collusion with/a real supplier/the internal person provides the supplier with advance information on changes to the quantity purchased/thereby corrupting the need phase of the acquisition/resulting in higher project costs.

From a fraud data analytics analysis, the scenario provides the fraud auditor with the blueprints on how to write the data interrogation routine.

IDENTIFYING THE KEY DOCUMENTS AND ASSOCIATED DATA

The starting point is the purchase order, which indicates an item was procured. Purchase orders may have line items or no line items. If no line items on the purchase order, then the supplier invoice should provide the specifics on what was purchased.

Procurement Process Documents:
- Request for proposal is the document provided to the supplier describing the goods or services that is the basis of the supplier's bid.
- Bid list is a listing of all suppliers that were requested to submit a bid or all the suppliers that were provided a bid.
- Submitted bid document is a listing prepared at time of opening the bids as to all suppliers that submitted a bid.
- Supplier bid is the document that provides all the representations made by the supplier.
- Bid analysis file is all the documents prepared to analyze the submitted bids. The existence of this file usually depends on the nature of the purchase.

Payment Process Documents:
- Purchase orders—both original and changes to purchase orders.
- Supplier invoices.
- Line items for the purchase order and the invoice.

FDA Planning Reports for Procurement Fraud

The planning reports depend on the scope of the audit project and the focal point of the fraud data analysis. Is the project focusing on bid avoidance, favoritism, or after-the-fact analysis? Is the audit focusing on the procurement function or a targeted expenditure area? As with the other chapters, the purpose of the planning reports is to provide high-level information regarding the audit scope.

OVERALL FRAUD APPROACH FOR CORRUPTION IN THE PROCUREMENT FUNCTION

To build a fraud data analytics plan for corruption, we will need to define the attributes of corruption from a data perspective versus a legal perspective.

The key data attributes are avoidance of bidding procedures or favoritism in the awarding the bid. Favoritism analysis can occur through the pattern of purchase awards or through after-the-fact analysis. Within the data definition, the fraud auditor will need to distinguish between policy abuse with no corrupt intent and policy abuse with corrupt intent.

Bid avoidance is defined as the intentional efforts of management to circumvent the bidding procedures through false statements, splitting a large purchase order into small purchase orders to avoid the bidding dollar threshold requirements, purchase order extension, or simply purchasing directly with the supplier. As a guideline, all purchases that exceed the bid level are excluded from the analysis.

Favoritism is defined as a corrupt relationship between a supplier and an internal person. Our fraud data analytics approach is designed to search for favoritism in the award of a purchase order or comparing the award decision to the after-the-fact analysis of what was actually purchased. The first step is to identify the permutation of favoritism and then determine which fraud action statement is relevant through additional data analytics or through document examination. As a guideline, all purchases below the bid level are excluded from the analysis.

Favoritism is also defined as a corrupt relationship between two suppliers with no internal involvement, often referred to as supplier bid rigging. Fraud auditing for supplier bid rigging requires a superior knowledge of the item procured.

Defective pricing and price reduction relates specifically to government contracts. Federal Acquisition Register (FAR), states that "purchases shall be made from, and contracts shall be awarded to responsible prospective contractors only." While a critical corrupt act within government acquisitions, the concept relates more to fraud auditing versus fraud data analytics, and therefore is beyond the scope of this book.

Mischarging, charging for products not used, product substitution, and kickback schemes are discussed in Chapter 7 regarding fraud scenarios in the disbursement function.

Clearly, the receipt and control of bid documents is not a fraud data analytics; however, corruption identified in the document phase may provide the fraud auditor with clues in how to modify or refine the fraud data analytics plan.

FRAUD AUDIT APPROACH FOR CORRUPTION

Once the appearance of favoritism is identified or once the intentional circumvention of the selection process is identified, the hard work of the fraud auditor starts. The fraud auditor must examine bid documents, interview employees, and offer opinions to management. There are six objectives of the fraud audit:

1. Determine how the parties corruptly influence an official act by identifying the fraud action statement.
2. Establish that the representation regarding the process, assumptions, documentation, qualifications, requirements, or management decision is false.
3. Determine that the parties making the representation knew or had knowledge, or should have had knowledge, that representation was false.
4. Determine the technique used to inflate the costs to fund the bribe tax. These techniques are described in Chapter 7 in the supplier overbilling section of the chapter.
5. Calculate the damages to the company due to the corrupt awarding of the purchase order.
6. Through an investigative process, determine that the purchasing manager received a bribe for influencing the awarding of the purchase order or a kickback through the administration of the purchase order.

Both favoritism and bid avoidance use circumstantial evidence (inference analysis) versus a direct evidence approach as a basis for sample selection. Circumstantial evidence is all evidence of an indirect nature when the existence of the principal fact (corrupt act) is deducted from evidentiary by a process or probable reasoning either alone or with other collateral facts (the fact in issue may be *inferred*). The inference in the data is that pattern and frequency is consistent with the fraud action statement.

WHAT DATA ARE NEEDED FOR FRAUD DATA ANALYTICS PLAN?

Prior to starting the conversation, it needs to be recognized that companies will follow different purchasing practices. Some companies have extensive data files regarding procurement data, whereas other companies may not have any procurement data as part of their database. The challenge for the fraud auditor in the planning stage is to identify what data are available in electronic form and then develop a plan to apply the strategy. In a perfect world, all the data are available; in the real world, the fraud auditor will need to work with the available data. When data are not available, maybe there is a control recommendation to improve the company's ability to monitor internal controls.

The first step is to determine whether the data needed to identify bid avoidance or favoritism is located in a paper file or an electronic file. There are four critical data elements:

1. What item was purchased? The goal is to be able to summarize like item purchases. In the ideal world your organization has adopted the use of a commodity code classification system. The commodity code will allow the fraud auditor to identify like items on a detailed basis. If the commodity code is not available, the next level is the line item description on each invoice or purchase order. If the line item description on the invoice is determined not to be sufficiently accurate, the last common linkage might be the general ledger code. Throughout this chapter, I will refer to line items as the basis for the specific item purchased to avoid repeating specific item.

2. Who purchased the item? In the ideal world, your company has a purchasing function that procures items for the company. If so, then we use the buyer's identification code. If purchasing does not function in that role, then we will need to use department code.

3. What bidding practice was followed? In the ideal world, each purchase order has a *bid code*. The purpose of the bid code is to describe what competitive purchasing practice was followed for the acquisition. If the bid code does not exist, it should be your first recommendation to management. Absent a bid code, the competitive purchasing practice will need to be determined at time of document examination.

4. Purchase order data and supplier invoice data become the basis for identifying both bid avoidance and favoritism in the fraud data analytics phase of the fraud audit. The key data item is whether the electronic document is entered in total or line items. Second is the quality of the description in the line item. This is an important aspect of the availability, reliability, and usability phase of the fraud data analytics plan.

The second step is to determine the time period of the fraud data analytics plan. Purchasing fraud data analytics generally requires at least two years of data. A caveat to the two-year requirement is based on the duration of purchase orders within your organization. The fraud auditor will have to have both purchase order information and invoice information.

The third step is to determine what data are needed for the overall strategy of the fraud data analytics plan. The strategy selected is the final determination of the primary and secondary data tables. There is no magic answer to the strategy question. The choice is based on your knowledge of company purchasing practices, internal complaints, or the judgment of the auditor. The fraud data-mining strategies applicable for corruption in the selection process are:

- Internal control avoidance strategy is for bid avoidance. The process is a direct identification of transactions that are structured to evade bidding. Whether the avoidance was with corrupt intent or control arrogance is determined in the examination of documents, interviews, and other research. The necessary data are the purchase order and supplier invoice with line-item descriptions.
- Data interpretation strategy is used for favoritism in awarding a purchase order. The reasoning process starts with the summarization of data based on analysis of purchase order information or analysis of supplier invoice information. The data interpretation will be based on inference analysis that can be defined as the principal fact (favoritism) is deducted from the data by a process of probable reasoning. The probable reasoning is the process of selecting a sample for audit examination of documents versus the specific identification of a corrupt act. The necessary data are the purchase order and supplier invoice with line-item descriptions.
- Specific identification strategy is used for favoritism in the after-the-fact approach. The necessary data are the purchase order and supplier invoice data with line-item descriptions.
- Specific identification approach for targeted expenditures. The starting point is the general ledger numbers for the targeted expenditure. The necessary data are the purchase order and supplier invoice with line-item descriptions.
- The fourth step is to determine what paper documents are available for the purpose of the fraud audit procedures:
  - Bid file contains the request, listing of bids received, bid analysis, and correspondence related to the bidding procedures.
  - A bid document becomes the basis of determining the representations made by the supplier.
  - Purchase order or contract document becomes the basis of determining what was purchased from the supplier.

Remember, fraud data analytics is about creating the sample of transactions meeting the fraud data profile, and the fraud audit procedure is about gathering evidence to formulate a conclusion based on the supporting documents.

FRAUD DATA ANALYTICS: THE OVERALL APPROACH FOR CORRUPTION IN THE PROCUREMENT FUNCTION

There are four overall approaches for searching for corruption through fraud data analytics. The list is not in order of priority:

1. The first fraud data analytics approach is to search for bid avoidance. The inference is that bidding was avoided because the internal person intentionally circumvented the bidding process to select a specific supplier. The difficulty is in establishing whether the circumvention occurred for corrupt reasons versus internal control arrogance.

2. Bid avoidance. Each purchase is below the dollar level for bidding but the aggregate dollar level for the item acquired exceeds the dollar level for bidding. The bid avoidance permutations are:
   a) Same supplier is issued multiple purchase orders all under the bidding dollar level for the same item.
   b) Hidden supplier is one supplier operating under different names and supplying the same item.
   c) Contract extension extends the time period of the contract.
   d) Budget owners purchase directly from the supplier, thereby avoiding the purchase function.
   e) False statement regarding sole source selection. Absent a bid code, false statement schemes are identified in the document examination phase.

3. The second fraud data analytics approach is to search for favoritism in the selection process. The favoritism in the selection process uses purchase order information or electronic bid files. From a data analytics perspective there are two types of favoritism. The first type of favoritism occurs through a continuing relationship with a supplier to purchase a specific item. The second type of favoritism is a change in a continuing relationship with a supplier that correlates to the same buyer or a change in the buyer. The change in the buyer might be the beginning or end of the corrupt relationship. The favoritism approach requires the fraud auditor to examine all the facts and circumstances to determine if the relationship is either corrupt or a smart business practice.

4. Favoritism in the award of purchase orders shows up in four ways:
   a) Continued relationship with the historical supplier.
   b) Change in existing relationship with the historical supplier, same buyer.

   c) Change in existing relationship with the historical supplier, different buyer.

   d) External suppliers in collusion to corrupt process with no internal person involved.

5. The third fraud data analytics approach for favoritism is the after-the-fact approach. The after-the-fact approach is using purchase orders and supplier invoice data. Prior to receipt of the bids, an internal person communicates to one supplier that actual purchases will differ from the projected purchases in the bid documents. The changes are either in quantity of items or the actual items purchased. Depending on how the data are stored, the summarization can occur through a purchase order change transaction or through summarization by purchase order number and by supplier invoice line items that linked to the purchase order number. The fraud auditor will need to recalculate the bidding process with actual purchases versus the projected purchases in the bid documents.

6. The permutations for after-the-fact analysis are that the purchase order is issued based on dollar level for bidding; however, changes occur after the bid, causing purchase order costs to increase:

   a) Change in total cost.

   b) Change in quantities.

   c) Change in unit price.

   d) Change in the mix of items.

   e) Primary supplier is unable to fulfill a line item on the purchase order and the second lowest price supplier fulfills the item.

7. The fourth approach and the easiest from a fraud data analytics perspective is the targeted expenditure approach. By its nature, the fraud auditor is starting with a homogeneous data set. Once identified, the first three previous strategies are used to analyze the data. The focus of the fraud data analytics is on the pattern and frequency of suppliers selected for the targeted expenditure.

   a) Favoritism in the award of the purchase order

   b) After-the-fact analysis

   c) Bid avoidance

8. Within bid avoidance and favoritism analysis, the second phase of the fraud data analytics is to determine which secondary fraud action statement was used to corrupt the purchase decision. If the electronic data are not available, then the fraud auditor must examine all the available paper documents to determine if there is credible evidence that one of the fraud action statements has occurred.

LINKING THE FRAUD ACTION STATEMENT TO THE FRAUD DATA ANALYTICS

The following provides a brief synopsis of how the primary fraud action statement links to the fraud data analytics plan:

1. Bid avoidance scheme is the process of structuring the purchase to avoid the bidding process.

   FDA Plan: The data-mining strategy is the control-avoidance strategy.

2. A false bid document created by an internal person scheme is the process of an internal person preparing and submitting a fictitious bid in the name of a noncomplicit supplier. The internal person is in collusion with the favored supplier.

   FDA Plan: The fraud data analytics is able to identify purchases that meet the favoritism model, bid avoidance model, or purchases exceeding a dollar level.

3. A false bid document created by supplier's scheme occurs when the suppliers colluded among themselves to determine which supplier will have the winning bid. The assumption in this scheme is that no internal person is involved.

   FDA Plan: Assuming the purchase files as to suppliers requested to bid and the supplier awarded for the bid are in electronic format, the fraud data analysis would search for favoritism. The fraud data analytics is better suited for targeted expenditure analysis because the data are a homogeneous data file and the ability to observe a bid-rigging pattern.

4. Issuing, receipt, and control of bid proposal scheme is the process of corrupting the bid process by destroying supplier bids, accepting a supplier bid after the bid-open process, or allowing one supplier to change its bid after the bid opening or shortening the duration of the bid process.

   FDA Plan: Not applicable to this fraud action statement; however, the favoritism analysis would be a starting point.

5. Establish false need scheme is the process of market timing; acquire something not required; excess quantity; unnecessary purchases; or advance communication of future changes to one supplier.

   FDA Plan: Fraud data analytics depends on whether the false need is embedded in the data or the documents. The use of retrospective analysis to summarize the actual purchases for comparison to projected purchases to identify false needs schemes.

6. Structuring specification scheme is the process of structuring the specifications to advantage of a supplier or creating vague or restrictive specifications to allow the manipulation of the selection process.

   FDA Plan: The plan could search for vague product descriptions in the line item description of the invoice or purchase order. A restrictive specification is a byproduct of the favoritism analysis.

7. Identify unqualified entity scheme is the process of intentionally including unqualified suppliers within the bid process to provide the favored supplier with an unfair advantage.

   FDA Plan: Assuming the bid analysis file is stored in an electronic format, would create a report by supplier indicating the number of items a supplier was requested to bid and the number of times the supplier was awarded a bid.

8. False evaluation of supplier scheme occurs when the selection team makes false conclusions regarding the supplier's qualifications or cost proposal.

   FDA Plan: A plan is not directly applicable to this fraud action statement; however, the favoritism analysis would be a starting point.

9. Favored negotiating of terms and conditions schemes occurs when part of the process allows for negotiating of bids after the bid opening.

   FDA Plan: A plan is not directly applicable to this fraud action statement; however, the favoritism analysis would be a starting point.

10. False selection of supplier occurs through corrupting the selection criteria or corrupting the evaluation process.

    FDA Plan: A plan is not directly applicable to this fraud action statement; however, the favoritism analysis would be a starting point.

BID AVOIDANCE: FRAUD DATA ANALYTICS PLAN

Same supplier is one supplier that is issued multiple purchase orders all under the bidding dollar level for the same item. The first report should provide two columns of data: summary of purchase orders under the bid level and summary of purchase orders exceeding the bid level. The first report is for informational purposes.

The second data analytics report should summarize by supplier purchase orders under the bid level as to the number of purchase orders (frequency), the dollar value of purchase orders, and the average purchase order amount. Purchase orders exceeding the bid level should be excluded from this analysis. The purpose of the second report is to identify suppliers that in the aggregate exceed the bid level, or the average purchase order is high, which implies a pattern of avoiding the bid levels. For those suppliers that appear to be circumventing the bid levels in the aggregate, their invoices should be summarized by line item to determine if a specific line item exceeded the bid level. A word of caution: Layering the purchases over a multiyear period would hamper the effectiveness of the analysis. Consideration should be given to using two years of data.

Hidden supplier is one supplier operating under different names that supplies the same item. The first fraud data analytics report is to search for duplicate master file data to determine if there are two suppliers with duplicate identifying information. The fraud data analytics process to locate hidden suppliers was described in Chapter 6. Once identified, the second step is to summarize the duplicate supplier's invoices by line item. The report should provide unit price, quantity, and the extended dollar value. The third step is to determine if there are matching line items between the two suppliers that would exceed a dollar bid level.

Purchase order extension extends the time period of the contract and there is an increase in dollar amount. The key to identifying this practice directly correlates to the data maintained in the data system. The first data item is a purchase order extension date field. If there is no purchase order extension date field, then search the change files for a date change transaction. If your system does not keep an audit trail of date changes, then search for dollar changes that may correlate to a date change.

Operations personnel circumvent the purchasing department by purchasing directly from a supplier, thereby avoiding the purchase function or the required bid levels. The first report is a summary of supplier invoices supported by a purchase order number and supplier invoices with no purchase order number. The purpose is to identify a supplier that is routinely used by company personnel that was not sourced by the purchasing department. The analysis can be enhanced by comparing the purchase order date to the invoice date. The avoidance would then include all invoices with no purchase order number and invoices where the purchase order date either equals or is greater than the invoice date.

The second approach to bid avoidance is a variation of targeted expenditures by identifying a specific department that is circumventing the purchasing function. The first homogeneous data file is all supplier invoices with no purchase order number. The supplier invoices should be summarized:

■ By line item, to determine if a supplier on a companywide basis is circumventing the purchasing department.

■ By department by line item, to determine if a specific department operating in collusion with a supplier is circumventing the bid levels.

FAVORITISM IN THE AWARD OF PURCHASE ORDERS: FRAUD DATA ANALYTICS PLAN

Favoritism occurs at two levels. The favored status may have occurred by virtue of a personal relationship or an extended business relationship with the company or the buyer. The favored supplier may also have preferred status though a purchasing process of identifying preferred suppliers. There is no bribe or kickback, so the fraud action statement might be a manipulation of the purchasing process versus committed with corrupt intent. The second favored status occurs with corrupt intent, resulting in a bribe or kickback.

The fraud data analytics for favoritism is based on identifying purchases that require bidding procedures based on the dollar value of the purchase order. Then fraud data analytics for favoritism is searching for either a continued relationship with one supplier over an extended period of time or a change in a supplier that links to a buyer. Remember, bid avoidance is designed to search for purchases that avoided the bidding process.

The purpose of fraud data analytics is to identify a buying relationship that meets the criteria of favored status. So, the starting point is to identify what constitutes a favored relationship in terms of the aggregate dollars or purchasing a like item for an extended period of time. The next step is to determine how to identify like purchases. The use of a commodity code is the easiest approach. If no commodity code is available, then use purchase order line item or a general ledger account.

Continued Relationship with the Same Historical Supplier

The continued relationship is defined as purchasing a specific item from the same supplier for a specific period of time. The analysis should be for a minimum of two years. The second assumption is that the analysis is not searching for bid avoidance. Therefore, purchase orders below the bid level are excluded from the summary. The first report should summarize by supplier providing the number of purchase orders and the dollar value of the purchase order by the line item or department code. The first report is primarily informational, to understand the volume of activity that requires bidding. Due to the volume of data, the analysis is more manageable when using a targeted expenditure strategy.

The first analysis is a summary of purchase orders for a minimum of a two-year period. The first report should summarize by line item by supplier by year. The report should provide the number of purchase order (frequency), the aggregate dollar value, and the average purchase order amount. When line items are not used or deemed unreliable, summarize purchase order activity by general ledger code by year by supplier by year. The selection criterion is a line item or general ledger code that has only one supplier for three-year period or a high concentration of one supplier.

Once the suppliers meeting the criteria are identified, the fraud auditor uses the primary and secondary fraud action statements to evaluate the purchases to determine the method used to corrupt the purchasing process.

Change in Purchasing Relationship from Historical Supplier to New Supplier but the Same Buyer

In this scenario, we are searching for a change from the historical supplier to either a new supplier or an existing supplier on the master file. The first step is to identify all suppliers that were active and now the spend level is zero. The difficulty is in establishing criteria for identifying how to determine a zero spending level. If the relationship ended at the close of the fiscal year, then comparing two years of data would easily answer the question. For purposes of programming, you will need a definition or parameters to identify the zero spend level. (Most likely, the parameter will not be perfect.) The second step is to identify the item that was purchased from the historical supplier.

To identify the new suppliers, the easy way is to use the creation date. If the creation date is in the scope period, either the new supplier replaced a historical supplier or is providing a new item. The second step is to identify the item that is purchased from the new supplier. Using the purchase order line item, match the old and new supplier for the line item.

A second approach to identifying a change in suppliers is to perform the analysis on a purchase order line item basis, summarizing purchase order activity by line item by supplier, providing the frequency and aggregate dollar value. Using the first record and the last record feature of the software, identify the first and last record for the line item using purchase order date.

If purchase order line items are not in the data, the analysis can also occur using the general ledger codes. However, the general ledger approach will require manual data interpretation to identify the change in supplier. Clearly, the general ledger code approach should use the targeted expenditure strategy.

Once the change in supplier is identified and correlated to the buyer, the next step is to identify a change in the unit price that has occurred. The sample selection is based on a change in unit price consistent with your fraud theory.

Assuming the buyer code is in the purchase order data, the sample selection is based on a change in historical supplier and the same buyer code. If the buyer code is not in the data, then the fraud auditor will need to interview procurement management to determine the timelines of buyers' procurement responsibilities.

Change in Purchasing Relationship from Historical Supplier to New Supplier but a Different Buyer

The analysis is the same as the previous analysis except that the change in supplier is linked to a change in buyer.

External Suppliers in Collusion to Corrupt Process with No Internal Person Involved

Supplier bid rigging is the process of the suppliers colluding among themselves to determine which supplier will be awarded the purchase order. These schemes do not usually include an internal person. The difficulty in using fraud data analytics is that the information needed to identify the patterns of supplier bid rigging is the lack of data in the purchase order or invoice files. The schemes include:

- Unresponsive bids to provide the impression of competitive bidding where, in reality, suppliers agree to submit token bids that are usually too high.
- Bid suppression—suppliers agree among themselves either to abstain from bidding or to withdraw bids. The suppliers know the company has to get its supplies from someone; thus, by suppressing the bids, they inflate the bidding in the long run.
- Bid rotation is employed, whereby the preselected supplier submits the lowest bid on a systematic or rotating basis. This fraud happens when there are like projects up for bid on a continual basis. Instead of harming profits by bidding low, suppliers collude to ensure high bids are received. The scheme depends on the bids being high enough to offset the awarding of projects at low bids in the aggregate.
- Market division is an arrangement among suppliers not to compete in designated geographic regions or for specific customers. You tend to see this type of fraud happening where corporations split up the country because of distribution routes. Less shipping time and distance means higher profits.

If the company bidding files are in an electronic format, the company has a commodity code as part of the data file; fraud data analysis may be able to identify a pattern consistent with the four primary supplier bid-rigging strategies. The use of data interpretation is critical in the analysis.

Search for Corruption Using After-the-Fact Analysis

Using after-the-fact analysis was first introduced in Chapter 7 in the discussion of a budget owner falsely administering a properly issued purchase order. The purchase order is issued based on a bidding procedure. The purchase order is issued based on the total dollar level for all items (unit price multiplied by quantity) for bidding; however, changes occur after the bid, causing the purchase order costs to increase based on the mix of items.

The first step is to identify all purchase orders that require bidding and the purchase order is for more than one item. The fraud data analytics summarizes the supplier invoices by line item as to quantity and unit price for each purchase order. The analysis is searching for change through the invoice file:

- Quantities change. The quantity is simply a summary of line item quantity and dollar value. The dollar value is to allow reconciliation to the original purchase order. The actual quantity is used to recalculate the bids submitted by each supplier to determine if the change in quantity purchased would have changed the bid results.
- Unit price changes. The process is to determine the actual unit price for each item purchased. The report should summarize by line item by unit price. The report should calculate the total purchases by line item by unit price. The actual cost of the purchases should be compared to winning bid to determine how the total cost of the purchase order changed from the original bid.
- The winning supplier is unable to fulfill a specific line item and use of secondary supplier to provide the line item. In this scheme, the suppliers have colluded to allow each supplier to provide those items that the supplier will have the highest margins on the line item. The first report is to summarize supplier invoice activity linked to the purchase order number. If a secondary supplier is identified, the second report is to summarize by line item to determine which items were provided by the second supplier. The fraud auditor should examine the bid documents to determine the difference between the two unit prices.

Targeted Expenditure: Fraud Data Analytics Plan

Targeted expenditure is based on a department or a specific expenditure (i.e., printing); operational services; cost of sales. Targeted expenditures can also be used in validating the assumptions used by management on the use of preferred suppliers. The value of the targeted expenditure approach is that the data start with a homogeneous data file. In the targeted expenditure approach, the fraud data analytics is searching for both bid avoidance and favoritism.

SUMMARY

Locating corruption through data analytics is the most difficult analysis for the fraud auditor. Once identified, the fraud auditor through document examination and interviews must gather credible evidence that the process was corrupted versus poor management practices. The fraud auditor will need a superior knowledge of company practices and industry knowledge of the items procured to identify corrupt purchasing practices.

For your first try at using fraud data analytics to search for corruption in procurement, I would strongly recommend using the targeted expenditure review strategy. In this way, you will be able to concentrate on learning how to use the techniques described in the book without being overwhelmed by the sheer amount of data and the difficulties you will encounter with the availability, reliability, and usability of your company's data.

If not the targeted expenditure review, start with bid avoidance, because it uses the specific identification strategy versus favoritism, which requires a greater use of data interpretation. The document examination is easier because the conclusion is based on whether the item purchased should have followed bidding procedures versus management judgment on selecting the supplier.

CHAPTER TWELVE

Corruption Committed by the Company

P aying a bribe for a corrupt purpose is considered illegal in countries around the world. So, if you believe that it is a normal and customary business practice to pay bribes in a country, then stop reading. The main purpose of this chapter is to provide a framework for building a fraud data analytics plan to search your company's books for fraud scenarios for transactions associated with bribes. The secondary purpose is to provide knowledge of where and how to look for the bribes. Trust me, the task is not easy, but it is not impossible when using strategies designed to search the general ledger.

In this chapter, the expression *bribes* is intended to include all forms of payments that are intended to corrupt an individual. The bribe maybe a direct payment to the individual, payment for services, travel and entertainment expenses paid for the benefit of the individual, and various forms of indirect payments. Since a bribe is a legal conclusion, within this book a bribe payment will be referred to as a questionable payment.

There is legislation around the world that makes paying a bribe for a corrupt purpose illegal. The most recognized laws are the Foreign Corrupt Practices Act or the UK Bribery Act of 2010. The purpose of this chapter is not to evaluate the legal aspects of the law, but rather, use the enforcement actions and court cases as a basis for developing a fraud data analytics plan to search for transactions that link to a corrupt act. The fraud auditor needs to understand the legislation, court cases, and FCPA Procedures Opinions to be able to effectively search and create a sample of transactions that have a higher probability of being related to a corrupt payment.

The making of questionable payments occurs either on or off the company's books. The expense is either recorded in the proper general ledger account or the true nature of the expense is mischaracterized or recorded in the wrong general ledger account. Your company may directly receive the sales contract or your company maybe a subcontractor to the sales contractor. Your company is paying the questionable payment to obtain the sales contract or is paying the questionable payment for the benefit of another party. Your company description of expense is either clearly stated or disguised. Typically, senior management is involved in the cover-up and there is a certain degree of collusion to conceal the questionable payment. Due to management override implications, reliance on internal controls to mitigate questionable payments is greatly reduced from a fraud data analytics perspective. A test of control procedures will provide a greater insight into how and where transactions are recorded.

It is critical before starting your fraud data analytics project that the scope is clearly defined, the purpose is understood, and the objectives are clearly defined. The fraud risk assessment or the corruption risk assessment is prescribed for this analysis. The plan will need to decide to search for risks that have a high residual risk or search for risks that correlate to their understanding of their company.

The fraud data analytic plan could be based on compliance with company policies, prior enforcement actions by the government, or by searching for credible evidence that your company has made a questionable payment through either an on- or off-the-book approach.

FRAUD SCENARIO CONCEPT APPLIED TO BRIBERY PROVISIONS

The methodology or components for writing a fraud scenario for corrupt payments under the bribe statute is the same as described in Chapter 2. What differs are the fraud action statement and the fraud impact statement. The following guidelines should be followed in writing a fraud action statement and the impact statement:

1. Start with the concept of how the questionable payment occurs or how the recordkeeping requirements are violated.

2. The questionable payment fraud action statement must consider:
   a) The entity is false or real.
   b) The payment is on or off the books.
   c) The business system used to make the questionable payment—that is, accounts payable, payroll, or other systems.
3. The fraud action statement may relate to a specific transactional issue deemed to be a questionable payment by prior enforcement actions.
   a) The provision of authoritative cases, regulations of rulings associated with a specific transactional issue should be incorporated into the statement.
   b) Describe the transaction consistent with the authoritative source.
4. The recordkeeping provision should focus on these elements:
   a) The improper transaction is recorded on or off the company books.
   b) The true nature or purpose of the transaction is disguised.
   c) Transaction is recorded in a general ledger account that disguises the true purpose of the transaction.
5. The impact statement should focus on the concept of obtaining or retaining business.

The following provides examples of how to write a fraud scenario for a fraud data analytics plan searching for internal corruption consistent with the associated bribe statute.

1. Management causes a real person who is considered a politically exposed person to receive payroll payments resulting in a questionable payment to be recorded on the books in a disguised manner for the benefit of a government official authorizing a contract for services (questionable payment on the books).
2. Management causes a shell company to be set up in accounts payable and causes payments to the shell company so the shell company can make questionable payments off the company books for the benefit of a government official authorizing a contract for services (questionable payment off the books).
3. Management causes travel payments that are associated with a product demonstration that are considered lavish, excessive, beyond company travel policy, and beyond the government employees' travel policy to be paid through a booking agency for the benefit of a government official authorizing a contract for services (questionable payment associated with a specific transactional issue on the books in a disguised manner).

As an overall guideline, the fraud scenario must have sufficient detail to instruct the fraud auditor where and how to find the transactions in the company books. Once the transactions are identified, the fraud auditor through document examination and interviews will formulate a conclusion regarding the identified transactions.

CREATING THE FRAMEWORK FOR THE SCOPE OF THE FRAUD DATA ANALYTICS PLAN

There is no one approach to building a fraud data analytics plan to search for payments that would constitute a questionable payment consistent with the law. The scope should start with using an authoritative source. Authoritative sources are laws, regulations, court cases, company policy, and published internal control standards. The reason for using the authoritative source is to create a basis for sample selection. First, the authoritative source provides a basis for comparing the recorded transaction to a definitive source for the purpose of determining whether either sales transactions or expenditures meet the criteria of the authoritative source. Second, the authoritative source provides clues as to where in the general ledger the transactions are recorded.

For an example, prior enforcement actions have indicated that expenditures related to travel have constituted questionable payments. By reading the authoritative source, the fraud auditor understands the facts and circumstances of what constitutes a questionable payment. Now, the fraud auditor builds a fraud data analytics plan searching for the questionable payment cited in the authoritative source.

The following authoritative sources are useful in building the fraud data analytics framework:

- FDA for compliance with company policies
- FDA based on prior enforcement actions using transactional issues
- FDA based on the internal control attributes of DOJ opinion release 04-02 or the UK Bribery Act: Guidance on Internal Controls

The scope of the fraud data analytics is also based on how your company is structured: one company or multiple companies or locations around the world. The scope should be based on where sales transactions occur that could have compliance issues with customers that meet the criteria in the applicable corruption laws. An authoritative source for the level of corruption in a country is the corruption index for high-risk countries. The first step is to identify where in your company sales contracts occur in a country that meets the criteria of high-risk countries. Caution: Prior enforcement actions have indicated the questionable payment did not need to result in the issuance of a sales contract. As a reminder, understanding the legal aspects is important; otherwise, the fraud auditor might have missed the concept of offer versus completed contract.

Within the scope identified through your company's sales efforts, the fraud data analytics plan is based on either compliance with an authoritative source or the search for a questionable payment.

If the purpose is compliance, then the fraud data analytics will use specific identification to search for sales transactions or expenditure transactions that relate to company policy or internal control avoidance strategies.

If the purpose is searching for questionable payments, then there are four categories of questionable payments that are recorded in the general ledger:

1. FDA based on questionable payments that are recorded in the books.
2. FDA based on company funds that are removed from the books to allow for questionable payments. These schemes are typically asset misappropriation schemes committed by management for the direct purpose of concealing a questionable payment.
3. FDA based on transactions that fail the recordkeeping provision.
4. FDA based on false description of the business purpose.

If the purpose is based on the recordkeeping provisions, then the fraud data analytics is searching for violations of the recordkeeping provisions of the relevant statute.

While the fraud data analytics plan may include one, two, three, or four strategies, the fraud auditor should be aware of all four aspects.

PLANNING REPORTS

A key provision of the law is the concept of obtaining or retaining business. The planning reports should summarize sales data to determine where sales have occurred that would come under the provisions of the FCPA:

- Identify all sales contracts to government entities as defined in the relevant statute as to amount, date, and any customer names in the contract.
- Identify all sales contracts to government entities as defined in the relevant statute where your company is a subcontractor.

- Summarize the expenditures by the relevant general ledger accounts, or preferably, a sales contract number by vendor, providing the frequency, aggregate expenditure level, maximum, minimum, and average payment.

The purpose of the planning reports is to identify sales transactions that meet the criteria of the bribery law. The knowledge of the sales transactions and the associated expenditures then become a necessary part of the fraud data analytics that is searching for questionable payments.

PLANNING THE UNDERSTANDING OF THE AUTHORITATIVE SOURCES

The starting point is to be familiar with the relevant bribery statute that is the scope of the fraud data analytics. The following should not be considered a legal treatise on the provisions but provide a background on the elements. The reader is encouraged to study the published literature to obtain a complete understanding of the laws, regulations, and court cases.

Using the FCPA, the law has two major provisions: prohibit corrupt payments to foreign officials and the recordkeeping and internal controls provision. The Act also provides affirmative defenses in regard to the difference between a questionable payment and a facilitation payment. The bribery provision has the following elements:

1. Payment, promise to pay, an offer to pay money, or anything of value
2. To a foreign official
3. For a corrupt purpose
4. To assist in obtaining or retaining business

The recordkeeping and internal control provision has the following elements:

1. Maintain books and records in reasonable detail.
2. Properly describe the transaction and how the assets were used.

FDA FOR COMPLIANCE WITH COMPANY POLICIES

The starting point is to identify and understand company policies regarding bribery and corruption policies and procedures. The fraud auditor should review the literature on FCPA enforcement actions, then read the company policy and procedures and determine their understanding of an appropriate expenditure and appropriate documentation. Then fraud auditors should meet with legal counsel and reconcile their understanding of an appropriate expenditure and appropriate documentation.

A key aspect of the compliance plan is to determine compliance both before obtaining the sales contract and the subsequent due diligence of the sales contract.

The compliance audit starts with identifying all sales efforts and sales contracts with organizations that meet the criteria of the FCPA statement of "obtaining or retaining business for or with, or directing business to, any person."

The second phase of the compliance audit is identifying payments that would cause a foreign official, within the definition of the law, to assist your company in securing any improper advantage.

The FDA plan should extract expenditures using specific identification strategy consistent with company policy for sample selection. The use of control avoidance FDA strategy can be used to search for expenditures that were processed and recorded to avoid company policy scrutiny.

FDA BASED ON PRIOR ENFORCEMENT ACTIONS USING TRANSACTIONAL ISSUES

The FCPA was enacted in 1977. Since that time, there are many cases and rulings that provide a fraud data analytics plan with a playbook. I would encourage the fraud auditor to obtain copies of the documents that are available on the Internet. Use the following search phrase to locate the documents: DOJ FCPA Review Procedure Releases and Opinion Procedure Release Summaries.

Commissions, royalties, consultant fees, agents, sales and marketing expenses, contributions both political and charitable, gifts, travel and entertainment, cash withdrawals, payments to politically exposed persons (PEPs), leasing of automobiles, apartments, buying assets above fair market value, and selling assets below fair market value—for FDA purposes, these disbursements are referred to as *expenses of interest*. The audit examination may raise the concept of questionable payment.

The fraud data analytics using the prior enforcement action strategy is based on focusing on those expenditures that the Justice Department or the SEC has questioned and the question resulted in an enforcement action against a company. The FDA plan should identify the applicable general ledger accounts that link to enforcement actions as the starting point of the FDA plan.

The first step is to identify the general ledger accounts for the expenditure areas that link to expenditures that are associated with known enforcement actions: commissions; royalties; consultant fees; travel and entertainment; contributions that are either political or charitable; sales or marketing expenses and rebates.

The fraud data analytic plan is a simple extract and summarizes routine by general ledger account by vendor number. These are the expenses that are properly coded to the correct general ledger account and are called the *known vendors*. Using data interpretation, the fraud auditor can select a sample from the known expenditures. The fraud auditor would examine the relevant documentation to determine if an expense violates known FCPA enforcement actions.

FDA BASED ON THE INTERNAL CONTROL ATTRIBUTES OF DOJ OPINION RELEASE 04-02 OR THE UK BRIBERY ACT: GUIDANCE ON INTERNAL CONTROLS

The starting point is to select the internal control standard that is the basis of the fraud data analytics plan. In this book, I will use the DOJ opinion 04-02 because the standard has been in place for a greater period of time. Obviously, not all aspects of the opinion relate directly to fraud data analytics. The purpose of fraud data analytics is to determine how robust your internal controls are for your compliance program. The primary categories are:

1. Commitment from senior management
2. Code of conduct and compliance procedures
3. Oversight, autonomy, and resources
4. Risk assessment
5. Training and continuing advice
6. Incentives and disciplinary measures
7. Third-party due diligence and payments
8. Confidential reporting and internal investigations
9. Continuous improvement: Periodic testing and reviews

Risk assessment from a fraud data analytics perspective is the searching for revenue-based transactions to customers that would be associated with a foreign official consistent with the legal definition. Using the common terms associated with the risk assessment the analysis should focus on:

- Country risks
- Sector risks
- Transaction risk
- Business opportunity risk
- Business partner risk

The goal with the analysis is to identify revenue transactions meeting the previous profiles and then determine the extent of oversight performed by management in the client acceptance phase and client monitoring phase.

Transactional risk is focusing on those transactions that have previously been linked to known enforcement actions.

Training and continuing advice uses the specific identification strategy by selecting all expenditures associated with the internal control objective, determining compliance with company policies and whether the training meets the expectation of the control standard.

Third-party due diligence and payments uses the specific identification strategy to identify all payments associated with a sales contract to determine compliance with company policies and whether the due diligence meets the expectation of the control standard.

BUILDING THE FRAUD DATA ANALYTICS ROUTINES TO SEARCH FOR QUESTIONABLE PAYMENTS

The fraud scenario is the starting point for the fraud data analytics plan. The objective of the transaction analysis determines where and how to search for questionable payments. The *where* question is: Is the questionable payment located on the books or have company assets been removed from the books? The *how* question is which specific scenario was used by management to make the questionable payment. The fraud action statement in the fraud scenario provides the necessary details to write the data interrogation routine. The second aspect of the plan is linking the fraud audit procedure to the fraud data analytics plan.

In Chapter 4, building the fraud data analytics plan step 10 stated: What is the design of the fraud audit test for the selected sample? The answer to this question is critical in examining documents that link to the transactions selected in the fraud data analytics. As a general guideline, initial fraud audit procedure should be based on the framework of the project. As additional information is gleaned, the fraud audit procedure will be revised based on the facts and circumstances learned through the audit examination.

A second aspect of the audit test is when the fraud auditor should become a fraud investigator under the supervision of an attorney. Although the answer to this question is beyond the scope of this book, I would be remiss in not advising the fraud auditor to build this step into their audit program.

FDA FOR QUESTIONABLE PAYMENTS THAT ARE RECORDED ON THE BOOKS

A questionable payment on the company books is made through the corporate bank account and is recorded in the company general ledger. The payment may occur through accounts payable, payroll, and company credit cards. The expenditure may also have a false description. The expenditure may or may not be recorded in the correct general ledger account.

A starting point for the brainstorming is to identify the sales contracts between your company and government entities. The dates of the contracts are critical to identify a time period when a questionable payment would most likely be paid. The second aspect is to identify all company employees that had a direct involvement in winning the contract. The background information is useful in the sample selection process.

The methods of making the questionable payment and then concealing the true nature of the payment is a very long list. To start the fraud data analytics plan, the fraud auditor should brainstorm as to the various methods a questionable payment could be paid on the company books. Previous chapters have described asset misappropriation fraud scenarios that could be used to fund questionable payments. Those scenarios would be a starting point for the brain-storming.

From a planning perspective the following categories can be used to develop the plan:

1. Paid directly to the individual.
2. Paid directly to the individual's business.
3. Payments that inure to the benefit of the recipient.
4. Payments associated with transactions previously associated with enforcement actions.

5. Payments identified as facilitation payments.
6. Payments that occur through an on-the-books asset misappropriation scheme.

The following illustrates the type of data interrogation routines that would be associated with the category:

- Questionable payment is made directly to the recipient of the questionable payment or the questionable payment is paid directly to a family member, friend, or acquaintance. Using the OFAC list, the vendor master file and payroll file should be matched to the OFAC list to determine if any payments are to companies or individuals on the list. All matched should be selected for testing.
- Questionable payment is paid directly to a business owned by the recipient. Without direct knowledge of the business name, this is in fact difficult. The fraud data analytics may search for vendors that are:
  - Subcontractors associated with a government contract.
  - New vendors within a date range of government contracts.
  - Word search on key terms in the invoice description.
- Disbursements that are not paid directly to the recipient but inure to the benefit of the recipient of the questionable payment. A common location in the general ledger for these expenses is typically travel, meals, and entertainment:
  - Search for expenses that are outside the geographic radius of the corporate or sales office paid through accounts payable or company credit card (e.g., office is in Singapore but the hotel expense is in Hong Kong).
  - Search for expenses associated with entertainment (e.g., a concert or Broadway play).
  - Search for expenses paid to a travel tour company or a booking agency.
  - Search for credit card charges with an MCC code associated with entertainment.
  - Credit cards that do not link to a company employee.
  - Credit card chapter (Chapter 9) provided other examples of how to conceal the true nature of the expenditure.
- Disbursements to charitable organizations have been associated with questionable payments. The government official or a family member of the government official is a board member or employee of the charitable organization.
- Disbursements to distributors and resellers have been associated with questionable payments. If the business purpose of the payment is a

disguised questionable payment, then either the questionable payment or recordkeeping provision may apply.

- Disbursement is characterized or described as a facilitation payment. Any payment that is characterized must be identified and examined by the fraud auditor.
- An asset misappropriation scheme through payroll using a real person on the payroll that performs limited or no services. A fictitious ghost would be a questionable payment scheme off the books.

FDA FOR FUNDS THAT ARE REMOVED FROM THE BOOKS TO ALLOW FOR QUESTIONABLE PAYMENTS

Off-the-books questionable payment starts on your company books with a business transaction; however, the goal is to transfer company funds to another company or another bank account (slush fund bank account) for purposes of making the questionable payment. Off-the-book questionable payments are a form of reverse money laundering. The process starts with clean money, which is transferred to another organization with the appearance of a legitimate business purpose. Then one or more layering transactions occur to conceal the original source. The final stage is the questionable payment is made to the recipient or the funds are deposited in a slush fund bank account. Management is an active participant in the scheme or management is the person committing the fraud scenario.

The following techniques are typically used:

1. Asset misappropriation scheme is committed by management for the sole purpose of transferring company funds to an off-the-books bank account controlled by management. The scenarios described in Chapters 7 to 10 can all be used by management to move funds off the company books. Shell companies, ghost employees, and theft of revenue schemes have all been used to transfer company funds to an off-the-books bank account for the purposes of making questionable payments.
2. The questionable payment is layered through a real company that may or may not be knowingly complicit under the law. Typically, the real company hires the second company (recipient of questionable payment) as a subcontractor to the project. Then the real company disburses the funds to the subcontractor for work allegedly performed. Based on previous cases,

professional fee expenditures or commissions are often associated with this scheme.

3. Management sells company assets and receives currency for the asset. The currency is then deposited in the slush-fund bank account or the currency is provided to the recipient. Scrap sales and equipment sales are common areas for this scheme.
4. Management sells company assets below fair market value either to a recipient or through a disguised recipient.
5. Management incurs a charge on the company credit card and the vendor provides currency to the cardholder and retains a commission for processing the credit card transaction. Either the charge may have a valid business purpose but the credit card charge is of a greater value than the event, or the charge has no valid business purpose other than cash conversion.
6. Vendor rebates or refunds are deposited directly in the slush fund bank account.
7. Customer pass-through schemes occur when your company sells a product to a controlled customer at a deep discount. The controlled customer then sells the product to the intended customer at a higher price. The difference between the two selling prices is used to make the questionable payment.

To illustrate how to build a fraud data analytics plan for shell companies associated with off-the-books questionable payments:

Identify new vendors added to the master file consistent with your scope and the planning reports associated with sales contracts. The fraud data analytics should also identify dormant vendors that have become active in the time period with changes to addresses, bank accounts, telephone numbers, or email addresses. For the first fraud data analytic plan, I would suggest using the last 36 months as a time period. Other factors that could be used are management turnover statistics, dates of significant government contracts, new business lines, new high-risk countries, etc.

- Create a report of disbursements by new vendors or dormant vendors providing the aggregate spend level, the frequency of disbursements, and the maximum, minimum, and average invoice. The report should also provide date the vendor was added to the master file and the invoice number and date of the first invoice.
- The second report is similar to the first report but the summary is by disbursements by general ledger accounts by vendor.
- A common search technique is using word searches on the invoice description field. The report should summarize by key words as to frequency of use

and aggregate dollar value. The reader can find lists of key words through simple Internet searches.

- Identify vendors that are individuals versus corporations. This is easier said than done. Some companys have a special sequence of vendor numbers used for individuals. If your company does not have this process, it is a good process for monitoring payments to individuals. Assuming your company does not have this process, the following strategies can be useful:
  - Depending on the master file size, a manual review of the name column.
  - Matching the vendor file to both the human resources file and the customer file.
  - Search the government identification number column for number patterns consistent with an individual versus a corporation.
  - Search the government identification number column for blanks, on the theory that a government identification number for corporations is necessary for tax reporting.

OVERALL STRATEGY FOR THE RECORD-KEEPING PROVISIONS

The fundamental phrase is *reasonable detail* that would satisfy the reasonable or prudent person regarding their own personal affairs. Caution: There is no materiality requirement for the provision. The provisions articulate a difference between knowingly making a false statement versus the honest mistake. Record-keeping cases typically fall into:

1. Failure to record the questionable payment is covered under the questionable payments recorded off the books.
2. The company records that disguise some aspect of the transaction but are otherwise recorded properly in the general ledger is covered in questionable payments recorded on the books.
3. Falsified records that disguise the true purpose of the questionable payment. The recordkeeping provisions are all-inclusive of all company records. The discussion in the section will focus solely on how the disbursement is recorded in the general ledger.

The fraud auditor will still need to examine the books and records to determine if the manner of how the transaction was recorded rises to the level of a questionable payment.

FDA FOR QUESTIONABLE PAYMENTS THAT FAIL THE RECORD-KEEPING PROVISION AS TO PROPER RECORDING IN THE GENERAL LEDGER

The test of controls for compliance with company's policies and procedures is the starting point for ensuring the transactions are properly recorded. However, since violation is recording transactions improperly, the fraud data analytics needs to search for transactions that are not recorded in the proper account.

Summarize transactions by vendor by general ledger account providing a frequency and aggregate dollar value by general ledger account by vendor. The purpose of this test is to search for disbursements that are hidden in a different general ledger account or the general ledger account that does not seem consistent with the vendor's name. Remember, one of the enforcement strategies is to demonstrate that the corporation did not maintain a proper set of books that would satisfy a prudent businessperson in the conduct of their own business.

Summarize transactions by vendor number for the selected accounts associated with prior enforcement actions. Then search the remaining general ledger for the same vendor numbers in a general ledger account other than the selected general ledger accounts.

Summarize transactions by general ledger account by the line on vendor invoice. This report will be large, so data filtering is critical in using this report. The use of keywords would be one filtering strategy.

FDA FOR QUESTIONABLE PAYMENTS THAT HAVE A FALSE DESCRIPTION OF THE BUSINESS PURPOSE

The purpose of this test is to identify a payment that on its face was for a legitimate purpose; however; the true intent of the payment is a disguised questionable payment. Many of the previous routines already will provide this analysis. However, focusing on payments to employees may reveal other questionable payments.

Company employee directly receives a payment that is characterized as a legitimate business purpose. However, the employee uses the money for making the questionable payment. A few search routines are:

- Bonuses paid to employees associated with sales contract.
- Advances to employees that are eventually written off.

- Significant changes in sales per diems.
- Credit card charges on a company credit card that is a disguised cash-conversion scheme.

SUMMARY

One strategy for all chief audit directors is the concept of focusing on high-risk areas. Violations of bribery statutes cases are extremely costly for organizations when considering the legal associates connected with defending the corporation, the internal investigation costs associated with determining whether the event occurred, potential fines, and the adverse publicity.

In some ways, the fraud data analytics for corruption committed by the company can be very easy. Specific identification is based on transactional history for compliance with standards. In other ways, the fraud data analytics is the most challenging because of where and how questionable payments are recorded, on the books or off the books. So, before you start the project, make sure your scope and objectives are clearly defined and the purpose is understood.

CHAPTER THIRTEEN

Fraud Data Analytics
for Financial Statements

This chapter will explain a methodology for using fraud data analytics in the search for fraud scenarios in financial statement accounts. Chapters 14 and 15 will explain how to use the methodology for revenue and journal entry testing.

This chapter will focus on uncovering fraud scenarios that are recorded in the general ledger or omitted from the general ledger either in a source journal or through a manual journal entry. This chapter will not focus on standards of care required by the professional auditing standards to uncover material misstatement through an intentional error. It is assumed the reader has knowledge of GAAS and will incorporate the standards into the data analytics plan.

I would encourage the reader to study the known financial statement frauds that occurred to improve their personal knowledge of how management has misstated financial statements. The knowledge will assist the auditor in the data interpretation aspect of the methodology. It is always easier to see a fraud scenario the second time versus the first time. Through the study of previous financial statement fraud cases, the auditor will learn the concept of fraud predictability or the logic of building the fraud analytics plan.

In one publicly traded company, revenue was materially overstated through a series of small-dollar general journal entries that in the aggregate caused a material misstatement. Therefore, financial statement history has taught the profession that fraud can be recorded in one large transaction or a series of transactions in the aggregate that can cause a misstatement of a financial statement account. In one publicly traded company, management intentionally failed to write off damaged or lost assets. Once again, history has taught the profession, the absence of a write-off journal entry would have highlighted this fraud scenario. Remember the famous phrase: Knowledge is power.

The methodology for fraud in financial accounts is the same as described in the first five chapters but needs to be adapted for the nuances of fraud in financial statements versus asset misappropriation or corruption. The fraud scenario statement has the same four components. However, the concept of a material overstatement or understatement must be included in the fraud scenario. The fraud action statement needs to be adapted for how, where, and when the fraudulent transaction is recorded in the general ledger.

The auditor is responsible for detecting misstatements, whether caused by error or fraud in the financial statements that are material and would impact an investor's decision to purchase the stock or for a bank to provide a loan to a company. The auditor is not responsible for uncovering all fraud but fraud that is material. Therefore, the fraud data analytics plan should incorporate the concept of fraud and materiality.

Lastly, because fraud in financial statements requires the intent to conceal the fraud, the element of concealment needs to be considered in building the fraud data analytics plan. Remember from our discussion in Chapters 2 and 3 that concealment is separate from the fraud scenario. Concealment also has three levels of sophistication.

Within this chapter, there are two overall approaches for searching for fraud in financial statements. First, search for the fraud data profile of the recorded fraud scenario. Second, search for the predictable concealment strategies associated with the fraud scenario. Before we start the discussion, we need to explain a few terms associated with financial statement misstatement.

WHAT IS AN ERROR?

An *error* is a mistake in the recognition, presentation, or disclosure in the financial statements. The error could be caused by a mistake in applying GAAP, internal control weakness resulting in improper recognition, or an error in judgment or assumptions. In one sense, the list is endless. However, an error does not occur with intent to misstate the financial statements. Therefore, there is no desire to conceal the error at the time the error occurs. However, the error may result in a material misstatement of the financial statements. Fraud data analytics can assist the auditor in searching for an error by searching for the fraud data profile of the transaction. However, fraud data analytics will not detect the misstatement through the search for the predictable concealment strategies because there was no intent to conceal the truth.

To illustrate, let's assume expenses were understated at year-end. The search for 2016-dated vendor invoices in the 2017 purchases journal would detect the error. If the error was intentional, the 2016 invoices would be recorded in the journal after the opinion date or with a 2017 date versus the correct date.

WHAT IS EARNINGS MANAGEMENT?

The concept has many terms associated with the phrase: *income smoothing, cookie jar, creative accounting,* and *aggressive accounting.* By whatever name, *earnings management* is a strategy used by management to achieve a predefined earnings target. It usually occurs through changes in accounting practices or through aggressive estimates for accruals or adjustments. It can either result in understatement in the current year to assist in achieving next year's earnings or result in overstatement in the current year through aggressive accounting practices.

Earnings management is sometimes called the gray area between errors causing misstatement and intent by management causing misstatement of the financial statements. It may not be a clear violation of GAAP but does distort the true financial picture of the company or a material misstatement. The planning reports may highlight areas of misstatement but fraud data analytics is not really intended to search for the type of misstatement caused by earnings management through the improper application of GAAP.

WHAT IS FINANCIAL STATEMENT FRAUD?

Financial statement fraud is the process of intentionally misleading the reader of the financial statements. It is the deliberate misrepresentation, misstatement, or omission of financial data to provide the impression that the organization is financially sound.

The key aspect in determining whether the misstatement is fraudulent is through establishing the intent of management. Is there clear and convincing evidence that management intended to misstate the financial statements, or the misstatement was caused by an unintentional error? The job of the fraud data analytics auditor is to identify the fraud scenario in the general ledger. The job of the fraud auditor is to offer that opinion that the scenario occurred with intent to conceal the fraud scenario and whether the fraud scenario is material to the financial statements.

HOW DOES AN ERROR DIFFER FROM FRAUD?

The answer is simple. An error is a mistake, whereas fraud is an intentional act that management conceals from the auditor. For this reason, using the predictable concealment strategies is an effective method for searching for misstatement through fraudulent efforts.

The starting point for building the fraud data analytics plan is for the fraud auditor to understand the inherent fraud scheme concept, and how to write a fraud scenario for the inherent fraud scheme.

INHERENT FRAUD SCHEMES AND FINANCIAL STATEMENT FRAUD SCENARIOS

The inherent fraud scheme concept for financial statement fraud or the methodology for writing a fraud scenario described in earlier chapters is the same for financial statement fraud scenarios. What changes is the addition of the financial account, which is impacted by the fraud scenario, type of misstatement, and how to write the fraud action statement. In Chapter 14 and 15, respectively, we will describe the nuances of writing fraud scenarios for revenue and journal entries.

Let's review the component of fraud scenario for financial statement fraud:

1. *Person committing* is less critical for financial statement fraud versus asset misappropriation and corruption. Based on most fraud statistics, financial management or senior management is responsible for most financial statement fraud. Therefore, a simple statement of the controller or senior management would suffice. However, those schemes involving other members of management should identify at the minimum the department or function responsible for committing the fraud scenario.

2. *Direction of misstatement* is whether the general ledger account is overstated or understated. The type of misstatement is critical to understanding which operating year to search for the fraud scenario. This statement also describes when the transaction is recorded to achieve the desired misstatement.
3. *General ledger account* is the financial account that is the focus of the fraud data analytics plan. This tells the fraud auditor where the transaction is recorded or where to search for the concealment technique.
4. *Type of entity*—the same structure identified in the shell company chapter is relevant for financial reporting. The one difference is that the entity is not always a legal entity. For example, in inventory, the entity is sku number versus a legal entity such as a vendor. However, the sku number is either false or real.
5. *Fraud action statement* is the basis for developing the fraud data interrogation routine. The statement describes how the fraud scenario occurs and how the transaction is recorded in the financial account. The fraud action statement describes whether the transaction is false or real, whether the entity is false or real, and whether the transaction is recorded through a source journal or journal entry. The type of entity and fraud action statement describes how the transaction is recorded.
6. *Impact statement*—as a matter of style, the fraud auditor may use a generic statement, causing the financial statements to be materiality misstated, or a specific impact statement, causing revenue to be misstated. Remember, the direction of misstatement is described in the first part of the fraud scenario.

The following provides examples of how to write a financial statement fraud scenario using the prescribed format:

1. Controller intentionally/overstates/revenue/by recording false sales through a false customer/in the sales journal/causing the financial statements to be materially misstated.
2. Controller intentionally/overstates/revenue by recording false sales through a real customer/in the sales journal/causing the financial statements to be materially misstated.
3. Controller intentionally/overstates/revenue by recording real sales (improper recognition) through a real customer/in the sales journal/causing the financial statements to be materially misstated.

All three fraud scenarios involve overstatement of revenue by the controller. However, the important point is to understand that the fraud data analytics for the three scenarios is very different. As follows for each scenario:

1. The fraud data analytics for scenario one can search for a false customer, a false revenue transaction, or the eventual reversal of the false revenue.
2. The fraud data analytics for scenario two can search for false revenue transaction or the eventual reversal of the false revenue.
3. The fraud data analytics for scenario three must search the current-year source journal for the specific technique used to prematurely record the revenue transaction in the source journal.

The proceeding three scenarios demonstrate the concept that the fraud data analytics must be designed for a specific fraud scenario.

ADDITIONAL GUIDANCE IN CREATING THE FRAUD ACTION STATEMENT

Creating the fraud scenario requires the fraud auditor to be able to identify the fraud action statement in order to build the fraud interrogation routine. To repeat, a fraud action for financial statement fraud has the following components:

1. Where is the transaction recorded: revenue or expense/asset or liability or equity?
2. Is the entity real or false?
3. Is the transaction real or false?
4. For a real transaction, the method of improper recognition must be stated.
5. GAAP requirements must be understood and stated. Remember, fraud in the financial statement is an intentional error in GAAP, so this aspect of the fraud action statement is critical.
6. Is the transaction recorded through a source journal?
   a) Was the initial transaction recorded in the balance sheet or the income statement?
   b) Was the transaction recorded in the right account for purposes of misstatement, or will the transaction need to be reclassified?
   c) Was there a failure to record a real transaction?

7. Is the event recorded through a journal entry?
   a) Was there a failure to adjust an account balance?
   b) Was there a failure to adjust or reclassify a previously recorded transaction?
   c) Was there a failure to write off the transaction that was previously recorded?
8. Location of the transaction on the financial statement. Depending on the size and complexity of the financial statement, the fraud action statement may also include the section of the financial statement, such as cost of sales, operating expenses, or other expenses.

Building the fraud action statement starts with creating the list of permutations by changing the variables and then changing the generic permutations to be account-specific. Once the permutation analysis is understood, the fraud auditor then links the specific technique to the person committing the fraud scenario.

Starting with the concept of using generic permutation analysis to create fraud action statements:

1. Recording a false transaction to a false entity in the source journal.
2. Recording a false transaction to a real entity in the source journal.
3. Recording a real transaction to a real entity in the source journal.
4. Failure to record a real transaction for a real entity in the source journal.
5. Recording a false event associated with a real entity through a journal entry.
6. Recording a real event associated with a real entity through a journal entry.
7. Failure to adjust or reclassify a real event initially recorded from a source journal with a general journal entry.
8. Failure to write off the transaction previously recorded.

Remember, the fraud auditor does not know which fraud scenario the controller is going to commit, but the fraud auditor does know all the fraud scenarios the controller *can* commit. By starting with the generic fraud action statement and applying the generic statement to the specific account, the fraud auditor is assured regarding the completeness of the fraud scenario listing. Using the generic fraud action statement, we will identify the applicable fraud scenarios to be included in our fraud data analytics plan. Let's assume the balance sheet has an asset entitled capitalized advertising expenditures.

306 Fraud Data Analytics for Financial Statements

1. Controller intentionally overstates assets by recording a **false** operating expense incurred from a **false** vendor through the **purchase journal** as a capitalized expenditure, causing the capitalized advertising expenditures to be materially misstated.
2. Controller intentionally understates assets by failing to record a real operating expense incurred from a **real** vendor through a **general journal entry or purchase journal** as a capitalized expenditure, causing the capitalized advertising expenditures to be materially misstated.
3. Controller intentionally overstates assets by recording a **real** operating expense incurred from a **real** vendor through the **purchase journal** as a capitalized expenditure, causing the capitalized advertising expenditures to be materially misstated.
4. Controller intentionally overstates assets by recording a **false** operating expense incurred from a **real** vendor through the **purchase journal** as a capitalized expenditure, causing the capitalized advertising expenditures to be materially misstated.
5. Controller intentionally overstates assets by recording a **false** operating expense incurred from a **real** vendor through **a general journal entry** as a capitalized expenditure, causing the capitalized advertising expenditures to be materially misstated.
6. Controller intentionally overstates assets by recording a **real** operating expense incurred from a **real** vendor through a **general journal entry** as a capitalized expenditure, causing the capitalized advertising expenditures to be materially misstated.
7. Controller intentionally overstates assets by failing to adjust or reclassify a **real** operating expense incurred from a **real** vendor through a **general journal entry** as a capitalized expenditure, causing the capitalized advertising expenditures to be materially misstated.
8. Controller intentionally overstates assets by failing to write off a **real** operating expense incurred from a **real** vendor through a **general journal entry** as a capitalized expenditure, causing the capitalized advertising expenditures to be materially misstated.

The first step is now completed. The fraud auditor has built the foundation of the fraud data analytics plan by identifying the permutations of the fraud scenario. GAAS will require the fraud auditor to assess the likelihood of the scenarios. Assuming the likelihood assessment has labeled the fraud scenario as an identified fraud risk for purposes of testing, the fraud auditor knows the answers to the *where*, *when*, and *how* questions in order to build the data interrogation routine. The astute auditor understands that the list of previous scenarios can be easily converted to each asset account by adapting the fraud action statement for the financial account.

The second step is to incorporate the GAAP implications into the fraud scenario. As a matter of style, the GAAP assertion can be written into the fraud scenario or documented as part of the overall plan. The problem with incorporating GAAP into the statement is that the fraud scenario may become too wordy.

HOW DOES THE INHERENT FRAUD SCHEME STRUCTURE APPLY TO THE FINANCIAL STATEMENT ASSERTIONS?

The GAAS standards as described in SAS #106 (audit evidence) discusses the concept of the risk of material misstatement at the financial statement and assertion levels. The fraud data analytics plan must link to the assertions described in the standard. The following illustrates how the fraud action statement links to the assertion statements for class of transactions and events:

1. *Occurrence.* Transactions have been recorded that have occurred and relate to the company. The search is for false transactions in the general ledger.
2. *Completeness.* All transactions that should have been recorded are recorded. The search is for improper recognition in the general ledger.
3. *Accuracy.* All transactions have been recorded appropriately. Incorporating the GAAP implications into the fraud scenario.
4. *Cutoff.* Transactions have been recorded in the proper period. The planning associated with the right operating year to search for the fraud scenario or the associated concealment technique.
5. *Classification.* Transactions are recorded in the proper account. The planning associated with the direction of testing and the impact statement.

Answering the fraud action statement questions of *where, when,* and *how* will help the auditor achieve the goals of SAS #106.

DO I UNDERSTAND THE DATA?

Effective financial statement analysis and interpretation begins with an understanding of the types of questions that a fraud auditor needs to ask concerning where, when, and how the financial statements maybe misstated. The profession abounds with ratios and variance analysis, both vertical and horizontal analysis. Fraud data analytics is another tool for the auditor to understand the data. One difference between the traditional tools and the fraud data analytics tool is that the fraud auditor is searching for an intentional error that is material and embedded in the transactional history of a source journal or a general journal entry. A second difference is that fraud data analytics is looking at all transactions versus a random sample of transactions. Fraud data analytics should complement the existing tools versus replace the traditional tools.

Understanding the data starts with understanding what transactions created the account balance. The use of disaggregated analysis of an account balance is a powerful tool for the fraud auditor to determine what journal created the account balance. The tool allows the auditor to understand whether the account was created through a source journal or a general journal entry. This knowledge tells the auditor from a materiality factor whether it is more predictable that the scenario is embedded in the source journal or general journal entry.

The trial balance is the starting point of understanding where, when, and how the financial statements are misstated through fraud scenarios. The first report should be an analysis of each general ledger account as to whether the balance was created through a source journal or through a journal entry. The analysis should provide a net summary of the debits and the credits that compose each financial account through the source journals and the general journal entries.

The purpose of the report is to understand how the account balance was created. All account balances are created through a source journal or a general journal entry. By understanding the composition and the dollar value of the recorded transactions, the fraud auditor can start to develop the fraud data analytics plan. The analysis does require the fraud auditor to understand whether the account balance should be created from a source journal or through general journal entries.

- A control account such as accounts receivable should be created through source journals; therefore, a general journal entry in the control account would be suspicious.
- If the inventory is seasonal, such as the apparel industry, the lack of a journal entry to write down inventory would be suspicious.

For a simple illustration, if 95 percent of the revenue total is created from a source journal and 5 percent of total revenue is created from general journal entries, then the most likely location for a material overstatement is in the source journal. If the source journal is the primary source of the balance, then the most likely fraud scenarios are associated with either false revenue or improper recognition of real revenue. The next round of reports would be designed to determine the likelihood of false revenue or improper recognition.

For key financial statement accounts supported by a sub-ledger, the use of disaggregated analysis would recreate the control account balance by each account in the sub-ledger. The second level of disaggregated analysis is to determine whether the sub-account was created by source journal or general journal entries. The purpose of the analysis is to determine where the material entries are located in the sub-ledger. Is the source journal creating the account balance or a general journal entry?

To illustrate the concept, using the work-in-process inventory account, let's assume the disaggregated analysis indicates that a general journal entry is creating 60 percent of the balance for three accounts in the sub-ledgers. Then the analysis would perform a disaggregated analysis on the journal entry. In another example, we will assume that the analysis indicates that 100 percent of the account balance for one account in the sub-ledger was created from the accounts payable source journal. Furthermore, the disaggregated analysis of the accounts payable transaction reveals that one vendor invoice from a real vendor for $500,000 was recorded on December 31. Should this be suspicious?

The second tool is the data summarization feature of existing software to summarize journal activity based on a specific criterion:

- Summarize expenditures by vendor by debits and credits. Large credits may indicate that accounts payable was overstated by posting false or real invoices in the wrong period. The credit is reversing the vendor invoice.
- Summarize journal entries by dollar control level, which may indicate fraud in the aggregate if there is a high frequency of small-dollar journal entries.
- Summarize journal entries by key accounts in the last month and journal entries after year-end by dollar control level. Compare the summary to the previous year. A significant difference between the two years may indicate management is attempting to reach a financial target.

The understanding the data concept is the same concept described in earlier chapters in the planning reports section. The purpose of this stage of fraud data analytics is to improve the predictability of the planning stage of the audit by highlighting those accounts or transactions that have the highest predictability of being associated with a fraud scenario.

WHAT IS A FRAUD DATA ANALYTICS PLAN FOR FINANCIAL STATEMENTS?

In Chapter 4, we discussed the steps of building a fraud data analytics plan. The same steps apply for financial statements; however, due to the unique nature of financial statements, we need to answer additional questions to build a comprehensive plan to detect fraud scenarios in the financial accounts.

Fraud Brainstorming for Significant Accounts: Assets, Liabilities, Equity, Revenue, or Expenses

The planning stage requires the auditor to brainstorm by discussing the susceptibility of a financial account in having a material error arising from either an error or fraud. From the fraud perspective, the discussion should include the fraud scenarios that could impact a significant account balance and how the fraud scenario would be concealed in the account balance, or, said another way, the red flags of the scenario or red flags of the concealment technique.

The starting point is to identify which accounts individually or in the aggregate are deemed to be a significant account balance. For assets, are we focusing on inventory, accounts receivable, or capitalized expenses? The brainstorming should identify the financial account and discuss the type of scenarios that would be predictable for the account and the company. The focus of the discussion is on the fraud action statement as to how the type of error would occur and be concealed.

The six primary techniques used to overstate an asset are:

1. Recording an asset that does not exist.
2. Recording a real asset that is not owned by the company.
3. Recording a real asset before the liability occurs.
4. Improper capitalization of a false expense.
5. Improper capitalization of a real expense.
6. Reporting the asset in the wrong section of the balance sheet.

The four primary techniques used to understate an asset are:

1. Failure to record a real asset.
2. Failure to capitalize a real expense.
3. Failure to record an asset in the proper period.
4. Reporting the asset in the wrong section of the balance sheet.

The four primary techniques used to overstate an expense are:

1. Recording false expense.
2. Recording a real expense before the liability occurs.
3. The failure to capitalize a real expense.
4. Reporting the expense in the wrong section of the income statement.

The four primary techniques used to understate an expense are:

1. Improper capitalization of the expense.
2. Failure to write off or write down and asset.
3. Failure to record a liability in the proper period.
4. Reporting the expense in the wrong section of the income statement.

The second aspect of the brainstorming should be the predictable conceal-ment techniques used to conceal the fraud scenario and what is the fraud data profile of the concealment technique. To illustrate, if management is overstat-ing inventory, what are the concealment techniques, and what is the fraud data profile?

In one famous inventory fraud scheme, management tricked the auditors by transferring inventory from one physical location to the physical location where the auditor was performing test counts. Therefore, the fraud data analyt-ics would search for inventory transfers at year-end (the fraud action) or search for the reversal of the transfer after year-end (fraud concealment). The next step is to incorporate the GAAP implications.

WHAT ARE THE ACCOUNTING POLICIES FOR ASSETS, LIABILITIES, EQUITY, REVENUE, AND EXPENSE ACCOUNTS?

The accounting policies identify how a transaction should be recorded to comply with GAAP. The auditor needs to ensure that the accounting practices comply with GAAP. However, from a fraud data analytics perspective, the company's accounting policies will identify how a transaction should be recorded. Therefore, an anomaly can be described as a transaction recorded contrary to the company's accounting guidelines.

Within the Financial Statement, Which Fraud Scenarios Are We Trying to Uncover?

The process starts with the fraud risk assessment prepared as part of the planning process. One of the goals of the fraud risk assessment is the process of identifying those fraud risks that could have a material impact on the financial statement. For purposes of this book, we will refer to the identified fraud risk concept as a fraud scenario. From a GAAS perspective, a fraud scenario is called an identified fraud risk.

The second step of the process is the planning reports used in the understanding of the data step. If the planning reports do not suggest material amounts associated with the fraud data profile, then more than likely, that scenario is not occurring.

What Are the Overall Strategies for Fraud Data Analytics?

The correct overall strategy is dependent on many variables, ranging from the nature of the industry to how the general ledger is maintained. The correct answer to the question is determined on a scenario-by-scenario basis. This is why understanding how to write a fraud scenario becomes the basis for developing the fraud audit plan for searching for a material error in the financial statement. In practice, you will learn that one fraud data analytics plan will link to several fraud scenarios. It is the completeness of the thought process that is critical to the exercise of judgment in building the fraud audit approach for financial accounts.

1. Is the fraud data analytics searching for the fraud data profile of the fraud scenario or the concealment technique to hide the fraud scenario?
2. Is the fraud data analytics focusing on the recording of the transaction or based on disaggregated analysis of an account balance to spot the most likely location of the error?
3. As a general guideline for transactional analysis:
   a) False transactions can be identified through a fraud data profile of the false transaction or the eventual reversal of the transaction.
   b) A real transaction recorded through a source journal is all about recording the transaction in the right period and the right section of the financial statement. Therefore, dates and general ledger accounts are important.
   c) Failure to record a transaction is about the absence of a transaction.
4. Guidelines for journal entries are discussed in Chapter 15.

What Are the Steps to Designing a Fraud Data Analytics Search Routine for Financial Statements?

Your initial use of this process will seem overly bureaucratic; however, eventually the process will become just a way of thinking. The thought process is important to understand what your data analytics plan is designed to detect and what the data analytics plan will not detect. The following steps are necessary to build the data interrogation routines:

1. Which financial account is the focus of the fraud data analytics?
2. Are we searching for understatement or overstatement in the financial account?
3. How does the opinion date correlate to our ability to analyze the general ledger?
4. How is the fraud scenario recorded, through a source journal or a journal entry?
5. Is the fraud data analytics searching for a fraud scenario?
6. Based on the fraud scenario, should our data interrogation occur through the recording of the transaction or through disaggregated analysis of the general ledger account?
7. Is the fraud data analytics searching for the concealment strategy to hide the fraud scenario?
8. Are we searching for a large error or many small errors that in the aggregate are material?
9. Which data-mining strategy is appropriate for the scope of the fraud audit?

Which Financial Account Is the Focus of the Fraud Data Analytics?

GAAS provides guidance on which accounts should be the focus of the audit. We will assume for purposes of illustration that the GAAS analysis has indicated that inventory is a significant account balance. The fraud scenario for illustration is:

Controller overstates inventory by failing to write off obsolete inventory, causing the financial statements to be materially misstated.
Controller understates cost of goods sold by failing to write off obsolete inventory, causing the financial statements to be materially misstated.

As the auditor understands, the impact of one fraud scenario typically impacts another financial account. The beauty of the double entry system is that the fraud scenario can be detected through two accounts. Yes, a matter of style, yes, a matter of double entry accounting, but ultimately, the fraud data analytics is searching for the fraud scenario or the fraud scenario concealment strategy.

Are We Searching for Understatement or Overstatement in the Financial Account?

The direction of testing is a critical question that must be considered in the planning stage. The fraud risk factors or conditions of fraud used in the planning stage of the audit should provide the auditor with clues as to the direction of testing. The primary purpose of the direction of testing question is to determine if the fraud data analytics is searching for overstatement or understatement. From a simple perspective, if the fraud auditor is performing a valid test on the wrong year of data, then the fraud data analytics will not uncover the fraud scenario.

The direction of misstatement will also provide a clue as to which year to look for the misstatement. From a fraud data analytics perspective, there are three years that should be considered in building the fraud data analytics plan. Assuming the year of audit is the calendar year ending December 31, 2016, the following describes the direction of testing for over- or understatement:

2016 year to perform substantive testing on the account balances.
2016 year if searching for overstatement of an account balance.
2016 year if searching for the failure to write down an asset.
2017 year if searching for reversals of entries.
2017 year if searching for understatement of an account balance.
2016 year if using retrospective analysis to test the methodology for estimates.

To further illustrate the concept, we will assume a year-end of December 31, 2016, fiscal year. The year under audit, 2016, is a collection of all transactions recorded in the general ledger through either a source journal or general journal entries. Said another way, all of the fraud scenarios committed by management are either recorded in the general ledger or not recorded in the general ledger (i.e., the general ledger reflects the absence of a transaction that should have been recorded). The real question for the fraud auditor is to determine in which year to search for the fraud scenario causing the over- or understatement. The examples will assume the primary focus is the balance sheet accounts while understanding the impact on the other side of the entry:

1. False transactions are recorded in the 2016 year. From a fraud data analytics perspective, there are two subsets of false transactions. The first subset is transactions that have an aging analysis, such as revenue or loan receivables. The subset is typically recorded in a balance sheet. In the 2017 year, the transaction will need to be reversed or the aging falsified. The fraud data analytics can search for the false transaction in the 2016 year, false aging concealment techniques in the 2016 ledger, or reversal of the transaction in the 2017 year.

2. The second subset of false transactions is accounts that have no aging analysis; therefore, there is no need to reverse the transaction or conceal the transaction in the 2017 year. The fraud data analytics must search for the false transaction in the 2016 year. If the account has a subledger, then search through the use of disaggregated analysis of the 2016 subledger.

3. The overstatement of financial accounts through the source journal is caused by posting 2017 real transactions in the 2016 source journal or 2015 real transactions in the 2016 general ledger. The fraud data analytics should search either the beginning or end of the 2016 year.

4. The overstatement of financial accounts through a general journal entry is caused by recording the general journal entry in the 2016 year, whereas the real transactions that are the basis of the accrual are recorded in a source journal in the 2017 year. The fraud data analytics should search the 2017 source journal or the recorded 2016 journal entries.

5. The overstatement of financial accounts is caused by the failure to adjust or write off an asset. The fraud data analytics should search for the absence of the journal entry or through the use of disaggregated analysis of the subledger.

6. The overstatement of a specific financial account is caused by the failure to record the transaction in the right account or the failure to reclassify a real transaction to the proper account. The fraud data analytics should search the 2016 ledger.

7. The understatement of financial accounts through the source journal is caused by posting 2016 real transactions in the 2017 year. The fraud data analytics should search the 2017 source journal.

8. The understatement of financial accounts through a journal entry is caused by recording the general journal in the 2016 year, whereas the

real transactions are recorded in the 2017 year. The fraud data analytics should search the 2017 general ledger or use disaggregated analysis of the 2016 subledger.

9. The understatement of financial accounts through a journal entry is caused by the failure to adjust an account or reclassify a recorded transaction. The understatement of a specific financial account is caused by the failure to classify the transaction in the proper account. The fraud data analytics should search for the absence of the journal entry in the 2016 year.

Using the previous fraud scenario:

Controller overstates inventory by failing to write off obsolete inventory, causing the financial statements to be materially misstated.

The fraud data analytics would search for the absence of a journal entry in the 2016 year or through disaggregated analysis of the 2016 inventory subledger.

The overstatement or understatement question is an important one for building the fraud data analytics plan. Without considering the question, the fraud data analytics does not know which year of data to use in the search for the fraud scenario.

How Does the Opinion Date Correlate to Our Ability to Analyze the General Ledger?

GAAS requires the auditor to consider the nature, timing, and extent of the audit procedures. The correlation of the opinion date and the year-end has a direct impact on the timing of the fraud data analytics.

The next consideration is the proximity of the opinion date to the financial statement date or the timing of the fraud data analytics. As the opinion date moves closer to the financial statement date, the ability to search 2017 for overstatement or understatement in the 2016 financial statement accounts becomes difficult. Therefore, performing the fraud data analytics during the midyear time period or through the use of retrospective analysis becomes a more viable approach. The *when* and *where* questions will depend on the opinion date proximity to the financial statement date and which financial statement account we are interrogating.

Let's first consider the *when* question using two assumptions:

Opinion date is January 31, 2017. In this situation the data interrogation will test the December 31, 2015, estimates by searching transactions recorded in the first quarter of 2016. The reason is simple; if management is intentionally misstating the financial statements, then management will ensure the 2016 transactions recorded in the 2017 source journal will occur after the opinion date.

Opinion date is April 1, 2017. In this situation, the data interrogation will test the December 31, 2016, estimates by searching the first quarter 2017 source journals. In this situation, there are sufficient data and time to analyze the year-end estimates.

Using the previous fraud scenario and assuming a January 31, 2017, opinion date:

Controller overstates inventory by failing to write off obsolete inventory, causing the financial statements to be materially misstated.

The opinion date does not provide sufficient time to use 2017 data; therefore, the analysis must focus on the 2016 ledger. The procedure most likely will need to be performed earlier in the year.

How Is the Fraud Scenario Recorded—Through a Source Journal or a Journal Entry?

Financial statements are prepared from the general ledger unless management is creating top-sided journal entries. General ledgers are a summary of source journals and manual journal entries. Therefore if a fraud scenario is lurking in the general ledger, the fraud scenario had to be recorded through a source journal or through a journal entry. The exception to the following statement is the transaction or journal entry that is not recorded.

The answer to this question tells the fraud auditor which journal to search for the fraud scenario. That is why understanding the data question, previously discussed, is so critical.

Using the previous scenario:

Controller overstates inventory by failing to write off obsolete inventory, causing the financial statements to be materially misstated.

In this scenario, it is the absence of the journal entry that is causing the overstatement, whereas the concealment technique is lurking in the subledger caused by a false movement either in the inventory journal or sales journal.

Is the Fraud Data Analytics Searching for a Fraud Scenario?

The fraud data analytics searches for either the recorded scenario or how the fraud scenario is concealed in the general ledger. The decision is made on a scenario-by-scenario basis on an account-by-account basis. The following guidelines are useful in determining which approach:

- Transactions recorded in a general ledger through a source journal can use either the fraud scenario approach or the concealment approach.
- The decision is impacted by the timing of the procedure. Will the fraud data analytics have the right data to find the recorded fraud scenario?
- Failure to record a transaction or a journal entry should use the concealment approach.

Using the previous fraud scenario:

Controller overstates inventory by failing to write off obsolete inventory, causing the financial statements to be materially misstated.

For this scenario, the overstatement occurs due to the failure to record a transaction. Therefore, the fraud data analytics will search for evidence on how obsolescence is concealed in the subledgers.

Based on the Fraud Scenario, Should Our Data Interrogation Occur through the Recording of the Transaction or through Disaggregated Analysis of the General Ledger Account?

The decision is both a matter of style and based on the data interpretation of the planning reports. The first planning reporting is the disaggregated analysis of each general ledger account that is intended to describe what journal created the account balance or what journals created the change from the beginning balance to the ending balance. The review of this report should provide some direction to answer the question.

The answer to the question will depend on the stage of the audit as to testing internal controls or substantive testing of account balances. The answer will also depend on the fraud scenario and the associated concealment strategy. Using the previous fraud scenario:

Controller overstates inventory by failing to write off obsolete inventory, causing the financial statements to be materially misstated.

For this scenario, there is no transaction recorded. Therefore, the summary of journal entries by account balance would reveal that no write-downs have occurred. The second analysis would use disaggregated analysis of the sub-ledger.

The disaggregated approach would compare beginning inventory to ending inventory, searching for inventory lines that have zero movement or minimal movement. A similar approach would use the sales journal and summarize by product number. The exclusion theory would exclude all product lines having significant sales movement. The report would then compare sales by product line to the inventory movement report. The sample selection is based on inventory line items with no movement and no sales. This assumes that management has not attempted to conceal the lack of inventory movement.

Is the Fraud Data Analytics Searching for the Concealment Strategy to Hide the Fraud Scenario?

As described in earlier chapters, fraud concealment is different from the fraud scenario. Fraud concealment theory in financial statements is the same concept as described for asset misappropriation or corruption fraud schemes. The difference is that the method of concealment is recorded in the general ledger in the 2015, 2016, or 2017 year. Second, history has taught us that each financial account has predictable concealment strategies.

Concealment is an integral part of hiding the fraud scenario from the fraud auditor. The general concealment may occur by: how the transaction is recorded; how the transaction is reversed; when the transaction is recorded; or which section of the financial statement the transaction is recorded. The specific concealment strategies are those actions taken by management to falsify the financial statement assertions. An integral part of the concealment is the documentation supporting the transaction. However, the documentation aspect is not critical to the fraud data analysis plan but is critical to developing the fraud audit program.

The second consideration to identifying the concealment strategies is to understand the accounting principles associated with the fraud scenario and the financial account. Using each accounting principle for the financial account, the fraud auditor would brainstorm how management would provide the illusion of compliance with the accounting principles.

Consistent with Chapter 3, there are two types of concealment strategies. There are general concealment strategies and the concealment strategies that directly correlate to creating the illusion that the fraud scenario complies with GAAP or complies with the company's accounting practices.

Illustrations of General Concealment Strategies

How is the transaction recorded?

- Small-dollar transactions; however, the transactions in the aggregate are material.
- Layering a transaction through multiple cost centers or subsidiaries.
- Transaction is recorded directly to the financial account through a source journal.
- False customers or false vendors are created to provide the illusion of a valid transaction.

How is the transaction reversed?

- Transaction is reversed after the audit opinion date.
- Reversal is hidden in a source journal.
- Use of a contra transaction in a source journal.
- Transaction is written off to another general ledger account.

When is the transaction recorded?

- Transaction is recorded after the audit opinion date.
- Transaction is recorded in a source journal and later transferred to another general ledger account through a journal entry.

In which section of the financial statement is the transaction recorded?

- A financial statement has various sections; the income statement has revenue, cost of sales, operating expenses, other expenses, and extraordinary expenses. Another description is above the line or below the line.
- Balance sheet assets and liabilities have current, long term, and intangibles.

What is the concealment strategy which creates the illusion of compliance with GAAP?

- Shipping dates are falsified.
- Perpetrator commits a variation of a lapping scheme to conceal a bad-debt write-off.
- Operating expenses are posted to Property, Plant, and Equipment accounts.

Consideration of Specific Concealment Strategies

The discussion starts with the specific fraud scenario and focuses on the fraud action statement and the accounting practices for proper recognition of the transaction. The goal of management is to create the illusion of compliance with GAAP and record the transaction in a way to hide the truth from the fraud auditor.

To illustrate the concept, we will explain the techniques to conceal obsolete inventory from the fraud auditor. In the example, the company accounting practice does not recognize a reserve for obsolescence and uses the direct write-off method at time of obsolescence. The accounting practice is to review inventory usage reports to determine which inventory items should be written off. We will further assume the accounting policy is correct.

Using the previous fraud scenario:

Controller overstates inventory by failing to write off obsolete inventory, causing the financial statements to be materially misstated.

The following concealment techniques allow the controller to hide the fraud scenario from the fraud auditor:

- Create the illusion of inventory movement. The concealment technique is to ship the item to another company warehouse through a zero-dollar invoice. Record the inventory at the second location under a new inventory number. The data analytics should search for zero-dollar invoices with the shipping location to a company warehouse. The data analytics should search for new inventory items and determine whether the new item was created from a transfer of inventory versus a receiving transaction.
- Create the illusion of inventory movement through inventory transfers. The concealment is the same as the zero-dollar invoices. The data analytics should search for transfers within the company with a change in the inventory description.

- Conceal the timing of the write-off to a later accounting period. Create a false customer and sell the item. The scheme shifts the asset from inventory item to accounts receivable. The controller effectively delays the operating expenses to a later period.
- Shift the expense from cost of goods sold to an operating expense such as bad-debt expense, marketing and promotions, or donations. As to bad expenses, the fraud data analytics should match bad-debt write-off to the associated inventory record. As to other operating expenses, search for debits from the inventory system other than cost of goods sold. The transfer could also occur through a manual journal entry.

Are We Searching for a Large Error or Many Small Errors That in the Aggregate Are Material?

Financial statements are overstated or understated by a single intentional error or a series of intentional errors in the aggregate. The fraud error is the fraud scenario. Many high-profile financial statement frauds involve either one major fraud scenario or many small fraud scenarios. The fraud scenario may have been committed by one large transaction in one account or many smaller transactions in one account that in the aggregate are material.

The concept of a large error needs to be defined through a general ledger account(s) associated with the materiality concept for a financial statement or financial account. Using inventory, the trial balance may indicate that there are many accounts associated with the amount of inventory reported on the financial statement.

The large error may be hidden in raw materials, work in process, and finished goods or spread throughout all the inventory accounts. The fraud data analytics plan must understand how to link the concept of a large error associated with a fraud scenario to a series of general ledger accounts. The fraud data analytics will create a homogeneous data set of large-dollar transactions as defined through the materiality concept. For a large-dollar transaction the clue is amount of the transaction and the posting date of the transaction.

The concept of a small error has the same linkage to the general ledger accounts associated with the material number on the financial statement. However, in the small error scheme, there are many transactions posted. The fraud data analytics will create a homogeneous data set of small-dollar transactions, as defined through the materiality concept. The first report is a summary report linked to the inventory line item providing aggregate dollar value, record count, largest dollar, smallest dollar, and average dollar.

For a series of small transactions the clue is the high frequency and the high aggregate dollar value.

The reason for the two data files correlates back to Chapter 4 with the use of the inclusion and exclusion theory regarding shrinking the size of the haystack. Spotting an error in a small homogeneous data set is easier than spotting an error in a large collection of data that has limited commonality. In this question, the commonality of data is the dollar amount of the transaction.

Using the previous fraud scenario with a minor change to include damaged inventory:

Controller overstates inventory by failing to write off obsolete or damaged inventory (raw, work in process, or finished), causing the financial statements to be materially misstated.

The sample selection should use the materiality amount as the focus of the analysis. Large transactions are those transactions that exceed the materiality amount for the account balance or are within a percentage of the materiality amount. The small transactions are the remaining transactions. The large transactions will use the specific identification strategy, whereas the small transactions would start with using a summary of transactions to search for materiality.

Which Data-Mining Strategy Is Appropriate for the Scope of the Fraud Data Analytics Plan?

As a reminder, the right data-mining strategy is based on both fraud data analytics strategy and answers to all the previous questions. As a reminder:

- Specific identification, the sample selection is based on the testing criteria in the fraud action statement.
- Internal control avoidance, the sample selection is based on transactions that avoid the internal control designed to mitigate the fraud action statement.
- Data interpretation, the sample selection is based on the auditor's judgment consistent with the fraud scenario and the associated fraud concealment strategies.
- Number anomaly, the sample selection is based on the type of number anomaly that is defined in the fraud test: round numbers, recurring numbers, or contra numbers.

Using the previous fraud scenario, what is the right fraud data analytics strategy?

Controller overstates inventory by failing to write off obsolete or damaged inventory (raw, work in process, or finished), causing the financial statements to be materially misstated.

Specification identification is the starting point to search for the fraud scenario, the concealment strategy, and the inclusion and exclusion theory. The sample selection would either use the materiality factor of the specific identification or use data interpretation using the auditor's understanding of the industry and company.

How Will the Fraud Auditor Design the Fraud Test?

The fraud data analytics plan must be linked to the audit program. Integrating fraud testing into the audit plan requires a sample plan designed to search for fraud but also testing techniques designed to pierce the concealment strategy associated with the fraud scenario.

 ## SUMMARY

The purpose of this chapter was to describe a methodology for creating a fraud data analytics plan for financial accounts. The next two chapters will describe how to apply the methodology to the revenue source journal and general journal entries. The fraud auditor will need to adapt the methodology to their industry and their company. Issues such as nature, timing, and extent of audit procedures will impact the success of fraud data analytics in searching for the material error. However, those issues are under the control of the auditor.

The good news is that financial statement fraud is in the general ledger. The bad news is, financial fraud is in the general ledger. The sheer amount of transactions and journal entries recorded in a general ledger makes it imperative that auditors use fraud data analytics. Generally speaking, the fraud auditor has access to all the data necessary to locate financial statement fraud scenarios, whereas in asset misappropriation schemes and corruption schemes the fraud auditor does not have all the necessary data or information to formulate a conclusion.

CHAPTER FOURTEEN

Fraud Data Analytics for Revenue and Accounts Receivable Misstatement

S
AS no. 99 states that you "should ordinarily" presume there is risk of material misstatement due to fraud relating to revenue recognition. If you do not identify improper revenue recognition as a risk of material misstatement due to fraud, you should document the reasons supporting this conclusion. The assumption in this chapter is that you are searching for material misstatement of revenue in the source journal. I should clarify that the phrase *sale of goods* will be used throughout the chapter to indicate revenue earned from the sale of tangible goods, services, or rental income.

Chapter 13 described the methodology for building a fraud data analytics plan for financial accounts. Using the plan, this chapter will focus on the fraud data analytics search routines for fraud scenarios in the source journal.

Revenue is the candy jar of choice used by management to misstate the financial statements. The candy jar has many different types of candy to cause revenue to be over- or understated. Fraudulent revenue may be recorded through a source journal or through a journal entry. Management may decide to misapply GAAP, thereby causing the recorded transaction to misstate the financial statements.

For the auditor, revenue recognition requires an understanding of the industry and the organization. The auditor needs to have the ability to apply and interpret the principles of revenue recognition to the audit program. It sounds simple; however, there are many widely accepted revenue recognition procedures and many situation-specific ways to interpret and apply each of these procedures. Just as organizations are different, the kinds of revenues they generate are different. Consequently, these different types of revenues need different recognition and different reporting methods. Therefore, each revenue system also needs an audit program tailored to its uniqueness.

 ## WHAT IS REVENUE RECOGNITION FRAUD?

The fundamental revenue recognition concept is that revenues should not be recognized by a company until the revenue is earned and realized or realizable. Revenue is earned if your company has fulfilled its obligations under the revenue contract. Revenue is realized when there is a real expectation that the customer will pay for the goods or services provided by your company.

Therefore, revenue recognition fraud occurs when revenue is recognized on the financial statements and the revenue is not earned or there is no expectation that the customer will fulfill its obligation to pay for the services. The second aspect is that management has concealed the fact that the revenue is not earned or the receivable is not realizable.

 ## INHERENT FRAUD RISK SCHEMES IN REVENUE RECOGNITION

It is generally recognized that misstating revenue is the most common fraud technique used by management to misstate the financial statements. The auditing standards created the phrase that improper revenue recognition is a presumed fraud risk. Therefore, it is critical that fraud auditors understand the fraud scenarios used by management to create fraudulent revenue:

1. False revenue and false customer scheme is the process of creating a false customer and recording through the source journal a false revenue transaction for the false customer.
2. False revenue and real customer scheme is the process of recording through the source journal a false revenue transaction that a real customer did not order. In this scheme, the real customer may retain the goods or may return the goods.

3. Real customer and improper recognition of revenue schemes through historical schemes:
   a) Holding the books is simple; the revenue is shipped in the subsequent period but recorded in the current period.
   b) Channel stuffing is more abstract than holding the books open. In channel stuffing, the customer is real, the goods have been delivered, and the terms of sale are achieved. Channel stuffing is referred to as accelerating sales by causing a real customer to order more goods than a customer would normally purchase through the offering of inducements that are intended to shift revenue versus a normal marketing technique. The traditional inducements are deep discounts, rebates, and extended payment terms.
   c) Sham sales transactions occur with the recording of a revenue transaction with a real customer; however, there is no economic benefit for either party. Typically, tendencies in sham transactions are that there are no cash transfers between the two parties; the two parties have a relationship; and both parties tend to be in the same industry. The sole purpose of sham transactions is to increase revenue versus create an economic benefit.
   d) Soft sale is recording a revenue transaction through the source journal before a fully executed contract exists between the two parties.
   e) Undisclosed return policy scheme is recording a revenue transaction through the source journal when the customer has a right to return the product.
   f) Incomplete terms schemes is recording a revenue transaction through the source journal before all terms and conditions of the sales contract are fulfilled.
   g) Upfront fees are for services provided over a period of time. The fraud scheme is recognizing the upfront fee as current revenue versus amortizing the revenue over the life of the contract.
   h) Non-operating revenue recognized as operating revenue occurs when a cash receipt from a non-operating revenue source is recorded as operating revenue.
4. Revenue is misstated because of the misapplication of GAAP in relation to the customer contract. These schemes need to be identified as part of the brainstorming based on how your company achieves the five criteria of revenue recognition.
5. Revenue created through changing GAAP without disclosure.

6. Revenue recognized through improper application of GAAP related to specific accounting statements:
   a) Percentage of completion schemes
   b) Bill-and-hold schemes
   c) Income recognized on consignment sales
7. Falsifying accounts receivable aging or the failure to write off uncollectable receivables.
8. Revenue created through accrued revenue: journal entries schemes.

All of these schemes have been committed by management in some company. The study of prior schemes by the fraud auditor will enhance their practical application of the suggested fraud data analytics routines.

INHERENT FRAUD SCHEMES AND CREATING THE REVENUE FRAUD SCENARIOS

For ease of reading, the following will repeat the guidance in earlier chapters.

1. Person committing: The starting point is to understand how revenue is reported and how internal persons are held accountable for meeting sales numbers in the company. The person committing would start with financial management. In a regional sales environment, the misstatement may occur through one division or one sales region.
2. Direction of misstatement: Most reported fraud schemes result in the overstatement of revenue. Therefore, overstatement is the most predictable direction of misstatement. However, GAAS fraud risk factors need to be considered in determining the direction of misstatement. If the fraud auditor is focusing on a specific region versus the company as a whole, then the direction of testing is dependent on the historical success of the region. A highly successful region is more likely to understate revenue as a form of cookie jar, whereas a region having difficulty in meeting internal goals is more likely to overstate its revenue.
3. General ledger account: What is critical about revenue recognition is which accounts are used for the sales journal and which accounts are used for revenue accrual journal entries.
4. Type of entity: The same structure identified in the shell company chapter is relevant for financial reporting.
5. Fraud action statement: Describes how the fraud scenario occurs in the financial account. The fraud action statement describes whether the

transaction is false or real, whether the entity is false or real, and whether the transaction is recorded through a source journal or journal entry.

6. A GAAP implication focuses on either whether the recorded revenue transaction achieved the five criteria of revenue recognition or how management concealed the failure to achieve the five criteria.

7. Impact statement for revenue recognition should provide specifics to the impact on the financial statements.

IDENTIFYING KEY DATA ON KEY DOCUMENTS

The revenue system has more diversity than any other core business system. The industry will impact the documents that will comprise the system. Think about the difference between retail, health care, telecommunications, wholesale, and construction. Within each industry and within each company the revenue system is more unique than payroll, which is somewhat standardized throughout all industries. In this chapter, we will present the methodology for detecting revenue fraud in the financial accounts.

The revenue cycle comprises sales order, which is a customer purchase order or internal sales order; shipping records; internal sales invoice; customer payment; and customer return or customer sales adjustment. The understanding of the information on these documents becomes the basis of the fraud data analytics plan. Consistent with Chapter 3 the documents all have a control number, control date, sales invoice amount, and a description of what was ordered that is posted to a general ledger account. Furthermore, in the revenue cycle, in contrast to the expenditure cycle, the documents may originate from an internal source or an external source.

Sales order is the document that starts the sales process. The sales order may originate from an internal salesperson or from a customer's purchase order system. If the document originates from the customer's purchase order system, then the consistency of information is by customer versus internal systems. This will impact the usability question in the planning phase.

Shipping process occurs through an internal fleet of trucks or through an external fleet of vehicles. If the shipping occurs through an external source, the critical issue is how to match the internal records to the external shipping records. If the shipping records are internal, then fraud data analytics for improper recognition is possible.

Internal sales invoices are created either through one centralized billing system or through billing systems that are decentralized by location. The sales invoice becomes the central point of the fraud data analytics.

Customer payments depending on the industry may originate from currency, credit card, paper check, electronic transfer, or via a loan transaction. Is the payment applied to a specific invoice or to an account balance?

Customer return or sales adjustment is the contra entry to a customer payment transaction. These transactions are associated with reversing false transactions.

Now that the fraud auditor understands the documents that comprise the system and the information on the documents, the fraud auditor can start the process of building the fraud data profile.

Do I Understand the Revenue Data?

The planning reports are a form of analytic review. In the accounting profession we use ratio analysis to determine if relationships and changes are consistent with our understanding of the company. We also use the data as part of our planning process to determine how to tailor our audit program to detect a material error. This stage is no different from historical analytic review. The major difference is that the fraud auditor is creating the revenue report from raw data versus from the prepared financial statements.

The planning reports should be designed around the most logical grouping of data that is associated with a specific fraud scenario. Many fraud schemes have occurred by management recording false revenue to a false customer. Therefore, a report summarizing sales by new customers would indicate what percentage of revenue was derived from new customers. If the amount is material, then the predictability of false revenue being recorded in new customers goes up. If the revenue amount is not material, then look somewhere else.

Creating the reports is a two-step process. First, summarize the revenue data in some common grouping. Second, link the report to a fraud scenario. I need to stress the importance of the second step. Without defining the purpose of the report, the auditor will not know how to interpret the report or offer any logical conclusions regarding the information.

The common grouping analysis for false revenue starts with creating a homogeneous data file based on type of customer commonly associated with fraud scenarios. The second grouping for false revenue starts with the data attributes associated with the sales transaction. For improper revenue recognition, the common grouping needs to be linked to the specific technique. For improper recognition, change analysis becomes a large part of designing the report.

For simplicity, we will assume a December year-end for our discussions on planning reports and our discussions will focus on an annual reporting process versus a quarterly process. The purpose of the planning reports is to identify where material revenue is recorded and the material amount associated with a predictable fraud scenario.

The first report is an analysis of all revenue accounts to determine what percent of revenue was posted from a source journal and what percentage of revenue was posted from a manual journal entry. The purpose is to describe the source of all revenue postings. My preference is to create the report by general ledger account with the appropriate totals and record counts.

The second report is an analysis of revenue posted in the source journal by customer. The report should provide sales by the first three quarters and the final quarter. The purpose of the report is to identify customers whose sales reflect a large increase in the fourth quarter.

The report design can be modified in various ways:

- New customers created in the current year have a focus on false revenue transactions.
- Sales recorded in a dormant customer that now has sales activity have a focus on false revenue transactions.
- Sales recorded in what is labeled as house accounts have a focus on false revenue transactions.
- Sales recorded in customer account not assigned to a sales representative have a focus on false revenue transactions.
- December sales for all customers as compared to the fourth quarter sales for all customers have a focus on both false revenue and improper recognition of revenue.
- Sales by a meaningful business unit, by region, by division, by geographic area, or by subsidiary, may indicate that a particular unit is committing an improper revenue recognition scheme.
- Sales by product line with special emphasis on new sales items.
- Sales by product line with a comparison to the previous year's sales by product line may indicate a concealment technique associated with obsolete inventory.
- Sales by product line with the associated cost of goods sold may indicate sham transactions.

Creating the right planning reports to highlight a potential fraud scenario is as important as performing the right ratio analysis. Your ability to interpret the report as to fraud predictability is as important as your ability to interpret what are the implications of the change in working capital. The planning reports are part of the process of the identified fraud risk process defined in the auditing standards.

What Is the Fraud Data Analytics Plan for Revenue?

In Chapter 13, we discussed the steps of building a fraud data analytics plan for financial statements; the same concepts apply when the auditor is drilling down to a specific account in the financial statements. In applying the methodology to revenue, the auditor must have a solid understanding of the revenue recognition principles.

FRAUD BRAINSTORMING FOR REVENUE

The proper recognition of revenue is defined in IFRS 15, Revenue from Contracts with Customers. As a disclaimer, the intent of this section of the chapter is not to be an authoritative discussion of the new accounting standard, but rather, the importance of understanding how to use the standard in the search for a fraud scenario or the associated concealment strategy. Fraud data analytics brainstorming starts with understanding the basic framework for proper revenue recognition:

1. Persuasive evidence of an arrangement exists—this is intended to ensure that an understanding exists between the two parties and that a final understanding of the terms and conditions is achieved.
2. Delivery has occurred or services have been rendered—this assumes that the customer takes title and assumes the benefits and risks of ownership.
3. The seller's price to the buyer is fixed or determinable as to payment terms, right of return, discounts, and rebates.
4. Collectability is reasonably assured because all the terms and conditions are achieved and the customer has the ability to fulfill its obligations.

To illustrate the concept of fraud brainstorming for fraud data analytics, let's focus on the collectability concept. So, how could management conceal the collectability concept or how can we find data that indicate the collectability concept was falsified? From a data perspective we will focus on the concept of the probability of whether the customer will pay for a recorded revenue transaction at the recorded amount.

For discussion purposes, we will focus on three different situations. There are two types of revenue transaction from the collectability perspective: false revenue or real revenue.

- False revenue to a false customer. Clearly your company will not collect from a fictitious customer. However, there are cases that management has used their personal funds to create the illusion of collection. Among management's fraud strategies:
    - Record the revenue at year-end so the false revenue does not appear on the aging report.
    - Reverse the revenue transaction after opinion date.
    - Clear the false revenue transaction with a sales adjustment or return transaction.
    - Use a rebilling scheme to create a current date on the false revenue.
    - Use a variation of a lapping scheme to cause the aging report at year-end to reflect the balance as paid.
    - Apply a dormant credit to the false revenue transaction.
- False revenue to a real customer. The assumption is that the customer did not order the item and the customer will not accept the item:
    - Since the transaction is a false revenue transaction, the previous concepts apply.
    - Conceal the return of the item from the customer that indicates the return is posted to the customer account after the opinion date. In one publically traded company, management concealed the returns by making false statements to the customer regarding the shipment. Then management had the items returned to a secret warehouse to conceal the return from the auditors.
    - Crediting the customer account with a false sales adjustment versus a sales return transaction.
- Real revenue to a real customer. The assumption is that the contract is valid and the sales transaction is complete. The focus is on the probability the customer will remit the required funds under the terms of the contract. In one sense all customers are the same; however, from a collectability perspective customers are very different.
    - New customers with credit limits that exceed normal credit limits for new customers.
    - Existing customers:
        - Active customers with no history of delinquent payments should be excluded from this analysis; the exception is for channel stuffing.
        - Nonactive customers with a history of delinquent payments and a change to credit amount or creditworthiness should be the focus of the analysis.
    - Improper application of GAAP.

From a GAAP perspective, let's use price concessions on tangible goods to brainstorm how revenue can be overstated and concealed from the auditors. For purposes of discussion, price concessions are: rebate, allowance or a price reduction, or other terms of agreement. Since our discussion is on revenue our discussions will not focus on other accounts such as a potential liability. The price concession discussion assumes collectability; the question focuses on the total amount of consideration to be received and the proper reporting of the event.

The starting point is to understand how the transaction should be recorded from a GAAP perspective. The second aspect is a review of standard customer contracts to ensure the contract is consistent with GAAP. Assuming management's accounting policies are GAAP compliant, now the fraud auditor can start building the fraud data analytics plan.

The next important step is to discuss how management could conceal the over- or understatement of revenue. Using the rebate concept, the rebate could be recorded as a marketing expense versus a contra revenue account. Management could hire a marketing company to pay the rebates and record the disbursement as a marketing expense.

Remember, the purpose of the brainstorming session is to assist the auditor in developing the fraud action statement. Consistent with Chapter 13, the following fraud action statements are the generic list, which needs to be converted for the GAAP implications of the revenue transaction.

The primary techniques used to overstate revenue are:

1. Record false revenue through either a false customer or a real customer.
2. Record real revenue in the wrong period or account.
3. Record accrued revenue that is false or improper recognition of revenue through a journal entry.
4. Record contra revenue as an operating expense.
5. Record non-operating revenue in operating revenue.
6. Consideration should also be for uncollectable revenue hidden in the accounts receivable.

The primary techniques to understate revenue:

1. Record real revenue in the wrong period.
2. Record through a journal entry improper recognition of revenue.

What Are the Accounting Policies for Revenue?

The accounting policies identify how a transaction should be recorded to comply with GAAP. The auditor needs to ensure that the accounting practices comply with GAAP. However, from a fraud data analytics perspective the company's accounting policies will identify how a transaction should be recorded. Therefore, an anomaly can be described as a transaction recorded contrary to the company's accounting guidelines.

Within the Revenue Accounts, Which Fraud Scenarios Are We Trying to Uncover?

As stated in Chapter 13, the process starts with the fraud risk assessment, which is an integral part of determining which fraud scenarios are relevant to the fraud data analytics plan. The understanding data step is intended to help the auditor by identifying revenue data at a high level, which is consistent with the fraud theory associated with the fraud scenario. Therefore, the decision should be based on the likelihood analysis from the control assessment and likelihood analysis from the planning reports.

What Are the Overall Strategies for Revenue Fraud Data Analytics?

The fraud data analytics plan has two choices. Search for the fraud scenario in the source journal by building the fraud data profile or search for the concealment strategy in the source journal or general ledger used to conceal the improper recognition of revenue.

The Data Analytics Is Based on the Mechanics of the Fraud Scenario

The following provides a brief synopsis of the fraud data analytics approach based on the inherent scheme structure.

In false customer schemes, the data analytics plan should use the same approach as the outlines in the chapter on shell companies, tailored for customers versus vendors.

In false revenue schemes for false customers, the data analytics should search for the data profile of false revenue or through the subsequent reversal of the false revenue in the next operating period.

A false revenue scheme for a real customer depends on whether the real customer accepts the false revenue or rejects the false revenue. If the real customer rejects the revenue, the search should focus on the subsequent operating period and focus on the reversal of the transaction. If the real customer accepts the revenue, the data analytics should search for the data profile of false revenue.

Improper recognition schemes involve real customers that may or may not be complicit in the scheme and real revenue transactions. Typically the recorded transaction complies with company policies at least on the face of the transaction. The key to building the fraud data analytics plan is to understand the fraud action statement as it relates to the improper recognition inherent fraud scheme.

To illustrate the improper recognition inherent fraud scheme for channel stuffing, the concept suggests an accelerated sales pattern at year-end. Therefore, the planning report would compare December sales history to last year's December sales history or fourth-quarter sales to the previous three quarters. Often, the sales transaction has extended payment terms. The fraud data analytics would compute the average number of days the customer remits payment for the first nine months and the last quarter average number of days for remittance. The inclusion and exclusion theory would focus on those customers having an elevated sales pattern in the fourth quarter.

Is the Data Analytics Is Based on the Concealment Strategy?

When either false revenue or real revenue is materially misstated in the financial statement management needs to conceal the fact from the auditors. Later in the chapter, the common concealment techniques used by management are discussed. The advantage of using the concealment technique is that when the concealment technique is identified the probability of fraud occurring increases dramatically. The second aspect is the key difference between revenue error and revenue fraud is the intent to conceal factor.

What Are the Steps to Designing a Fraud Data Analytics Search Routine for Improper Recognition Fraud Risk?

Chapter 13 provided the methodology for creating a fraud data analytics plan for financial statements. For easy reference, the questions are repeated and the discussion will focus on the nuances related to revenue.

1. Which financial account is the focus of the fraud data analytics?
2. Are we searching for understatement or overstatement in the financial account?
3. How does the opinion date correlate to our ability to analyze the general ledger?
4. How is the fraud scenario recorded, through a source journal or a journal entry?
5. Is the fraud data analytics searching for fraud scenario?

6. Based on the fraud scenario should our data interrogation occur through the recording of the transaction or through disaggregated analysis of the general ledger account?
7. Is the fraud data analytics searching for the concealment strategy to hide the fraud scenario?
8. Are we searching for a large error or many small errors, which in the aggregate is material?
9. Which data-mining strategy is appropriate for the scope of the fraud audit?

Using the previous questions, the fraud data analytics plan is as follows:

FDA FOR FALSE REVENUE SCENARIOS

False revenue schemes either occur through a false customer or through a real customer. In false customer schemes, the search starts with fraud data analysis for shell customers and then proceeds to the transactional analysis. In real customer schemes, the fraud data analytics searches for clues in the sales journal or returns and adjustments in the subsequent period.

FDA for False Customers

The analysis for false customers is very similar to shell companies; however, the fraud data analysis needs to be tailored for customers. The additional fields that should be examined are:

- Credit limit. To record a material amount of false sales that customer will need a higher credit limit. The fraud data analytics should search for a change in credit limit or a higher credit than normal for a new customer.
- Sales representative assigned to the customer. The fraud data analytics is looking for customers that have no sales representative assigned to the account.
- New customers are more prone to be used in the scheme; therefore, search for new customers' material sales in the final quarter.
- Dormant customers are real customers; however, management has assumed the identity of the customer. The fraud data analysis should search for customers with address changes and material sales in the final quarter.

▫ Ship-to address. Since false customers have no physical location the ship-to address has to be an address controlled by the company. The fraud data analytics should search for duplicate shipping addresses and different customer names and physical locations that link to company operations. There are schemes where management used a freight forwarding company to provide the illusion of delivery of the goods.

FDA for False Revenue for False Customers

The first assumption in the analysis is that the customer is either new or a dormant customer that has become active. The second assumption is that the sales transaction will not be attributable to a sales representative. So, the fraud data analytics should focus on:

▫ Sales transactions that have no commission code. The analysis will need to be tailored to the sales force's compensation and how their performance is measured.
▫ Sales order number anomalies. The list should include: no sales order number; low sales order numbers, even-number sales order (e.g., 1,000), and a sequential pattern of sales order numbers.
▫ Round or even sales invoice amounts.
▫ Recurring sales invoices; the focus is on materiality in the aggregate versus a single sales invoice.
▫ Products that were not selling in the first half of the year suddenly reflect an accelerated sales movement.

FDA for Real Customers

For real customers, the fraud data analytics should search for increases in customer credit limits in the final quarter or use the beginning of the year credit amount and the end of the year credit amount. If management is recording a material amount of false revenue through a real customer, then the credit limit will need to be increased to allow for both the real and false revenue. Also search for the addition of a new shipping address for the real customer when the false revenue is not shipped to the real customer.

FALSE REVENUE FOR FALSE CUSTOMERS THROUGH ACCOUNTS RECEIVABLE ANALYSIS

Since false customers seldom pay for false revenue transactions, the fraud data analytics should search for customers with material sales and no posting from cash receipts. The design of the report would in essence recreate the accounts receivable account. The report would have eight columns of data providing both dollar amount and frequency of postings:

- All debits originating from a sales journal
- All other debits
- All credits originating from a cash receipts journal
- All other credits

While the analysis will detect the false revenue, the issue becomes the timing of the procedure. If the opinion date is after the first quarter of the next year, perform the procedure at year-end, otherwise the procedure must be performed midyear. In the midyear approach, the search for the false revenue scenario should be performed on final quarter sales.

The report will have a few phases before the report reveals the false revenue. Start with summarizing the data as recommended. Exclude those customers with no sales or minimal sales. Then exclude those customers reflecting a significant amount of postings from the cash receipts journal. The first search is for customers that have no cash receipts posting and recorded sales. If the false sales were recorded through the year, then the report will reflect significant other credits. If the false sales are recorded at the end of the year, then the account will only reflect sales journal postings.

Remember, one of the concealment strategies is a form of lapping. If the lapping scheme is being used, then the customer will have cash receipts posting. However, since the posting must be transferred to the true customer, the customer account should also have a material amount in the other debits and credits column.

FDA for False Revenue through Real Customers

False revenue posted to real customers has two approaches. The first is the fraud data profile of the sales transactions or the subsequent return of the product. The sales transaction fraud data profile should focus on:

- The customer order number may be blank or there is an anomaly with the number. Common anomalies are round numbers, number contains alpha or a special symbol, or the order number is less than earlier numbers.
- Quantity order amounts are different than previous order amounts. Common anomalies are round numbers, quantity is larger than average quantity amounts.
- No sales representative number assigned to the sale.

· Customer number links to an internal house account versus a real customer.

· Shipping address is different from the shipping address for all other customer invoices.

· Speed of processing by comparing the sales order date to the invoice date.

The sales returns and adjustments approach will focus on returns and adjustments posted in the subsequent period. The fraud data analytics should create a file of all sales returns and adjustments in the subsequent period and link the transactions to the related sales invoice. The sample selection is based on sales transactions in the year of audit that were returned in the subsequent period. If there is an accrual for returns and adjustments, then the analysis would compare the actual return rate to the accrued amount.

FRAUD CONCEALMENT STRATEGIES FOR FALSE REVENUE FRAUD SCENARIOS

The second approach to search for a fraud scenario is through the concealment strategy used by management. The following concealment strategies all can be found through the study of historical fraud stories:

· The weakness in the false revenue schemes is the realization principle. False customers typically do not pay for goods and services. There are published cases where financial management used personal funds to create the illusion of customer payment. In some way and at some time, the false receivable will need to be cleared.

· Lapping is typically associated with an asset misappropriation scheme. However, the technique can be used to hide the false revenue from the aging schedules. The concept is simple: Apply a real customer's payment to a false customer's account payment at the end of the year. After the aging report is created, the customer payment is transferred back to the real customer. The fraud data analytics should search for transfer of customer payments between customer accounts after the creation of the aging schedule.

· The astute auditor should see how the concealment techniques can be used in different industries. In the banking industry, management or a loan officer might be trying to hide an uncollectable loan. The lapping technique would conceal the bad loan from the delinquency report. Similar but different, the delinquent loan could be concealed by rolling over the loan using internal bank funds. Also, see the discussion on rebilling in what follows.

- In accounts receivable, there are dormant credits associated with both dormant customers and active customers. The dormant credit is transferred to clear the false revenue. The fraud data analytics searches for the transfer of an aged credit to a customer's account.
- Rebilling is a technique to hide a delinquent invoice from the aging report. The concealment technique is concealing a true delinquency for a real customer with real revenue. The financial management is trying to hide the bad-debt expense. The technique is also used to hide false revenue.
- In the rebilling scheme the delinquent invoice is credited with an adjustment or return, thereby removing the customer invoice from the aging report. A second invoice is created for the same customer with a current date. The adjustment or sales return is recorded through a source journal and is posted to the correct general ledger account. The fraud data analytics is first matching sales adjustments to aged sales invoices. The second step is to search for a current duplicate invoice for aged invoice. The use of a customer order number or line item descriptions on the invoice is a useful technique for the matching.
- A more sophisticated approach to hide the sales adjustment is to post the sales adjustment as a contra transaction in the sales journal, thereby concealing the adjustment in the sales journal. The search for a contra entry in the sales journal is an easy technique using the number anomaly strategy.
- Returns and adjustments is the most common technique to clear false revenue. The return or adjustment is typically posted after the opinion date. There are many variations of the returns and adjustments scheme. Instead of clearing the false revenue with the sales return, which the auditor is looking for, the false revenue is cleared with a sales adjustment transaction and the inventory is added back as an inventory adjustment. The fraud auditor needs to understand the different systems or transactions that exist in the revenue system to clear a customer invoice.
- Shipping concealment strategies vary by the organizational structure of the company. The first step is to ship the inventory somewhere. The shipment location for the false revenue schemes maybe another company warehouse, public warehouse, freight forwarder location, etc. The fraud data analytics should summarize sales by customer by shipping address, providing aggregate dollar value and the frequency of the invoice. Depending on the number of customers, the fraud auditor will need to determine how to shrink the report.
- There are many other concealment strategies associated with fraudulent revenue schemes. However, not all schemes are useful in fraud data

analytics. The undisclosed terms and conditions scheme is often associated with fraudulent revenue; however, the concept does not lend itself to fraud data analytics. As a reminder, it is important to understand what you can find and what you cannot find with fraud data analytics.

FDA for Improper Recognition Schemes

Holding the books open scheme occurs when delivery and acceptance occurs in the subsequent period but the revenue is recorded in the current year. The good news is, the homogeneous file is small because the fraud data analytics is only focusing on sales transactions that are recorded at the end of the operating period. The bad news is that the scenario includes real customers and real sales. The fraud data analytics must use either shipping records or inventory records for comparison analysis.

Shipping records are either internal or external. The ease of the analysis will depend on whether the shipping date is available in the electronic format. If so, compare the invoice date to the shipping date. The sample selection is either sales invoices with a subsequent shipping date or sales invoices at year-end. If using sales at the end of the period, then the audit procedure is finding the scenario versus the fraud data analytics.

FDA for Channel Stuffing

Channel stuffing is referred to as accelerating sales by causing a real customer to order more goods than a customer would normally purchase through the offering of inducements, which are intended to shift revenue versus a normal marketing technique. The traditional inducements are deep discounts, rebates, and extended payment terms.

The first clue for channel stuffing is the planning report that looks for anomalies in the fourth-quarter sales. The fraud data analytics for channel stuffing should focus on the inducements to cause the customer to agree to accept large sales:

- Compare unit price on the sales invoice to the unit price on the product master file. The search is looking for deep discounts, which are the inducement to order the large amount.
- Rebates may occur through sales adjustments or through accounts payable. The first step is to compare the customer list to the vendor list. This step is useful for round-tripping and possibly for related-party activity. If the customer is on the vendor master file, then identify the transactions

looking for a rebate, commission, and adjustment. Remember, the rebate may occur in the fiscal year or in the subsequent year.

- Sales adjustments that are in essence a rebate would be posted to accounts receivable. The fraud data analysis should search for sales adjustments that correlate to a customer invoice in the fourth quarter.
- Compute the average order quantity for the customer for the first 11 months and compute the average order amount for the last month. The sample selection is based on order amounts reflecting a large increase.
- Compute the average number of days for customer payment on the first 11 months and the last month. Compare the two calculations searching for a significant increase.

FDA for Sham Sales

Sham sale is the recording of a revenue transaction with a real customer; however, there is no economic benefit for either party. There are a few different approaches to searching for sham sales:

- The analysis of accounts receivable described in the false revenue section would identify customers with material sales and no cash receipts postings.
- Compare the vendor master to the customer master file to identify customers that are also vendors or possibly related parties.
- Search for a loan or other receivable associated with the customer.
- Compare the sales invoice amount to the cost of sales amount for the transaction. The search is for sales transactions that have no gross profit or a gross profit significantly below the gross profit on the financial statements.

FDA for Soft Sale

Soft sale is recording a revenue transaction through the source journal before a fully executed contract exists between the two parties. The fraud data analytics for soft sales would depend on whether the customer eventually executes the contract or the customer does not accept the contract. If the customer rejects the contract, then there would be a reversal or a return in the subsequent period. If the customer executes the contract in the subsequent period, then the fraud data analytics should search for the following:

- Customer order number. Since the customer has not issued a purchase order before year-end, the order number for the recorded soft sale should be greater than the last customer order for the fiscal year.

- Date on the customer order. If there is no attempt to conceal the soft sale, then the sales order date will be for the subsequent year versus the current year.
- Shipping data. If the soft sale has been recorded but not shipped, then the shipping date would be in the subsequent year.

FDA for Undisclosed Return Policy

Undisclosed return policy scheme is recording a revenue transaction through the source journal when the customer has a right to return the product. The difficulty in this fraud scheme occurs because there are no data in the customer file or the sales transaction file that would highlight this fraud scheme. If the customer accepts the goods and pays for the goods, then fraud data analytics would not be successful in identifying the scheme. If the customer does return the item, then the sales return test would disclose the fraud scheme.

FDA for Incomplete Terms

Incomplete terms scheme is recording a revenue transaction through the source journal before all terms and conditions of the sales contract are not fulfilled. The fraud data analytics plan should identify the specific terms and search for the event in the subsequent period. To illustrate, let's assume the tangible goods require an installation of the item. Search the installation expenditures in the subsequent period and match the expense to the sales contract.

FDA for Upfront Fees

Upfront fees are for services provided over a period of time.

The fraud data analytics will depend on how the upfront fees are recorded. Approach one would be to create a sales invoice through the sales journal and post the upfront fees. Approach two would be to post to a general ledger account directly from the cash receipts journal.

Fraud data analytics for approach one is that the sales invoice would most likely be a manual invoice versus an automated invoice. Under that theory, the fraud data analytics would search for manual sales invoices. In the second approach, the product description on the sales invoice would most likely not have a product number for upfront fees. Therefore, the description field on the sales invoice would have no product number or no product alpha description. A second approach is to use an alpha search on the description field on the sales invoice or the cash receipts journal for the term used by the company to describe upfront fees.

The third approach is to summarize the cash receipts journal for credits to accounts other than the accounts receivable control account. The first report would summarize the debits from the cash receipts journal by general ledger account, providing the aggregate dollar amount, frequency, maximum posting, minimum posting, and average dollar value of the postings.

FRAUD DATA ANALYTICS FOR PERCENTAGE OF COMPLETION REVENUE RECOGNITION

In revenue recognition, there are specific accounting pronouncements for specific revenue transactions. It would be impossible for this book to describe the fraud data analytics for all the statements. Therefore, to illustrate the use of the methodologies, we have selected percentage of completion.

While there are different variables that are considered in percentage of completion revenue recognition, this discussion will focus on the incurred cost account. The account is typically composed of a subledger of projects, and the expenditures are posted from either a source journal or a journal entry. The first report is a summary of the subledger by total expenditures. The sole purpose is to identify the material account balances or changes in material balances. The report can be enhanced by creating a comparison report (i.e., total expenditures at third quarter by account to fourth quarter by account) and calculating a dollar change and percentage change.

The use of disaggregated analysis would summarize which journals created the account balance for all accounts in the subledger: accounts payable, payroll, other, and general journal entry. The purpose of the report is to identify which journal created the account balance. The first sample selection is based on accounts that have a material general journal entry posting. The journal entry should be selected and summarized by account posting. The second analysis is material postings from the accounts payable journal. Summarize the accounts payable by vendor, providing aggregate dollar value, aggregate frequency, maximum invoice, minimum invoice, and average invoice for the final month (or final quarter) of the report period. The sample selection starts with a fraud data profile of a false vendor invoice.

FDA for Non-operating Revenue

Non-operating revenue recognized as operating revenue occurs when a cash receipt from a non-operating revenue source is recorded in operating revenue. The fraud data analytics starts with identifying all revenue accounts. The second analysis is searching for material cash receipts postings to the revenue accounts. The journal entry testing would search for transfers from a non-operating revenue account to operating revenue accounts.

The FDA for False Aging of Accounts Receivable

The fraud data analytics is searching for real revenue that was earned but the customer has failed to pay the invoice for whatever reason. The fraud data analytics would use the fraud concealment approach to search for the concealment techniques. The techniques are described in the chapter in the fraud concealment strategies for false revenue.

- ⬚ Lapping. Search for cash receipts transfers between customer accounts in the subsequent period.
- ⬚ Rebilling. First search for a duplicate transaction with different dates. If management was sophisticated, the second invoice was slightly changed. Then search by customer all invoices that were cleared by a noncash receipts transaction. Using this created file, match the cleared invoice to a subsequent invoice, using the description field or customer order number.
- ⬚ Dormant credits. The analysis is similar to the lapping analysis.
- ⬚ Changing data. The easiest way to make the invoice current is to change the invoice date. Using the invoice number and the invoice date search for invoice number that the invoice date is out of order with the sequence of numbers.

 SUMMARY

The purpose of this chapter was to describe a methodology for searching for fraud scenarios in the sales journal. Consistent with Chapter 13, the fraud auditor will need to adapt the methodology to their industry and company. A second aspect is the unique issues associated with fraud in GAAP interpretation. The fraud data analytics plan will need to be further adapted to search for fraud in GAAP.

As a reminder, the fraud audit procedure must be linked to the fraud scenario and the fraud data analytics.

CHAPTER FIFTEEN

Fraud Data Analytics
for Journal Entries

The auditing standards for journal entry testing must be the basis of selecting journal entries. An understanding of standards and the exercise of professional judgment can never be replaced. The following fraud data analytics methodology is intended to create a framework to help the auditor meet the intent of the professional standards of auditing. To assist the reader, we will start with an excerpt from the standard:

> The auditor should design procedures to test the appropriateness of journal entries recorded in the general ledger and other adjustments. More specifically, SAS no. 99 requires the auditor, in all audits, to (a) obtain an understanding of the entity's financial reporting process and controls over journal entries and other adjustments; (b) identify and select journal entries and other adjustments for testing; (c) determine the timing of the testing; and (d) inquire of individuals involved in the financial reporting process about inappropriate or unusual activity relating to the processing of journal entries or other adjustments (Statement of Auditing Standard (SAS) no. 99, *Consideration of Fraud in a Financial Statement Audit*).

This chapter will discuss how to use the fraud scenario approach for journal entries and then provide seven different frameworks to create an overall fraud data analytics plan for journal entry testing for financial accounts. The last section will illustrate my experiences with how controllers have used journal entries to conceal asset misappropriation schemes.

Journal entries are the tool of choice when management wants to cause the financial statements to be misstated. The reason is that it is simple: Debit receivables for a million and credit revenue a million. It is that easy.

FRAUD SCENARIO CONCEPT APPLIED TO JOURNAL ENTRY TESTING

The methodology or components for writing a fraud scenario for financial accounts is the same as writing a fraud scenario for a specific financial account. What differs is the guidance as to use of the components of the fraud scenario in creating a fraud data analytics plan. First what are the similarities?

1. Person committing the scenario is the same as in Chapter 13. However, since history has taught us that senior financial management or the CEO are involved directly or indirectly special emphasis should be applied to understanding how to identify journal entries either recorded by the CFO or caused to be recorded by the CFO or CEO.
2. Direction of testing as to overstatement or understatement is the same as Chapter 13.
3. General ledger account might be a specific general ledger account specific or relating to a section of the financial statement.
4. Fraud action statement is required, but how to write the fraud action is different.
5. Impact statement is the same as Chapter 13.

What differs is the concept of creating the fraud action statement and the fraud data profile. First, let's look at the similarities for creating a fraud action statement:

1. The journal entry is recorded to a financial account: revenue or expense/ asset or liability or equity.
2. GAAP requirements must be understood and stated. Remember that fraud in the financial statements is an intentional error in GAAP, so this aspect of the fraud action statement is critical.

3. The event was recorded through a journal entry.
   a) Was there a failure to adjust an account balance?
   b) Was there a failure to adjust or reclassify a previously recorded transaction?
   c) Was there a failure to write off the transaction that was previously recorded?
4. Understanding the location of the transaction on the financial statement is the same as in Chapter 13.

So, what is the difference in creating the fraud action statement? The difference is the fundamental difference between a source journal and a general journal entry. The source journal is a series of individual transactions that are posted in total to the general ledger. The general journal entry was created by a person for a reason. In previous chapters, we discussed the concepts of *how*, *when*, and *where*. For journal entries, the *why* question becomes the critical aspect of creating the fraud action statement. Other obvious differences are the following:

- There is no entity concept for a journal entry.
- The real or false transaction does not apply. However, the concept of false assumption, false estimate, or false purpose of the journal entry is substituted for the concept of a false or real transaction.
- The *how* question is not critical as to how a journal entry is posted; however, the *how* question does relate to how the person conceals the fraudulent journal entry: individual entry; series of smaller entries; compound entries to conceal the fraud amount; convoluted entries; layering the fraudulent amount, and the list goes on.

The following provides examples of how to write a financial statement fraud scenario using the prescribed format:

- Controller records a journal entry that intentionally overstates accrued revenue by overstating the estimate of accrued revenue by recording several small-dollar entries recognizing income when the contract has not been completed, causing revenue to be overstated.
- Controller records a journal entry that intentionally understates the estimate of future price rebates earned on completed contracts that are recorded through a journal entry at year-end, causing the contra revenue account to be understated.

- Controller intentionally understates cost of sales by failing to record a journal entry recognizing inventory that the market value is less than the original cost, causing cost of sales to be understated.
- Controller fails to reclassify advertising expenses posted from the source journal to the balance sheet consistent with the accounting manual, causing the overstatement of net operating income.

For purposes of illustration, I have intentionally written the previous fraud scenarios with a different style. Remember, style is in the eye of the beholder, whereas content of the scenario is required by the methodology. I would encourage the audit unit to adopt a writing style purely from an efficiency standpoint.

THE *WHY* QUESTION

The fraud action statement should include the *why* reason for posting the journal entry. The reason for recording the entry is a critical aspect of the fraud action statement. The reason is based on the assumption for recording the entry. Typical reasons correlate to the types of journal entries: accrue, adjust, reclassify, and reverse:

- To accrue a revenue contract that is earned but is not recorded in a source journal.
- To adjust the account balance of accrued revenue based on management's estimation formula.
- To reclassify or correct a previously posted transaction from a source journal.
- To reverse a previously recorded journal entry.

THE *WHEN* QUESTION

The question is simple. Was the journal entry posted before year-end or after year-end? What is the proximity of the journal entry to the opinion date? Was the account balance reversed? Should the journal entry be tested now, or should retrospective analysis of the journal posted after year-end? The answer to the *when* question has a major impact on the timing of the fraud data analytics plan. I also think the *when* question is a critical part of the predictability consideration as to where management records the fraudulent journal entries.

UNDERSTANDING THE LANGUAGE OF JOURNAL ENTRIES

To be clear, in this chapter we are not discussing journal entries that post a source journal to the general ledger. This chapter is about journal entries that are created by a person to adjust an account balance, reclassify a transaction, or reverse a journal entry from a previous period. Our discussion will focus on year-end reporting, although the methodology is the same for any reporting period. From a GAAS perspective, there are four types of journal entries:

1. *Routine transactions.* Recurring financial activities are reflected in the accounting records in the normal course of business.
2. *Nonroutine transactions.* Activities occur only periodically. A distinguishing feature of nonroutine transactions is that data involved are generally not part of the routine flow of transactions.
3. *Estimation transactions.* Activities involve management judgments or assumptions in formulating account balances in the absence of a precise means of measurement.
4. *Top-sided transactions.* These are journal entries that are recorded in the financial statement but not in the general ledger. Therefore, top-sided journal entries are not part of the fraud data analytics plan.

From a fraud data analytics perspective, I will use the following terms to describe the journal entries:

- *Adjusting entries* are designed to change, alter, or adjust an original transaction or change an estimate associated with an account balance.
- *Reversal entries* are designed to reverse a period-end adjusting entry.
- *Reclassifying entries* are designed to transfer a transaction from one general ledger account to another general ledger account.
- *Consolidating entries* are designed to consolidate two or more companies' financial statement. The entry is also designed to eliminate intercompany activity.

OVERALL APPROACH TO JOURNAL ENTRY SELECTION

Auditors select journal entries for the purpose of testing internal controls for recording a journal entry and to perform substantive procedures on account balances. GAAS provides guidance on determining the nature, timing, and extent of substantive testing of journal entries. This book will not duplicate that guidance, but rather provide fraud data analytic procedures to assist the fraud auditor in the detection of journal entries that are intended to materially misstate the financial statements.

Planning Reports for Journal Entry Testing

The first report was described in Chapter 13, which was a summary of the trial balance by the source of the entry and the debits and credits, which form the account balance. This report is very useful in targeting accounts that are composed solely of journal entries. The report will also allow the auditor to ensure the completeness of the population because the accounts totals produced from the report will need to be reconciled or matched to the general ledger produced from the company's automated system.

The second report is a summary of journal entry activity by individual. The summary should focus on:

- Aggregate dollar value of journal entries and frequency of journal entries. The FDA should use the value of the debits or credits.
- Stratify dollar value of journal entries by control levels and provide frequency of journal entries.
- Stratify journal entries before year-end and after year-end.

The third report is a summary of journal entries by type of journal entry. The type field is dependent on the codes used by the company. The first report should be a summary by type, providing the aggregate dollar value, frequency of posting, maximum dollar, minimum dollar, and the average dollar. Based on the company, the report could be summarized by:

- Company
- Account
- Individual

The remaining reports should be designed for the concept of data availability, reliability, and usability:

- Test for gaps in the journal entry numbers.
- Test for duplicate journal entry numbers. Remember, duplicates can be masked by alpha or special symbols. The cleaning process cleans the journal entry numbers of alpha and special symbols and records the cleansed number in a virtual field for duplicate testing.

- Test for journal entry numbers that have no numeric integers. Be careful, a simple test for blanks would not reveal a dash.
- Test for off-period journal entries.

What Are the Overall Strategies for General Journal Entry Fraud Data Analytics?

The following fraud data analytics approaches are designed to locate a fraud scenario recorded through a general journal entry:

- The defined anomaly attribute of the journal entry using the scoring sheet concept.
- The use of disaggregated analysis on general ledger accounts and sub-ledgers to identify which journal entry or entries would have a material impact on the general ledger account.
- The historical approach, using the red flags from previously reported fraud schemes in other companies.
- The absence of a journal entry, when a journal entry should be recorded.
- The timing of the journal entry.
- The alpha description explaining the purpose of the journal entry.
- The *why* question.

FRAUD DATA ANALYTICS FOR SELECTING JOURNAL ENTRIES

The nature, timing, and extent of journal entry testing are an important question. The difference between internal control testing of journal entries and the search for journal entries that have a fraudulent material impact on a financial account is also a critical question. The combination of the two important questions must be incorporated into the fraud data analytics plan.

The fraud data analytics plan for journal entries is not one-dimensional. It is not just picking one strategy but considering all the strategies consistent with the auditor's understanding of the entities' financial reporting process.

Approach One: What Is an Anomaly General Journal Entry Using the Scoring Sheet Concept?

The simple answer is that the journal entry is an extreme deviation from the standard journal entry. The answer is perfectly accurate but perfectly useless. By the way, that is a variation of an old accounting joke. The question, however, is a critical question in the development of a data interrogation plan.

The answer to the question starts with the fraud scenario; the remaining parts of the answer are: the financial account; materiality; the general anomalies; and the company-specific anomalies. The sample selection is then based on a composite score of the journal entry.

The scoring sheet concept was first introduced in Chapter 6 and referred to in many chapters. The concept is simple: The auditor identifies a series of attributes, assigns a risk rating to the attribute (1, 2, or 3), and then calculates a score for each journal entry within the analysis. The sample selection is based on the journal entries with the highest score.

The system works best on a specific account or combination of accounts. The system starts with the fraud scenarios. The next considerations are the direction of testing, materiality, general attributes of journal entries, and at least one company-specific consideration. The direction of testing and materiality are a requirement of the scoring sheet. It is recommended that at least three common or company-specific attributes are used to minimize false positives. However, in reality, the fraud auditor needs to exercise judgment on the number of attributes to use:

- The **first attribute** should be the materiality concept. If the entry is not material individually or in the aggregate, then the journal entry most likely will not have a material impact on the financial account.
- The materiality concept should be consistent with the direction of testing for overstatement or understatement.
- General journal entry that the debits exceed a predetermined dollar amount is searching for one journal entry that has a material effect on the financial account.
- General journal entries that have a high frequency of occurrence and a material dollar value in the aggregate is searching for journal entries that appear to be circumventing the intent of the internal control process and would have a material effect on the financial account.
- The **second attribute** should be a specific account or the class of accounts. Remember the definition of an anomaly and the concept of shrinking the haystack. To some degree, the first and second attributes are a lot like the question, Which comes first, the chicken or the egg?
- The **third attribute** is the general attributes of the financial reporting process. The following are intended to be examples of general attributes that would cause a journal entry to be selected.
  - General journal entries to control accounts such as cash, accounts receivable, or accounts payable is searching for journal entries that should not occur.

- General journal entries that shift transactions to another section of the financial statement. Examples are debit-capitalized advertising expenses and credit operating expenses. While the entry may be correcting a posting error, the entry moved a transaction from the income statement to balance sheet, which effectively increased operating income.
- General journal entries where the debit or credit side of the journal entry is illogical, such as debit equipment and credit accrued revenue.
- General journal entries transferring transactions from one company to another company.
- General journal entries that occur at off-period times. *Off-period* needs to be defined by off-period for your company versus a generic standard. The fraud data analysis links to the internal control avoidance strategy.
- General journal entries that are posted after all source journal entries are posted are searching on the timing of the entry.
- General journal entries originated or approved by senior financial management includes entries searching for management override or using the auditor's historical knowledge of prior financial frauds.
- General journal entries where the journal number has a number, special symbol, or alpha characters that are not consistent with normal journal number identification is searching for entries that have been tagged in a unique manner.
- General journal entries are round numbers or recurring numbers to the same general ledger account. The fraud data analysis links to the number anomaly strategy.
- General journal entries where the description contains words consistent with the concept of recording bogus entries.
- The company-specific journal entries are determined by the fraud auditor's understanding of the company's financial reporting process and internal controls for general journal entries.

Approach Two: Disaggregated Analysis of General Ledger Account Balance

Every financial statement has key operating statistics, by which investors or bankers evaluate the financial soundness of the company. Each operating statistic links to a general ledger account. The first step is to understand which accounts are most likely to be misstated. The second step is to understand the accounting policies and GAAP surrounding those accounts. The disaggregated approach is not intended for every general ledger account, but rather the key general ledger account or accounts that are comprised of a subledger by design, such as accounts receivable. The planning report for the trial balance is the first disaggregated report.

Many journal entries look like any other journal entry on face value—there are debits and credits. They tend to be large numbers that post to a general ledger control account. Behind that control number is a subledger that typically comprises many subaccounts. Those subaccounts comprise transactions from a source journal and transactions from journal entries. The disaggregated approach is to dissect the general ledger account into its smallest component. In this way, the large journal entry with a large number becomes a smaller journal entry with a lot of small numbers posted to individual accounts. The analysis uses summary features by both dollar and record count, using the subledger impact versus the control account impact.

The sample selection can be either solely on materiality or based on data interpretation using the red flag concept.

Approach Three: Historical Red Flag of Fraudulent Journal Entries

The fraud data analytics approach is based on the study of previous financial statement frauds. The knowledge is invaluable for the fraud auditor in both the internal control testing and the substantive testing performed by the auditor.

In internal control testing, the red flag approach should be called *educated skepticism methodology*. The knowledge tells the auditor that the observable event has been linked to prior financial statement frauds. Thereby, the knowledge would alert the auditor to the susceptibility of intentional misstatement of a financial account.

The red flag has two approaches—red flag associated with an individual journal entry or red flag associated with a general ledger account where fraudulent journal entries are oftentimes posted. The journal entry red flag is most effective for control testing, whereas the general ledger red flag is most effective for substantive testing.

In fraud data analytics, the red flag can be used to design a specific search criterion. The historical red flag approach can occur at the journal entry level or the impact on an account level. From a practical perspective, the methodology is easy to use. The following is a list of historical red flags that have occurred in previous companies in no specific order.

Historical Red Flags of Fraudulent Journal Entries:
Movement of asset, liability, equity, revenue, or expense accounts consistent with fraud theory of overstatement or understatement. This should be called the overall red flag.

Timing of when the entry is recorded. Entries recorded at late or early morning hours, entries recorded on a holiday.

End-of-quarter or end-of-year entries.

Entries recorded after closing routine journals.

Manual entries or nonroutine entries recorded in new general ledger accounts or seldom-used general ledger accounts.

Entries initiated or recorded by senior financial management.

Journal entry for which the total amount of the entry is a round amount or even amount.

Multiple journal entries recorded on successive dates or times.

Multiple manual entries initiated by same individual.

Reversal entries that cause the account balance to have a material change in balance.

Journal entry number is out of sequence with standard numbering.

Journal entry reference contains numbers, letters, or symbols not consistent with standard identification.

Journal entries that transfer the transaction between two operating companies, which are not considered a consolidating entry.

Journal entry reclassifies a recorded transaction between two general ledger accounts with no logical reason for the reclassification.

Journal entry reclassifies a transaction from the other revenue account to operating revenue.

Journal entry reclassifies a transaction between operating expenses to non-operating expense account.

Revenue entry having other side of entry having debits or credits to unusual accounts.

Historical Red Flags of General Ledger Accounts Containing Fraudulent Journal Entries:

Account without entries from a source journal.

Account used solely for period-end adjustments.

Account used for solely for reserves.

Account for intercompany transactions.

Account adjusted to a zero balance.

Account where the reversal entry causes a zero balance account to have a material balance.

Account with a significant year-end change.

Account not reconciled on a timely basis.

Account where the opposite side of the entry is nonstandard or unusual by the nature of the entry.

Account where the net movement of the account balance is consistent with fraud theory.

New general ledger account numbers containing only journal entries.

Account having an unusual activity of journal entries and all journal entries are below the control threshold.

Approach Four: The Absence of a Journal Entry

Journal entry testing by its nature indicates that we are selecting journal entries for either control testing or substantive testing. However, many high-profile financial statement frauds occurred because an entry was not posted. The following two situations will illustrate the concept. I have intentionally not identified the company.

The business plan for a corporation in the retail industry called for expansion and building of new retail locations. The accounting practice was to record all costs associated with inspecting new sites into property, plant, and equipment ledger directly from the purchases journal. When a decision was made not to build at the site, a journal entry transferring the costs from an asset account to an operating expense account was never recorded. The absence of a journal entry overstated operating net income.

A corporation in the business of renting home furnishings and office furniture intentionally did not write off any assets held for rental that were damaged or stolen by the renter. When the results of the physical inventory internal control revealed that rental furnishings were destroyed or missing, senior management instructed staff not to record a journal entry recognizing the write-off of the rental assets. The absence of a journal entry overstated operating net income.

The absence of an entry requires the fraud auditor to understand the company's business and the accounting practices for the specific general ledger account. The fraud data analytics then targets the specific accounts, searching for accounts where there is an absence of journal entry when a journal entry would be expected.

Approach Five: The Timing of the Journal Entry

One of the problems in falsifying the financial statements is that financial management does not know how much to misstate the financial account until the source journals are recorded. At that point, financial management knows what is necessary to meet their numbers. However, after the financial statements are issued, the process of falsifying the statements starts over. The strategies for timing analysis are:

- Journal entries posted after all source journals are posted.
- Journal entries' proximity to the opinion date.
- Reversal entries.

Approach Six: The Alpha Description Describing the Purpose of the Journal Entry

Each journal entry has a written description explaining the purpose of the journal entry. Similar to the word searching approach used in FCPA audits, the fraud data analytics could search the description field for anomalies or keywords. The fraud theory is that journal entries that are created with an evil motive are more likely to be brief or vague.

The first step is to understand the business practices of the accounting department in writing the journal entry description. Is the business practice to write a brief or verbose description in the description field?

The second step is to perform an alpha count on the description field to determine the average number of alpha positions in the description field. Using the alpha count, the fraud data analytics creates a file of journal entries that contain less than the average number of alpha positions. The second step is to summarize the journal entries by a logical grouping, such as by person, by timing, or by account. The sample selection can either be journal entries that contain less than x number of alpha positions or through the data interpretation strategy using the auditor's business knowledge and the listing of historical red flags.

Another approach is to search on keywords in journal entry description field. Once again, the auditor needs to understand the normal accounting practices for the description field. The approach can focus on either common words such as *estimate* or *estimation* or specific words such as *correct* or *fix*.

Approach Seven: The *Why* Approach

The focus of the why approach is to study journal entries that occur for a specific purpose and correlate to a specific category of accounts. As stated in the anomaly testing, an anomaly is a deviation from the norm. So, the first step is to create a common grouping of journal entries over a period of time. I would encourage you to use a complete accounting cycle. To illustrate the concept, we will use accrued revenue. Let's further assume the general ledger has multiple accounts associated with accrued revenue. The fraud data analytics would create a summary of the journal entries impacting only those accounts. The last decision is whether to use the balance sheet account or the revenue account. I would encourage the use of the balance sheet account. The analysis should further segregate reversals of the prior month from the entry that created the accrued revenue. The summary is by the person recording the entry or by a logical grouping of accounts:

- By person recording the journal entry, providing dollar and frequency summary data.
- By each account associated with accrued revenue, providing dollar and frequency summary data.

Approach Eight: Concealing the Theft of Assets

In my experience, when financial management is involved in asset misappropriation schemes, they understand that the theft has an impact on the bottom line. They also understand the financial audit process. The predictability of the audit process has been identified as one of the reasons for audit failure. The following red flags are common with asset misappropriation schemes:

- Reclassify posted theft transactions from the income statement to the balance sheet to hide the theft loss. In two privately held companies, the balance sheet was overstated by 75 percent. In case one, the company was audited, and in case two, the company received a review opinion.
- Net adjusting entries to "fix" a balance sheet that was purportedly unreconciled when in fact the theft losses were hidden in the account. The auditor focused on the account balance reconciliation rather than the *why* question.
- Convoluted journal entries that are so complex in the audit trail of the transaction that following the entry from beginning to end caused the auditor to give up. The convoluted aspect effectively concealed the technique used by the controller to commit the asset misappropriation scheme. In this scheme, the controller misappropriated $1.4 million.
- The write-off of an asset from the balance sheet to an illogical account where the write-off is not visible. The inventory was written off to marketing-related expenses. The journal entry description indicated sales promotions.

▪ Layering the theft through small-dollar entries affecting many accounts, effectively using the lack of materiality of the transactions as a concealment technique. The controller was reimbursing himself for out-of-pocket expenses totaling $120,000. The reimbursement was included in his net payroll. The journal entry description indicated "reimbursement of out-of-pocket expenses." The expenses were spread through many operating expense accounts so that no one entry appeared to be material.

SUMMARY

The beginning of the chapter stated that journal entry fraud was simple—debit receivables for a million and credit revenue a million. It is that easy. Unfortunately, locating the entry is not so easy. General ledgers today are massive, and the ledger contains millions of transactions. The process of building a fraud data analytics plan for locating the adjusting, reversal, or reclassifying journal entry requires a superior knowledge of the industry and company accounting practices. The timing of journal entries that cause a material impact on the financial statement is usually near the opinion date. The opinion date is therefore an important consideration for the CPA offering the opinion. If there are no opinion date considerations, then designing the plan becomes much easier.

The chapter has provided several strategies for designing the fraud data analytics plan. Most likely, the final plan will be based on the nature of the general ledger accounts in the plan. The timing of the analysis will be determined by the purpose of the plan. The use of the different strategies will be based on the knowledge and judgment of the auditor. Good luck.

APPENDIX A

Data Mining Audit Program for Shell Companies

I. Background on the project.

The purpose of this audit program is to provide an illustration of how to develop a fraud data analytics audit program for shell companies. The same format should be used for the remaining chapters and for your future fraud data analytics projects.

The audit program will need to be tailored to your organization. I have also included in the program different concepts to illustrate different ways you can tailor the program; please look for the "Note comment."

The background section should describe the purpose of the audit assignment and provide the necessary background for the project.

II. Definition of terms. (Note: Definitions should be a standard element in fraud data analytics audit programs.)

a) Shell company: is a legally created entity that has no active business or is intended to conceal the true identity of the real company operating through a shell company. In essence, a shell corporation exists mainly on paper, has no physical presence, employs no one, and produces nothing.

b) Created company (shell company) committing a false billing scheme: is a shell company that was created by an internal person and the internal person causes false invoices to be paid through the accounts payable system (typically services).

c) Created company (shell company) committing a pass-through billing scheme: is a shell company that was by created by an internal person and the company receives the goods or services (typically goods or rental).

d) Assumed identity shell company: is a real vendor that has become dormant and an internal person takes over the identity of the company and causes false invoices to be paid through the accounts payable system.

e) Hidden company: is a created or real company operating under different names in the accounts payable file.

f) Limited company: Company procedures have identified that one-time or limited-use vendors bypass routine vendor setup procedures. Internal person submits an invoice in the name of the company and the internal person approves the vendor invoice. Note: The limited-use company maybe legally created or exists in name only. Note: For reader, this process goes by different names in different companies.

g) Conflict of interest: is a legally created company that provides a service to the company but the company is legally owned or beneficially owned by an internal person and the ownership is not properly disclosed. Typically this vendor has one customer. Note: Conflict of interest occurring through the purchasing process is not within the scope of this project.

h) False invoice: is an invoice for which no goods or services were provided and the invoice links to a created company, assumed-identity company, or a limited-use company.

i) Real invoice: is an invoice that links to a hidden-identity company or a conflict-of-interest company.

j) Identify level of concealment for master file data:
   i. Low indicates that an exact match using master file data will identify red flag.
   ii. Medium indicates that a close match using master file data will identify red flags. Document the criteria for the close match.
   iii. High indicates that no match will occur through master file data and that the search will be based on transactional data.

    k) Identify level of concealment for transactional data:

        i. Low indicates that an exact match using the transactional data will identify the red flag.

        ii. Medium indicates a close match on the transactional data. Document the criteria for the close match.

        iii. High indicates that match will occur through the data interpretation strategy. Document the criteria for the data interpretation.

III. Identify scope and time period of the examination.

    a) Identify the date of the master file for testing file.

    b) Note: Date for master file data should correlate to the ending period of primary table.

    c) Identify the primary table and time period for expenditure testing. Note: Preference is to use two years of data and avoid use of partial years. Helps in the reconciliation process.

    d) Identify the secondary tables and time periods for expenditure tables.

        i. Purchase order extraction should correlate to the lowest purchase order number.

        ii. Payment extraction should correlate to the payment of all invoices in the primary table.

        iii. If purchase order table or payment table will not result in a match to all invoices, document the reasons.

IV. Identification and selection of data from primary and secondary tables.

    a) Document the primary table and date range of extraction.

    b) Document the secondary tables and date range of extraction.

V. Review fraud risk assessment.

    a) Review fraud risk assessment and identify all scenarios with high residual risk rating.

    b) Review fraud risk assessment and identify all other scenarios that should be included in the fraud data analytics project based on auditor judgment. Document the reasons.

    c) Fraud scenarios related to shell companies:

        i. Senior member of management acting alone or in collusion with a direct report causes a shell company to be set up on the vendor master file, processes a contract, and approves a fake invoice for goods or services not provided, causing the diversion of company funds.

ii. Budget owner acting alone or in collusion with a direct report causes a shell company to be set up on the vendor master file, processes a contract, and approves a fake invoice for goods or services not received, causing the diversion of company funds.

iii. Accounts payable function acting alone or in collusion with a direct report causes a shell company to be set up on the vendor master file, processes a contract, and approves a fake invoice for goods or services not received, causing the diversion of company funds.

iv. Accounts payable function acting alone takes over the identity of a dormant vendor, creates a fake invoice, and processes the invoice against a dormant contract or a no-contract invoice transaction for goods or services not received, causing the diversion of company funds.

v. Accounts payable function acting alone takes over the identity of a real vendor on a temporary basis, creates a fake invoice, and processes the invoice against a dormant contract, a no-contract invoice transaction, or a current open contract for goods or services not received, causing the diversion of company funds.

vi. Budget owner acting alone or in collusion with a direct report causes a shell company to be set up on the master file, places orders for goods or services through the shell company, the shell company places an order with a real supplier, the real supplier ships directly to the budget owner company, the real supplier invoices the shell company, and the shell company invoices the budget owner company at an inflated price, causing the diversion of company funds.

vii. Senior member of management acting alone or in collusion with a direct report causes a shell company to be set up on the master file, places orders for goods through the shell company, the shell company places an order with a real supplier, the real supplier ships directly to the senior member of management company, the real company invoices the shell company, and the shell company invoices the senior member of management at an inflated price, causing the diversion of company funds.

viii. Sales representative at a real supplier sets up a shell company and convinces the budget owner or senior member of management to purchase from the shell company versus the real supplier. The budget owner places orders for goods through the shell company, the shell company places an order with a real supplier, the real supplier ships directly to the budget owner company, the real company invoices the shell company, and the shell company invoices the budget owner at an inflated price, causing the diversion of company funds.

    d) Cross-reference fraud scenarios to fraud data analytics.

VI. Data files requested.

    a) Using the standard naming table list meet with IT and identify the exact name of the table in the database and the online system screen name for:

        i. Vendor master file data.

        ii. Expenditure primary data table.

        iii. Purchase order data table.

        iv. Payment data table.

        v. Vendor master file change table. Note: Should be consistent with audit scope. If not, change file obtain vendor master file data at beginning and end of scope period for comparison.

        vi. Human resources data table for required employee information.

    b) Based on meeting with IT update standard naming table list with actual names used in the database table.

    c) Review online system for vendor master file, invoice screen, purchase order screen, and payment screen and update to the standard naming table list with actual screen names.

    d) Based on review of online system, are there additional fields that should be requested for project?

VII. Reconciliation reports.

    a) Compare IT record count for vendor master file extraction to field statistic report as to record count.

    b) Compare IT record count on primary table to field statistic report.

    c) Reconcile aggregate dollars in extraction to the general ledger.

VIII. Data availability, reliability, and usability for master file data.

    a) Data availability analysis for master file data.

        i. Note: Performance of this analysis before data testing is critical to avoid false positives and for the reliability of test results.

        ii. Perform record count for each master file field for blanks or effective blanks.

        iii. Prepare data availability report for each data field providing total record, blank fields, available fields, and percent of available fields.

    iv. Prepare conclusion statement as to effect of blanks on planned testing.

  b) Data reliability analysis for master file data.

    i. Sort high to low and low to high, searching for overt data integrity issues.

  c) Data usability conclusion for master file data.

    i. Conclude on data availability and reliability impact on planned testing.

IX. Data availability, reliability, and usability for primary table data.

  a) Data availability analysis for primary table.

    i. Determine the number of invoices that have no purchase order number.

    ii. Determine the number of invoices that have no payment record.

  b) Data reliability analysis for primary table.

    i. Review date field and identify number of invoices where the invoice date is not consistent with scope period.

    ii. Review vendor invoice number for overt data integrity issues.

    iii. Review vendor invoice number field for alpha text.

    iv. Review line-item description for integrity of description field.

  c) Data usability conclusion for primary table.

    i. Conclude as to impact of data reliability for invoice date, invoice number, and line-item description.

    ii. Conclude on impact of invoices with no purchase order.

    iii. Conclude on impact of invoices with no payment record.

X. Perform walkthrough testing on data files.

  a) Select entries from the master file and verify the information.

  b) Select entries from the primary table and compare information to original source document.

  c) For selected entries from secondary table, compare to original source document.

XI. Clean up of data files.

  a) Merge primary table to vendor master file table. Note: Procedure is for ease of future data interpretation.

  b) Perform reconciliation on record count and aggregate dollars.

  c) Match secondary tables to primary table.

  d) Identify all primary table entries that have no match to secondary tables.

  e) Perform data availability summary as to:

    i. Frequency of primary table not matching to a secondary table.

   ii. Determine the aggregate dollar value and number of records having no match transactions.
   iii. Determine reasons for the lack of data match.
   iv. Conclude on the impact of lack of data match on planned testing.
   f) Identify reversal transactions using the exact match precision.
   g) Determine how telephone field, bank account, email are recorded in data file. If fields are not split, then create a separate data file for the:
      i. Country code, area code, and telephone number
      ii. Bank routing number and bank account number
      iii. Email name and server name
      iv. Determine procedures for populating blank fields:
         1. If zero or dash
         2. If blank
   h) Review date fields for proper format for analysis purposes.
XII. Understanding the data reports.
   a) Purpose of planning reports is to provide an overview of the data files that are being used in the fraud data analytics project.
   b) Create statistical reports for each table included in project:
      i. Record count.
      ii. Aggregate dollar: Provide positive and negative numbers.
   c) Identify all vendors on the master file that are active and inactive.
      i. By activity code or
      ii. By summarizing transactions by vendor number and identify all vendors with no spend level.
      iii. Conclude as to whether inactive vendors should be excluded from data interrogation.
   d) Create spend-level report providing vendor number, vendor short name, creation date of vendor, frequency of records, aggregate dollar value, maximum, minimum, and average invoice amount (referred to as maximum, minimum, and average report).
      i. Purpose is to provide high-level overview of spend level by vendor.
      ii. Through review of report, determine if any vendors should be excluded from reports. Document reasons. Note: See discussion in book regarding nuisance vendors.
   e) Create purchase order comparison report comparing purchase order date to invoice date. Create report by vendor number, providing aggregate dollars and frequency.

      i. Purpose is to determine the frequency of circumvention of the purchase order system.
      ii. Purchase order date before invoice date.
      iii. Purchase order date equals invoice date.
      iv. Purchase order date greater than invoice date.
  f) Identify all invoices with no purchase order.
      i. Purpose is to determine effectiveness of purchase order system and identify invoices that routinely circumvent the purchase order system.
      ii. Create the maximum, minimum, and average report.
      iii. Based on review of report, determine how to further refine the report to identify routine circumvention.
  g) Create comparison of expenditures from last year to this year.
      i. Purpose is to identify change in buying relationships. Note: Change may relate to pass-through schemes or one-person conflict-of-interest schemes.
      ii. Calculate dollar change.
      iii. Calculate percent of change.
  h) Identify the number of payments that are in electronic format and how many are in paper check format.
      i. Summarize by vendor number payments in electronic format and number payments in paper; check format and provide aggregate dollars and frequency.
XIII. Data interrogation routines based on master file data.
  a) Specific identification of master file data for created shell companies based on missing data.
      i. Purpose of analysis is to identify vendors where communication with vendor is limited by available data in master file.
      ii. Note: Each report created should have a documented purpose of the report.
      iii. Identify level of concealment: low, medium, or high.
      iv. Create the missing data scoring report using the street address, city, state, bank account number, telephone number, government registration number, email address, and contact person.
      v. Review data availability report and determine impact of availability on fields.
      vi. Risk rate each field using a score of 1, 2, and 3.
      vii. Based on scoring total create a separate file and create the maximum, minimum, and average report.

    viii. Based on scoring total summarize invoices by department, searching for vendors that are used solely by one department or person.

    ix. Other reports are the invoice range report and speed of payment report. (Note: Reference other reports associated with specific scheme. Often a shell company will appear on more than one report. Based on reviewing the data, the fraud auditor will need to perform additional analysis.)

    x. Note: Document the programming steps used to create the report. This procedure should be performed for each fraud data analytics report. It is also useful for recurring audit assignments.

    xi. Note: Transaction analysis is for high concealment in master file data, or the transactional analysis should be linked to the master file, testing for low and medium concealment.

    xii. Note: Document the report title and filename for each report and file.

  b) Specific identification of master file data for created shell companies.

    i. Purpose is to identify vendors created in the scope period.

    ii. Identify level of concealment: low, medium, or high.

    iii. Using the creation date field, identify all vendors created in the last X number of months.

    iv. Create separate file and create the maximum, minimum, and average report. (Note: With whichever strategy, specific identification or through data interpretation, the program should explain the review process.)

    v. Review report for anomalies associated with a created shell company.

      1. Note: Illustration of incorporating red flags into the audit program.

      2. Maximum dollar invoice is below dual signature threshold.

      3. Number of records is fewer than 25 (judgmental).

      4. Limited range between maximum and average invoice amount.

      5. Number anomaly as to even numbers. (Note: Example of review process.)

      6. Recurring amount by vendor. (Note: May be indicative of a pass-through company for equipment rental.)

      vi. Other reports are the invoice range report and speed of payment report.

  c) Specific identification of master file data for created shell companies.

      i. Purpose is to identify vendors that have an exact match on vendor address and employee match.

      ii. Identify level of concealment: low, medium, or high.

      iii. Compare vendor address to address in human resources using the exact match.

      iv. Consider matching on bank account number and telephone number.

      v. Note: For scenarios committed by accounts payable function consider a close match using a Zip code radius and creation date that correlates to position date for function.

  d) Internal control avoidance master file data for created shell companies.

      i. Purpose is to search for vendors that were created during an off-period time.

      ii. Identify level of concealment: low, medium, or high.

      iii. Identify all vendor created at off-hours:

         1. Based on work hours, determine off-period time.

         2. Include record creator.

      iv. Identify all vendor numbers created in the XX-month time period.

      v. Create separate files and create the maximum, minimum, and average report.

  e) Specific identification for assumed identity.

      i. Purpose is to search for the takeover of a dormant vendor. Note: Analysis may also indicate temporary takeover or a real vendor if two or more changes.

      ii. Identify level of concealment: low, medium, or high.

      iii. Using the change file identify all vendors with a change to the address or bank account field.

      iv. Create separate file and create the maximum, minimum, and average report based on transactions after the change date.

      v. Note: Using the payment table identify all vendors that have more than one payment address or bank account. (Note; Example of a different way to identify.)

  f) Specific identification for hidden company.

      i. Purpose is to identify a vendor that is operating under multiple names.

      ii. Identify level of concealment: low, medium, or high.

     iii. Create the duplicate scoring report for address, bank account number, telephone, email address, and government registration number.

     iv. All fields will have the same risk rating.

      v. Create separate file and create the maximum, minimum, and average report.

     vi. Review report for identified anomalies.

    vii. Consider use of fuzzy logic analysis on vendor name.

g) Specific identification for temporary companies.

      i. Purpose is to identify payments to vendors that occurred through the limited payment procedure.

     ii. Identify level of concealment: low, medium, or high.

     iii. Based on interviews determine method of identifying limited-use vendors.

     iv. Identify all vendors identified as temporary vendors.

      v. Create separate file and create the maximum, minimum, and average report.

     vi. Using the maximum, minimum, and average report review list for vendors that have three (number is judgmental) or less invoices.

h) Specific identification anomaly testing for master file data.

      i. Purpose is to identify anomalies that are indicative of a shell company but the anomaly may or may not be sufficient to cause a sample selection.

     ii. Identify level of concealment: low, medium, or high.

     iii. Identify all vendors where the address field and bank account field is blank.

     iv. Perform name test searching for names that have limited number of alpha positions.

      v. Identify all vendor email addresses that use a public email address (e.g., g-mail).

     vi. Search street address one and two for mailbox service companies based on suite number, file number, or cloud number.

    vii. Based on results of each test, determine additional data analysis.

XIV. Data interrogation routines based on primary table.

a) Create specific identification report by vendor number comparing the first invoice number by date to the last invoice number by date.

      i. Purpose is to identify vendor invoice patterns that are sequential or a limited range pattern in relationship to the date range.

The report will also identify vendor invoices starting with low or even numbers.

  ii. Provide vendor number, vendor short name, vendor creation date, aggregate dollars, and frequency of invoices.

  iii. Calculate invoice number range and date range.

  iv. Determine impact of alpha text in invoice number field.

  v. Determine impact by overt data integrity of invoice number.

  vi. Review the report:

    1. Note: Illustrative example of how to use the report.

    2. Review report for sequential patterns of invoice number by comparing record count to invoice number range.

    3. Sort first invoice number low to high, looking for low numbers or invoice number starting with 1,100 or 1,000.

b) Create specific identification report; identify all purchase orders with more than one invoice.

  i. Purpose is to identify open purchase orders. Open purchases by the nature of the transaction indicate the approval process is based on availability of dollars.

  ii. Summarize by vendor number, creating a separate line by vendor number and purchase order number.

  iii. Create maximum, minimum, and average report.

  iv. Review results and determine additional analysis for open purchase orders.

  v. Note: Remember the review of the first report often defines the second report. Fraud data analytics programs are a continually evolving process. But, you need a starting point.

c) Create internal control avoidance report for invoice splitting by vendor number using exact match by vendor number by invoice date. (Note: Report is not searching for duplicate payments.)

  i. Purpose is to identify invoice-splitting technique for the purpose of identifying a pattern of internal control avoidance.

  ii. Filter out all transactions below dollar approval level.

  iii. Note: Report may have a high volume of transactions because vendors by their nature issue multiple invoices on one day.

d) Create internal control avoidance report by identifying:

  i. An invoice that is recorded at off-period times.

  ii. Vendor invoices recorded at off-hours.

  iii. Vendor invoices recorded at off-hours by record creator.

  iv. Vendor invoices with dates that are Saturday or Sunday. (Note: Example of internal control avoidance using different criteria.)

e) Create internal control avoidance report by identifying invoices with a prescribed percentage of each control level.
   i. Purpose is to identify invoices within a certain dollar range of a key control level.
   ii. Identify all invoices within prescribed range:
      1. Summarize by vendor.
      2. Summarize by operating unit.
      3. Summarize by record creator.
f) Create internal control avoidance report by comparing invoice date to payment date.
   i. Purpose is to identify a pattern of vendor invoices that are paid faster than company payment policy.
   ii. Identify all invoices and payment dates are the same:
      1. Summarize by vendor number.
      2. Summarize by operating unit.
      3. Summarize by record creator.
   iii. Create average speed of payment by vendor. Stratify the report by invoices paid within terms and invoices paid faster than terms.
g) Create internal control avoidance report for the use of a dormant open purchase order in the system.
   i. Purpose: Identify payments to a vendor that occurred by matching the invoice to a dormant purchase order.
   ii. Identify purchase orders where there is X number of days between the last two vendor invoices applied to the purchase order. Note: Establish the number of days for the range as to sample selection.
h) Create a number anomaly report by invoice amount, summarize by invoice amount.
   i. Purpose is to search for a pattern of even amounts or recurring amounts that link to a particular vendor.
   ii. Note: Procedure should be performed on the merged master file and transaction data file.
   iii. Identify all round invoice amounts.
      1. Click on amount field and sort by vendor number. Using data interpretation review vendor invoice data for anomalies.
      2. Anomalies are: invoice number pattern, concentration associated with one vendor number, line-item descriptions. If noted, review vendor master file data for creation date.
   iv. Identify all recurring invoice amounts.
      1. Click on amount field and sort by vendor number. Using data interpretation review vendor invoice data for anomalies.

XV. Sample selection criteria.
  a) For each fraud data analysis document the sample selection criteria.
XVI. Fraud testing procedure.
  a) For each fraud data analysis report document the audit procedure performed to determine whether the transaction should be identified as a suspicious transaction.
  b) Note: Audit procedure should be linked to the specific fraud scenario.
  c) Note: Audit procedures for shell companies are explained in Chapter 6.
XVII. Conclusions.
  a) The conclusion statement for the data analysis is the identification of transactions that are consistent with the data analysis routine.
  b) The conclusion statement for the fraud testing procedure is:
    i. There is credible evidence that the specific fraud scenario is occurring and a recommendation for an investigation.
    ii. There is no credible evidence that the specific fraud scenario is occurring.
XVIII. End of document.

About the Author

L eonard W. Vona, CPA, CFE, is the CEO of Fraud Auditing and a world-renowned authority in fraud auditing. He has provided expert witness testimony in federal and state courts; consulted with corporations around the world; and is the author of *Fraud Risk Assessment: Building the Fraud Audit Program* and *The Fraud Audit: Responding to the Risk of Fraud in Core Business Systems* published by Wiley. A forensic auditor with more than 38 years of diversified forensic auditing experience, he has provided more than 1,500 days of fraud training around the world.

Index

Page references followed by *f* indicate an illustrated figure.

Abuse
asset misappropriation, contrast, 206–207
expenses submission, 206
Abusive purchase scenario, 218
Access security databases, usage, 198
Accounts, fraud brainstorming, 296–297
Accounts payable
clerk, duplicate payment scheme, 170
fraud scenario example, 33
function, collusion, 170, 352
usage, FDA (impact), 237–238
vendor, collusion, 168–170
Accounts receivable
analysis, usage, 324–326, 329
dormant credits, association, 327
false aging, FDA (impact), 332
falsification, 314
misstatement
documents data, identification, 315–318
fraud data analytics, usage, 311
Accrued revenue
controller overstatement, 335
recordation, 320
Action statement, 185–186
fraud, 30
services, performance (absence), 102
Active vendor, identity
(assumption), 67
Add-on charges, search, 167–168
Add-on purchase order, 174

Address field
example, 132*f*
fields, combination, 113
Address information, 212
Adjusting entries, change, 337
Adjustments
pattern/frequency, 233
technique, 327
Advertising expenses, controller
reclassification (absence), 336
After-the-fact analysis
permutations, 259
usage, 266
After-the-fact approach, 259
Aged documents, usage, 55
Aggregate amount, 75
Aggregate dollar value, 59
Alpha descriptions, 75–76
absence, 76
Alpha positions, 345
Alpha string, applicability, 113
Alpha transaction description, 69
Amount
field, 75
patterns, 75
Annual payroll summary table, 186
Anomaly
general journal entry, scoring sheet
concept (usage), 339–341
pattern, transaction identification, 66
specific data, 103
types, 133
Anomaly testing, 133, 141–142, 234
identification anomaly testing, 359
Arrangement, evidence, 318

Ascending/descending numbers,
    mixture, 70
Asset misappropriation, 74
    fraud data analytics, usage, 114–118
    general ledger account number
        category, 76
    real employee complicitness, 194
    scenarios, occurrence, 206
    scheme, 280
        lapping, association, 326
        management commitment, 280
    secondary category, consideration
        levels, 20
Assets
    accounting policies, 297–310
    controller overstatement, 292
    fraud brainstorming, 296–297
    identification, 180
    overstatement, techniques, 296
    theft
        company credit card, usage, 117
        concealment, 346–347
    understatement, techniques, 296
    write-off, 346
Assumed entity shell company, 129
    fraud data analytics, usage, 133–134
    usage, 228
Assumed identity employee, occurrence,
    185
Assumed identity, identification, 358
Assumed identity shell company, 350
Attendance reporting database, 186
Attributes, usage, 340
Audit
    knowledge, 14
    planning considerations,
        documentation process, 124–125
    procedure
        application, 4
        design, 100*f*
    program, 349
    scope, strategy selection, 91
    software, knowledge, 14
Authoritative sources, understanding
    (planning), 274
Authorization avoidance, concept, 28

Automated payments, total number
    (summarization), 188

Bad debt scenarios, 241
    hidden entity shell customer, usage,
        228
Bad debt write-off scenarios, 229
Balance sheet
    accounts, focus, 300–301
    assets, identification, 180
Bank account
    absence, 190
    number, fraud concealment example,
        46*f*
Banking industry (term loan inclusion),
    lapping (usage), 240–242
Bank routing number, 141
Bedford's law, 62
Believability factor, 25
Bid avoidance, 249, 252
    analysis, 259
    circumstantial evidence, usage, 255
    fraud data analytics plan, 261–263
    internal control avoidance strategy,
        257
    scheme, 260
    search, fraud data analytics approach,
        258
Bid criteria, internal person creation, 251
Bidding
    levels, avoidance, 176–177
    practice, 256
Bid proposal scheme,
    issuing/receipt/control, 260
Bid rotation, 265
Bid suppression, 265
Birthdate, 212
Bribery
    fraud risk, 29
    provisions, fraud scenario concept
        (application), 270–272
    scenarios, 229, 244–245
Bribes, 248
    payment, 13
Bribe tax (funding), cost inflation
    technique (determination), 255

Budget owner
  action, 352
  collusion, 117
  purchasing circumvention, 172
  scenario, 101
  vendor, collusion, 176–177
Business
  capacity test, 146
  opportunity risk, 277
  partner risk, 277
  questionable payment, direct payment,
    279
  systems, commonalities, 27
  transaction, data availability, 68, 69
  unit, sales, 317
Business purpose
  false description
    FDA basis, 273
    questionable payments, FDA basis,
      283–284
  scenario, 218–219

Cash conversion scenario, 222
Cash-equivalent purchase
  scenario, 220
Cash equivalent purchase scheme,
  occurrence, 208
Cash receipts journal, credit origination,
  325
Cash receipts theft
  data/documents, identification,
    229–231
  fraud data analytics, usage, 227
Certainty, degree (concept), 100
Certainty principle, 10–11
Change transactions, importance,
  121–122
Channel stuffing, 313
  FDA, impact, 328–329
Charitable organizations, disbursements,
  279
Circumvention fraud data analytics
  strategy, 176–177
Classification identification
  systems, 64
Close match, 51

Code of conduct, 276
Collectability, assurance, 318
Commission code, absence, 324
Commodity code, 216
  purchases, 212
Common fraud scenario, 5, 27
Common names, table (establishment),
  167
Company
  assets, management sale, 281
  company-specific anomalies, 340
  company-specific concept, 27
  company-specific fraud scenario, 5, 27
  corruption, 269
  credit cards
    charge, management creation, 281
    fraud data analytics, usage, 205
  data
    files, size, 95
    quality, improvement, 112
  files, merger (impact), 99
  funds
    diversion, 13
    FDA basis, 273
  internal controls, vulnerabilities
    (vendor exploitation), 165–168
  policies (compliance), FDA (impact),
    274–275
Compensation grade, 212
Completeness test, 87
Completion revenue recognition
  (percentage), fraud data analytics
  (usage), 331–332
Compliance procedures, 276
Concealment. See Fraud concealment
  higher sophistication, 210–211
  low sophistication, 210
  scheme, contrast, 209–211
Conditions schemes, favored
  negotiations, 261
Confidential reporting, 276
Conflict of interest, 350
  process, 150
  scenarios, 223
Conflict of interest company, defining,
  131

Conflict of interest entity
  analysis, 68
  pattern, 67
Consolidating entries, impact, 337
Construction (favoritism), real entity
    targeted statement, 252
Consultant, internal budget owner
    (collusion), 151
Consumption, company requirements
    (contrast), 180
Content, style (fraud scenario contrast),
    34–36
Continuous improvement, 276
Contra amount, 75
Contract
  award, 248
  execution, 248
  purchase/administration, internal
      source negotiation, 177–179
Contra entry deduction scenario, FDA
    plan, 200
Contra entry transaction, 63
Control account, 294
Control avoidance, 96
  internal control avoidance, 54–57
  strategy, 93
Controllers
  asset overstatement, 292
  format, 289
  overstatement, 299
Control number, 69, 77
  illogical range, 70
Control number patterns
  data anomaly, identification, 71–72
  existence, 70–71
  listing, 70
  occurrence, 69–70
  red flag, identification, 71–72
Conversion statement, 57
Convoluted journal entries, 346
Corporations. *See* Shell corporations
Corrupt act, intent, 248
Corrupt influence, 248
Corruption
  asset misappropriation, contrast, 206
  company corruption, 269

defining, 248
fraud approach, 253–254
fraud audit approach, 254–255
fraud data analytics, usage, 114–118,
    247
general ledger account number
    category, 76
procurement process, fraud data
    analytics (usage), 247
project
  examples, 84–86, 90–91, 98–100
  scope concept, 83–84
real employee complicitness, 194
scenarios, 206
schemes, 75, 118
search, after-the-fact analysis (usage),
    266
Cost of goods sold, expense (shift), 308
Cost of sales, controller understatement,
    336
Country risks, 277
Covert influence, 248
Created company (shell company),
    impact, 350
Created shell companies
  identification master file data,
      357–358
  internal control avoidance master file
      data, 358
Creation date, 73, 190
Credit cards
  expenditures, matching, 214
  information, human resources
      (linkage), 212
  purchases, file layout description,
      214–216
Credit limit, 323
Credit value, FDA usage, 338
Cumulative principal, 11
Currency conversion scenarios, 229,
    242–243
Customer
  account, sales recordation, 317
  address/bank account (change),
      internal person (impact), 238
  credit scenarios, theft, 228, 236–238

credits theft, assumed entity shell customer (usage), 228
documents, data elements (usage), 72
invoice, traditional lapping scenario (application), 239–240
number, internal house account (linkage), 326
open credits (theft), accounts payable (FDA impact), 237–238
order date, 330
order number, 325, 329
order quantity, computation, 329
pass-through schemes, occurrence, 281
payments, 316
  records, 230
remittances, planning reports, 230–231
sales records, 229–230
sales representative, assignation, 323

Data
  addition, 112
  dilemma, auditor decision, 121
  entry, errors, 71
  groups, creation, 65
  identification, 112
    primary/secondary tables, usage, 351
  integrity, identification, 121
  item
    control number pattern, occurrence, 69–70
    patterns, occurrence, 68
  mining strategy
    appropriateness, 309–310
    selection, 82, 85–86
  reports, understanding, 355–356
  selection, primary/secondary tables (usage), 351
  set
    cleaning, 93–94, 103
    error cleaning, 91
  summarization, 112
    feature, 295

  understanding, 82, 90–91, 293–295
    real-world perspective, 14–15
  usage process, understanding, 112–113
Data analytics
  basis, 321–322
  concealment strategy basis, 322
  phase, false positives minimization (avoidance), 121
  plan. See Fraud data analytics plan.
Data anomaly, 53
  identification/impact, 71–72
  pattern, impact, 68
Data availability, 68, 69, 82
  basis, 91
  cleaning, 93–94, 103
  concept, 338–339
  decisions, 86–90
  impact, 120–121
Database
  control number pattern, existence, 70–71
  credit card expenditures, matching, 214
  data, identification/addition, 112
  pattern, existence, 68
Data elements, 256
  identification, 51–54
  usage, 72
    process, guidance, 73–77
Data errors
  identification, 91
  impact, 88
  presence, 89
Data files
  cleanup, 354–355
  location, 186
  request, 353
  walk through testing, 354
Data interpretation, 51, 96, 103, 211
  challenge, 166–167
  exclusion, basis, 59, 62
  importance, 65
  scenario, 59–62
  selection, basis, 62

Data interpretation (*Continued*)
  strategy, 57–62, 93, 156, 218
  usage, 257
  usage, guidelines, 57–59
Data interrogation
  occurrence, 304–305, 323
  tests, 52
Data interrogation routines
  building, guidelines, 67–68
  development process, 68, 73–77
  filtering concept, 118–119
  master file data basis, 356–359
  primary table basis, 359–360
  selection criteria, establishment, 91
  type, illustration, 279–280
Data profile
  building. *See* Fraud data profile; Fraud
    scenario.
  circular view, 9*f*
Data reliability, 82
  basis, 91
  cleaning, 93–94, 103
  concept, 338–339
  decisions, 86–90
  impact, 120–121
Data usability, 82
  basis, 91
  cleaning, 93–94, 103
  concept, 338–339
  decisions, 86–90
Date, creation, 142
Date field, usage (examples), 74–75
Date format numbers, 70
Date patterns, 73
Debit value, FDA usage, 338
Delete transactions, importance,
    121–122
Delinquent payment history, absence,
    319
Delivery, occurrence, 318
Department number, 190
Department of Justice (DOJ)
  FCPA Review Procedure Releases and
    Opinion Procedure Release
    Summaries, 275

Opinion Release 04–02, internal
    control attributes (FDA basis),
    276–277
Description field, 89
  alpha/numeric considerations,
    75–76
Direct access, 30
Disaggregated analysis, 114
Disbursement, 279–280
  fraud, FDA planning reports (usage),
    153–154
  fraudulent disbursements, 149–152
  report, creation, 281
Disciplinary measures, 276
Discount amount, 69
Discounts, bribery scenarios, 244–245
Disguised compensation, occurrence,
    185
Disguised expenditures, 180–181
  fraud scenario, 216–217
  occurrence, 150
Distributors, disbursements, 279–280
Documents
  date, 73
  fraud data analytics, usage, 152–153
Dollar amount
  maximum, 59
  minimum, 59
Dollar levels, avoidance, 55
Dormant credits, 237
  usage, 240
Dormant customer
  accounts, FDA file (creation),
    237–238
  real customer, equivalence, 323
  sales recordation, 317
Dormant open purchase order, usage,
    361
Dormant vendor
  identity, assumption, 67
  impact, 99
Duplicate amount, 75
Duplicate information, 103
Duplicate invoice, submission, 168–170
Duplicate numbers, 70, 72
Duplicate purchase scenario, 221

Duplicate purchase scheme, occurrence, 208
Duplicate test (testing), 140, 141, 338

Earnings management, defining, 287
Educated skepticism methodology, 342
Electronic funds transfer (EFT), 3
Emergency contact person, absence, 190
Employee
    advances, writing off, 283
    bonuses, payment, 283
    classification systems, 187
    collusion, 196
    comparison, 222
    database, 234
    excessive hours, 197
    filtering, 188
    ghost employee, 189
    hours worked, overstatement, 196
    job function, 214
    no-show employee, 194
    overtime hours, cluster, 197
    payroll employee, collusion, 196
    purchases, 212
    reactivation, 193
    supervisor, collusion, 196
Employer fraud, 186
Employment status, 187
Entity
    availability, 87–88
    concept, absence, 335
    external entity, internal collusion (absence), 78
    false created employee, 102
    false entity, 31, 290
    hidden entity fraud scenario, 86
    identified entities, transactional data file (linkage), 135
    pass-through entities (search), limited range (usage), 72
    pattern, focus, 66
    permutations, understanding, 30–33
    real entity, 290
        impact, 31–32
    red flags, correlation, 10
    reliability, 87–88

structure, 30
    operation process, understanding, 158
    term, 30
    types, 289, 314
        data interrogation routines, building guidelines, 67–68
    verification, 143–147
Equipment sales, theft, 229, 243–244
Equity
    accounting policies, 297–310
    fraud brainstorming, 296–297
Error
    defining, 286–287
    fraud, contrast, 288
    GAAS recognition, 118
    scheme, 308
    search, 308–309
Estimation transactions, journal entry type, 337
Even amount, 75
Even number transaction, 62
Event recordation, journal entry (usage), 291, 335
Exact match, 51
Excessive purchase scenario, 218
Exclusion theory, 309
    data, usage, 113–114
    usage, 91, 95–96, 104
Expenditures
    comparison, creation, 356
    summarization, 295
Expenses
    accounting policies, 297–310
    fraud brainstorming, 296–297
    overstatement, techniques, 297
    understatement, techniques, 297
Expenses of interest, 275
External entity
    internal collusion, absence, 78
    internal source, collusion, 78–79
External perpetrator
    high sophistication, relationship, 138
    medium sophistication, relationship, 137

External perpetrator (*Continued*)
  permutation, low sophistication
    (relationship), 137
External suppliers (collusion), internal
  person involvement (absence),
  265–266

False add-on charge
  inclusion, 167–168
  variation, 171–172
False adjustment deduction scenarios,
  199
False adjustment scenarios, 228,
  235–236
  FDA, impact, 236
False adjustment scheme, occurrence,
  186
False administration, 174–181
False aging, FDA (impact), 332
False bid document, creation, 260
False billing, 150
  red flags, ranking, 155
  scenario, tendencies, 155
  schemes, FDA (usage), 154–158
False created employee, 102
False customer
  false revenue, 319
    accounts receivable analysis, usage,
    324–326
    FDA, impact, 324
  FDA, impact, 323–324
  scheme, 312
False document scheme, 29
False entity, 31, 290
  example, 78–79
  schemes, transaction numbers
    (association), 65
  transactional data, association
    (guidance), 77
False invoice, 350
False need scheme, establishment, 260
False operating expense, 292
False positives, 72
  defining, 7–9
  minimization, avoidance, 121
  resolution, plan, 82, 99–100

False revenue, 319
  data profile, 321–322
  FDA, impact, 324
  fraud scenarios, fraud concealment
    strategies, 326–331
  recordation, 320
  scenarios, FDA (impact), 323–324
  scheme, 312
    weakness, 326
False sales transactions, recording, 202
False transactions
  application, absence, 335
  deduction scenario, FDA plan, 200
  recordation, 301
  subset, 301
False vendor scenario, 209, 223–224
Falsified records, usage, 282
FATF. *See* Financial Action Task Force
Favoritism, 252, 254
  after-the-fact approach, 259
  analysis, 259
  circumstantial evidence, usage, 255
  fraud data analytics approach, 259
  identification, 256
    strategy, usage, 257
  impact, 258–259
  search, fraud data analytics approach,
    258
FCPA. *See* Foreign Corrupt Practices Act
FDA. *See* Fraud data analytics
Federal Acquisition Register (FAR), 254
Federal identification, IRS verification,
  145
Fictitious employee
  nonexistence, 189–191
    FDA plan, 189–191
  occurrence, 185
Fictitious person, setup, 101
File layout description, 214–216
Filtering
  concept, 118–119
  techniques, 82, 97–98
    selection, 105
Financial account
  focus, 299–300
  overstatement, 301

understatement, 301–302
understatement/overstatement,
    search, 300–302
Financial Action Task Force (FATF), 194
Financial reporting
    fraud data analytics, usage, 114–118
    general ledger account number
        category, 76
    receiving report date, timing, 75
Financial statements
    assertions, inherent fraud scheme
        structure (impact), 293
    data, understanding, 293–295
    fraud data analytics plan, defining,
        296–297
    fraud data analytics search routine,
        design steps, 299
    fraud scenarios
        uncovering, 298
        writing process, 335–336
    transaction
        location, 291, 335
        recordation, 306
Financial statements fraud
    data analytics, 285
    defining, 287–288
    fraud scenario, components, 288–289
    scenarios, 288–290
        writing process, 289
Fitness issue scheme, 24
Footprint. *See* Perpetrators
Foreign Corrupt Practices Act (FCPA),
        269
    enforcement actions, 276
        literature review, 274–275
    Procedures Opinions, 270
    provisions, 273–274
    violation, 19, 206
Foreign nationals, country exit, 190
Fraud
    action, high-level description, 24
    auditor
        assumptions, 156–157
        choices, 116
    brainstorming, 296–297
    conversion, 25

data profile, building, 10
data programming, time allocation,
        121
detection
    audit procedure design, 100*f*
    data analytics strategies, 41
error, contrast, 288
impact, 24
knowledge, 14
materiality, impact, 118–119
perspective, data usage process
        (understanding), 112–113
primary/secondary categories,
        19–20
scope, defining (processing), 19–21
test, fraud auditor design process, 310
testing procedure, 362
Fraud action statements, 185–186,
        228–229, 289
    creation
        guidance, 290–293
        permutation analysis, usage
            (concept), 291
    impact, 314–315
    linkage, 260–261
    requirement, 334
    transactional issue, relationship, 271
    when question, 336
    why question, 336
Fraud audit
    fraud data analytics, usage, 109
        process, 111–114
    objectives, 255
    procedure, 125
        usage, 143–147
    scope, data mining strategy (selection),
        85–86, 323
    test, design, 82, 100–105
Fraud auditing
    defining, 4
        scenario, defining, 4–6
    purpose, 119
Fraud auditing, fraud scenario approach
        (integration process), 110–111
Fraud circle, 22–26
    flowchart, 22*f*

Fraud concealment, 25, 213
  actions, 43
  defining, 6
  high sophistication, 44–47, 49
  impact, understanding, 42–43
  low sophistication, 43–44, 48
  medium sophistication, 44, 48–49
  scheme, 29
  sophistication, 10
    shell companies, impact, 136–138
  tendencies, 45*f*
  usage, process, 119–120
Fraud concealment strategies, 46*f*
  basis, 322
  considerations, 307–308
  GAAP compliance, illusion (creation), 307
  illustrations, 306–307
  search, fraud data analytics (usage), 305–308
  usage, 326–331
Fraud data analytics (FDA), 12, 174
  assumptions, 10–11
  axioms, 15–16
  brainstorming, 235–236
  defining, 2–9
  financial account focus, 299–300
  focus, 298
  fraud action statement, linkage, 260–261
  fraud scenario, linkage process, 36–38
  impact, 196–198
  methodology, 9–11
  mistakes, 16
  multi-tiered approach, 178
  plan, 162, 164
  planning reports, usage, 122–124, 153–154, 253
  routines, building, 277–278
  scenario, 290
  scoring sheet, 136
  search routine, design steps, 82, 91–97, 299, 322–323
  selection criteria, usage, 96
  skills, requirement, 14–15
  specific identification, usage, 116

  strategies, 9, 51–54, 211
    defining, 298
    selection, 91, 93, 102–103
  test, building, 96
  testing, selection basis, 11
  usage, 154–158, 164–165
  work papers, requirement, 125
Fraud data analytics plan, 38, 261–263
  approaches, 213–214
  construction process, 81
  data, requirement, 255–257
  defining, 296–297
  fraud concealment, impact (understanding), 42–43
  fraud risk assessment, impact, 82, 84
  fraud scenario, linkage, 12–14
  payroll fraud scenarios, usage (example), 101–105
  planning, 212–213
  postponement, 89
  requirement, 125
  scope, 82–84
    data mining strategy, appropriateness, 309–310
    framework, creation, 272–273
  steps, 82
  usage, 131–132, 263–267
Fraud data profile, 96
  building, 138–143
    guidelines, 50
  search, 298
Fraud risk
  assumption memo, 125
  structure, 18, 18*f*
    categories, 249–251
    understanding, 171–173
Fraud risk assessment, 125
  impact, 82, 84
  review, 351–353
Fraud scenario, 9, 213
  approach, 11–14
    fraud auditing, integration process, 110–111
  basis, 304–305
  categories, 26–28

components, 29–30
 identification, 91, 101–102
conflict of interest, entity
  pattern, 67
data profile, building, 49–51
data, relationship/identification, 91,
  93, 102
defining, 4–6
 opposite, 28–29
disguised expenditure fraud scenario,
  216–217
examples, 33–34
flowchart, 36*f*, 124*f*
fraud data analytics
 linkage process, 36–38
 plan, linkage, 12–14
fraud data profile, linking, 10
hidden entity fraud scenario, 86
hiding, 305–308
identification, 17, 92
inherent schemes, 26
 conversion process, 252
links (location), data interrogation
  routine (development), 73–77
matrix, 39–40
 vulnerabilities, 25–26
mechanics, data analytics basis,
  321–322
patterns, linkage, 72
real company, entity pattern, 67
real entity, impact, 31–32
recordation process, 303–304, 322
resell fraud scenario, purchase,
  217–224
scheme, occurrence, 24–25
search, fraud data analytics (usage),
  304
selection, 58
shell company, entity pattern, 66–67
split purchase orders fraud scenario,
  85–86
statement, personnel involvement, 35
style, content (contrast), 34–36
supervisor fraud scenario, 221–222
types, 5
unauthorized access, 27–28

uncovering, 298, 321
writing, 29–30
Fraudulent action statement, 30
Fraudulent disbursements
 data identification, 151–152
 fraud data analytics, usage, 149
 inherent fraud schemes, 149–151
Fraudulent journal entries, historical red
  flag, 342–344
Fraudulent transactions
 location, success, 10
 selection, odds (improvement), 3*f*, 47*f*
Frequency analysis, 64–68
 transaction analysis, association, 65
Funds
 deposit, 13
 diversion, 33, 54
 removal, FDA basis, 280–282
Future price rebates (estimation),
  controller understatement, 335

General journal entry, 292
 off-period times, occurrence, 341
General ledger, 289
 account, 161
 analysis ability, opinion date
  (correlation process), 302–303
 record keeping provision, questionable
  payments failure, 283
General ledger account, 314
 balance, disaggregated analysis,
  341–342
 disaggregated analysis, 304–305
 historical red flags, 343–344
 number, 69, 76–77
  categories, 76
 usage, 334
Generally accepted accounting principles
  (GAAP), 19
 application, mistake, 286–287
 compliance, 297, 320–321
  illusion, creation, 307
 implication, 293, 297
  focus, 315
 misapplication, 311, 313–314, 319
 perspective, 320

Generally accepted accounting principles
(GAAP) (*Continued*)
  requirements, understanding, 290,
      334
  violation, 287
Generally accepted accounting standards
(GAAS), 82
  fraud risk factors, 314
  guidance, 299–300, 338
  knowledge, 285
  perspective, 298, 337
  provisions, 115
  requirements, 110, 292–293, 302
Ghost employee, 189
  schemes, FDA (usage), 189–196
Gift certificates, usage, 220
Goods
  charging, 172
  customer payment, avoidance, 241
  purchase, 180–181
Government entities, sales contracts
(identification), 273
Government identification number
  absence, 190
  discovery, 189–190
Government-preferred supplier, 162
Government registration
  date, 144
  number, 141
Grade level/title, pattern, 76
Gross payroll, 191
  false adjustments, FDA plan, 199

Health insurance code, absence, 190
Hidden company
  creation, 350
  identification, 358–359
Hidden duplicate invoice number,
      occurrence, 169–170
Hidden entity, 67
  fraud scenario, 86
  pass-through scheme operation,
      163–164
  scheme, 129
  shell company, 129–130

fraud data analytics, usage,
      134–135
  usage, 228
Hidden numbers, 70
High sophistication
  external perpetrator, relationship, 138
  internal perpetrator, relationship, 137
Hire date, 212
Historical supplier
  new supplier, purchasing relationship
      change, 264–265
Historical supplier, relationship
(continuation), 263–264
Homogeneous data files, creation, 104
  inclusion/exclusion theory, usage,
      95–96
Homogeneous data sets, 114
  creation, 180
    inclusion/exclusion theory, usage,
      91
Human resources
  credit card information, linkage, 212
  database, 186
    absence, 196
    employee, recording, 191
    payroll register, real person, 195
  error, 195
  files change, 186

IDEA software,
      maximum/minimum/average
      report, 60*f*–61*f*
Identification master file data, 357–358
Identification report, creation, 360
Identification strategy, 51–54, 93, 211
  examples, 53
  usage, 257
    guidelines, 53–54
Identified entities, transactional data file
(linkage), 135
Identity
  permanent takeover, 192–193
  schemes, search assumption, 68
  takeover, 191–192
Illogical product description, 76
Illogical range, 70

Illogical sequence, usage, 74
Impact statement, 35, 57, 289, 334
  focus, 271
Incentives, impact, 276
Inclusion theory, 309
  data, usage, 113–114
  usage, 91, 95–96, 104
Incomplete terms
  FDA, impact, 330
  schemes, recordation, 313
Indirect access, 30
Indirect influence, 248
Industry-specific concept, 28
Industry-specific fraud scenario, 5, 28
Information technology (IT) knowledge,
    14
Inherent fraud schemes, 149–151,
    184–187, 288–290
  revenue fraud scenarios, creation,
    314–315
  structure, 207
    impact, 293
Inherent scheme
  conversion process, 252
  structure, understanding, 21–22,
    171–172
Insurance, proof, 146
Intelligence information, summary, 147
Intentional duplicate payment, 171
Interest, expenses, 275
Internal budget owner
  consultant, collusion, 151
  internal collusion, assumption, 151
Internal control avoidance, 51, 54, 103,
    155–156, 211
  examples, 56
  master file data, 358
  report, creation, 360–361
  scenario, 56–57
  search process, automation, 112
  strategies, 55–56, 65
    focus, 65
    usage, guidelines, 56
Internal control inhibitor, 28
  fraud scenario, 5

Internal control procedure inhibitor,
    concept, 28
Internal controls, 25, 125
  anomaly, identification, 51–54
  assessment, 12
  attributes, FDA basis, 276–277
  circumvention, 74
    red flag, 73–74
  vulnerabilities, vendor exploitation,
    165–168
  vulnerability statement, 35–36
Internal investigations, 276
Internal perpetrator
  low sophistication, relationship,
    136–137
  medium sophistication, relationship,
    137
Internal person
  benefit, 181
  change, 179
  corruption, 250
  generic statement (bid avoidance),
    252
  goods purchase, 180–181
  impact, 238
  kickback acceptance, 241
  vendor, collusion, 171–173
Internal Revenue Service (IRS), federal
    identification verification
    assistance, 145
Internal sales invoices, creation, 315
Internal selection process, 19
Internal source
  external entity, collusion, 78–79
  vendor, collusion, 177–179
Internet
  database/search engine usage,
    145–146
  search companies, usage, 144
Internet Protocol (IP) address,
    information, 77
Inventory
  controller overstatement, 302, 305,
    307, 309
  movement, illusion (creation), 307
  overstatement, 299

Inventory (*Continued*)
  records, indication, 230
  seasonal usage, 294
  theft, resale, 229, 244
Invoice amounts, identification, 361
Invoice date, payment date (comparison), 361
Invoice numbers
  digits, addition/subtraction, 170
  hidden duplicate invoice number, occurrence, 169–170
  integers, transposition, 170
  tendencies, 154, 160–161
Invoices
  add-on charge searches, 167–168
  amount, 165–166
    tendencies, 154, 160
  date
    tendencies, 154, 161
    timing, 75
  description
    field, word searches (usage), 281–282
    tendencies, 154–155, 161
  file
    change, 175–177
    false administration, 174–181
  fraudulent disbursement data, 151–152
  identification, purchase order (absence), 356
  illogical order, 156
  layering, 156
  quantity, 168
  sales invoice number, 69
  small-dollar invoices, submission, 166
  submission, 165–166, 168
    false add-on charge, inclusion, 167–168
  unit price, 165–166
  vendor invoice, 69, 72, 146
Invoice splitting, internal control avoidance report (creation), 360
Item purchase, timing (determination), 256

Journal activity, summarization, 295
Journal entries
  absence, 344
  aggregate dollar value, 338
  controller recordation, 335–336
  convoluted journal entries, 346
  description, 337
  dollar value, stratification, 338
  entity concept, absence, 335
  fraud data analytics
    strategies, 339
    usage, 333
  fraudulent journal entries, historical red flag, 342–344
  language, understanding, 337
  purpose, alpha description, 345
  recordation, 334, 346
  selection
    approach, 337–339
    fraud data analytics, usage, 339–347
  stratification, 338
  summarization, 295
  testing
    fraud scenario concept, application, 334–336
    planning reports, usage, 338–339
  timing, 344–345
  types, 337
  usage, 291, 303–304

Keyword searches, 214
Kickback, 209
  acceptance, 241
  form, 213
  payment, 160
  receipt, 151, 183, 196
  scheme, 101
Knock-off scheme, 24

Lapping, asset misappropriation scheme (association), 236
Lapping scenarios, 229, 239–240
  traditional lapping scenario, FDA (impact), 239–240
Lapping, usage, 240–242

Legal existence, verification, 144
Legal pass-through, 210
  scenario, 217–218
  scheme, occurrence, 208
  usage, 210
Liabilities
  accounting policies, 297–310
  fraud brainstorming, 296–297
Likelihood conundrum, 12
Likelihood question, 123
Limited use shell company, 130
  fraud data analytics, usage, 135
Linkage factor, 11
Loan officer, term (usage), 240
Logging information, usage guidelines,
  77
Logical errors, identification, 91, 94–95,
  103–104
Low sophistication, 43–44
  external perpetrator permutation,
    relationship, 137
  internal perpetrator, relationship,
    136–137

Manual payments, total number, 188
Manual payroll disbursements, 185
  FDA, impact, 200–201
Manual payroll payments, FDA (impact),
  201
Manual transaction, 56
  analysis, 156
  importance, 121–122
Manufacturer false label scheme, 24
Market division, 265
Master file. *See* Vendor
Master file data, 102
  concealment level, identification,
    350
  data availability/reliability/usability,
    353–354
  guidance, 77
  identification anomaly testing, 359
  identification master file data,
    357–358
  internal control avoidance master file
    data, 358

interrogation routine basis, 356–359
  strategies, 66–67
Matching concept, precision, 51
Matching test, 140–142
Medium sophistication, 46, 48–49
  external perpetrator, relationship, 137
  internal perpetrator, relationship, 137
Merchant category code (MCC) codes,
    215–216
  purchases, 212
  usefulness, 220
Missing data analysis, 102
Missing test (testing), 140, 141
Misstatement, direction, 289, 314

Name field, 138–139
Net adjusting entries, 346
Net payroll, 191
  false adjustments, FDA plan, 200
New customers, creation, 317
New supplier, purchasing relationship
    change, 264–265
Nonactive customers, delinquent
    payment history, 319
Non-complicit vendor, disguised
    expenditure scenario, 207
Non-operating revenue
  FDA, impact, 331–332
  recognition, 313
  recordation, 320
Nonresponsible bids, acceptance, 251
Nonroutine transactions, journal entry
    type, 337
No-show employee, 194
Nuisance, identification, 153–154
Number anomaly, 51, 96, 157–158,
    211
  frequency, sufficiency, 65
  report, creation, 361
Number anomaly strategy, 62–64
  scenario, 64
  usage, guidelines, 63
Number transactions
  contra entry transaction, 63
  even number transaction, 62
  repeating number transaction, 62

Numeric descriptions, 75–76, 161
Numeric transaction description, 69

Odd amount, 75
OFAC list, 279
Official act, party corruption (influence),
   255
Off-period analysis, usage, 74, 156
Off-period overtime, 198
Off-period test, 13
Off-period transactions, 55
Off-the-book bank account, funds
   (depositing), 13
Off-the-book fraud scenario, 10
One-time entity, 67
One-time vendors, tagging, 135
On-the-book conversion, 25
Opinion date
   correlation, 322
   impact, 303
Opportunity files, search, 179–181
Order quantity, computation, 329
Outlier
   identification, data summarization,
      112
   pattern, focus, 66
Overbilling, 150, 165–173
   occurrence, 171–172, 177–179
   techniques, opportunity files search,
      179–181
   vendor overbilling scenario,
      222–223
Override transactions
   codes, usage, 56
   importance, 121–122
Overstatement, 115
Overt errors, data set (cleaning), 91
Overtime fraud, 185
   FDA, impact, 196–198
   FDA plan, 197–198
Overt influence, 248

Pass-through billing, 150
Pass-through customers
   fraud data analytics, 235
   fraud scenario, 233–235

purchases, 234
scenarios, 228
   FDA, impact, 234–235
schemes, 227
Pass-through customer scheme,
   traditional shell customer (usage),
   228
Pass-through entities
   external sales person, 159f
   internal person, 159f
   schemes, 158
   search, limited range (usage), 72
Pass-through schemes
   description, versions, 159–173
   occurrence, 281
   operation, understanding, 158–173
   tendencies, 161–162
Pass-through shell company operation,
   68
Pass-through stand-alone company,
   creation, 66
Pattern frequency, data interpretation,
   65
Pattern recognition, 64–68
Payment
   association, 278–279
   date, invoice date (comparison), 361
   fraudulent disbursement data,
      151–152
   number/amount, 69
   process documents, 253
   speed, 156
   tolerances, 52
PayPal, 208, 210, 217
Payroll
   adjustments schemes, FDA (impact),
      198–200
   calculation, understanding, 186–187
   checks, theft, 185
   employee, employee (collusion), 196
   frequency report, 188
   function, scenario, 101
   information, summary reports, 188
   inherent fraud schemes, 184–187
   manual payroll disbursements, FDA
      (impact), 200–201

payments
  summary report capture, 201
  theft, FDA (impact), 202–203
  payroll-related expenditures, 185–186
  records, data, 102
  systems, 184
Payroll fraud
  fraud data analytics, usage, 183
  planning reports, usage, 188
  scenario example, 34, 101–105
  statements, 185
Payroll register
  provisions, 191
  real person, 195
PEP. *See* Politically exposed person
Performance compensation, FDA
  (impact), 202
Performance criteria, decrease, 202
Permanent takeover, temporary takeover
  (contrast), 32–33
Permutation analysis, 23–24
  usage, 70
    concept, 291
Perpetrators, footprint
  high sophistication, 44–47
  low sophistication, 43–44
  medium sophistication, 44
Perpetrators, predictability (impact), 120
Personal expenses, 181
  identification, 150
Personal telephone number, absence, 190
Person committing, 23, 288
Persons, permutations, 249
Physical existence, verification, 144–146
Planning considerations, documentation
  process, 124–125
Planning reports, 273–274, 316,
  338–339
  usage, 122–124, 188
Politically exposed person (PEP), 194
  payments, 275
Population (shrinkage), sophistication
  factor (usage), 47–49
Postal code field, 140
Posted theft transactions, reclassification,
  346

Predictability factor, 115
Predictive analysis, form, 66
Pre-employment, 193
Preferential pricing, bribery scenarios,
  244–245
Pre-qualification procedures, 250
Price fixing, 19
Primary table data, availability/
  reliability/usability, 354
Prime contractor, FDA (usage), 164–173
Prior enforcement actions, transactional
  issues usage (FDA basis), 275–276
Procurement
  bypassing, 177–179
  card scenarios, FDA (impact),
    216–224
  fraud, FDA planning reports, 253
  process
    documents, 253
    involvement, 171–173
Procurement corruption
  documents/data, 253
  fraud data analytics, usage, 247
  internal person, impact, 250
Procurement function
  corruption
    fraud approach, 253–254
    fraud data analytics, 258–259
    inherent fraud schemes, 248–252
Products
  illogical product description, 76
  line, sales, 317
  number, absence, 76
  substitution scheme, 12–13
Programming routines
  identification, 104
  usage, 91, 97
Project numbers, 70
Public mailbox service company, labeling
  method (identification), 113
Public records
  filing, 146
  usage, 145
Purchase journal, 292
Purchase order, 248
  absence, 356

Purchase order (*Continued*)
  award, favoritism (impact), 258–259
    fraud data analytics plan, 263–267
  changes, 174
  comparison, 153
  data, basis, 256
  extension, 174
  false administration, 172
  fraudulent disbursement data,
    151–152
  identification, 173–174
    report, creation, 360
  illogical order, 156
Purchase scenarios, 218
  cash-equivalent purchase scenario,
    220
  duplicate purchase scenario, 221
  travel-related purchase scenario,
    219–220
Purchasing manager, bribe receipt
    (determination), 255
Purchasing procedures, compliance,
    176–177

Quantiles change, 266
Quantity order amounts, differences, 325
Questionable business purpose scheme,
    occurrence, 208
Questionable payment
  book recordation, FDA basis, 278–280
  direct payment, 279
  failure, FDA basis, 283
  FDA basis, 273
  fraud action statement, 271
  funds removal, FDA basis, 280–282
  layering, 280–281
  occurrence, 270
  recordation, failure, 282
  search, fraud data analytics routines
    (building), 277–278
  techniques, 280–281
  true purpose (disguising), falsified
    records (usage), 282

Random ascending/descending numbers,
    70

Real business
  FDA plan, 164
  shell company action, 164
Real companies
  business names, differences, 99
  defining, 131
  entity pattern, 67
  FDA approach, 163–164
  FDA plan, 162
  hidden entity, operation, 163–164
  multiple name operations, 68
  pass-through scheme
    composition, 158
    operation, 162
Real customers
  dormant customer, equivalence, 323
  false revenue, 319
    FDA, impact, 325–326
  FDA, impact, 324
  real revenue, 319
  schemes, 312, 313
  types, 228
Real employee, complicitness, 185, 194
  absence, 191–193
  FDA plan, 192
Real employee, direct deposit receipt, 195
Real entity, 290
  generic statement (bid avoidance), 252
  impact, 31–32
  scenarios, 50
  targeted statement, 252
  transactional data, association
    (guidance), 78–79
Real invoices, 350
  intentional duplicate items, 171
Realization principal, 326
Real operating expense, 292
Real person
  payroll payments (receipt),
    management (impact), 271
  payroll register, 195
  temporary employee, 195
Real revenue, recordation, 320
Real supplier, overbilling, 52
Real transaction, 290
  application, absence, 335

Real vendor
    addition, 67
    real operating expense, 292
Real vendor scenarios
    complicitness, 222–223
    vendor complicitness, 209
    vendor noncomplicitness, 207–208
Rebates (occurrence), sales
        adjustments/accounts payable
        (impact), 328–329
Receipt
    fraudulent disbursement data,
        151–152
    integrity, internal person corruption,
        250
Receiving report date, timing, 75
Reclassifications, occurrence, 55
Reclassifying entries, transaction
        transfer, 337
Recognition revenue schemes, 313
Recognition schemes, FDA (impact),
        328
Reconciliation reports, 353
Record count
    basis, 65
    establishment guidelines, 65
Record creator, ID, 142
Recordkeeping provision, focus, 271
Record keeping provision, questionable
        payments failure (FDA basis), 283
Record keeping provisions, strategy, 282
Recordkeeping requirements, violation
        process, 270
Records, aggregate number, 59
Recurring amount, 75
Recurring invoice amounts,
        identification, 361
Red flags
    close match, 51
    defining, 6–7
    exact match, 51
    examination, 50
    identification/impact, 71–72
    identifying, process, 10
    internal control circumvention, 73–74
    matching concept, precision, 51

ranking, 155
    related match, 51
Reference checking, 147
Related match, 51
Reliability test, 88
Remittance number, 69
Repeating number transaction, 62
Report design, modification, 317
Resellers, disbursements, 279–280
Resell fraud scenario, purchase,
        217–222
Resell fraud scheme, purchase, 208
Retirement code, absence, 190
Retrospective analysis (favoritism)
    real entity targeted statement, 252
    retrospective analysis, 252
Return scenarios, 228, 235–236
    FDA, impact, 236
Returns, technique, 327
Revenue
    accounting policies, 297–310
        defining, 320–321
    accounts, fraud scenario (uncovering),
        321
    creation, 313
    data, understanding, 316–318
    fraud brainstorming, 318–323
    fraud data analytics plan, defining, 318
    overstatement, techniques, 320
    scenarios, 229
Revenue fraud
    brainstorming, 296–297
    scenarios, creation, 314–315
Revenue misstatement
    documents, data identification,
        315–318
    fraud data analytics, usage, 311
    GAAP, misapplication, 313
Revenue recognition
    fraud, defining, 312
    GAAP, application problem, 314
    impact statement, 315
    inherent fraud risk schemes, 312–314
Revenue theft, 117
    data/documents, identification,
        229–231

Revenue theft (*Continued*)
  fraud data analytics, usages, 227
  inherent scheme, 228–229
  planning reports, 230–231
  sales transaction, recording, 231–233
Reversal entries, reversal design, 337
Reversals, occurrence, 55
Risk assessment, 276
Round invoice amounts, identification, 361
Routine transactions, journal entry type, 337

Sale of goods, 311
Sales adjustment
  hiding, 327
  rebate, equivalence, 329
Sales bonuses, occurrence, 185
Sales commissions, inflation, 185
Sales contracts, identification, 273
Sales invoice
  fraud data analytics, usage, 235
  number, 69
  unit price, comparison, 328
Sales journal, debit origination, 325
Sales order, 315
  number, 69
    anomalies, 324
Sales paid in currency, theft, 229, 242–243
Sales recordation, 317
Sales representative
  assignation, 323
  number, assignation (absence), 325
Sales transaction
  commission code, absence, 324
  recording, 231–233
Sample selection, 105
  basis, 82
  criteria, importance, 125, 362
  process (refinement), filtering techniques (usage), 97–98
Sampling strategy
  change transactions, importance, 121–122

delete transactions, importance, 121–122
fraud concealment, impact (process), 119–120
fraud materiality, impact, 118–119
manual transactions, importance, 121–122
override transactions, importance, 121–122
perpetrators, predictability (impact), 120
void transactions, importance, 121–122
SAS. *See* Statement of Auditing Standard
Scheme, concealment (contrast), 209–211
Scoring sheet concept, usage, 339–341
Scrap income, theft, 229, 243–244
Scrap sales, 281
Search process, one-dimensionality, 10
Search technique, 281–282
Sector risks, 277
Selection criteria
  identification, 97
  usage, 96, 104
Selection process
  basis, 98–99
  example, 38
Senior management, commitment, 276
Senior manager, vendor (collusion), 176–177
Sequential number, 70
Service
  charging, 172
  customer purchase, avoidance, 241
  records, indication, 230
  rendering, 318
  transaction, alpha description, 76
Sham sales, FDA (impact), 329
Sham sales transactions, occurrence, 313
Shell companies
  accounts payable setup, management (impact), 271
  assumed entity shell company, 129
  bank routing number, 141

categories, 128*f*
country/city/state, 140
customer operations, 142
data mining audit program, 349
date, creation, 142
defining, 130–131
email address, 141–142
employee operations, 143
entity pattern, 66–67
false billing schemes
  FDA, usage, 154–158
  internal control avoidance,
    155–156
fraud data analytics, 127
  plan, 131–132
fraud data profile, building, 138–143
fraud scenarios, relationship, 351
government registration number, 141
hidden entity shell company, 129–130
high sophistication, impact, 137–138
homogenous categories, 228
identification, 117
intelligence information, summary,
  147
internal person creation, 159–160
limited use shell company, 130
low sophistication, impact, 136–137
medium sophistication, impact, 137
name, 138–139
one-time use, 130
pass-through schemes, 158–173
  composition, 158
pass-through shell company operation,
  68
postal code, 140
profile information, 138–142
project, background, 349
record creator ID, 142
sales representative setup, 352–353
sophistication, impact, 136–138
street address, 139–140
telephone number, 140
temporary use, 130
terms, definition, 349–351
time, creation, 142
traditional shell company, 128

Shell corporations
  business capacity test, 146
  entity verification, 143–147
  identification, fraud audit procedures
    (usage), 143–147
  legal existence, verification, 144
  physical existence, verification,
    144–146
  reference checking, 147
Shipping address, differences, 326
Shipping concealment strategies,
  variation, 327
Shipping data, 330
Shipping documents, examination, 146
Shipping process, occurrence, 315
Shipping records, indication, 230
Site visit, 145
Small-dollar entries, theft
  layering, 347
Small-dollar invoices, 177
  submission, 166
Small-dollar purchase orders, 84
Small-dollar purchases, circumvention,
  177
Small-dollar transactions, 306
Society, changes, 72
Soft sale
  FDA, impact, 329–330
  recordation, 313
Sophistication
  factor, usage, 47–49
  levels, 44–47
Source journal, usage, 290, 303–304
Specification scheme, structuring, 261
Split purchase orders fraud scenario,
  85–86
Stand-alone company, 66
Statement of Auditing Standard (SAS)
  no. 99, auditor requirement, 333
  no. 106, 293
Street address field, 139–140
Style, content (fraud scenario contrast),
  34–36
Subcontractor, FDA (usage), 164–173
Supervisor
  employee, collusion, 196

Supervisor (*Continued*)
 fraud scenario, 221–222
  occurrence, 208
Suppliers
 documents, data elements (usage), 72
 external suppliers (collusion), internal
  person involvement (absence),
  265–266
 false selection, occurrence, 261
 historical supplier, relationship
  (continuation), 263–264
 invoice data, basis, 256
 line item fulfillment, inability, 266
 scheme, false evaluation (occurrence),
  261
System codes, usage, 55
System generated date, 73

Tangible good descriptions,
  alpha/numeric descriptions
  (inclusion), 76
Tangible items
 identification, 180
 resell value, 180
Targeted expenditures
 approach, 259
 fraud data analytics plan, 266–267
 fraud scenario, inherent scheme
  (conversion process), 252
 identification approach, 257
Targeted purchases, 213–214
Telephone number field, 140
Telephone verification, 144–145
Temporary companies, identification,
  359
Temporary employee, 195
Temporary entity, 67
Temporary takeover, permanent takeover
  (contrast), 32–33
Termination date, 73, 212
Term loans, lapping (usage), 240–242
Terms
 bribery scenarios, 244–245
 negotiation, internal person allowance,
  251
 schemes, favored negotiation, 261

Theft, layering, 347
Theft of sales paid in currency, 242–243
Theft scheme, committing (intent),
  180–181
Third-party due diligence/payments, 276
Time, creation, 142
Time record file, data, 102
Time reporting database, 186
Top-sided transactions, journal entry
  type, 337
Total acquisition, split, 211
Trade association, 144
Traditional lapping scenario, FDA
  (impact), 239–240
Traditional shell company, 128
 usage, 228
Transactional analysis, guidelines, 298
Transactional data
 concealment level, identification, 351
 example, 78–79
 false entity, association (guidance), 77
 file, identified entities (linkage), 135
 identification strategy, focus, 52–53
 real entity, association (guidance),
  78–79
Transactional red flags, 50
Transactions
 alpha description, 69
 amount, 69
 analysis
  fraud data analytics, usage, 235
  frequency analysis, association, 65
 availability, 88–89
 change transaction, importance,
  121–122
 data errors, presence, 89
 data file, strategies, 68–79
 data, guidance, 77
 date, 73, 77
 delete transactions, importance,
  121–122
 exclusion, 121
 FDA basis, 273
 identification, 112
  anomaly pattern, 66
  illogical sequence, usage, 74

illogical order, 55
location, 291, 335
manual transaction, 56
    importance, 121–122
numbers, 210
    false entity schemes, association,
        65
numeric description, 69
override transactions
    codes, usage, 56
    importance, 121–122
pattern, predictive analysis form, 66
population, shrinkage, 112
recordation, 304–305
    process, 306
    source journal, usage, 290
    timing, determination, 306
red flags, correlation, 10
reliability, 88–89
reversal, 306
risk, 277
speed, test, 73
time, 77
type, 24, 30
void transactions, importance,
    121–122
volume, 166–167
Transfers, occurrence, 55
Travel payments, management (impact),
    271
Travel-related purchase scenario,
    219–220
Travel-related purchase scheme,
    occurrence, 208
Trial balance, 294

UK Bribery Act, 269
    Guidance on Internal Controls,
        272
    internal control guidance, FDA basis,
        276–277
Unauthorized fraud scenario, 5
Undisclosed return policy
    FDA, impact, 330
    scheme, recordation, 313
Unit price changes, 266

Unqualified entity scheme, identification,
    261
Unresponsive bids, usage, 265
Upfront fees, 313
    FDA, impact, 330–331
Usability analysis, 89

Vendor
    accounts payable, collusion, 168–170
    bid rigging, 176
    budget owner, collusion, 176–177
    change, 179
        absence, 179
    complicitness, 209, 222–223
    country code, purchases, 213
    duplicate invoice, submission,
        168–170
    examination, 222
    expenditures, summarization, 295
    false vendor scenario, 209, 223–224
    file, matching, 103
    identification, 282
    ID number, purchases, 213
    internal person, collusion, 171–173
    internal source, collusion, 177–179
    master, comparison, 3329
    noncomplicitness, 207–208
    number
        invoice splitting, internal control
            avoidance report (creation), 360
        summarization, 167
        usage, 156
    overbilling, 24
        scenario, 222–223
    paper check/electronic payments,
        occurrence, 153
    procedures, weakness (impact), 99
    real vendor scenarios, vendor
        noncomplicitness, 207–208
    rebates/refunds, 281
    retail sites, usage, 211
    search, 113
    senior manager, collusion, 176–177
    usage, 156
Vendor invoice
    amount, 69

Vendor invoice (*Continued*)
  line items, 168
  number
    duplicate date/line item, 170
    sequential pattern, 72
  structuring, 155–156
  summary, 153
  usage, 146
Vendor master file
  duplicate address search, 113
  street address, matching, 113
  testing, 153
Voids, occurrence, 55
Void transactions, importance, 121–122
Voluntary deductions, absence, 191

Voluntary government tax withholdings,
    absence, 191

When question, 336
Who question, 184
Why approach, 345–346
Why question, 336
Word searches, usage, 281–282
Workforce, real employee departure,
    195
Work papers, requirement, 125
World Customs Organization, 216
Write-off
  journal entry, absence, 286
  timing, concealment, 308

Printed and bound by CPI Group (UK) Ltd, Croydon, CR0 4YY

23/04/2025

14661000-0003